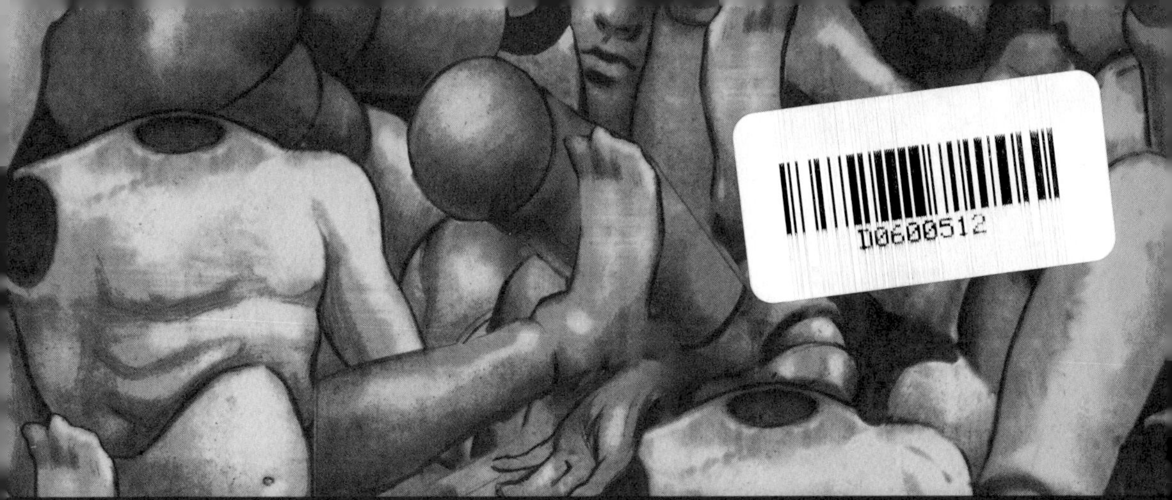

FABLES: HOMELANDS

FABLES CREATED BY BILL WILLINGHAM

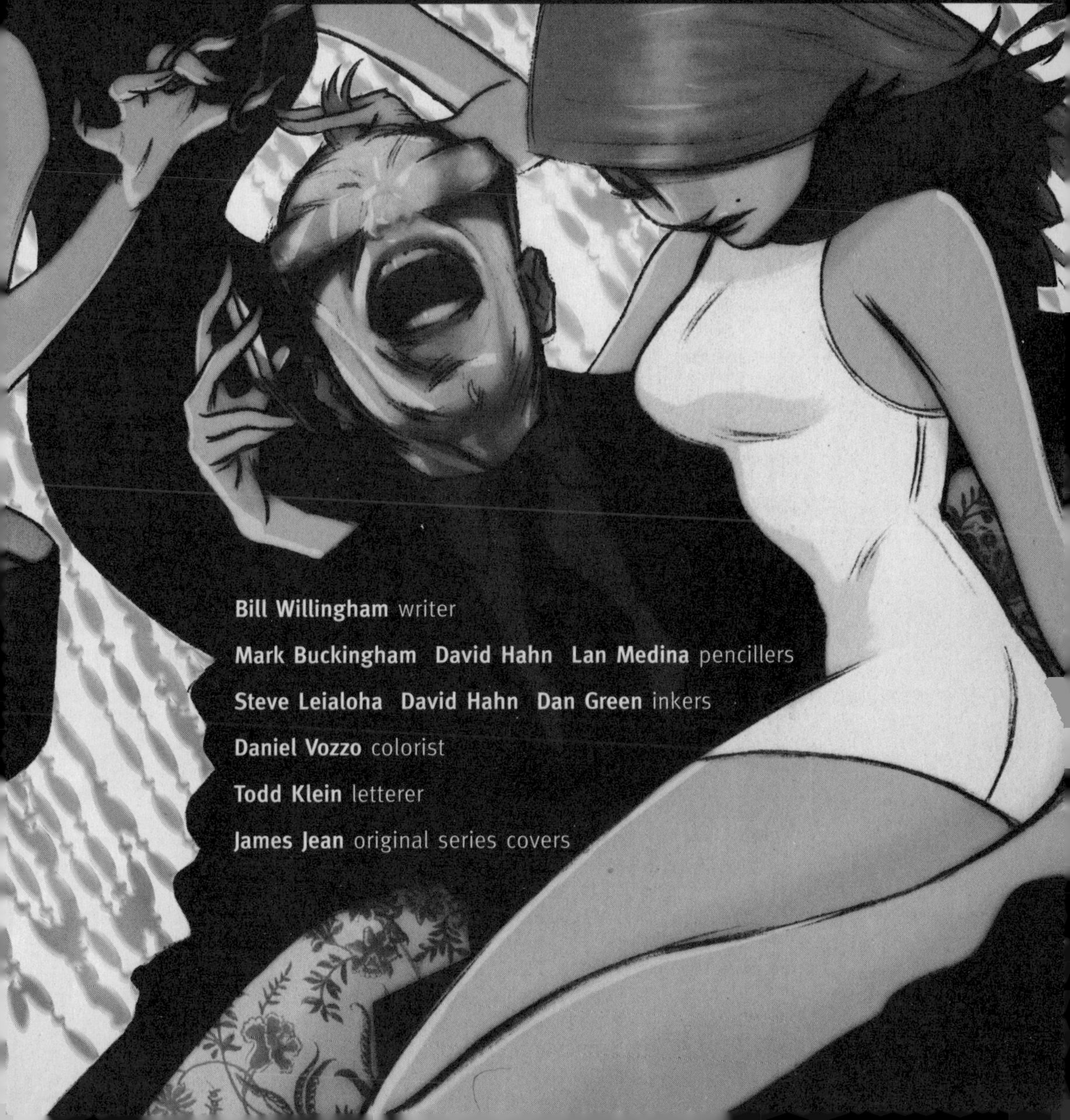

Bill Willingham writer

Mark Buckingham David Hahn Lan Medina pencillers

Steve Leialoha David Hahn Dan Green inkers

Daniel Vozzo colorist

Todd Klein letterer

James Jean original series covers

KAREN BERGER
VP-Executive Editor

SHELLY BOND
Editor-original series

MARIAH HUEHNER
ANGELA RUFINO
Assistant Editors-original series

SCOTT NYBAKKEN
Editor-collected edition

ROBBIN BROSTERMAN
Senior Art Director

PAUL LEVITZ
President & Publisher

GEORG BREWER
VP-Design & DC Direct Creative

RICHARD BRUNING
Senior VP-Creative Director

PATRICK CALDON
Executive VP-Finance & Operations

CHRIS CARAMALIS
VP-Finance

JOHN CUNNINGHAM
VP-Marketing

TERRI CUNNINGHAM
VP-Managing Editor

STEPHANIE FIERMAN
Senior VP-Sales & Marketing

ALISON GILL
VP-Manufacturing

RICH JOHNSON
VP-Book Trade Sales

HANK KANALZ
VP-General Manager, WildStorm

LILLIAN LASERSON
Senior VP & General Counsel

JIM LEE
Editorial Director-WildStorm

PAULA LOWITT
Senior VP-Business & Legal Affairs

DAVID MCKILLIPS
VP-Advertising & Custom Publishing

JOHN NEE
VP-Business Development

GREGORY NOVECK
Senior VP-Creative Affairs

CHERYL RUBIN
Senior VP-Brand Management

JEFF TROJAN
VP-Business Development, DC Direct

BOB WAYNE
VP-Sales

This volume is dedicated with respect
and gratitude to Mike Sinner, who
traveled these lands with me long before
I was privileged to write about them.

— Bill Willingham

Table of Contents

WHO'S WHO IN FABLETOWN

JACK HORNER

The famous Jack of the Beanstalk, Candlestick and many other tales, this incorrigible con artist skipped town after the Battle of Fabletown to seek his fortune in the mundane world.

PRINCE CHARMING

The current mayor of Fabletown, but not doing the most bang-up job of it.

BOY BLUE

He blows his horn, and not just when the sheep's in the meadow and the cows are in the corn. He's an office clerk with a past.

PINOCCHIO

Boy Blue's best friend. He was killed during the Battle of Fabletown, at which time his body reverted back to the form of a wooden puppet.

BEAUTY

The current deputy mayor of Fabletown. She took over from Snow White with the onset of Charming's new administration. She's been married for many years to...

BAGHEERA

The black panther of Jungle Book fame. He's been imprisoned up at The Farm since taking part in the attempted revolution several years ago.

THE STORY SO FAR

Since a mysterious being known only as the Adversary conquered their magical Homelands, many refugee Fables have lived in exile in our mundane world. In the aftermath of the Battle of Fabletown, Boy Blue has been secretly planning an unauthorized quest back into the Fable Homelands to rescue Red Riding Hood, his true lady love, from the Adversary and his minions. One night, without warning, Boy Blue stole the powerful Witching Cloak and

KAY

He has a shard of the Snow Queen's cursed mirror in his eyes, which allows him to see all the evil anyone has done in life. Often he gouges out his own eyes, to keep from seeing such terrible things — but they always grow back.

TRUSTY JOHN

The Woodland Building's loyal and trustworthy doorman.

FRAU TOTENKINDER

The Black Forest Witch of Hansel and Gretel fame. Recently she defeated the evil Baba Yaga in single combat.

BEAST

The current sheriff of Fabletown, who took over from Bigby Wolf when Charming won office.

BIGBY WOLF

The former sheriff of Fabletown. He disappeared after Beast succeeded him in office.

RED RIDING HOOD

Boy Blue's lost love from back in the Fable Homelands. Baba Yaga duplicated her in order to infiltrate Fabletown, which led to the Battle of Fabletown.

Vorpal Sword, plus the wooden body of Pinocchio, and then set out on his quest. In the meantime, the Fabletown authorities have come to suspect that the Adversary has at least one remaining undiscovered spy in their midst. Preliminary steps have been taken to uncover the spy's identity...

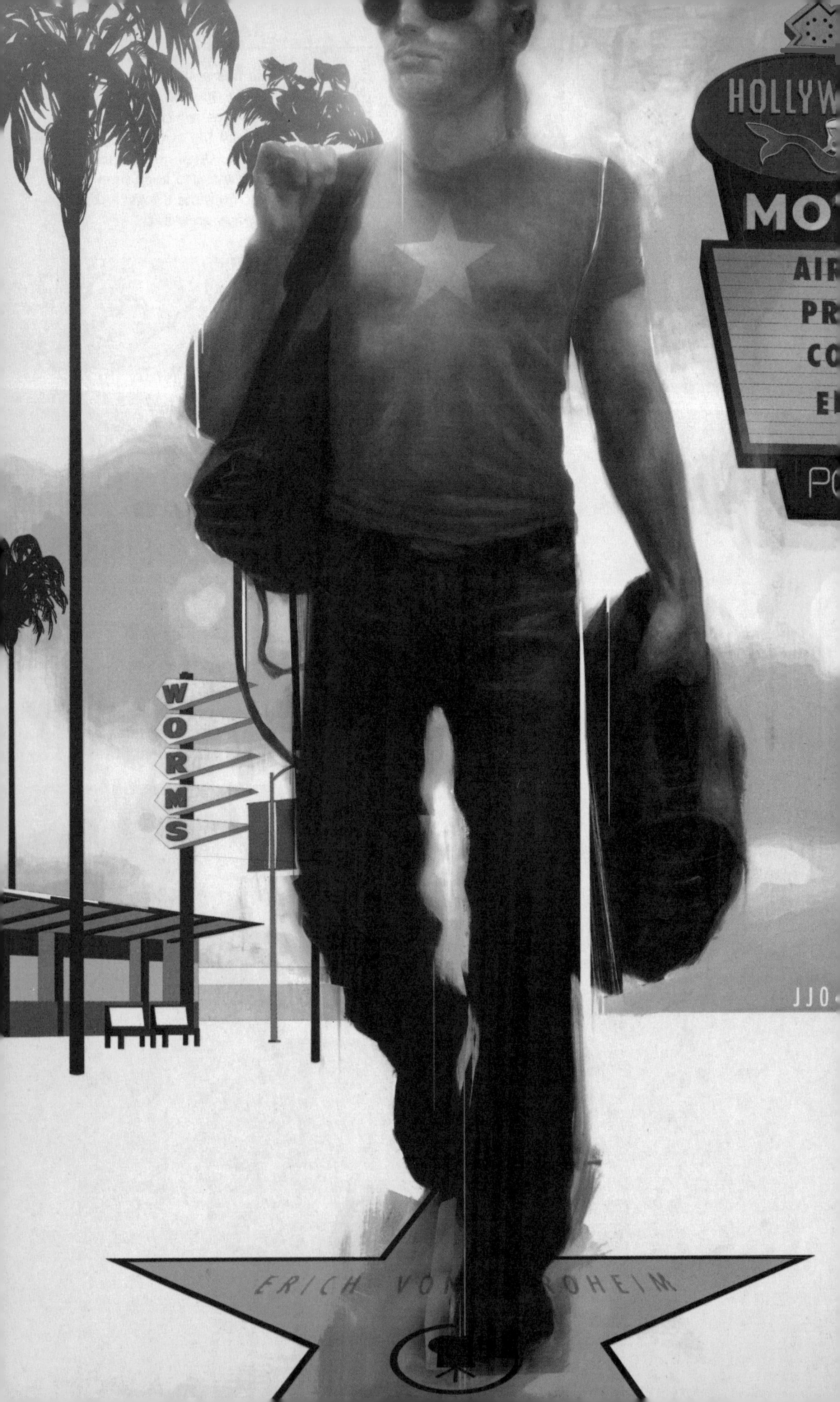
HOLLYW
MO
WORMS
ERICH VO
ROHEIM
JJO

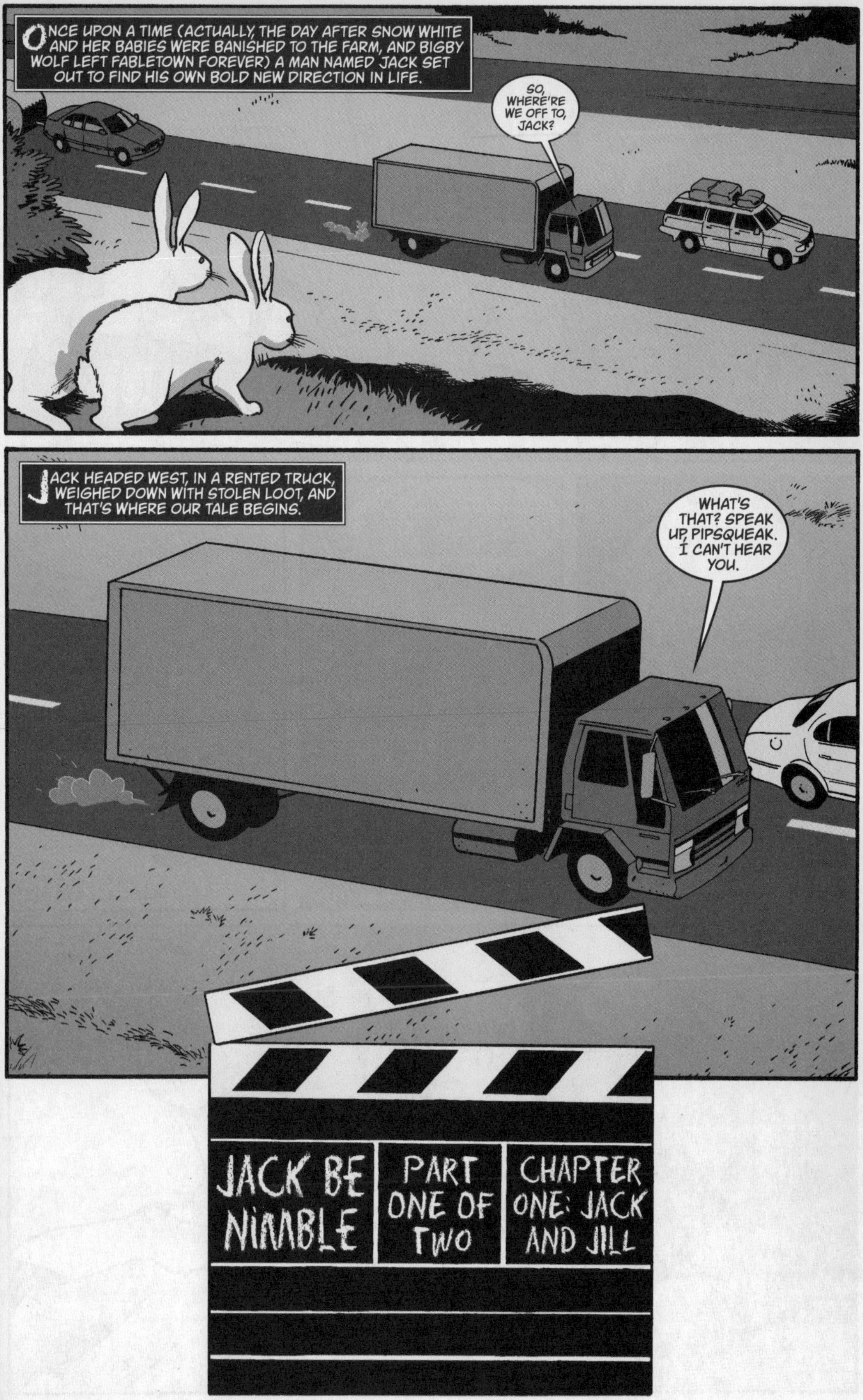
ONCE UPON A TIME (ACTUALLY, THE DAY AFTER SNOW WHITE AND HER BABIES WERE BANISHED TO THE FARM, AND BIGBY WOLF LEFT FABLETOWN FOREVER) A MAN NAMED JACK SET OUT TO FIND HIS OWN BOLD NEW DIRECTION IN LIFE.
SO, WHERE'RE WE OFF TO, JACK?
JACK HEADED WEST, IN A RENTED TRUCK, WEIGHED DOWN WITH STOLEN LOOT, AND THAT'S WHERE OUR TALE BEGINS.
WHAT'S THAT? SPEAK UP, PIPSQUEAK. I CAN'T HEAR YOU.
JACK BE NIMBLE
PART ONE OF TWO
CHAPTER ONE: JACK AND JILL

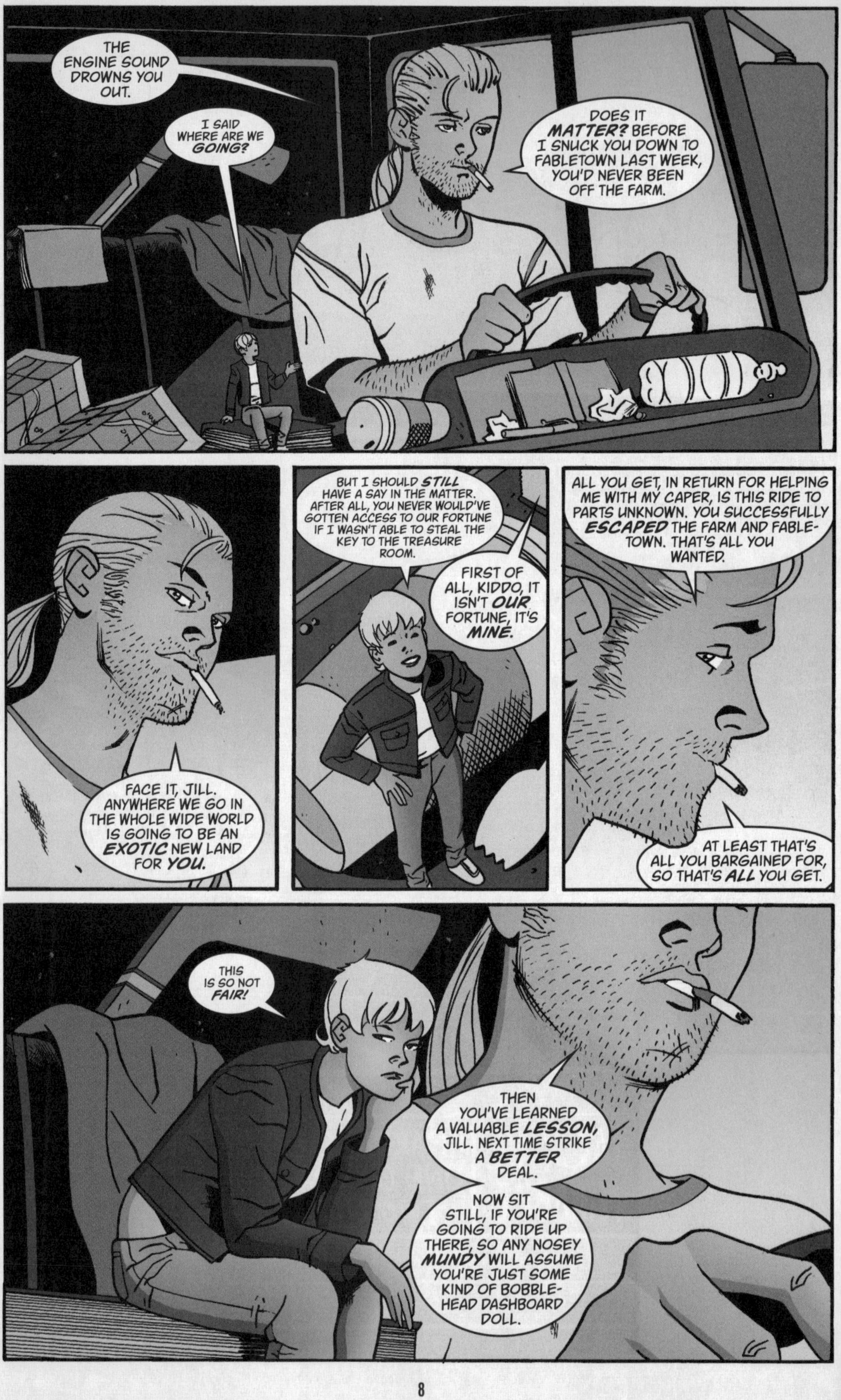
THE ENGINE SOUND DROWNS YOU OUT.
I SAID WHERE ARE WE GOING?
DOES IT MATTER? BEFORE I SNUCK YOU DOWN TO FABLETOWN LAST WEEK, YOU'D NEVER BEEN OFF THE FARM.
FACE IT, JILL. ANYWHERE WE GO IN THE WHOLE WIDE WORLD IS GOING TO BE AN EXOTIC NEW LAND FOR YOU.
BUT I SHOULD STILL HAVE A SAY IN THE MATTER. AFTER ALL, YOU NEVER WOULD'VE GOTTEN ACCESS TO OUR FORTUNE IF I WASN'T ABLE TO STEAL THE KEY TO THE TREASURE ROOM.
FIRST OF ALL, KIDDO, IT ISN'T OUR FORTUNE, IT'S MINE.
ALL YOU GET, IN RETURN FOR HELPING ME WITH MY CAPER, IS THIS RIDE TO PARTS UNKNOWN. YOU SUCCESSFULLY ESCAPED THE FARM AND FABLE-TOWN. THAT'S ALL YOU WANTED.
AT LEAST THAT'S ALL YOU BARGAINED FOR, SO THAT'S ALL YOU GET.
THIS IS SO NOT FAIR!
THEN YOU'VE LEARNED A VALUABLE LESSON, JILL. NEXT TIME STRIKE A BETTER DEAL.
NOW SIT STILL, IF YOU'RE GOING TO RIDE UP THERE, SO ANY NOSEY MUNDY WILL ASSUME YOU'RE JUST SOME KIND OF BOBBLE-HEAD DASHBOARD DOLL.

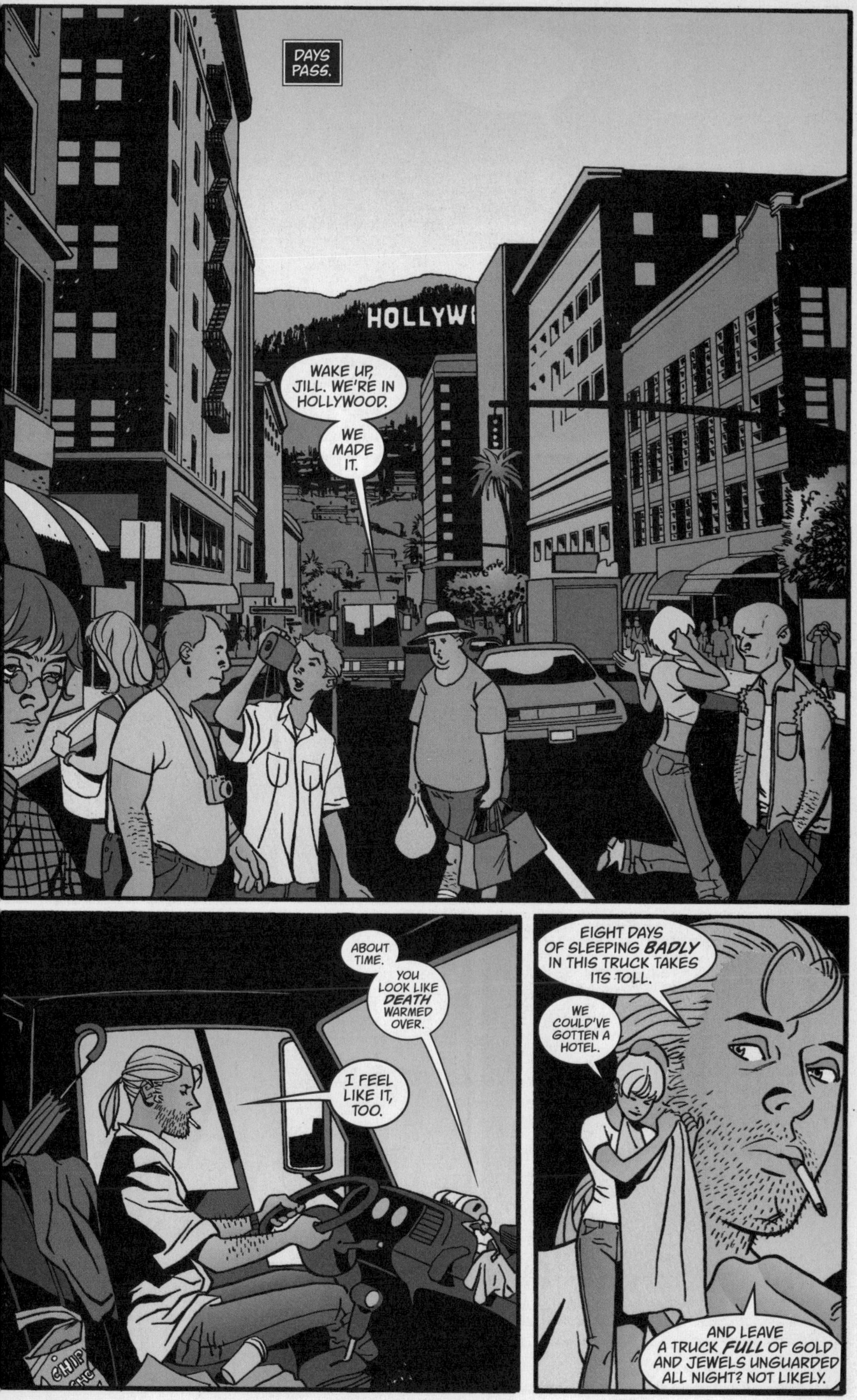
DAYS PASS.
HOLLYW
WAKE UP, JILL. WE'RE IN HOLLYWOOD.
WE MADE IT.
ABOUT TIME.
YOU LOOK LIKE *DEATH* WARMED OVER.
I FEEL LIKE IT, TOO.
EIGHT DAYS OF SLEEPING *BADLY* IN THIS TRUCK TAKES ITS TOLL.
WE COULD'VE GOTTEN A HOTEL.
AND LEAVE A TRUCK *FULL* OF GOLD AND JEWELS UNGUARDED ALL NIGHT? NOT LIKELY.

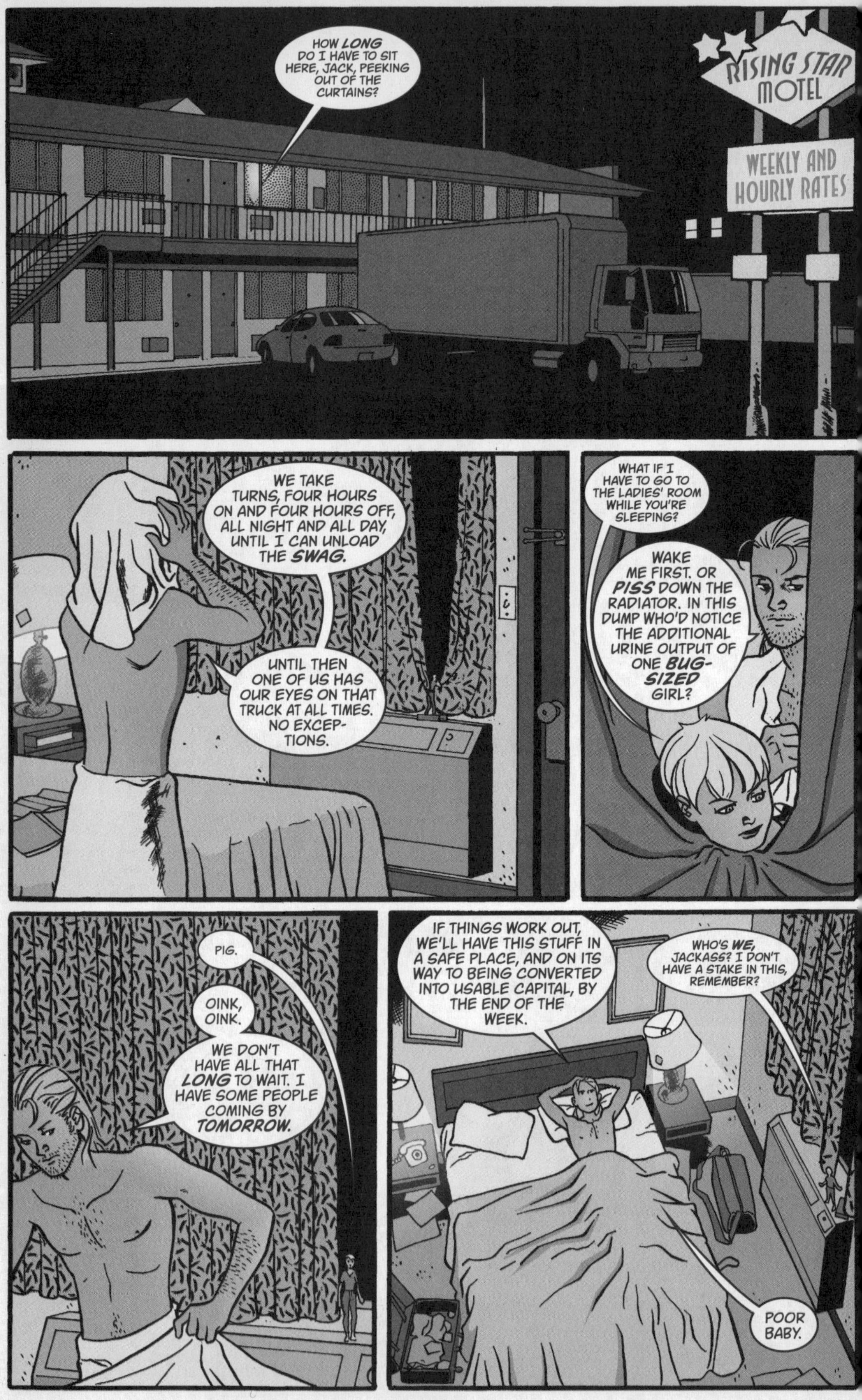

RISING STAR MOTEL
WEEKLY AND HOURLY RATES
HOW LONG DO I HAVE TO SIT HERE, JACK, PEEKING OUT OF THE CURTAINS?
WE TAKE TURNS, FOUR HOURS ON AND FOUR HOURS OFF, ALL NIGHT AND ALL DAY, UNTIL I CAN UNLOAD THE SWAG.
UNTIL THEN ONE OF US HAS OUR EYES ON THAT TRUCK AT ALL TIMES. NO EXCEPTIONS.
WHAT IF I HAVE TO GO TO THE LADIES' ROOM WHILE YOU'RE SLEEPING?
WAKE ME FIRST. OR PISS DOWN THE RADIATOR. IN THIS DUMP WHO'D NOTICE THE ADDITIONAL URINE OUTPUT OF ONE BUG-SIZED GIRL?
PIG.
OINK, OINK.
WE DON'T HAVE ALL THAT LONG TO WAIT. I HAVE SOME PEOPLE COMING BY TOMORROW.
IF THINGS WORK OUT, WE'LL HAVE THIS STUFF IN A SAFE PLACE, AND ON ITS WAY TO BEING CONVERTED INTO USABLE CAPITAL, BY THE END OF THE WEEK.
WHO'S WE, JACKASS? I DON'T HAVE A STAKE IN THIS, REMEMBER?
POOR BABY.

CHAPTER TWO: THE TESTIMONY OF BERNARD STEIN

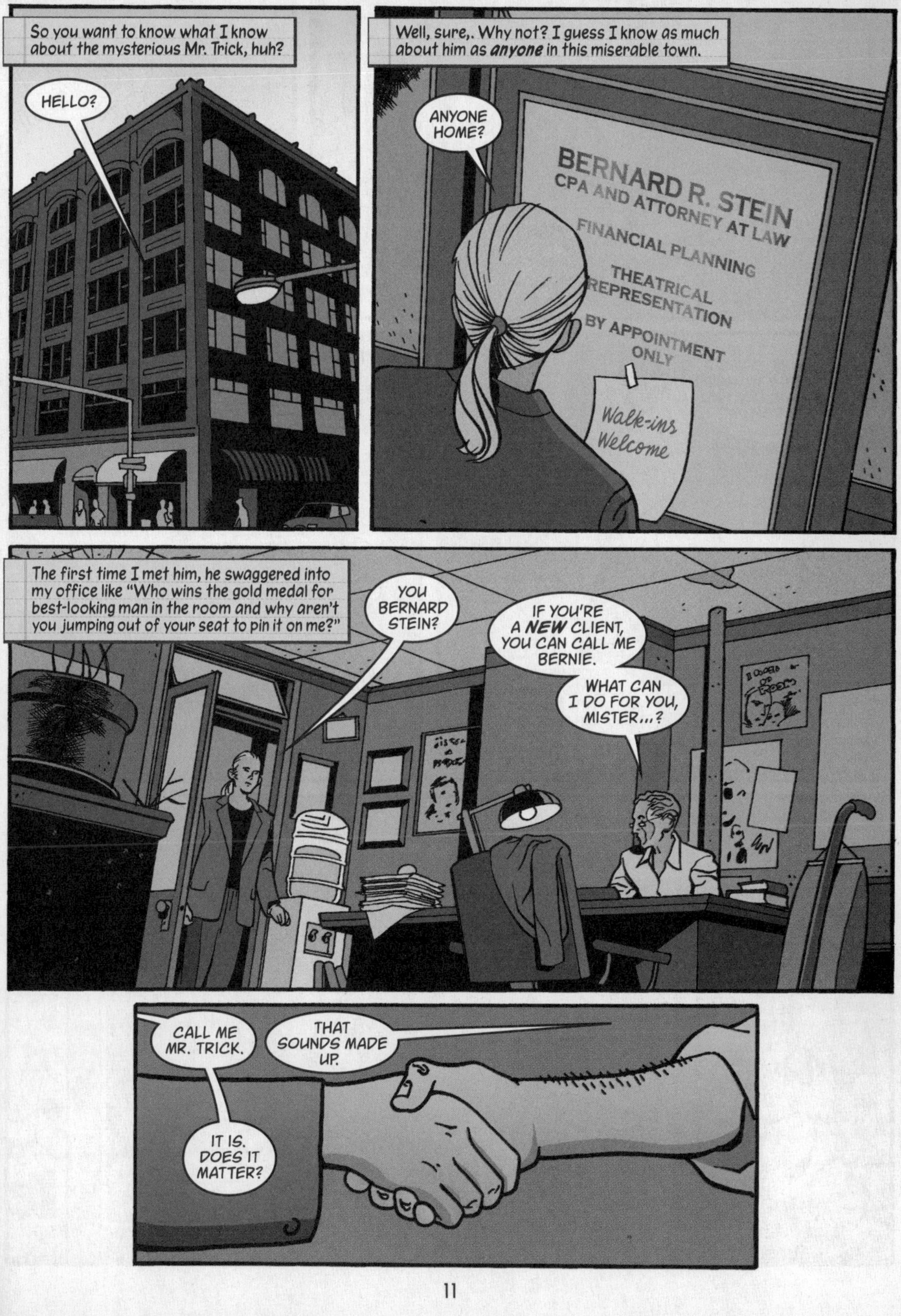
So you want to know what I know about the mysterious Mr. Trick, huh?
HELLO?
Well, sure,. Why not? I guess I know as much about him as *anyone* in this miserable town.
ANYONE HOME?
BERNARD R. STEIN
CPA AND ATTORNEY AT LAW
FINANCIAL PLANNING
THEATRICAL REPRESENTATION
BY APPOINTMENT ONLY
Walk-ins Welcome
The first time I met him, he swaggered into my office like "Who wins the gold medal for best-looking man in the room and why aren't you jumping out of your seat to pin it on me?"
YOU BERNARD STEIN?
IF YOU'RE A *NEW* CLIENT, YOU CAN CALL ME BERNIE.
WHAT CAN I DO FOR YOU, MISTER...?
CALL ME MR. TRICK.
THAT SOUNDS MADE UP.
IT IS. DOES IT MATTER?

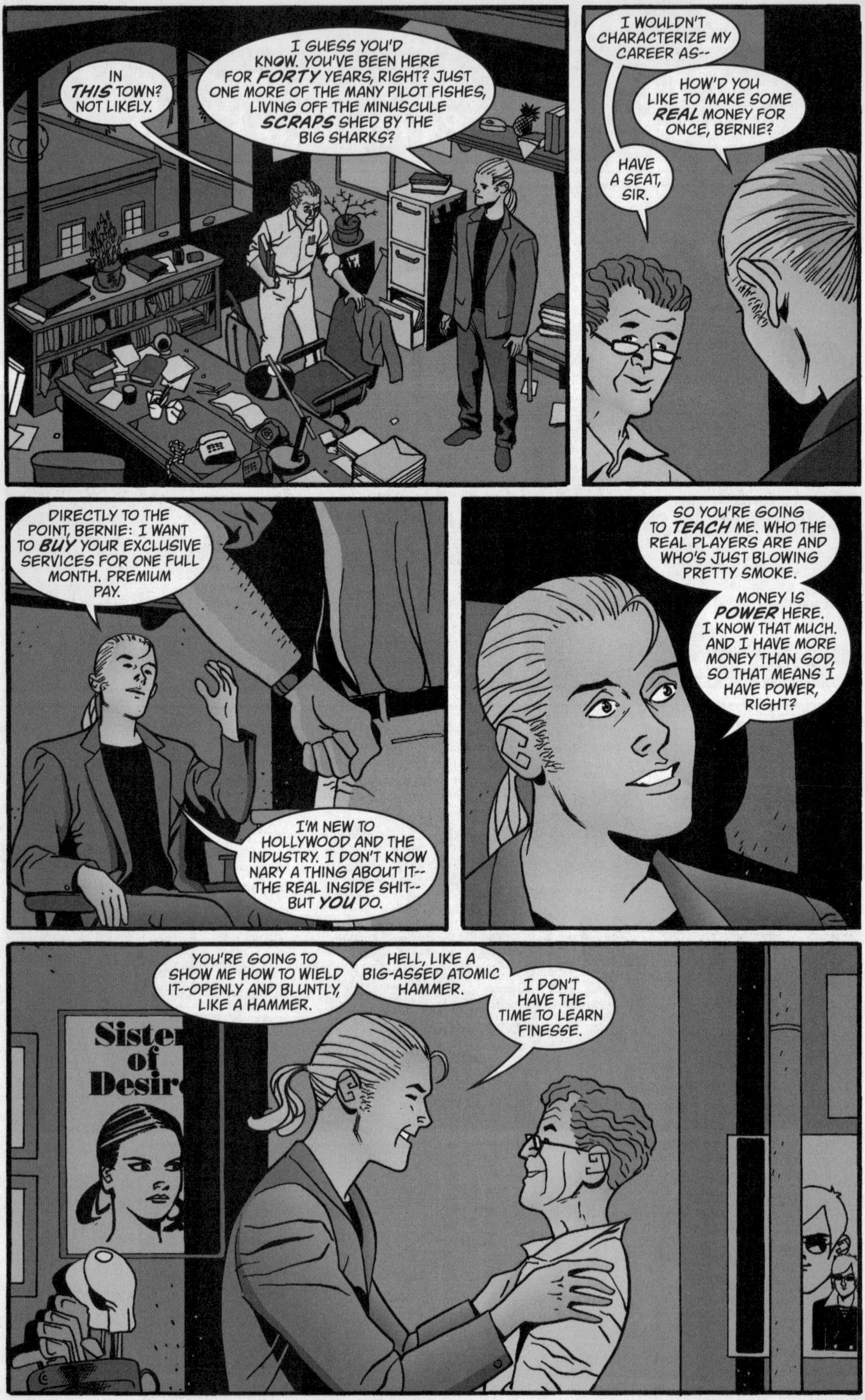
IN THIS TOWN? NOT LIKELY.
I GUESS YOU'D KNOW. YOU'VE BEEN HERE FOR FORTY YEARS, RIGHT? JUST ONE MORE OF THE MANY PILOT FISHES, LIVING OFF THE MINUSCULE SCRAPS SHED BY THE BIG SHARKS?
I WOULDN'T CHARACTERIZE MY CAREER AS--
HOW'D YOU LIKE TO MAKE SOME REAL MONEY FOR ONCE, BERNIE?
HAVE A SEAT, SIR.
DIRECTLY TO THE POINT, BERNIE: I WANT TO BUY YOUR EXCLUSIVE SERVICES FOR ONE FULL MONTH. PREMIUM PAY.
I'M NEW TO HOLLYWOOD AND THE INDUSTRY. I DON'T KNOW NARY A THING ABOUT IT-- THE REAL INSIDE SHIT-- BUT YOU DO.
SO YOU'RE GOING TO TEACH ME. WHO THE REAL PLAYERS ARE AND WHO'S JUST BLOWING PRETTY SMOKE.
MONEY IS POWER HERE. I KNOW THAT MUCH. AND I HAVE MORE MONEY THAN GOD, SO THAT MEANS I HAVE POWER, RIGHT?
YOU'RE GOING TO SHOW ME HOW TO WIELD IT--OPENLY AND BLUNTLY, LIKE A HAMMER.
HELL, LIKE A BIG-ASSED ATOMIC HAMMER.
I DON'T HAVE THE TIME TO LEARN FINESSE.
Sister of Desir

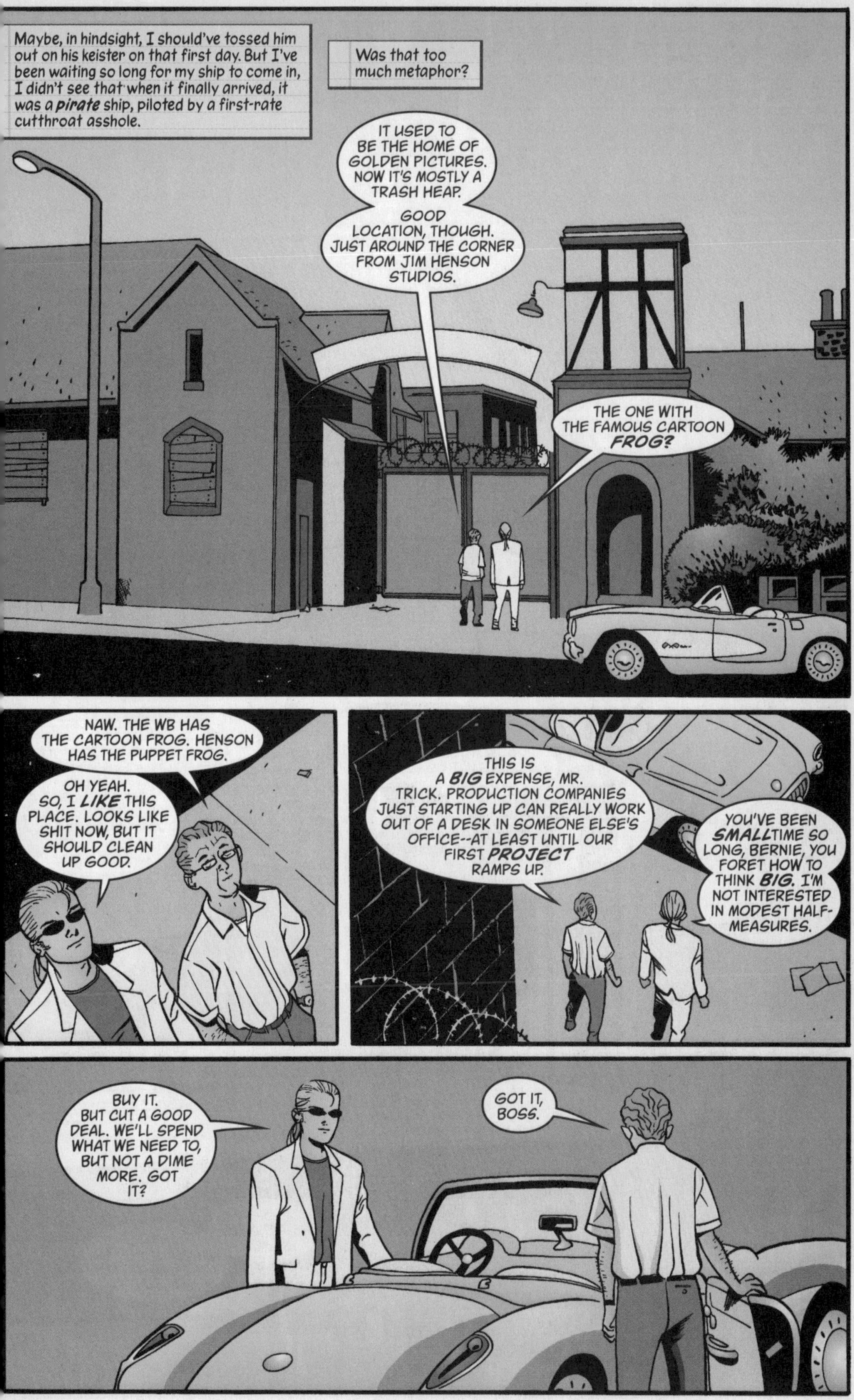
Maybe, in hindsight, I should've tossed him out on his keister on that first day. But I've been waiting so long for my ship to come in, I didn't see that when it finally arrived, it was a *pirate* ship, piloted by a first-rate cutthroat asshole.
Was that too much metaphor?
IT USED TO BE THE HOME OF GOLDEN PICTURES. NOW IT'S MOSTLY A TRASH HEAP.
GOOD LOCATION, THOUGH. JUST AROUND THE CORNER FROM JIM HENSON STUDIOS.
THE ONE WITH THE FAMOUS CARTOON *FROG?*
NAW. THE WB HAS THE CARTOON FROG. HENSON HAS THE PUPPET FROG.
OH YEAH. SO, I *LIKE* THIS PLACE. LOOKS LIKE SHIT NOW, BUT IT SHOULD CLEAN UP GOOD.
THIS IS A *BIG* EXPENSE, MR. TRICK. PRODUCTION COMPANIES JUST STARTING UP CAN REALLY WORK OUT OF A DESK IN SOMEONE ELSE'S OFFICE--AT LEAST UNTIL OUR FIRST *PROJECT* RAMPS UP.
YOU'VE BEEN *SMALL*TIME SO LONG, BERNIE, YOU FORET HOW TO THINK *BIG.* I'M NOT INTERESTED IN MODEST HALF-MEASURES.
BUY IT. BUT CUT A GOOD DEAL. WE'LL SPEND WHAT WE NEED TO, BUT NOT A DIME MORE. GOT IT?
GOT IT, BOSS.

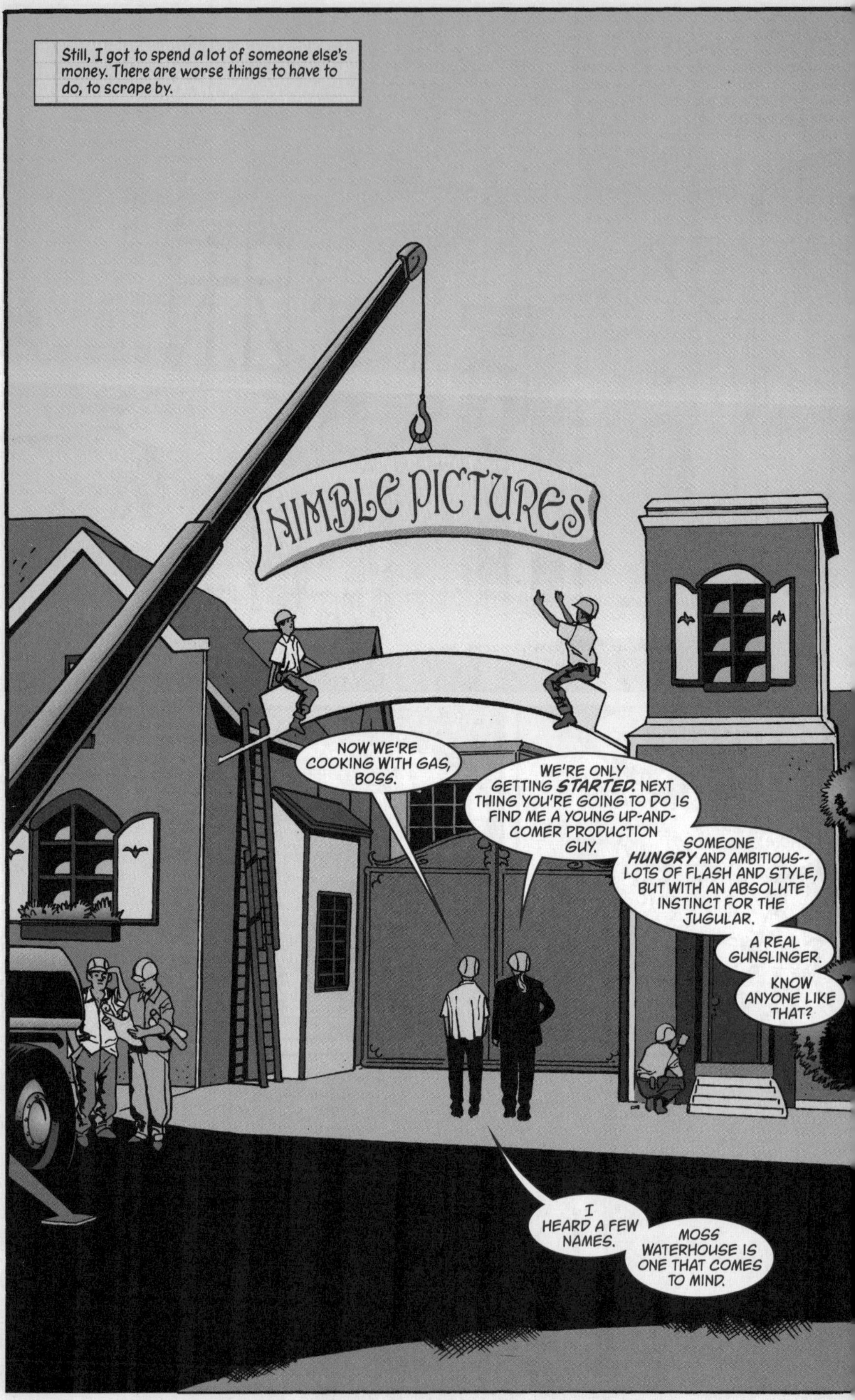
Still, I got to spend a lot of someone else's money. There are worse things to have to do, to scrape by.
NIMBLE PICTURES
NOW WE'RE COOKING WITH GAS, BOSS.
WE'RE ONLY GETTING STARTED. NEXT THING YOU'RE GOING TO DO IS FIND ME A YOUNG UP-AND-COMER PRODUCTION GUY.
SOMEONE HUNGRY AND AMBITIOUS-- LOTS OF FLASH AND STYLE, BUT WITH AN ABSOLUTE INSTINCT FOR THE JUGULAR.
A REAL GUNSLINGER.
KNOW ANYONE LIKE THAT?
I HEARD A FEW NAMES.
MOSS WATERHOUSE IS ONE THAT COMES TO MIND.

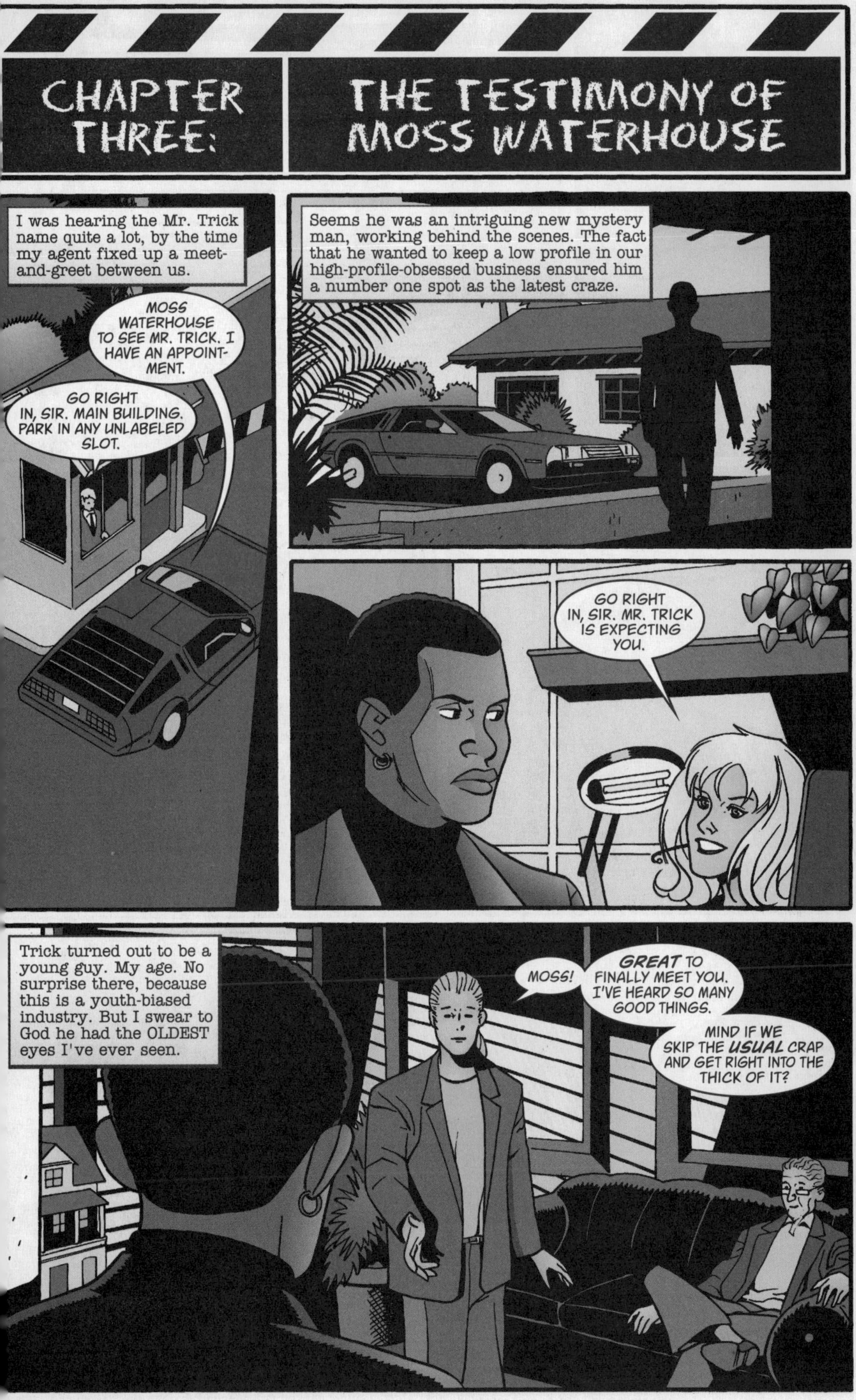
CHAPTER THREE:
THE TESTIMONY OF MOSS WATERHOUSE
I was hearing the Mr. Trick name quite a lot, by the time my agent fixed up a meet-and-greet between us.
MOSS WATERHOUSE TO SEE MR. TRICK. I HAVE AN APPOINTMENT.
GO RIGHT IN, SIR. MAIN BUILDING. PARK IN ANY UNLABELED SLOT.
Seems he was an intriguing new mystery man, working behind the scenes. The fact that he wanted to keep a low profile in our high-profile-obsessed business ensured him a number one spot as the latest craze.
GO RIGHT IN, SIR. MR. TRICK IS EXPECTING YOU.
Trick turned out to be a young guy. My age. No surprise there, because this is a youth-biased industry. But I swear to God he had the OLDEST eyes I've ever seen.
MOSS!
GREAT TO FINALLY MEET YOU. I'VE HEARD SO MANY GOOD THINGS.
MIND IF WE SKIP THE USUAL CRAP AND GET RIGHT INTO THE THICK OF IT?

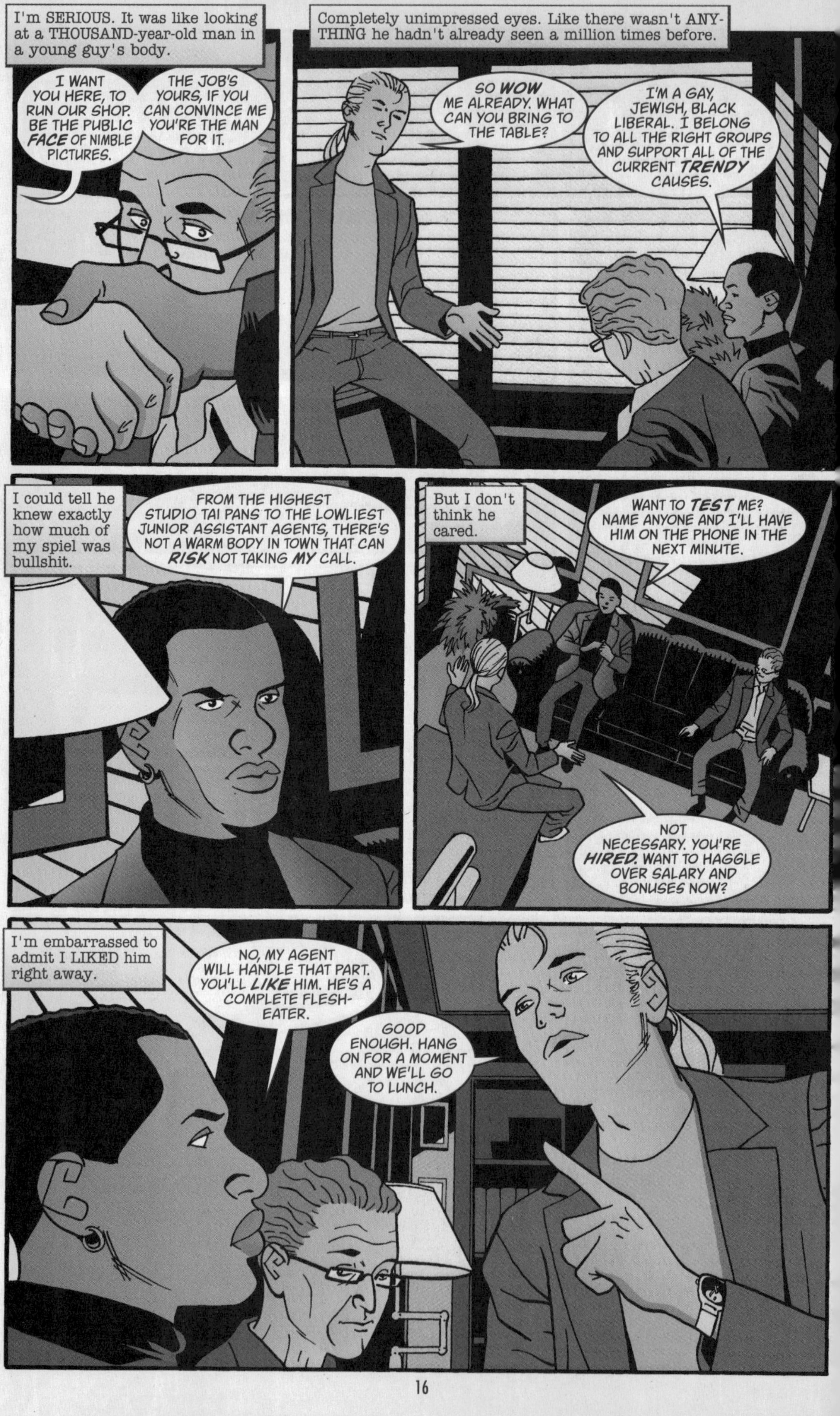

I'm SERIOUS. It was like looking at a THOUSAND-year-old man in a young guy's body.
I WANT YOU HERE, TO RUN OUR SHOP. BE THE PUBLIC FACE OF NIMBLE PICTURES.
THE JOB'S YOURS, IF YOU CAN CONVINCE ME YOU'RE THE MAN FOR IT.
Completely unimpressed eyes. Like there wasn't ANY-THING he hadn't already seen a million times before.
SO WOW ME ALREADY. WHAT CAN YOU BRING TO THE TABLE?
I'M A GAY, JEWISH, BLACK LIBERAL. I BELONG TO ALL THE RIGHT GROUPS AND SUPPORT ALL OF THE CURRENT TRENDY CAUSES.
I could tell he knew exactly how much of my spiel was bullshit.
FROM THE HIGHEST STUDIO TAI PANS TO THE LOWLIEST JUNIOR ASSISTANT AGENTS, THERE'S NOT A WARM BODY IN TOWN THAT CAN RISK NOT TAKING MY CALL.
But I don't think he cared.
WANT TO TEST ME? NAME ANYONE AND I'LL HAVE HIM ON THE PHONE IN THE NEXT MINUTE.
NOT NECESSARY. YOU'RE HIRED. WANT TO HAGGLE OVER SALARY AND BONUSES NOW?
I'm embarrassed to admit I LIKED him right away.
NO, MY AGENT WILL HANDLE THAT PART. YOU'LL LIKE HIM. HE'S A COMPLETE FLESH-EATER.
GOOD ENOUGH. HANG ON FOR A MOMENT AND WE'LL GO TO LUNCH.

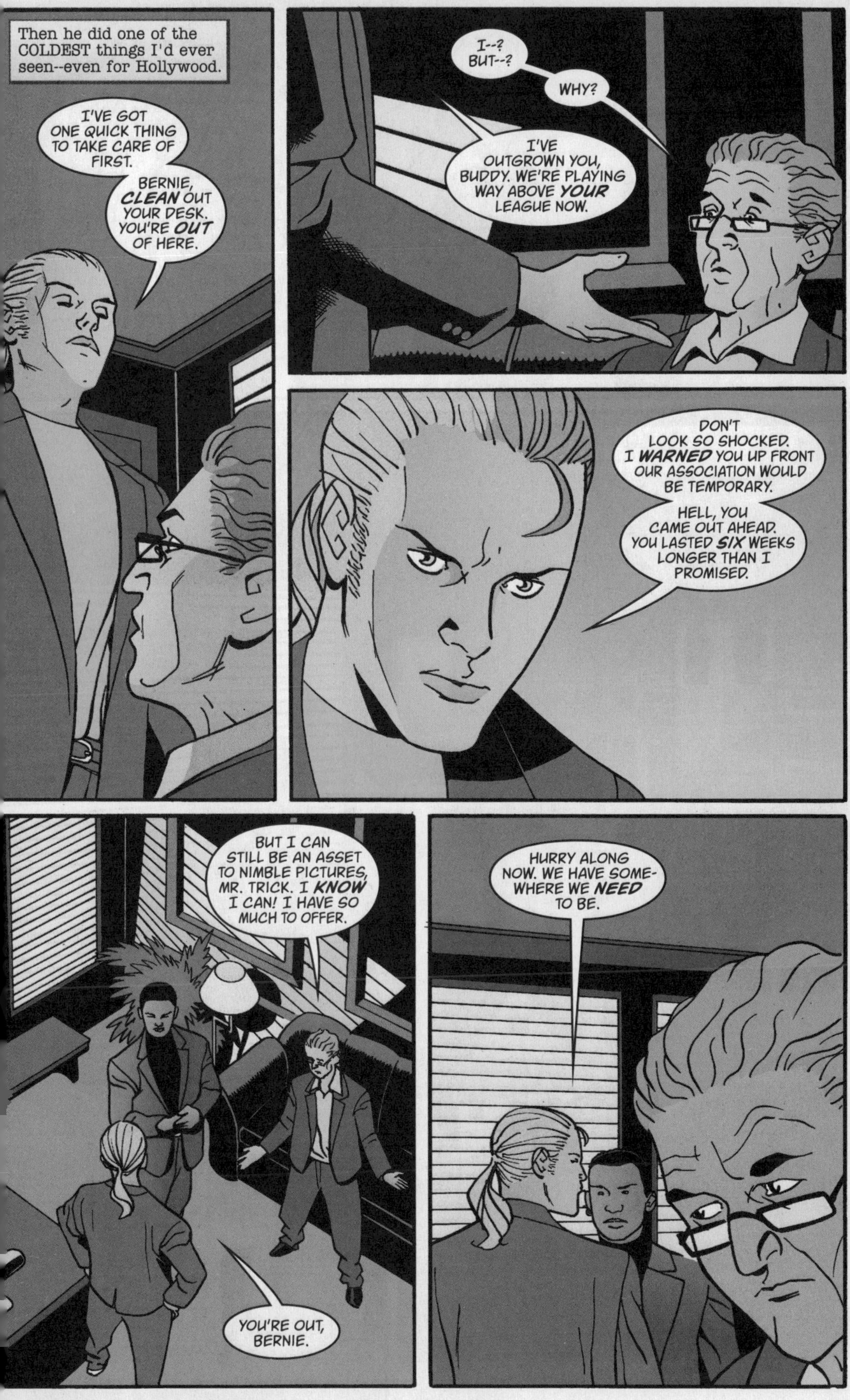

Then he did one of the COLDEST things I'd ever seen--even for Hollywood.
I'VE GOT ONE QUICK THING TO TAKE CARE OF FIRST.
BERNIE, CLEAN OUT YOUR DESK. YOU'RE OUT OF HERE.
I--? BUT--?
WHY?
I'VE OUTGROWN YOU, BUDDY. WE'RE PLAYING WAY ABOVE YOUR LEAGUE NOW.
DON'T LOOK SO SHOCKED. I WARNED YOU UP FRONT OUR ASSOCIATION WOULD BE TEMPORARY.
HELL, YOU CAME OUT AHEAD. YOU LASTED SIX WEEKS LONGER THAN I PROMISED.
BUT I CAN STILL BE AN ASSET TO NIMBLE PICTURES, MR. TRICK. I KNOW I CAN! I HAVE SO MUCH TO OFFER.
YOU'RE OUT, BERNIE.
HURRY ALONG NOW. WE HAVE SOME-WHERE WE NEED TO BE.

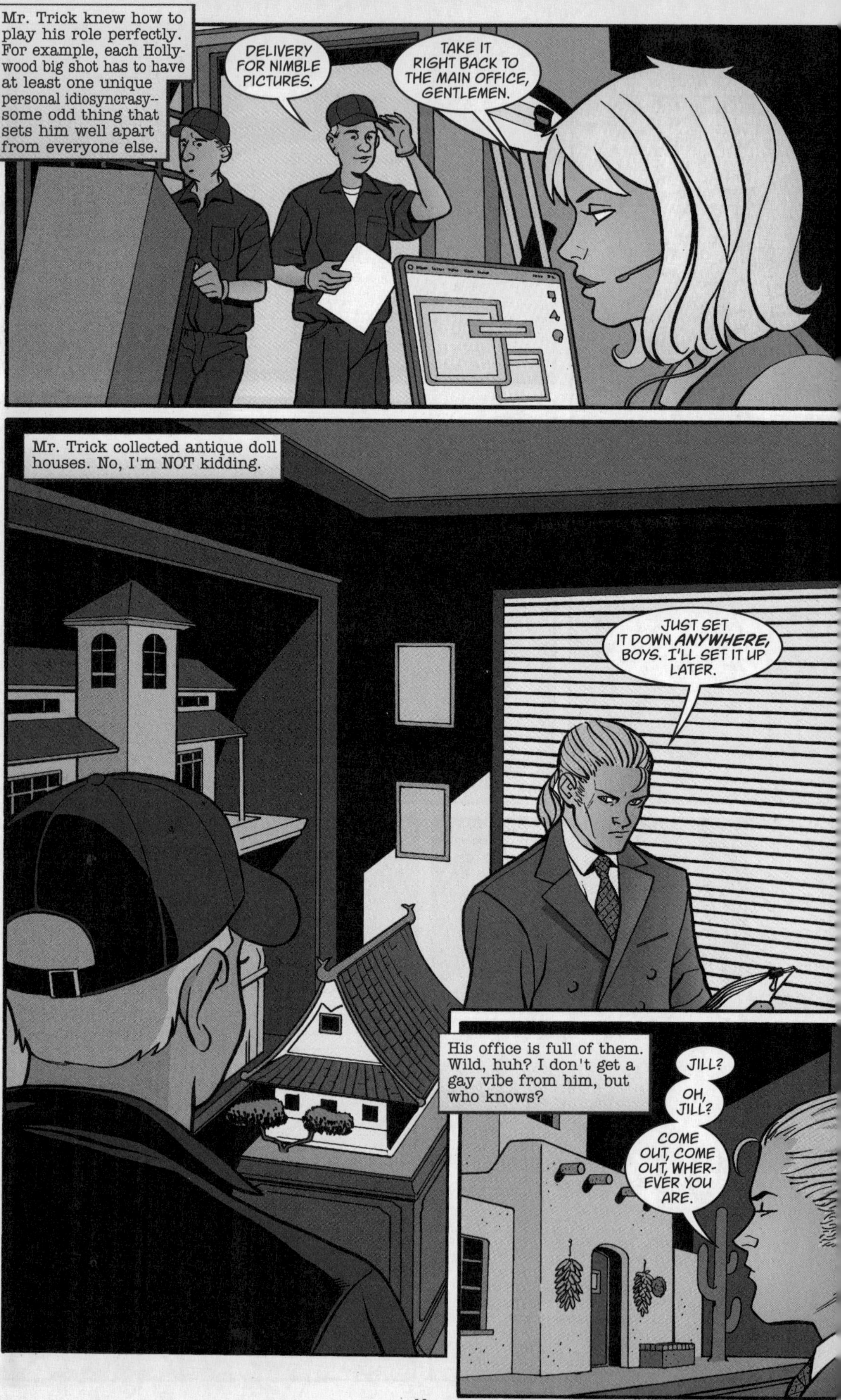
Mr. Trick knew how to play his role perfectly. For example, each Holly-wood big shot has to have at least one unique personal idiosyncrasy--some odd thing that sets him well apart from everyone else.
DELIVERY FOR NIMBLE PICTURES.
TAKE IT RIGHT BACK TO THE MAIN OFFICE, GENTLEMEN.
Mr. Trick collected antique doll houses. No, I'm NOT kidding.
JUST SET IT DOWN ANYWHERE, BOYS. I'LL SET IT UP LATER.
His office is full of them. Wild, huh? I don't get a gay vibe from him, but who knows?
JILL?
OH, JILL?
COME OUT, COME OUT, WHER-EVER YOU ARE.

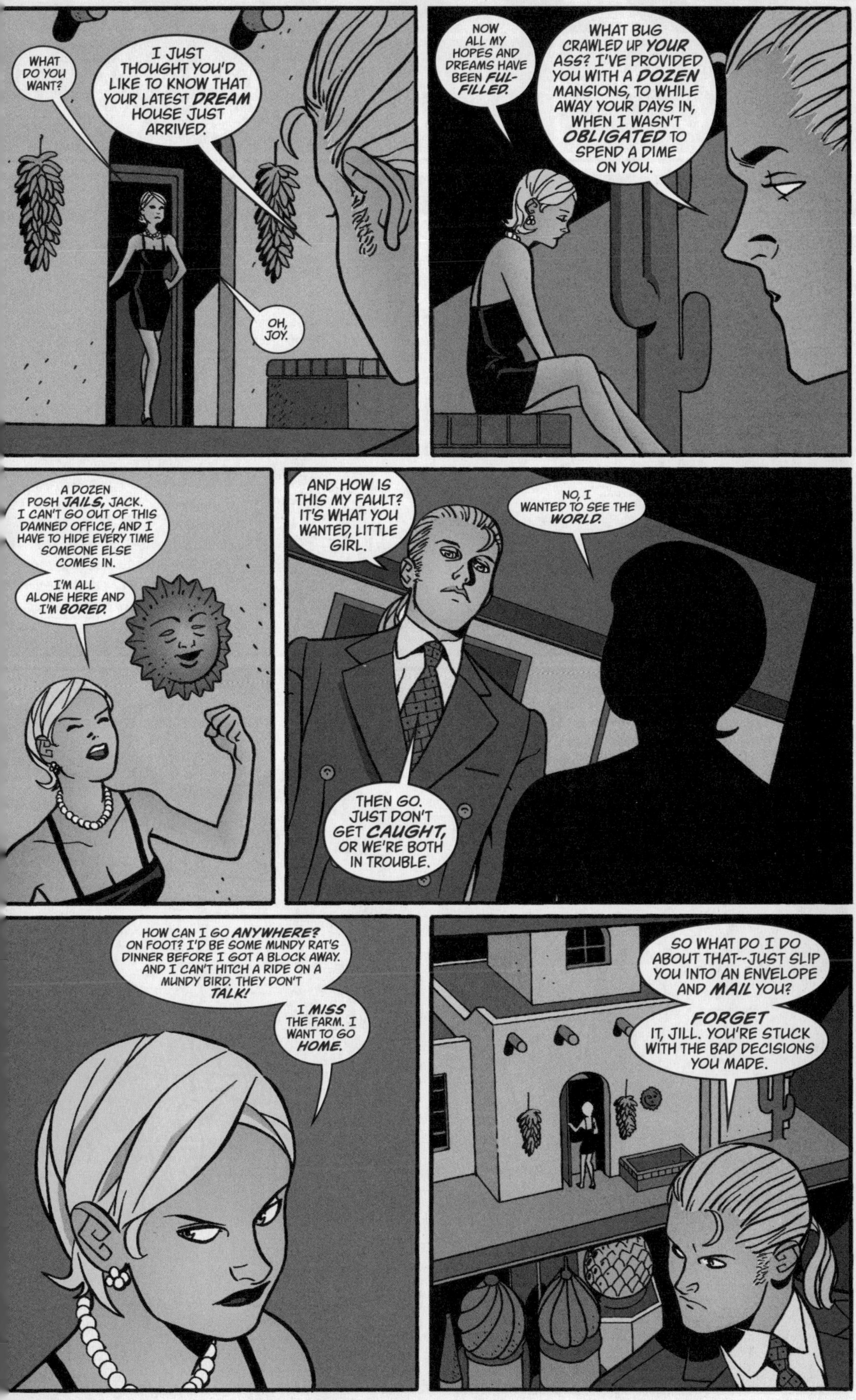

WHAT DO YOU WANT?
I JUST THOUGHT YOU'D LIKE TO KNOW THAT YOUR LATEST DREAM HOUSE JUST ARRIVED.
OH, JOY.
NOW ALL MY HOPES AND DREAMS HAVE BEEN FUL-FILLED.
WHAT BUG CRAWLED UP YOUR ASS? I'VE PROVIDED YOU WITH A DOZEN MANSIONS, TO WHILE AWAY YOUR DAYS IN, WHEN I WASN'T OBLIGATED TO SPEND A DIME ON YOU.
A DOZEN POSH JAILS, JACK. I CAN'T GO OUT OF THIS DAMNED OFFICE, AND I HAVE TO HIDE EVERY TIME SOMEONE ELSE COMES IN.
I'M ALL ALONE HERE AND I'M BORED.
AND HOW IS THIS MY FAULT? IT'S WHAT YOU WANTED, LITTLE GIRL.
NO, I WANTED TO SEE THE WORLD.
THEN GO. JUST DON'T GET CAUGHT, OR WE'RE BOTH IN TROUBLE.
HOW CAN I GO ANYWHERE? ON FOOT? I'D BE SOME MUNDY RAT'S DINNER BEFORE I GOT A BLOCK AWAY. AND I CAN'T HITCH A RIDE ON A MUNDY BIRD. THEY DON'T TALK!
I MISS THE FARM. I WANT TO GO HOME.
SO WHAT DO I DO ABOUT THAT--JUST SLIP YOU INTO AN ENVELOPE AND MAIL YOU?
FORGET IT, JILL. YOU'RE STUCK WITH THE BAD DECISIONS YOU MADE.

CHAPTER FOUR: THE TESTIMONY OF CHARLENE SPECK

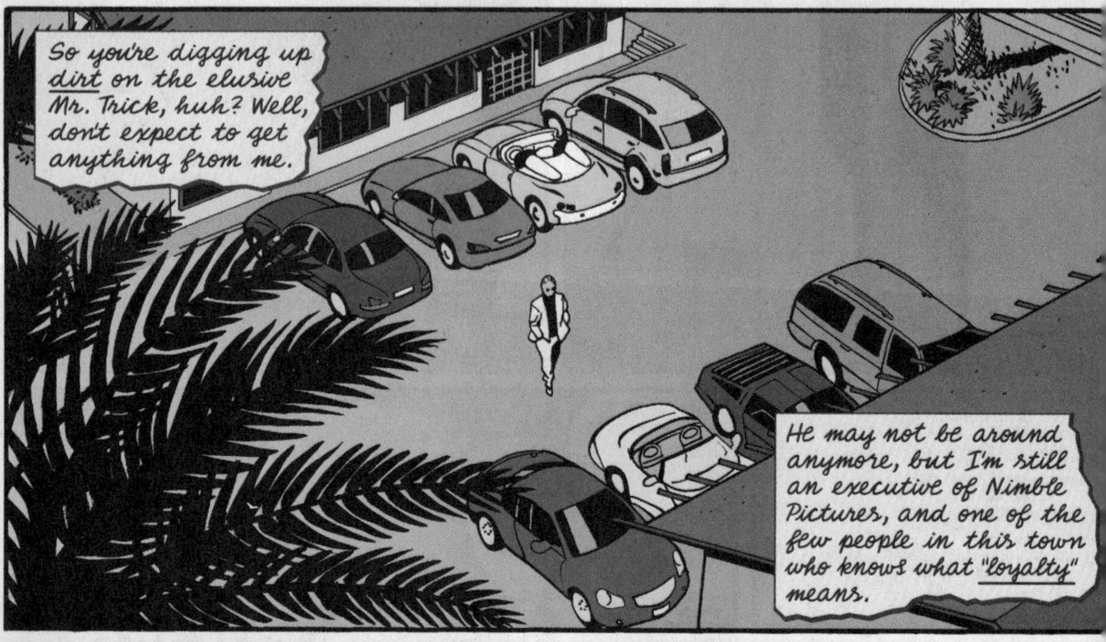

So you're digging up dirt on the elusive Mr. Trick, huh? Well, don't expect to get anything from me.
He may not be around anymore, but I'm still an executive of Nimble Pictures, and one of the few people in this town who knows what "loyalty" means.

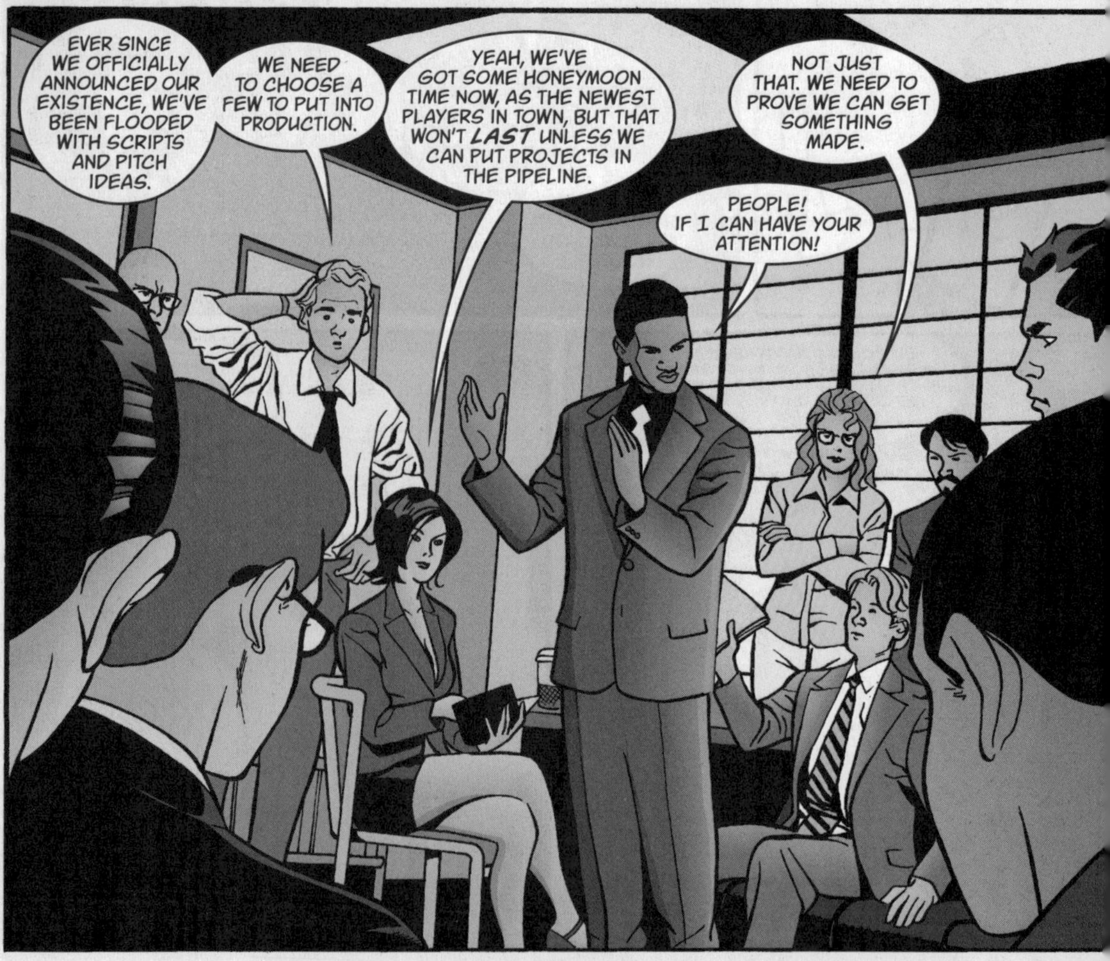

EVER SINCE WE OFFICIALLY ANNOUNCED OUR EXISTENCE, WE'VE BEEN FLOODED WITH SCRIPTS AND PITCH IDEAS.
WE NEED TO CHOOSE A FEW TO PUT INTO PRODUCTION.
YEAH, WE'VE GOT SOME HONEYMOON TIME NOW, AS THE NEWEST PLAYERS IN TOWN, BUT THAT WON'T LAST UNLESS WE CAN PUT PROJECTS IN THE PIPELINE.
NOT JUST THAT. WE NEED TO PROVE WE CAN GET SOMETHING MADE.
PEOPLE! IF I CAN HAVE YOUR ATTENTION!

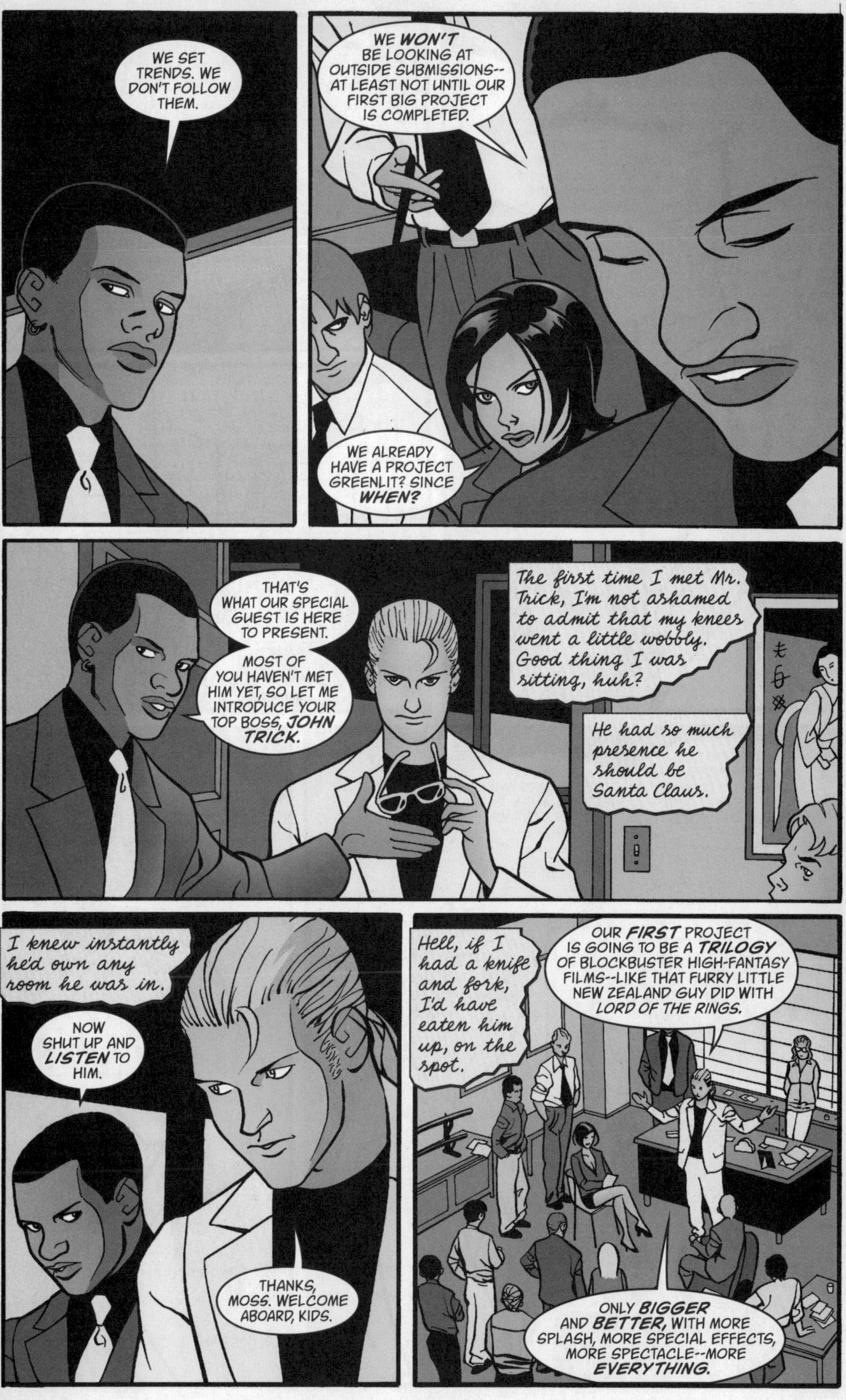

WE SET TRENDS. WE DON'T FOLLOW THEM.
WE WON'T BE LOOKING AT OUTSIDE SUBMISSIONS-- AT LEAST NOT UNTIL OUR FIRST BIG PROJECT IS COMPLETED.
WE ALREADY HAVE A PROJECT GREENLIT? SINCE WHEN?
THAT'S WHAT OUR SPECIAL GUEST IS HERE TO PRESENT.
MOST OF YOU HAVEN'T MET HIM YET, SO LET ME INTRODUCE YOUR TOP BOSS, JOHN TRICK.
The first time I met Mr. Trick, I'm not ashamed to admit that my knees went a little wobbly. Good thing I was sitting, huh?
He had so much presence he should be Santa Claus.
I knew instantly he'd own any room he was in.
NOW SHUT UP AND LISTEN TO HIM.
THANKS, MOSS. WELCOME ABOARD, KIDS.
Hell, if I had a knife and fork, I'd have eaten him up, on the spot.
OUR FIRST PROJECT IS GOING TO BE A TRILOGY OF BLOCKBUSTER HIGH-FANTASY FILMS--LIKE THAT FURRY LITTLE NEW ZEALAND GUY DID WITH LORD OF THE RINGS.
ONLY BIGGER AND BETTER, WITH MORE SPLASH, MORE SPECIAL EFFECTS, MORE SPECTACLE--MORE EVERYTHING.

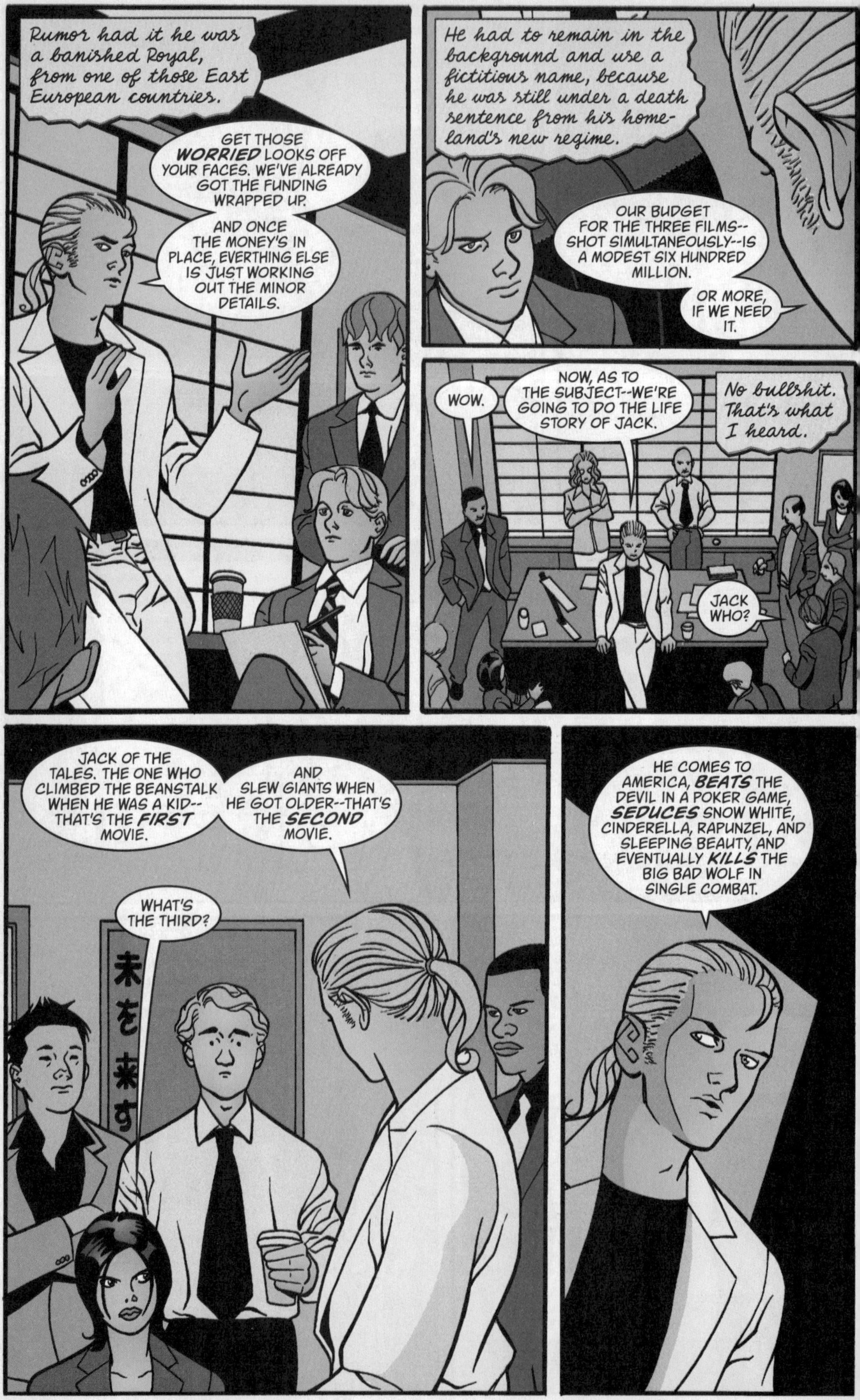

Rumor had it he was a banished Royal, from one of those East European countries.
GET THOSE WORRIED LOOKS OFF YOUR FACES. WE'VE ALREADY GOT THE FUNDING WRAPPED UP.
AND ONCE THE MONEY'S IN PLACE, EVERTHING ELSE IS JUST WORKING OUT THE MINOR DETAILS.
He had to remain in the background and use a fictitious name, because he was still under a death sentence from his homeland's new regime.
OUR BUDGET FOR THE THREE FILMS--SHOT SIMULTANEOUSLY--IS A MODEST SIX HUNDRED MILLION.
OR MORE, IF WE NEED IT.
WOW.
NOW, AS TO THE SUBJECT--WE'RE GOING TO DO THE LIFE STORY OF JACK.
No bullshit. That's what I heard.
JACK WHO?
JACK OF THE TALES. THE ONE WHO CLIMBED THE BEANSTALK WHEN HE WAS A KID--THAT'S THE FIRST MOVIE.
AND SLEW GIANTS WHEN HE GOT OLDER--THAT'S THE SECOND MOVIE.
WHAT'S THE THIRD?
HE COMES TO AMERICA, BEATS THE DEVIL IN A POKER GAME, SEDUCES SNOW WHITE, CINDERELLA, RAPUNZEL, AND SLEEPING BEAUTY, AND EVENTUALLY KILLS THE BIG BAD WOLF IN SINGLE COMBAT.

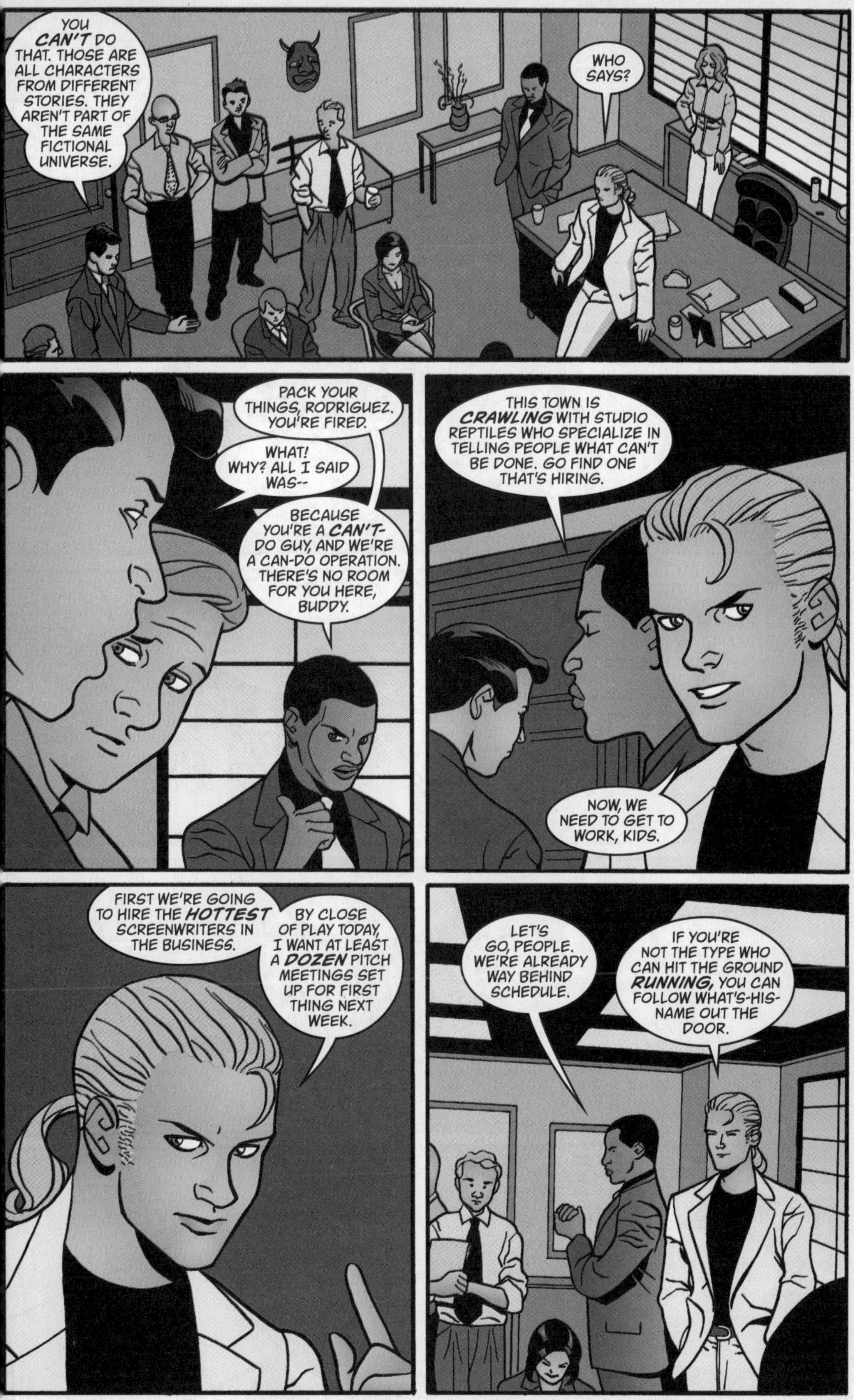
YOU CAN'T DO THAT. THOSE ARE ALL CHARACTERS FROM DIFFERENT STORIES. THEY AREN'T PART OF THE SAME FICTIONAL UNIVERSE.
WHO SAYS?
PACK YOUR THINGS, RODRIGUEZ. YOU'RE FIRED.
WHAT! WHY? ALL I SAID WAS--
BECAUSE YOU'RE A CAN'T-DO GUY, AND WE'RE A CAN-DO OPERATION. THERE'S NO ROOM FOR YOU HERE, BUDDY.
THIS TOWN IS CRAWLING WITH STUDIO REPTILES WHO SPECIALIZE IN TELLING PEOPLE WHAT CAN'T BE DONE. GO FIND ONE THAT'S HIRING.
NOW, WE NEED TO GET TO WORK, KIDS.
FIRST WE'RE GOING TO HIRE THE HOTTEST SCREENWRITERS IN THE BUSINESS.
BY CLOSE OF PLAY TODAY, I WANT AT LEAST A DOZEN PITCH MEETINGS SET UP FOR FIRST THING NEXT WEEK.
LET'S GO, PEOPLE. WE'RE ALREADY WAY BEHIND SCHEDULE.
IF YOU'RE NOT THE TYPE WHO CAN HIT THE GROUND RUNNING, YOU CAN FOLLOW WHAT'S-HIS-NAME OUT THE DOOR.

CHAPTER FIVE: OTHER TESTIMONIALS

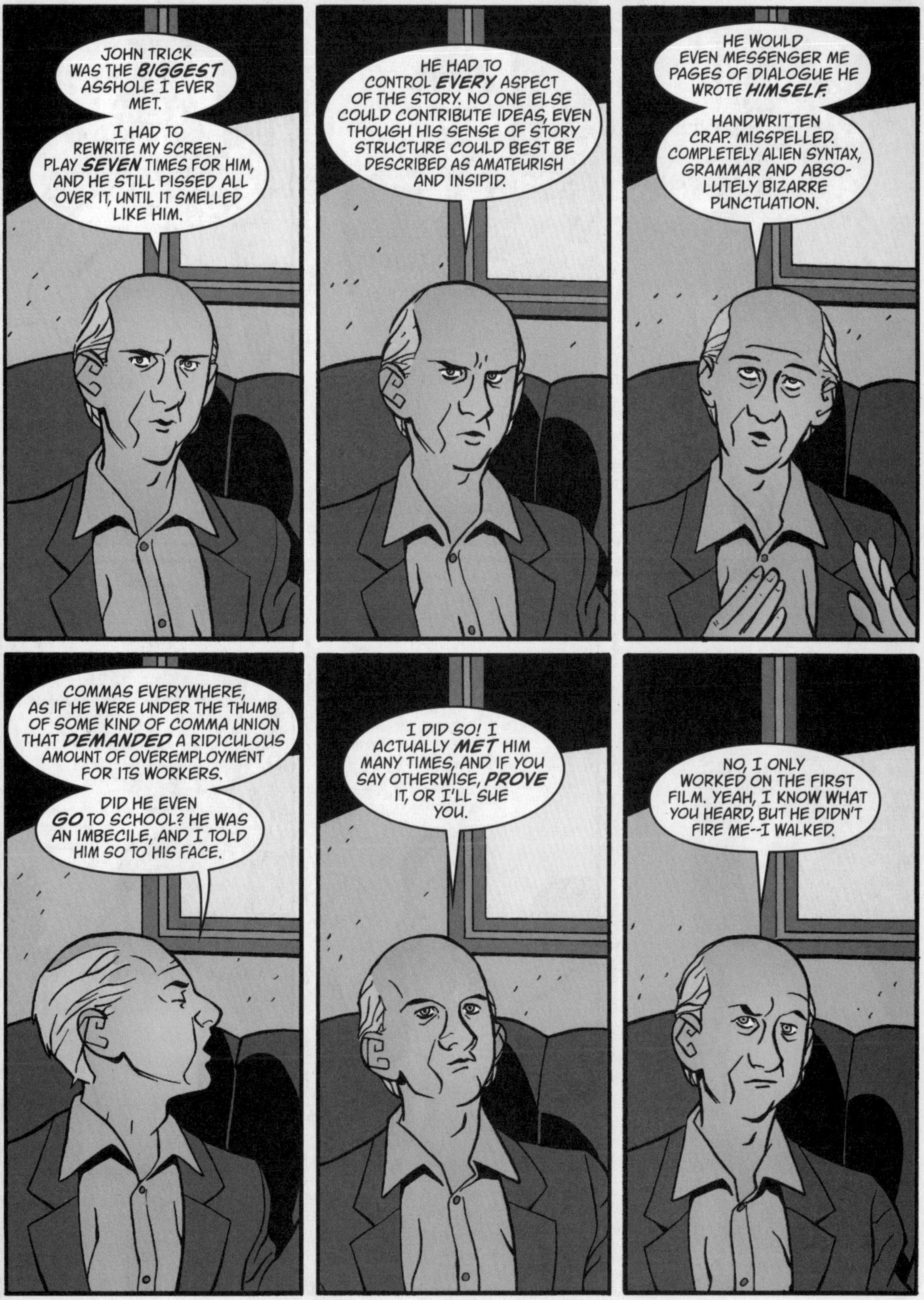
JOHN TRICK WAS THE BIGGEST ASSHOLE I EVER MET.
I HAD TO REWRITE MY SCREEN-PLAY SEVEN TIMES FOR HIM, AND HE STILL PISSED ALL OVER IT, UNTIL IT SMELLED LIKE HIM.
HE HAD TO CONTROL EVERY ASPECT OF THE STORY. NO ONE ELSE COULD CONTRIBUTE IDEAS, EVEN THOUGH HIS SENSE OF STORY STRUCTURE COULD BEST BE DESCRIBED AS AMATEURISH AND INSIPID.
HE WOULD EVEN MESSENGER ME PAGES OF DIALOGUE HE WROTE HIMSELF.
HANDWRITTEN CRAP. MISSPELLED. COMPLETELY ALIEN SYNTAX, GRAMMAR AND ABSO-LUTELY BIZARRE PUNCTUATION.
COMMAS EVERYWHERE, AS IF HE WERE UNDER THE THUMB OF SOME KIND OF COMMA UNION THAT DEMANDED A RIDICULOUS AMOUNT OF OVEREMPLOYMENT FOR ITS WORKERS.
DID HE EVEN GO TO SCHOOL? HE WAS AN IMBECILE, AND I TOLD HIM SO TO HIS FACE.
I DID SO! I ACTUALLY MET HIM MANY TIMES, AND IF YOU SAY OTHERWISE, PROVE IT, OR I'LL SUE YOU.
NO, I ONLY WORKED ON THE FIRST FILM. YEAH, I KNOW WHAT YOU HEARD, BUT HE DIDN'T FIRE ME--I WALKED.

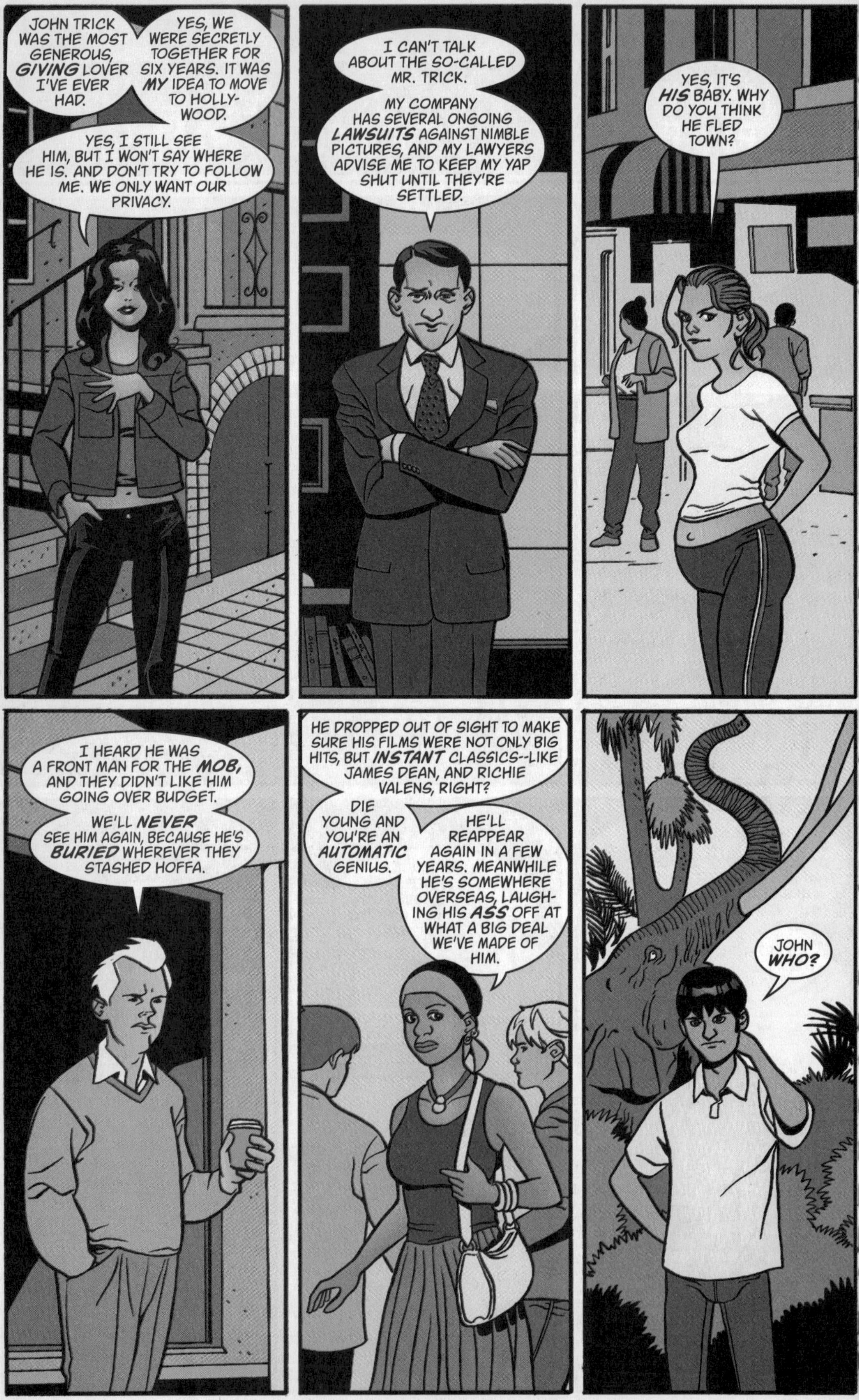
JOHN TRICK WAS THE MOST GENEROUS, GIVING LOVER I'VE EVER HAD.
YES, WE WERE SECRETLY TOGETHER FOR SIX YEARS. IT WAS MY IDEA TO MOVE TO HOLLY-WOOD.
YES, I STILL SEE HIM, BUT I WON'T SAY WHERE HE IS. AND DON'T TRY TO FOLLOW ME. WE ONLY WANT OUR PRIVACY.
I CAN'T TALK ABOUT THE SO-CALLED MR. TRICK.
MY COMPANY HAS SEVERAL ONGOING LAWSUITS AGAINST NIMBLE PICTURES, AND MY LAWYERS ADVISE ME TO KEEP MY YAP SHUT UNTIL THEY'RE SETTLED.
YES, IT'S HIS BABY. WHY DO YOU THINK HE FLED TOWN?
I HEARD HE WAS A FRONT MAN FOR THE MOB, AND THEY DIDN'T LIKE HIM GOING OVER BUDGET.
WE'LL NEVER SEE HIM AGAIN, BECAUSE HE'S BURIED WHEREVER THEY STASHED HOFFA.
HE DROPPED OUT OF SIGHT TO MAKE SURE HIS FILMS WERE NOT ONLY BIG HITS, BUT INSTANT CLASSICS--LIKE JAMES DEAN, AND RICHIE VALENS, RIGHT?
DIE YOUNG AND YOU'RE AN AUTOMATIC GENIUS.
HE'LL REAPPEAR AGAIN IN A FEW YEARS. MEANWHILE HE'S SOMEWHERE OVERSEAS, LAUGH-ING HIS ASS OFF AT WHAT A BIG DEAL WE'VE MADE OF HIM.
JOHN WHO?

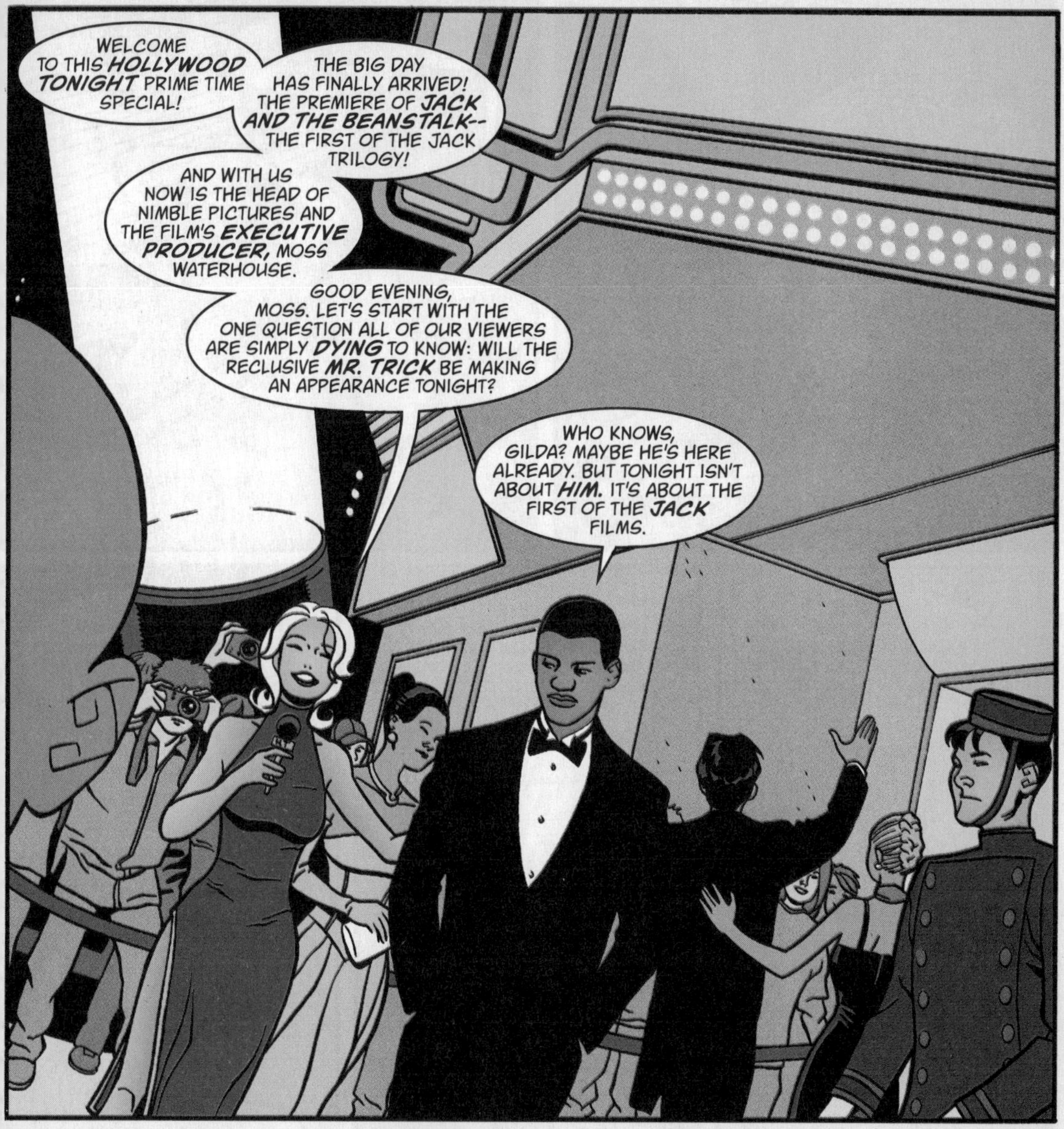
WELCOME TO THIS HOLLYWOOD TONIGHT PRIME TIME SPECIAL!
THE BIG DAY HAS FINALLY ARRIVED! THE PREMIERE OF JACK AND THE BEANSTALK-- THE FIRST OF THE JACK TRILOGY!
AND WITH US NOW IS THE HEAD OF NIMBLE PICTURES AND THE FILM'S EXECUTIVE PRODUCER, MOSS WATERHOUSE.
GOOD EVENING, MOSS. LET'S START WITH THE ONE QUESTION ALL OF OUR VIEWERS ARE SIMPLY DYING TO KNOW: WILL THE RECLUSIVE MR. TRICK BE MAKING AN APPEARANCE TONIGHT?
WHO KNOWS, GILDA? MAYBE HE'S HERE ALREADY. BUT TONIGHT ISN'T ABOUT HIM. IT'S ABOUT THE FIRST OF THE JACK FILMS.

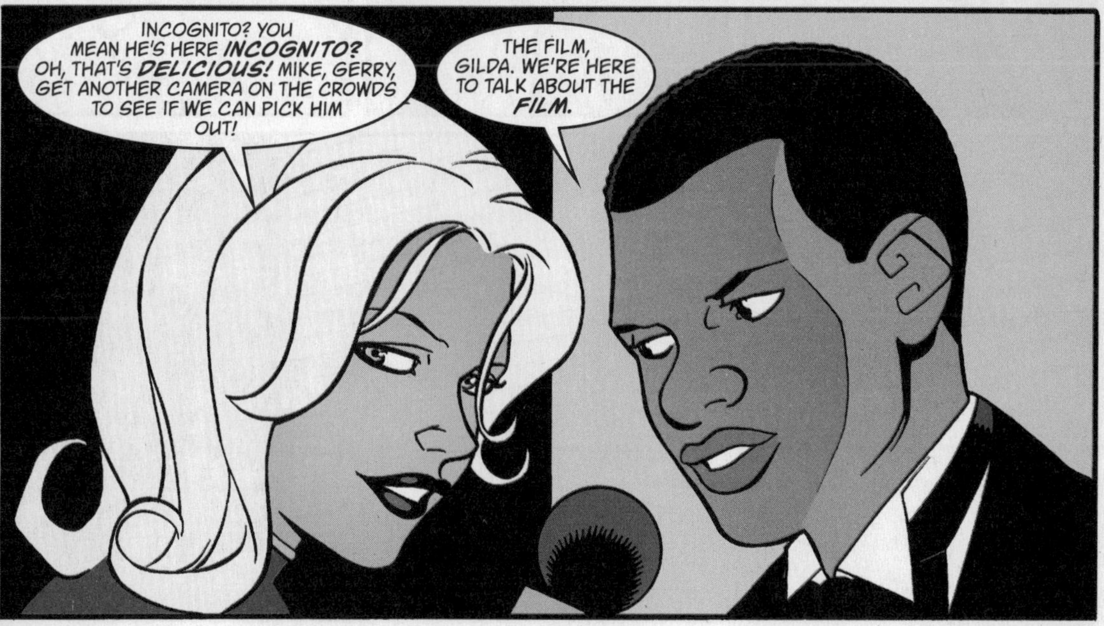
INCOGNITO? YOU MEAN HE'S HERE INCOGNITO? OH, THAT'S DELICIOUS! MIKE, GERRY, GET ANOTHER CAMERA ON THE CROWDS TO SEE IF WE CAN PICK HIM OUT!
THE FILM, GILDA. WE'RE HERE TO TALK ABOUT THE FILM.

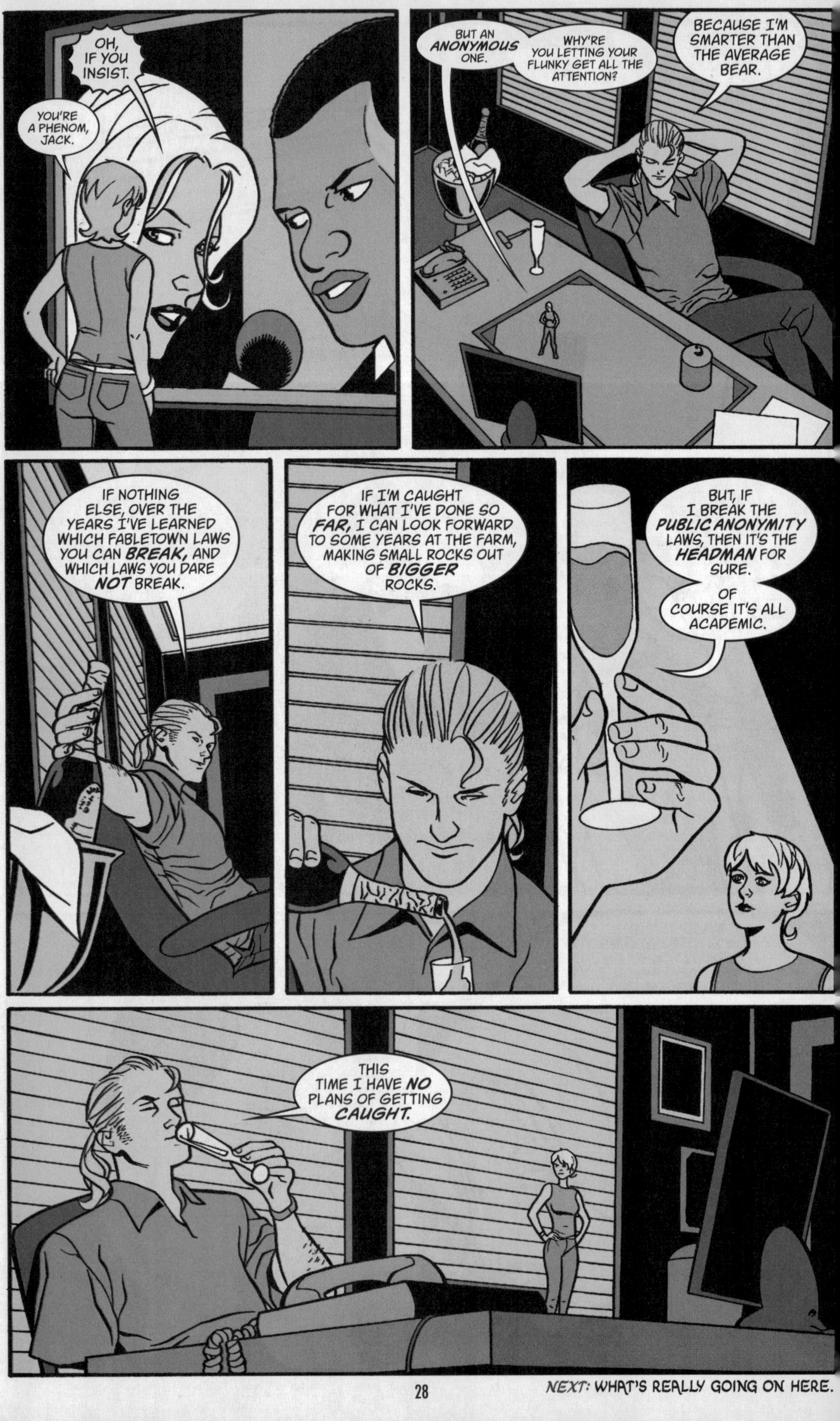
OH, IF YOU INSIST.
YOU'RE A PHENOM, JACK.
BUT AN ANONYMOUS ONE.
WHY'RE YOU LETTING YOUR FLUNKY GET ALL THE ATTENTION?
BECAUSE I'M SMARTER THAN THE AVERAGE BEAR.
IF NOTHING ELSE, OVER THE YEARS I'VE LEARNED WHICH FABLETOWN LAWS YOU CAN BREAK, AND WHICH LAWS YOU DARE NOT BREAK.
IF I'M CAUGHT FOR WHAT I'VE DONE SO FAR, I CAN LOOK FORWARD TO SOME YEARS AT THE FARM, MAKING SMALL ROCKS OUT OF BIGGER ROCKS.
BUT, IF I BREAK THE PUBLIC ANONYMITY LAWS, THEN IT'S THE HEADMAN FOR SURE.
OF COURSE IT'S ALL ACADEMIC.
THIS TIME I HAVE NO PLANS OF GETTING CAUGHT.

NEXT: WHAT'S REALLY GOING ON HERE.

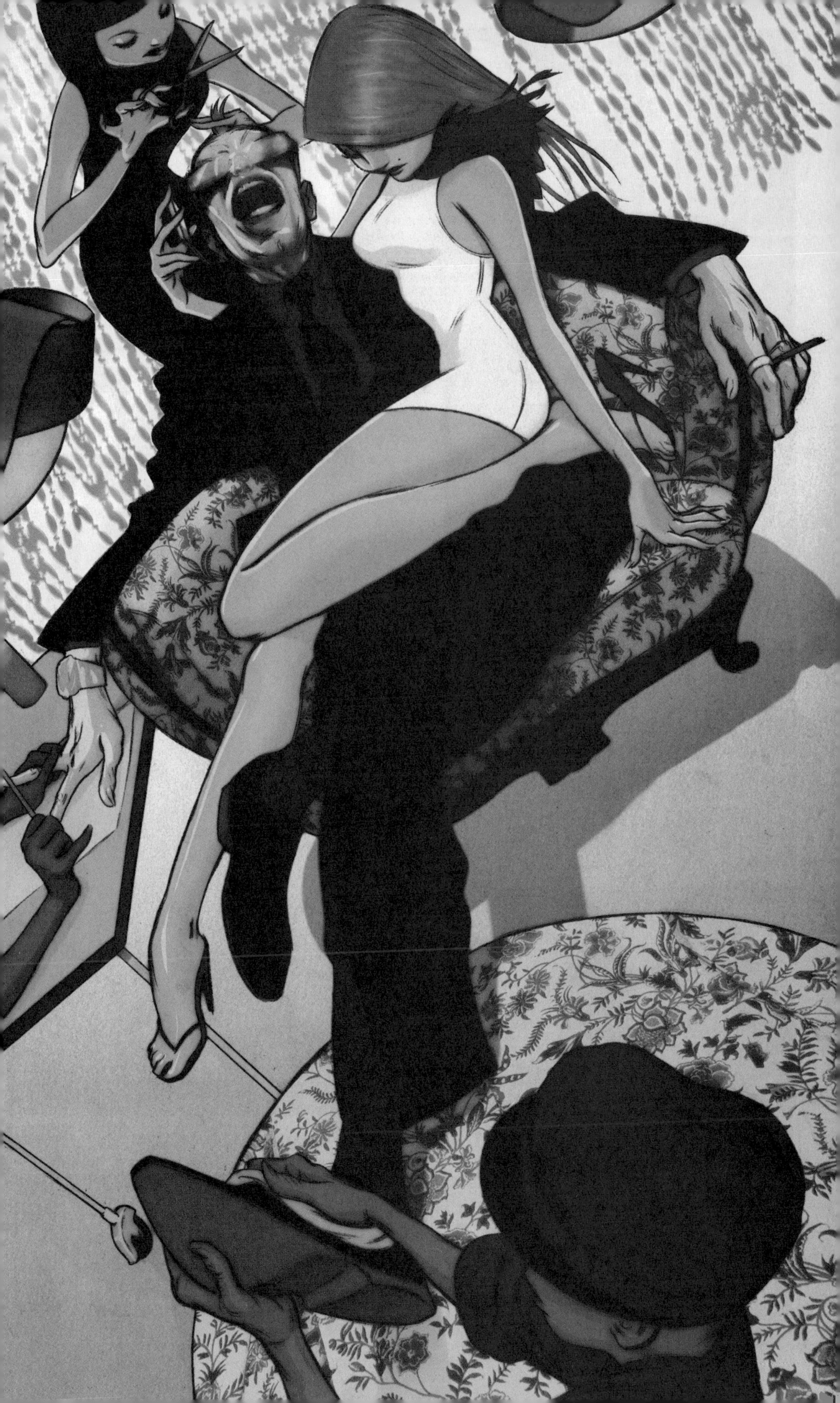

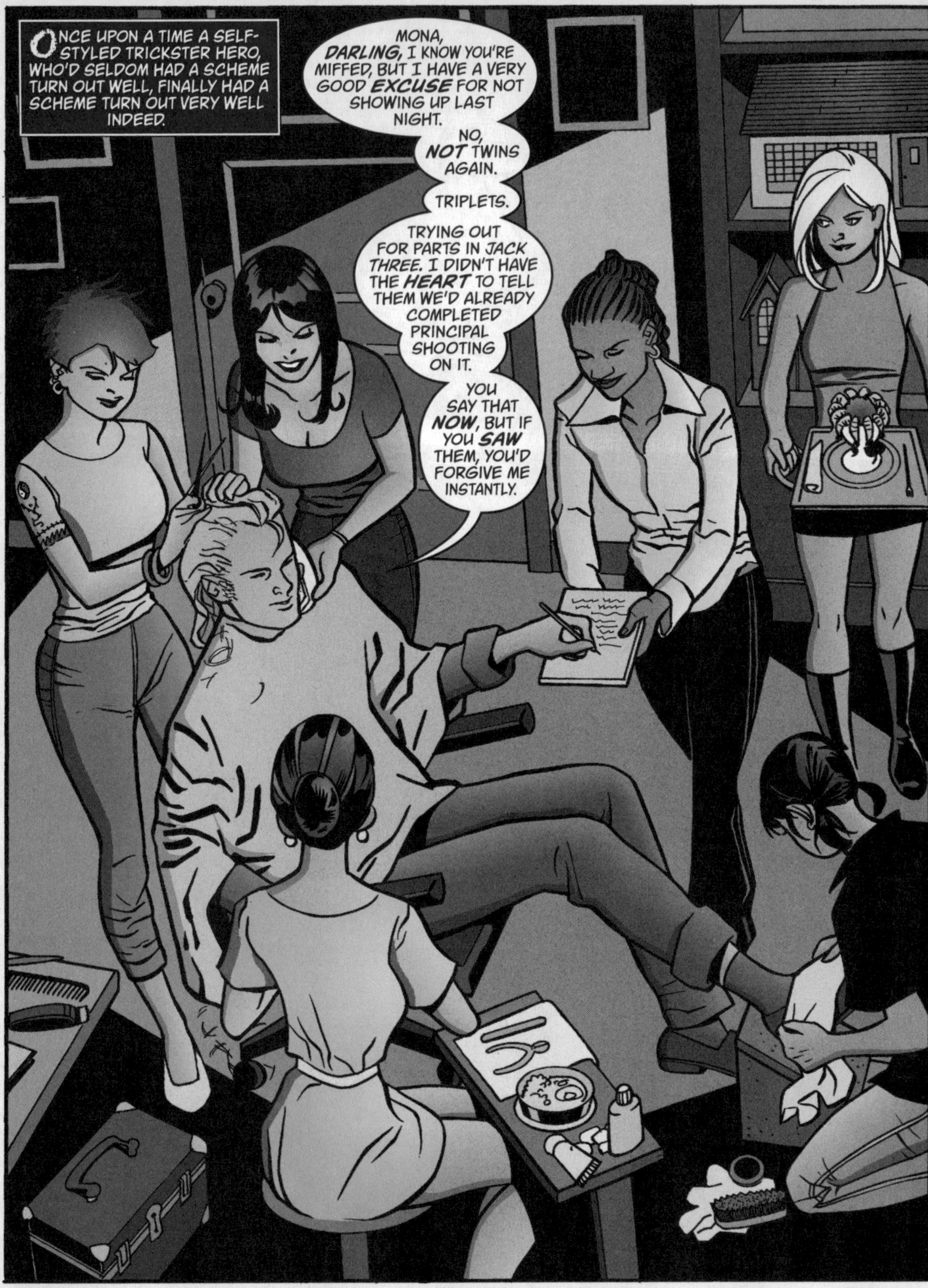
ONCE UPON A TIME A SELF-STYLED TRICKSTER HERO, WHO'D SELDOM HAD A SCHEME TURN OUT WELL, FINALLY HAD A SCHEME TURN OUT VERY WELL INDEED.
MONA, DARLING, I KNOW YOU'RE MIFFED, BUT I HAVE A VERY GOOD EXCUSE FOR NOT SHOWING UP LAST NIGHT.
NO, NOT TWINS AGAIN.
TRIPLETS.
TRYING OUT FOR PARTS IN JACK THREE. I DIDN'T HAVE THE HEART TO TELL THEM WE'D ALREADY COMPLETED PRINCIPAL SHOOTING ON IT.
YOU SAY THAT NOW, BUT IF YOU SAW THEM, YOU'D FORGIVE ME INSTANTLY.

JACK BE NIMBLE

PART TWO OF TWO

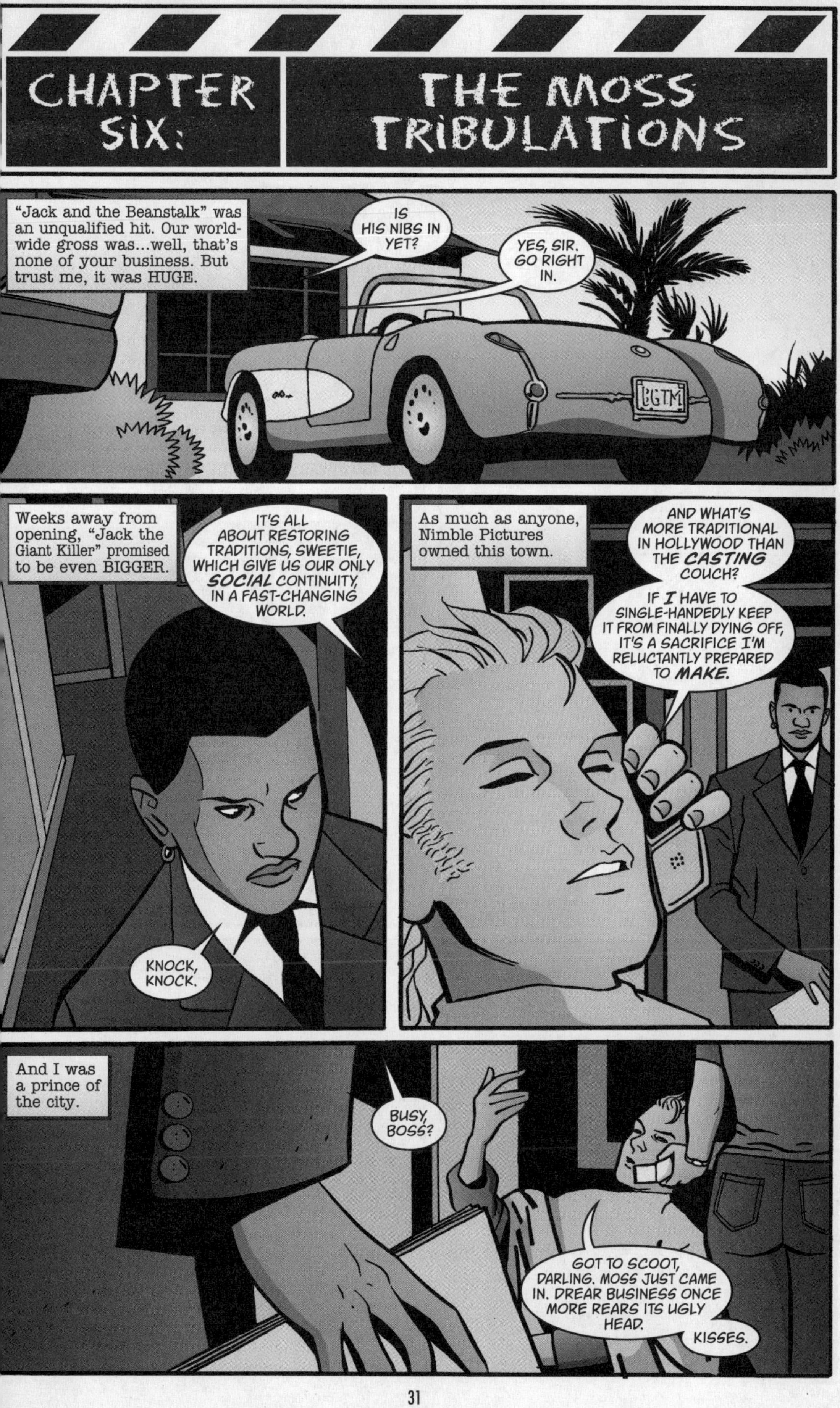
CHAPTER SIX:
THE MOSS TRIBULATIONS
"Jack and the Beanstalk" was an unqualified hit. Our world-wide gross was...well, that's none of your business. But trust me, it was HUGE.
IS HIS NIBS IN YET?
YES, SIR. GO RIGHT IN.
BGTM
Weeks away from opening, "Jack the Giant Killer" promised to be even BIGGER.
IT'S ALL ABOUT RESTORING TRADITIONS, SWEETIE, WHICH GIVE US OUR ONLY SOCIAL CONTINUITY, IN A FAST-CHANGING WORLD.
KNOCK, KNOCK.
As much as anyone, Nimble Pictures owned this town.
AND WHAT'S MORE TRADITIONAL IN HOLLYWOOD THAN THE CASTING COUCH?
IF I HAVE TO SINGLE-HANDEDLY KEEP IT FROM FINALLY DYING OFF, IT'S A SACRIFICE I'M RELUCTANTLY PREPARED TO MAKE.
And I was a prince of the city.
BUSY, BOSS?
GOT TO SCOOT, DARLING. MOSS JUST CAME IN. DREAR BUSINESS ONCE MORE REARS ITS UGLY HEAD.
KISSES.

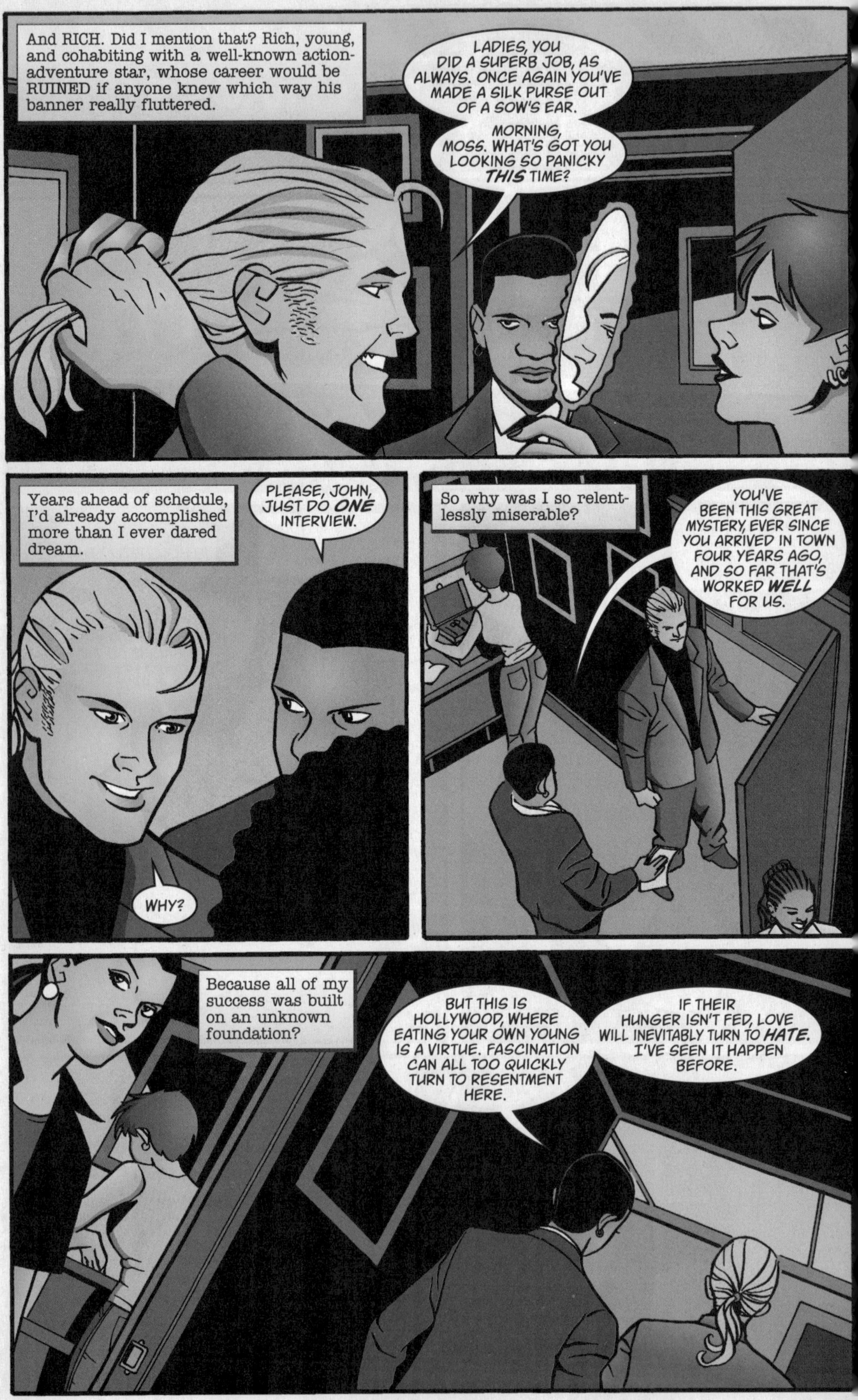
And RICH. Did I mention that? Rich, young, and cohabiting with a well-known action-adventure star, whose career would be RUINED if anyone knew which way his banner really fluttered.
LADIES, YOU DID A SUPERB JOB, AS ALWAYS. ONCE AGAIN YOU'VE MADE A SILK PURSE OUT OF A SOW'S EAR.
MORNING, MOSS. WHAT'S GOT YOU LOOKING SO PANICKY *THIS* TIME?
Years ahead of schedule, I'd already accomplished more than I ever dared dream.
PLEASE, JOHN, JUST DO *ONE* INTERVIEW.
WHY?
So why was I so relentlessly miserable?
YOU'VE BEEN THIS GREAT MYSTERY, EVER SINCE YOU ARRIVED IN TOWN FOUR YEARS AGO, AND SO FAR THAT'S WORKED *WELL* FOR US.
Because all of my success was built on an unknown foundation?
BUT THIS IS HOLLYWOOD, WHERE EATING YOUR OWN YOUNG IS A VIRTUE. FASCINATION CAN ALL TOO QUICKLY TURN TO RESENTMENT HERE.
IF THEIR HUNGER ISN'T FED, LOVE WILL INEVITABLY TURN TO *HATE.* I'VE SEEN IT HAPPEN BEFORE.

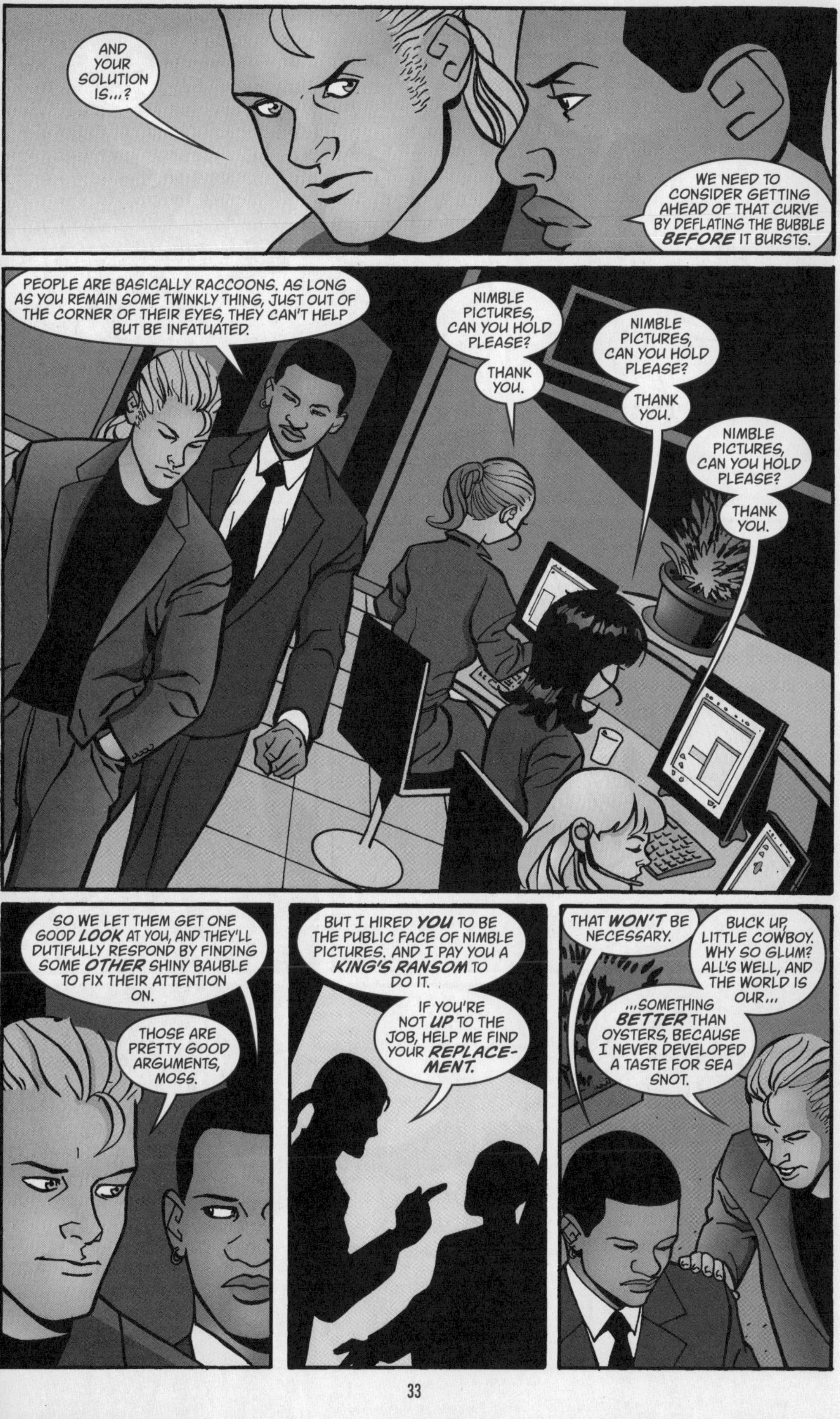
AND YOUR SOLUTION IS...?
WE NEED TO CONSIDER GETTING AHEAD OF THAT CURVE BY DEFLATING THE BUBBLE BEFORE IT BURSTS.
PEOPLE ARE BASICALLY RACCOONS. AS LONG AS YOU REMAIN SOME TWINKLY THING, JUST OUT OF THE CORNER OF THEIR EYES, THEY CAN'T HELP BUT BE INFATUATED.
NIMBLE PICTURES, CAN YOU HOLD PLEASE?
THANK YOU.
NIMBLE PICTURES, CAN YOU HOLD PLEASE?
THANK YOU.
NIMBLE PICTURES, CAN YOU HOLD PLEASE?
THANK YOU.
SO WE LET THEM GET ONE GOOD LOOK AT YOU, AND THEY'LL DUTIFULLY RESPOND BY FINDING SOME OTHER SHINY BAUBLE TO FIX THEIR ATTENTION ON.
THOSE ARE PRETTY GOOD ARGUMENTS, MOSS.
BUT I HIRED YOU TO BE THE PUBLIC FACE OF NIMBLE PICTURES. AND I PAY YOU A KING'S RANSOM TO DO IT.
IF YOU'RE NOT UP TO THE JOB, HELP ME FIND YOUR REPLACEMENT.
THAT WON'T BE NECESSARY.
BUCK UP, LITTLE COWBOY. WHY SO GLUM? ALL'S WELL, AND THE WORLD IS OUR...
...SOMETHING BETTER THAN OYSTERS, BECAUSE I NEVER DEVELOPED A TASTE FOR SEA SNOT.

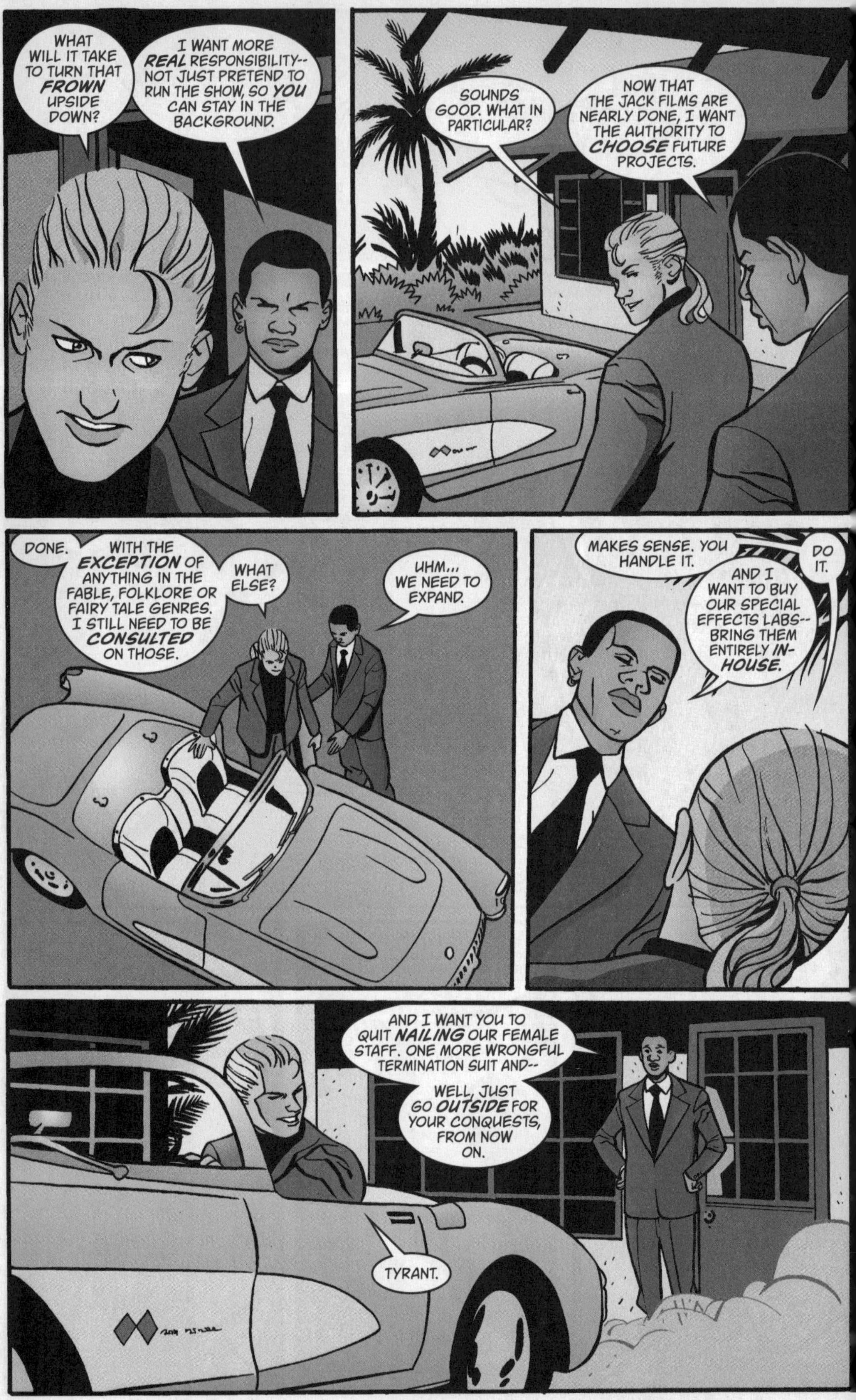
WHAT WILL IT TAKE TO TURN THAT FROWN UPSIDE DOWN?
I WANT MORE REAL RESPONSIBILITY-- NOT JUST PRETEND TO RUN THE SHOW, SO YOU CAN STAY IN THE BACKGROUND.
SOUNDS GOOD. WHAT IN PARTICULAR?
NOW THAT THE JACK FILMS ARE NEARLY DONE, I WANT THE AUTHORITY TO CHOOSE FUTURE PROJECTS.
DONE.
WITH THE EXCEPTION OF ANYTHING IN THE FABLE, FOLKLORE OR FAIRY TALE GENRES. I STILL NEED TO BE CONSULTED ON THOSE.
WHAT ELSE?
UHM... WE NEED TO EXPAND.
MAKES SENSE. YOU HANDLE IT.
AND I WANT TO BUY OUR SPECIAL EFFECTS LABS-- BRING THEM ENTIRELY IN-HOUSE.
DO IT.
AND I WANT YOU TO QUIT NAILING OUR FEMALE STAFF. ONE MORE WRONGFUL TERMINATION SUIT AND--
WELL, JUST GO OUTSIDE FOR YOUR CONQUESTS, FROM NOW ON.
TYRANT.

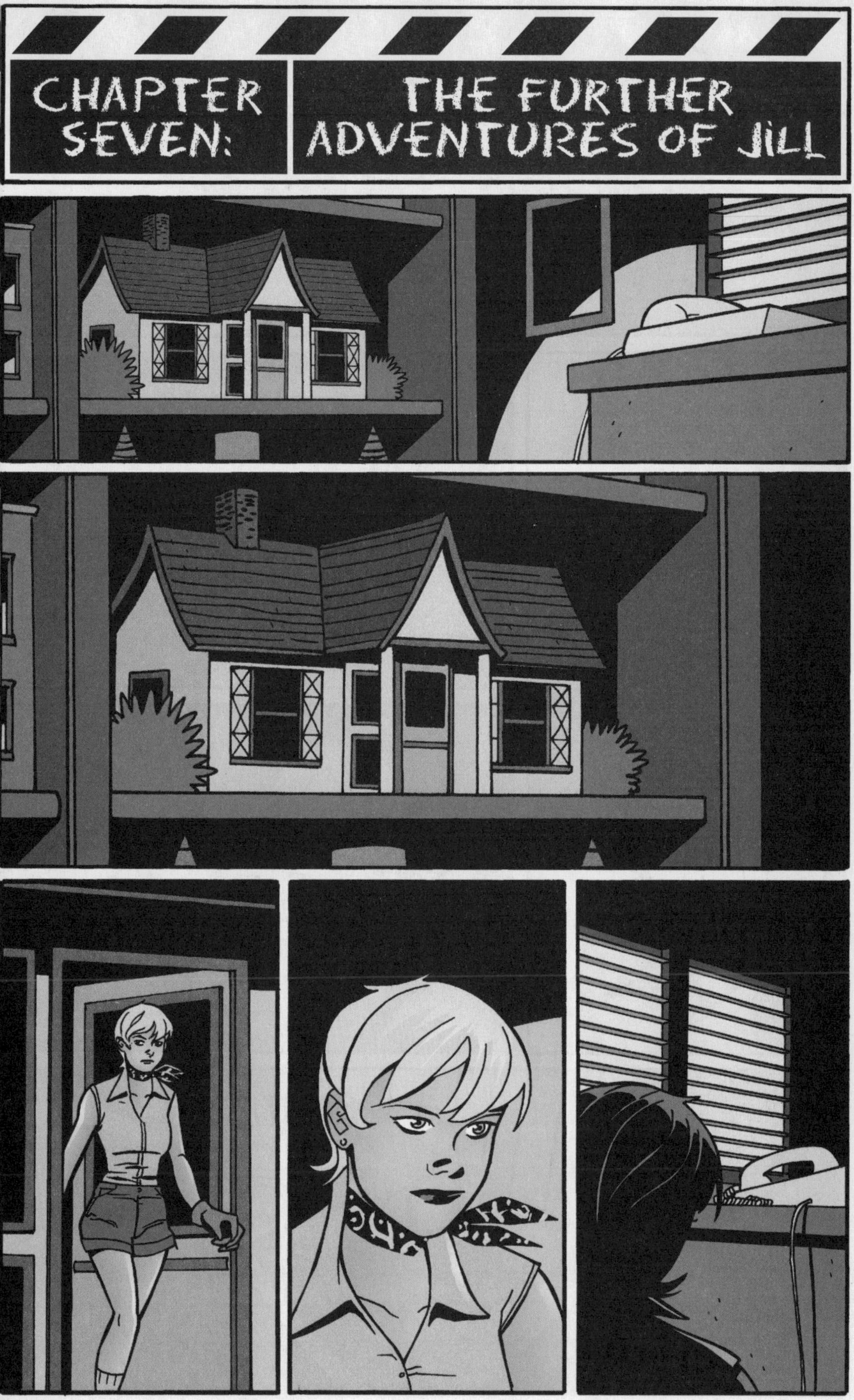
CHAPTER SEVEN:
THE FURTHER ADVENTURES OF JILL

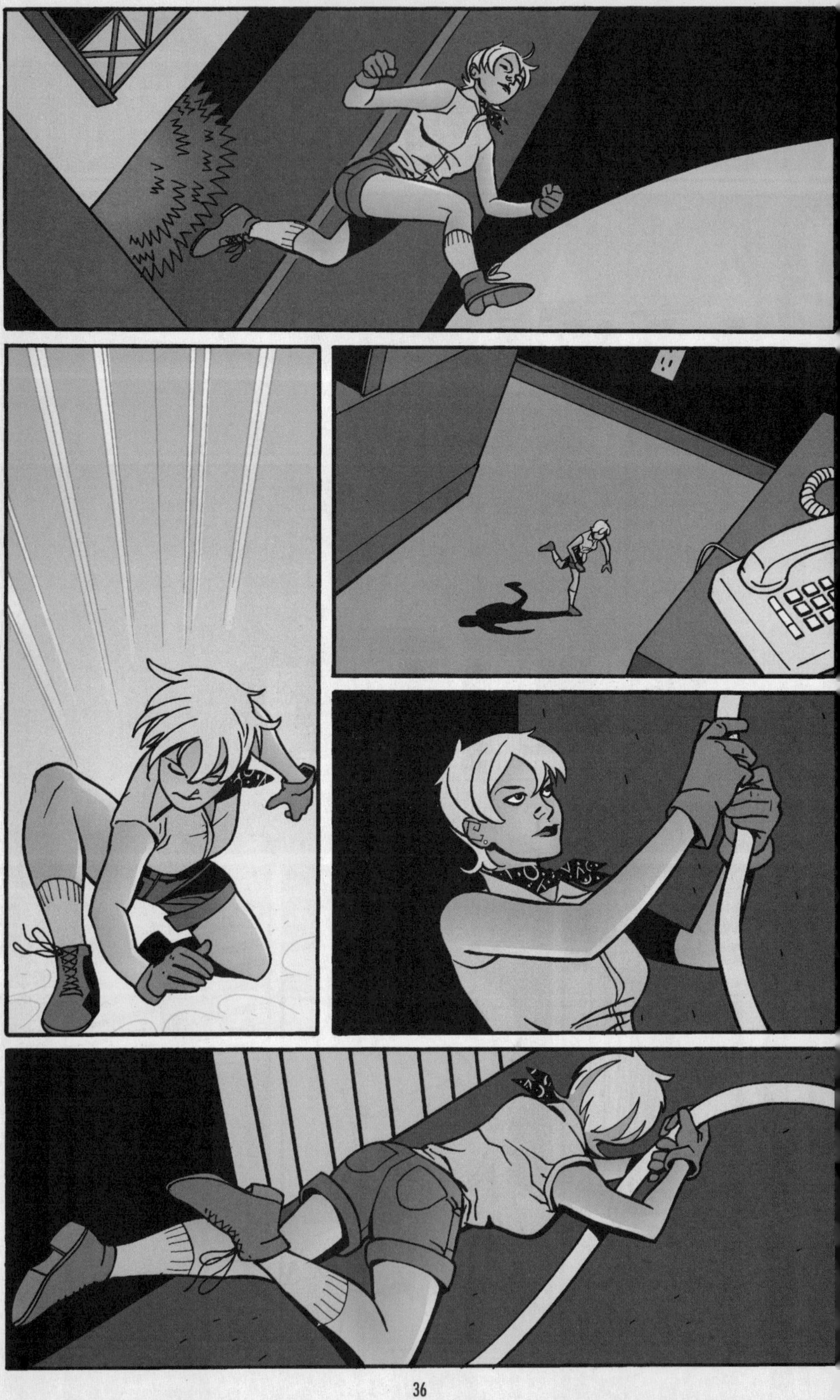

OKAY, LIFT, GIRL!

AND PUSH!

WAY TO GO, HOT MAMA!

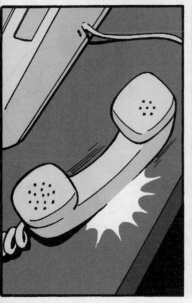

NOW FOR THE TRICKY PART--

--DIALING.

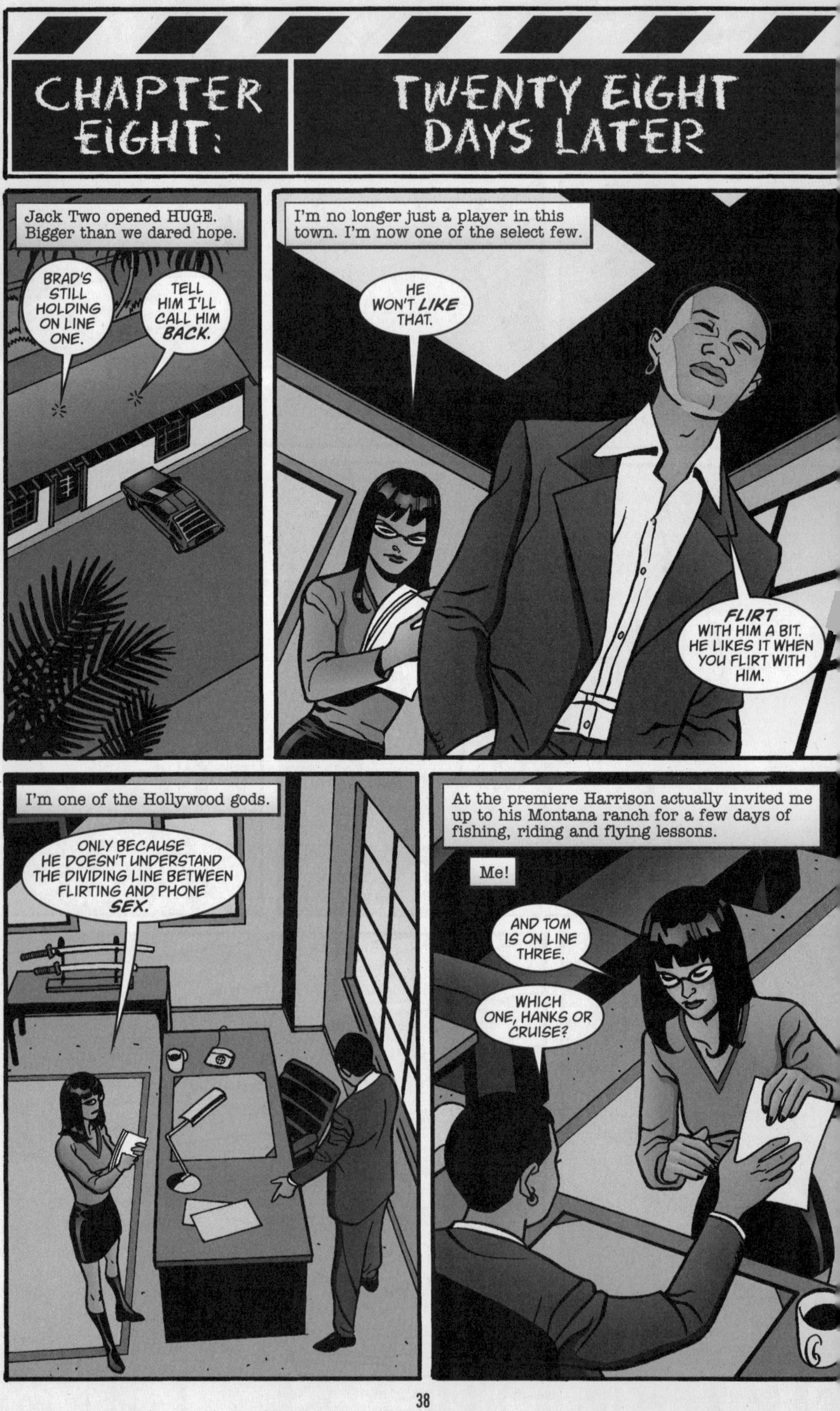
CHAPTER EIGHT:
TWENTY EIGHT DAYS LATER
Jack Two opened HUGE. Bigger than we dared hope.
BRAD'S STILL HOLDING ON LINE ONE.
TELL HIM I'LL CALL HIM BACK.
I'm no longer just a player in this town. I'm now one of the select few.
HE WON'T LIKE THAT.
FLIRT WITH HIM A BIT. HE LIKES IT WHEN YOU FLIRT WITH HIM.
I'm one of the Hollywood gods.
ONLY BECAUSE HE DOESN'T UNDERSTAND THE DIVIDING LINE BETWEEN FLIRTING AND PHONE SEX.
At the premiere Harrison actually invited me up to his Montana ranch for a few days of fishing, riding and flying lessons.
Me!
AND TOM IS ON LINE THREE.
WHICH ONE, HANKS OR CRUISE?

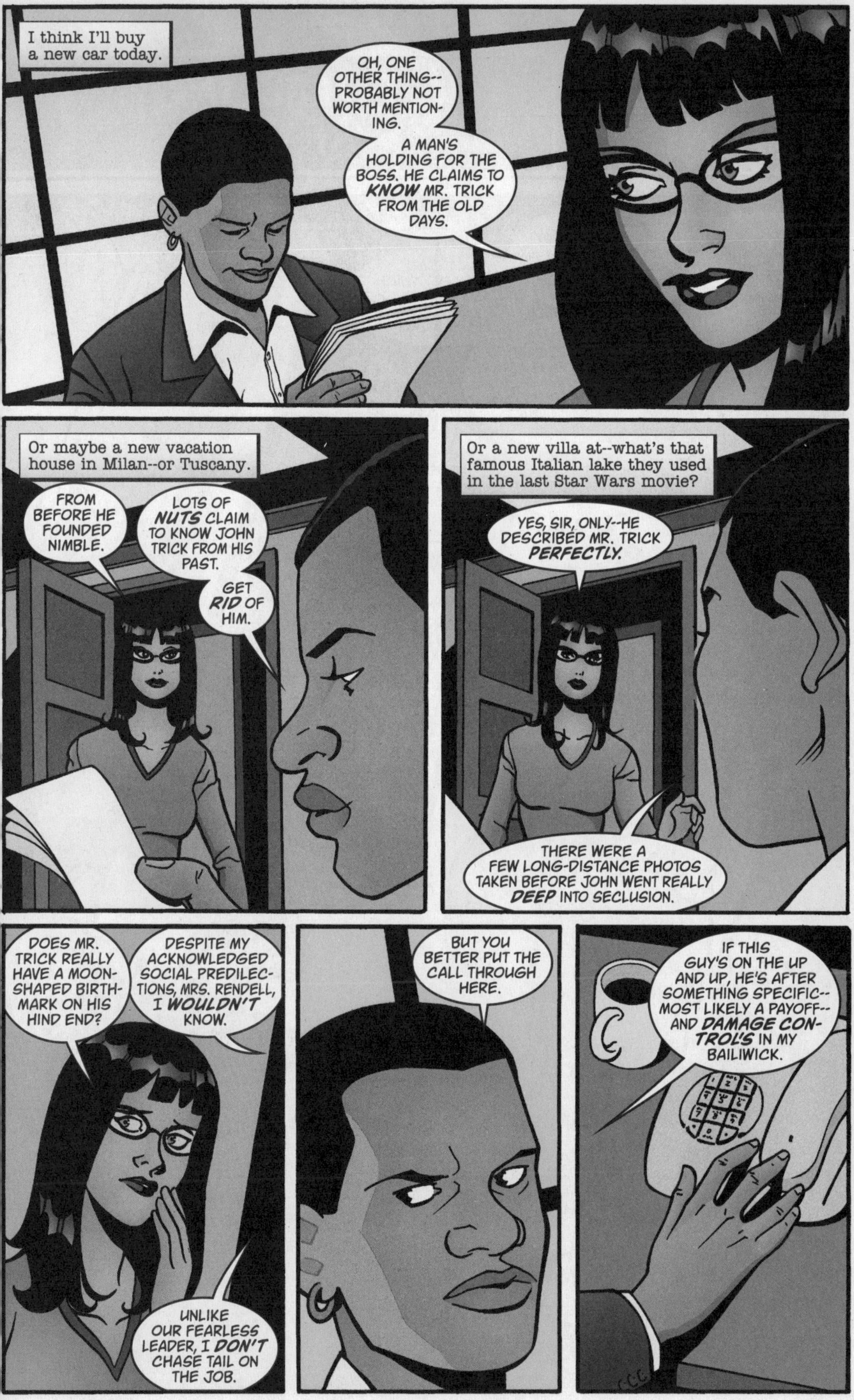
I think I'll buy a new car today.
OH, ONE OTHER THING--PROBABLY NOT WORTH MENTIONING.
A MAN'S HOLDING FOR THE BOSS. HE CLAIMS TO KNOW MR. TRICK FROM THE OLD DAYS.
Or maybe a new vacation house in Milan--or Tuscany.
FROM BEFORE HE FOUNDED NIMBLE.
LOTS OF NUTS CLAIM TO KNOW JOHN TRICK FROM HIS PAST.
GET RID OF HIM.
Or a new villa at--what's that famous Italian lake they used in the last Star Wars movie?
YES, SIR, ONLY--HE DESCRIBED MR. TRICK PERFECTLY.
THERE WERE A FEW LONG-DISTANCE PHOTOS TAKEN BEFORE JOHN WENT REALLY DEEP INTO SECLUSION.
DOES MR. TRICK REALLY HAVE A MOON-SHAPED BIRTHMARK ON HIS HIND END?
DESPITE MY ACKNOWLEDGED SOCIAL PREDILECTIONS, MRS. RENDELL, I WOULDN'T KNOW.
UNLIKE OUR FEARLESS LEADER, I DON'T CHASE TAIL ON THE JOB.
BUT YOU BETTER PUT THE CALL THROUGH HERE.
IF THIS GUY'S ON THE UP AND UP, HE'S AFTER SOMETHING SPECIFIC--MOST LIKELY A PAYOFF--AND DAMAGE CONTROL'S IN MY BAILIWICK.

CHAPTER NINE: TUMBLING AFTER

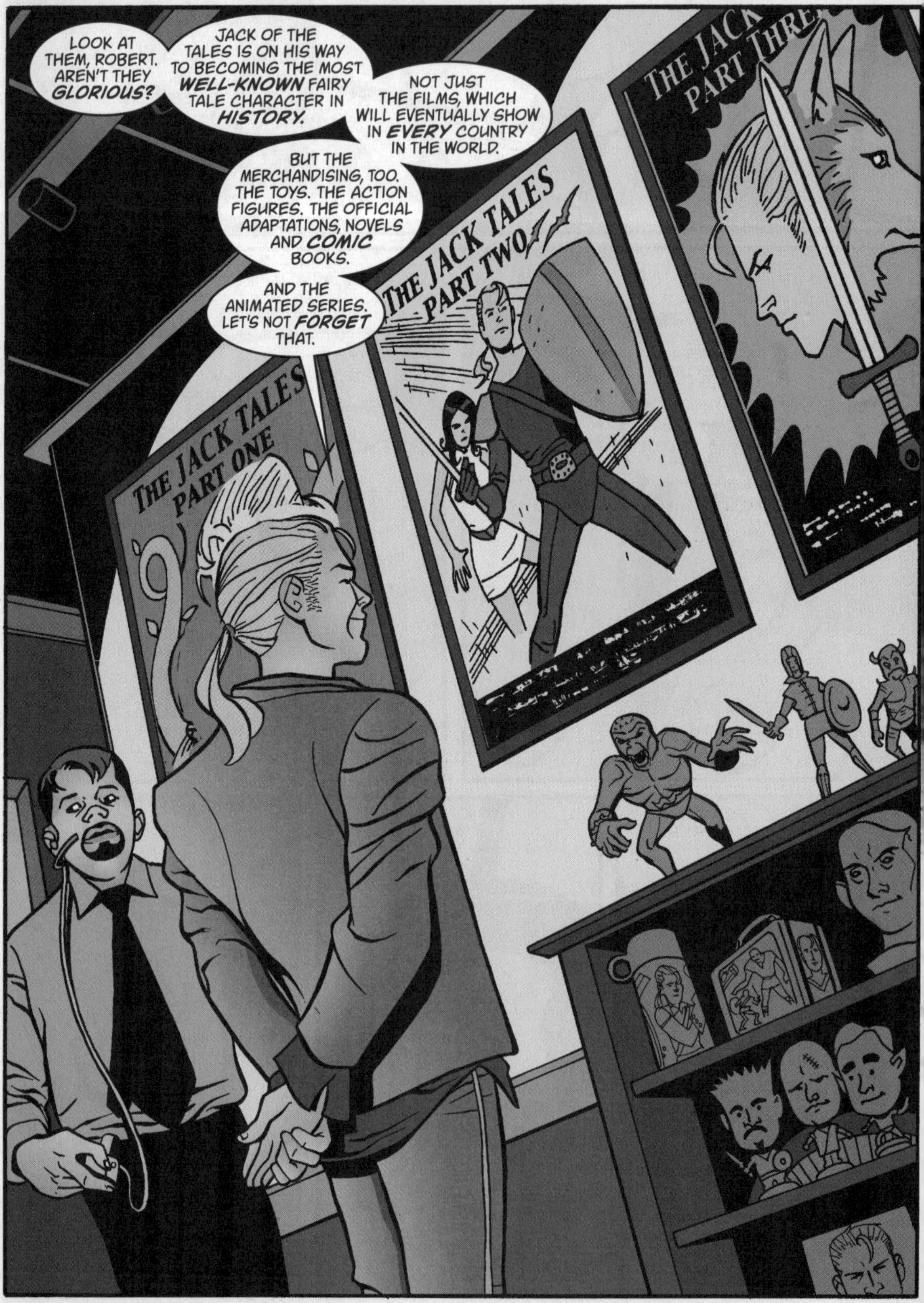

LOOK AT THEM, ROBERT. AREN'T THEY *GLORIOUS?*
JACK OF THE TALES IS ON HIS WAY TO BECOMING THE MOST *WELL-KNOWN* FAIRY TALE CHARACTER IN *HISTORY.*
NOT JUST THE FILMS, WHICH WILL EVENTUALLY SHOW IN *EVERY* COUNTRY IN THE WORLD.
BUT THE MERCHANDISING, TOO. THE TOYS. THE ACTION FIGURES. THE OFFICIAL ADAPTATIONS, NOVELS AND *COMIC* BOOKS.
AND THE ANIMATED SERIES. LET'S NOT *FORGET* THAT.
THE JACK TALES PART ONE
THE JACK TALES PART TWO

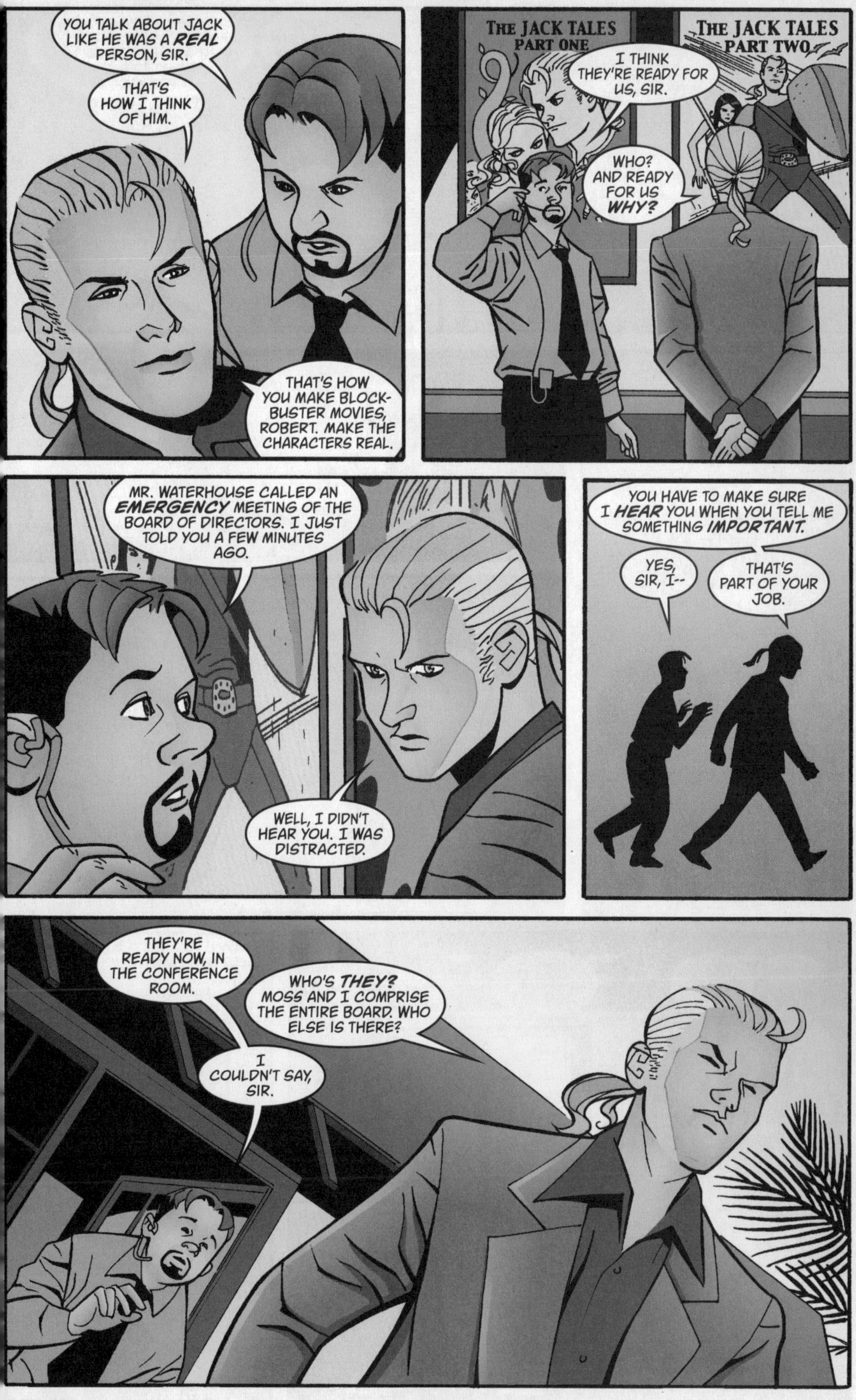

YOU TALK ABOUT JACK LIKE HE WAS A REAL PERSON, SIR.
THAT'S HOW I THINK OF HIM.
THAT'S HOW YOU MAKE BLOCK-BUSTER MOVIES, ROBERT. MAKE THE CHARACTERS REAL.
THE JACK TALES PART ONE
THE JACK TALES PART TWO
I THINK THEY'RE READY FOR US, SIR.
WHO? AND READY FOR US WHY?
MR. WATERHOUSE CALLED AN EMERGENCY MEETING OF THE BOARD OF DIRECTORS. I JUST TOLD YOU A FEW MINUTES AGO.
WELL, I DIDN'T HEAR YOU. I WAS DISTRACTED.
YOU HAVE TO MAKE SURE I HEAR YOU WHEN YOU TELL ME SOMETHING IMPORTANT.
YES, SIR, I--
THAT'S PART OF YOUR JOB.
THEY'RE READY NOW, IN THE CONFERENCE ROOM.
WHO'S THEY? MOSS AND I COMPRISE THE ENTIRE BOARD. WHO ELSE IS THERE?
I COULDN'T SAY, SIR.

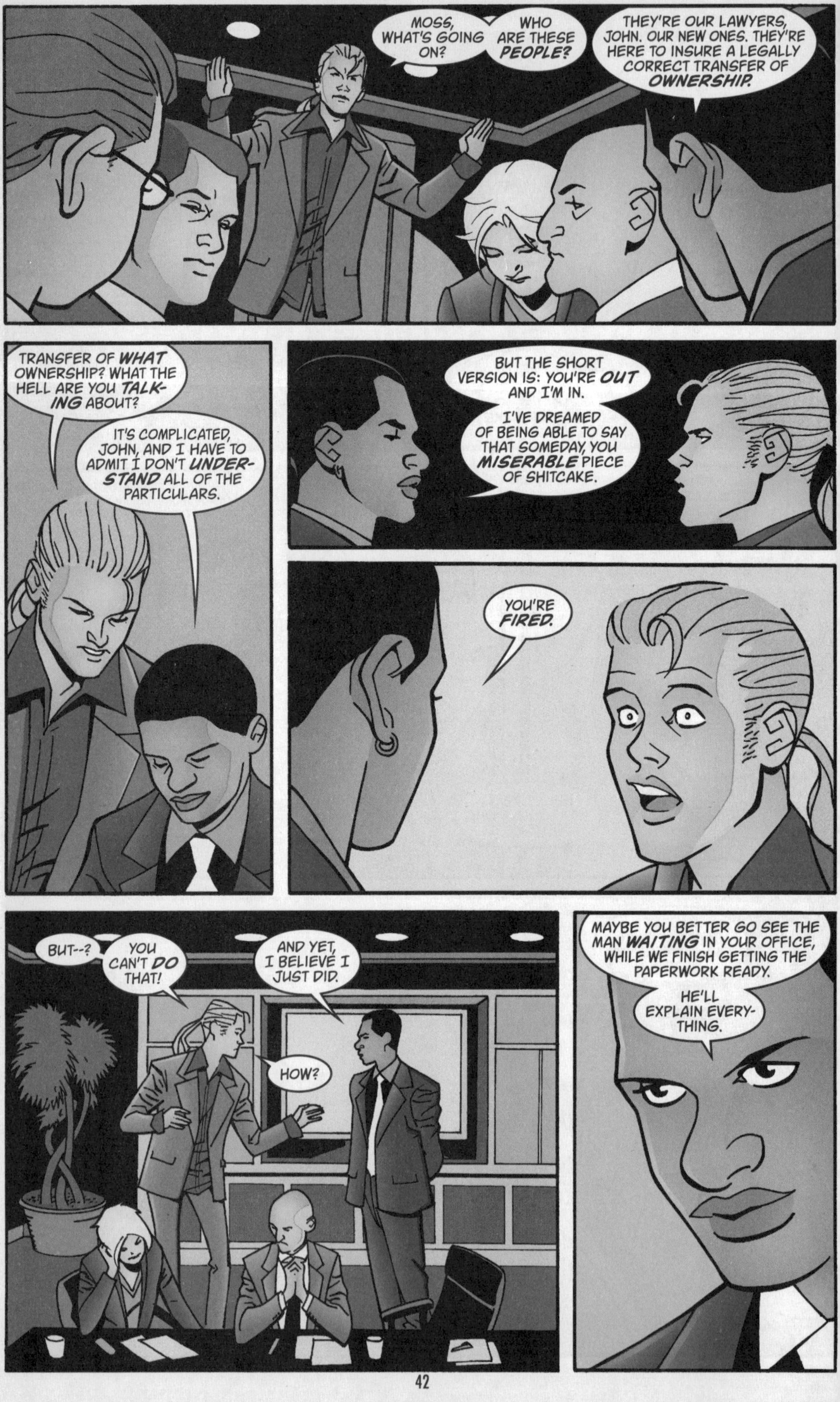
MOSS, WHAT'S GOING ON?
WHO ARE THESE *PEOPLE?*
THEY'RE OUR LAWYERS, JOHN. OUR NEW ONES. THEY'RE HERE TO INSURE A LEGALLY CORRECT TRANSFER OF *OWNERSHIP.*
TRANSFER OF *WHAT* OWNERSHIP? WHAT THE HELL ARE YOU *TALKING* ABOUT?
IT'S COMPLICATED, JOHN, AND I HAVE TO ADMIT I DON'T *UNDERSTAND* ALL OF THE PARTICULARS.
BUT THE SHORT VERSION IS: YOU'RE *OUT* AND I'M IN.
I'VE DREAMED OF BEING ABLE TO SAY THAT SOMEDAY, YOU *MISERABLE* PIECE OF SHITCAKE.
YOU'RE *FIRED.*
BUT--?
YOU CAN'T *DO* THAT!
AND YET, I BELIEVE I JUST DID.
HOW?
MAYBE YOU BETTER GO SEE THE MAN *WAITING* IN YOUR OFFICE, WHILE WE FINISH GETTING THE PAPERWORK READY.
HE'LL EXPLAIN EVERYTHING.

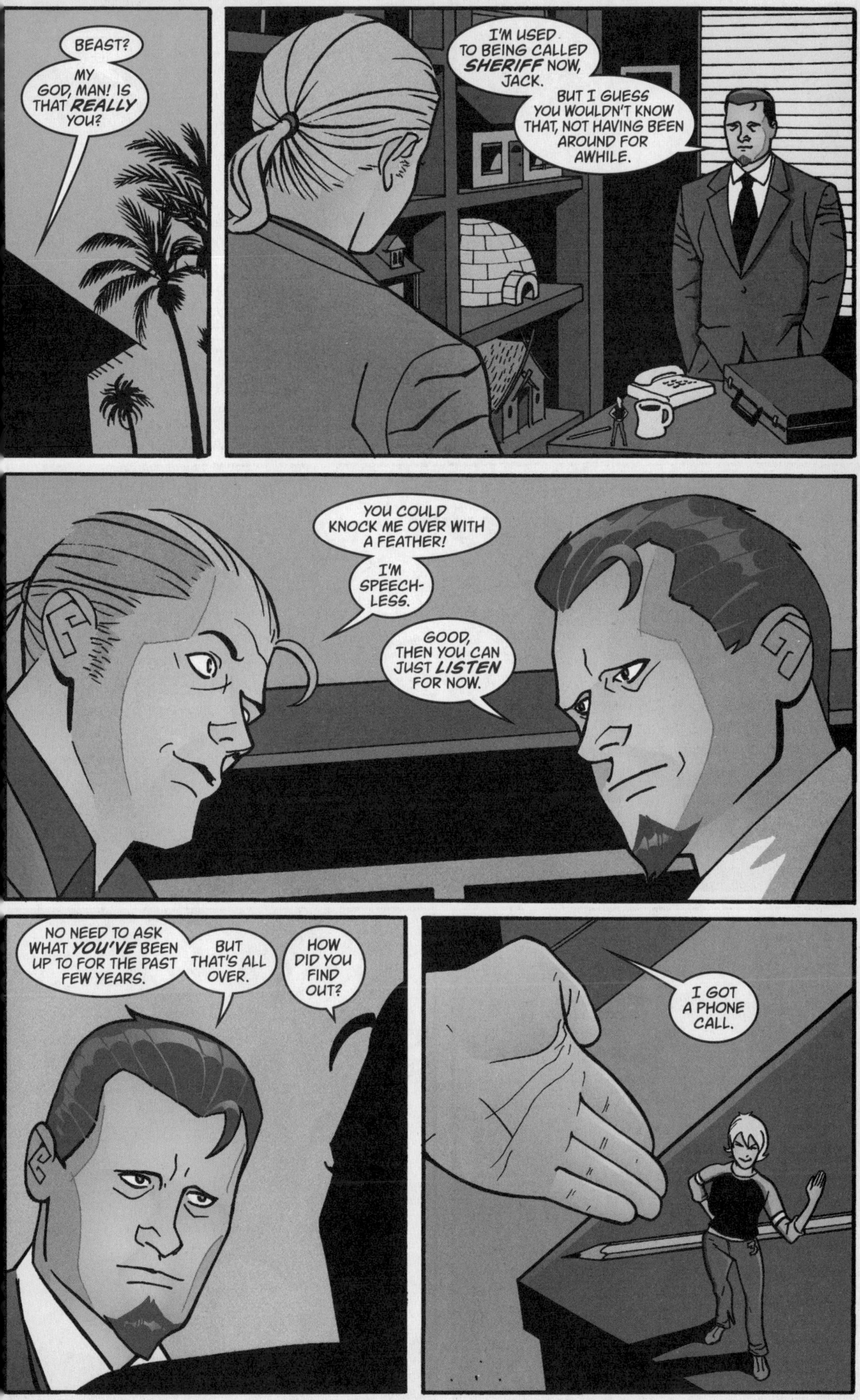
BEAST?
MY GOD, MAN! IS THAT REALLY YOU?
I'M USED TO BEING CALLED SHERIFF NOW, JACK.
BUT I GUESS YOU WOULDN'T KNOW THAT, NOT HAVING BEEN AROUND FOR AWHILE.
YOU COULD KNOCK ME OVER WITH A FEATHER!
I'M SPEECH-LESS.
GOOD, THEN YOU CAN JUST LISTEN FOR NOW.
NO NEED TO ASK WHAT YOU'VE BEEN UP TO FOR THE PAST FEW YEARS.
BUT THAT'S ALL OVER.
HOW DID YOU FIND OUT?
I GOT A PHONE CALL.

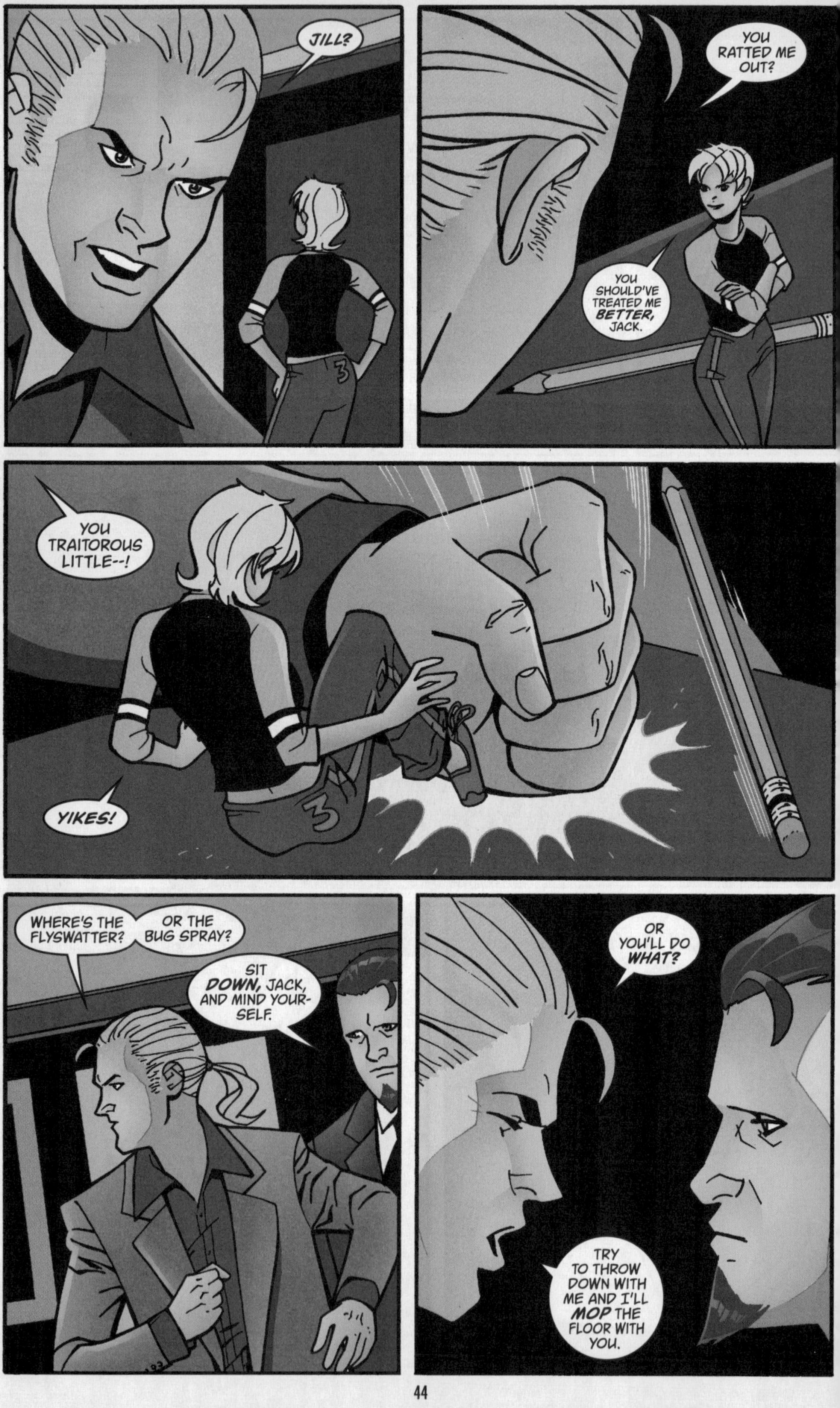
JILL?
YOU RATTED ME OUT?
YOU SHOULD'VE TREATED ME BETTER, JACK.
YOU TRAITOROUS LITTLE--!
YIKES!
WHERE'S THE FLYSWATTER?
OR THE BUG SPRAY?
SIT DOWN, JACK, AND MIND YOURSELF.
OR YOU'LL DO WHAT?
TRY TO THROW DOWN WITH ME AND I'LL MOP THE FLOOR WITH YOU.

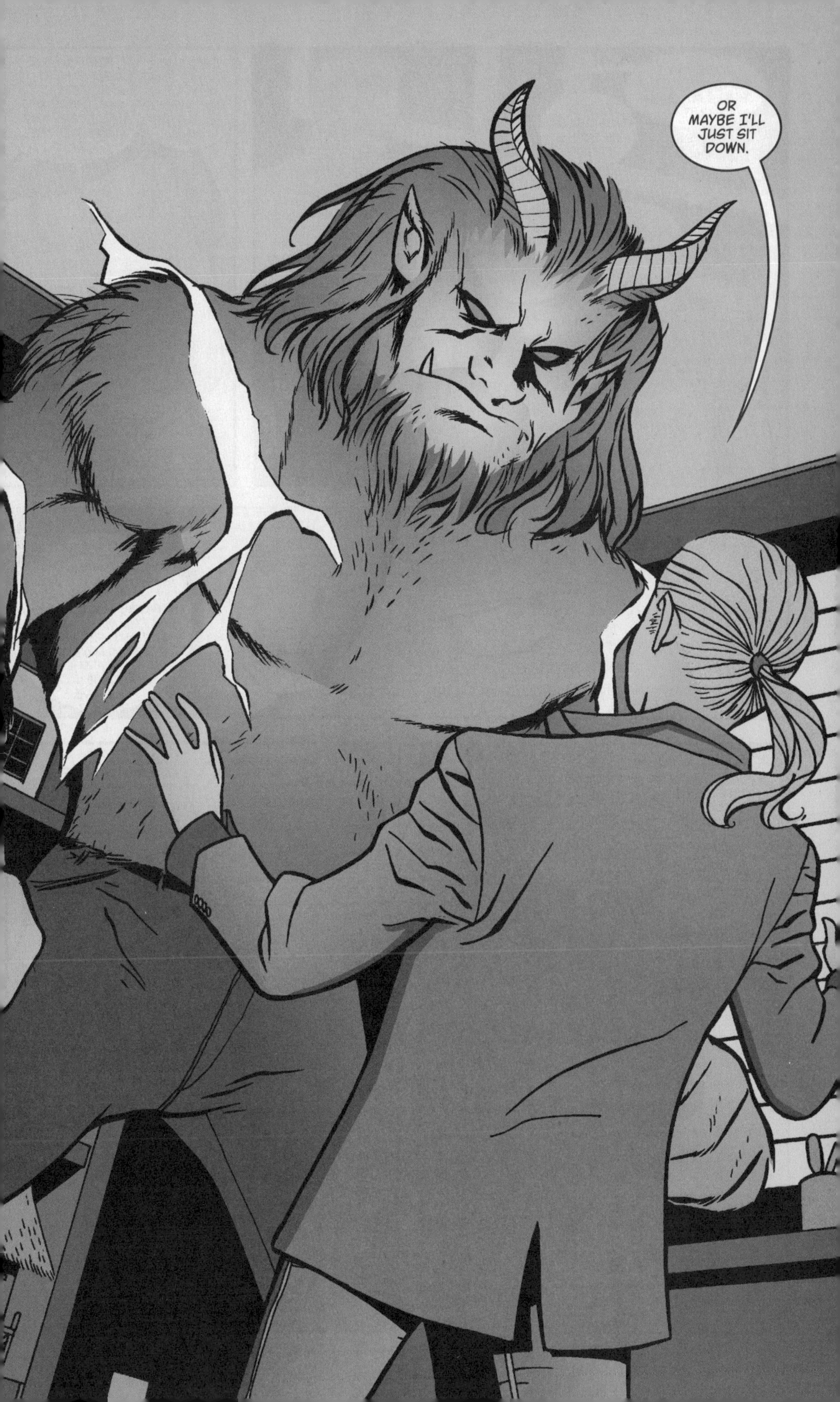

OR MAYBE I'LL JUST SIT DOWN.

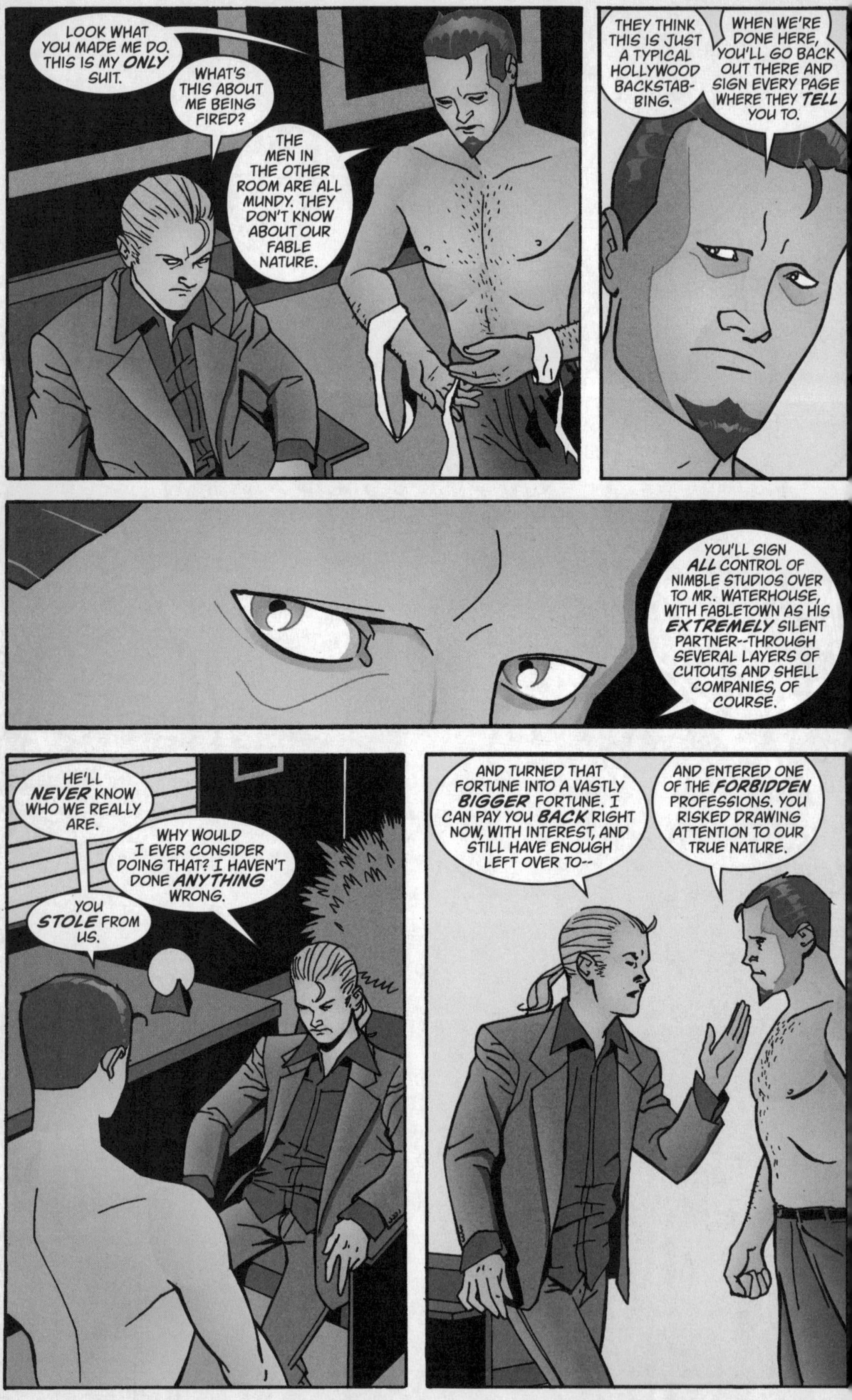
LOOK WHAT YOU MADE ME DO. THIS IS MY ONLY SUIT.
WHAT'S THIS ABOUT ME BEING FIRED?
THE MEN IN THE OTHER ROOM ARE ALL MUNDY. THEY DON'T KNOW ABOUT OUR FABLE NATURE.
THEY THINK THIS IS JUST A TYPICAL HOLLYWOOD BACKSTAB-BING.
WHEN WE'RE DONE HERE, YOU'LL GO BACK OUT THERE AND SIGN EVERY PAGE WHERE THEY TELL YOU TO.
YOU'LL SIGN ALL CONTROL OF NIMBLE STUDIOS OVER TO MR. WATERHOUSE, WITH FABLETOWN AS HIS EXTREMELY SILENT PARTNER--THROUGH SEVERAL LAYERS OF CUTOUTS AND SHELL COMPANIES, OF COURSE.
HE'LL NEVER KNOW WHO WE REALLY ARE.
WHY WOULD I EVER CONSIDER DOING THAT? I HAVEN'T DONE ANYTHING WRONG.
YOU STOLE FROM US.
AND TURNED THAT FORTUNE INTO A VASTLY BIGGER FORTUNE. I CAN PAY YOU BACK RIGHT NOW, WITH INTEREST, AND STILL HAVE ENOUGH LEFT OVER TO--
AND ENTERED ONE OF THE FORBIDDEN PROFESSIONS. YOU RISKED DRAWING ATTENTION TO OUR TRUE NATURE.

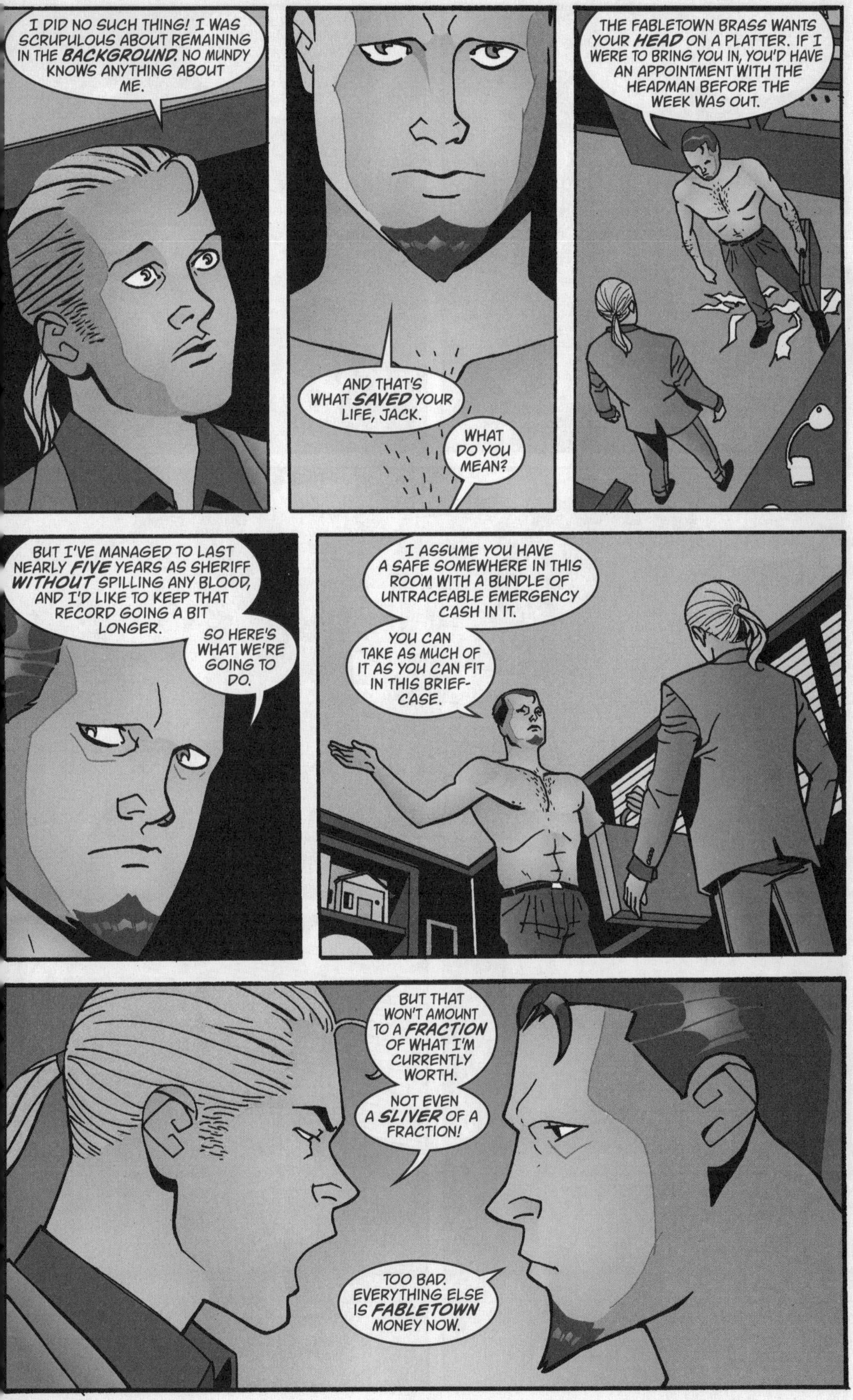

I DID NO SUCH THING! I WAS SCRUPULOUS ABOUT REMAINING IN THE BACKGROUND. NO MUNDY KNOWS ANYTHING ABOUT ME.
AND THAT'S WHAT SAVED YOUR LIFE, JACK.
WHAT DO YOU MEAN?
THE FABLETOWN BRASS WANTS YOUR HEAD ON A PLATTER. IF I WERE TO BRING YOU IN, YOU'D HAVE AN APPOINTMENT WITH THE HEADMAN BEFORE THE WEEK WAS OUT.
BUT I'VE MANAGED TO LAST NEARLY FIVE YEARS AS SHERIFF WITHOUT SPILLING ANY BLOOD, AND I'D LIKE TO KEEP THAT RECORD GOING A BIT LONGER.
SO HERE'S WHAT WE'RE GOING TO DO.
I ASSUME YOU HAVE A SAFE SOMEWHERE IN THIS ROOM WITH A BUNDLE OF UNTRACEABLE EMERGENCY CASH IN IT.
YOU CAN TAKE AS MUCH OF IT AS YOU CAN FIT IN THIS BRIEF-CASE.
BUT THAT WON'T AMOUNT TO A FRACTION OF WHAT I'M CURRENTLY WORTH.
NOT EVEN A SLIVER OF A FRACTION!
TOO BAD. EVERYTHING ELSE IS FABLETOWN MONEY NOW.

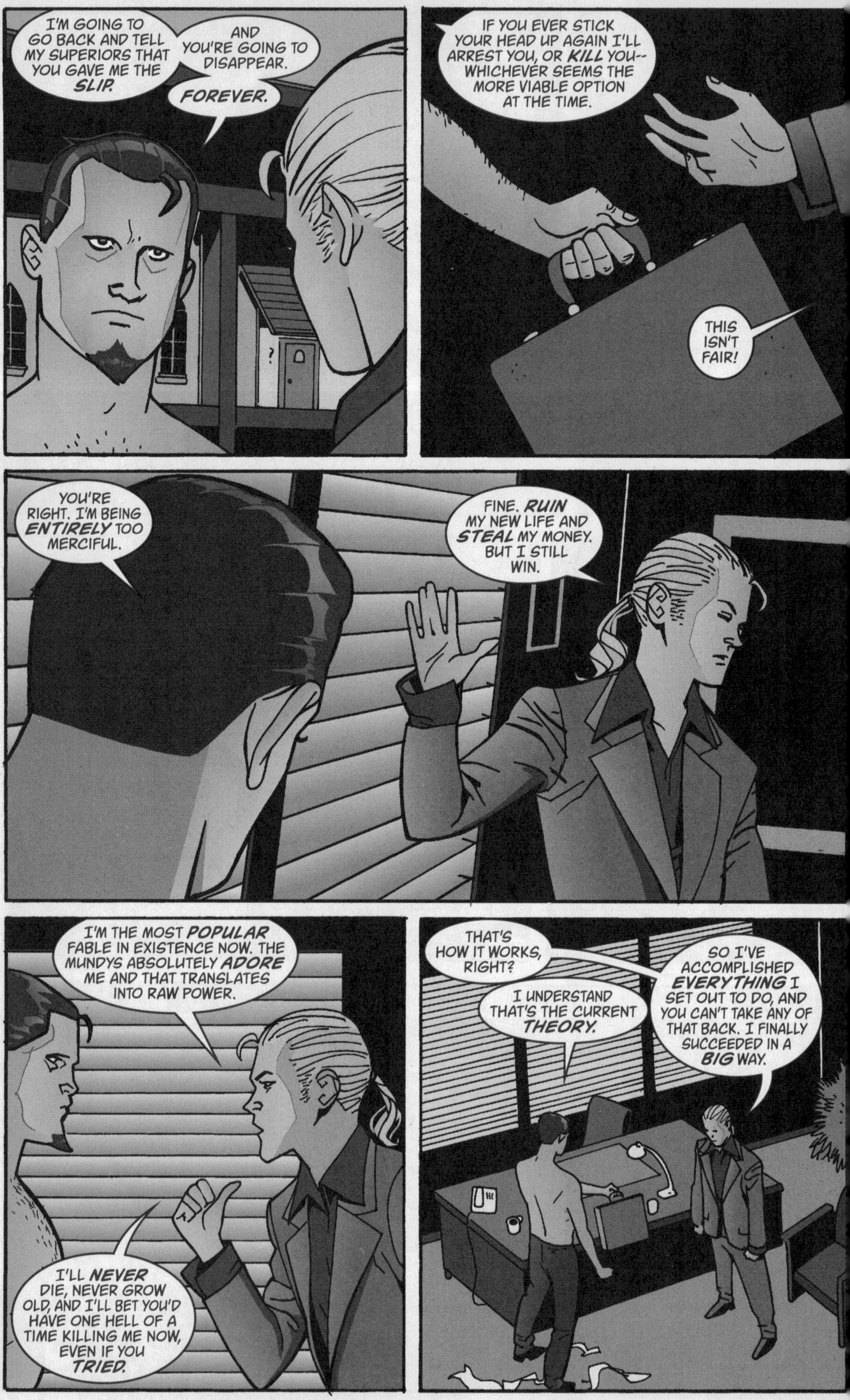
I'M GOING TO GO BACK AND TELL MY SUPERIORS THAT YOU GAVE ME THE SLIP.
AND YOU'RE GOING TO DISAPPEAR.
FOREVER.
IF YOU EVER STICK YOUR HEAD UP AGAIN I'LL ARREST YOU, OR KILL YOU-- WHICHEVER SEEMS THE MORE VIABLE OPTION AT THE TIME.
THIS ISN'T FAIR!
YOU'RE RIGHT. I'M BEING ENTIRELY TOO MERCIFUL.
FINE. RUIN MY NEW LIFE AND STEAL MY MONEY. BUT I STILL WIN.
I'M THE MOST POPULAR FABLE IN EXISTENCE NOW. THE MUNDYS ABSOLUTELY ADORE ME AND THAT TRANSLATES INTO RAW POWER.
I'LL NEVER DIE, NEVER GROW OLD, AND I'LL BET YOU'D HAVE ONE HELL OF A TIME KILLING ME NOW, EVEN IF YOU TRIED.
THAT'S HOW IT WORKS, RIGHT?
I UNDERSTAND THAT'S THE CURRENT THEORY.
SO I'VE ACCOMPLISHED EVERYTHING I SET OUT TO DO, AND YOU CAN'T TAKE ANY OF THAT BACK. I FINALLY SUCCEEDED IN A BIG WAY.

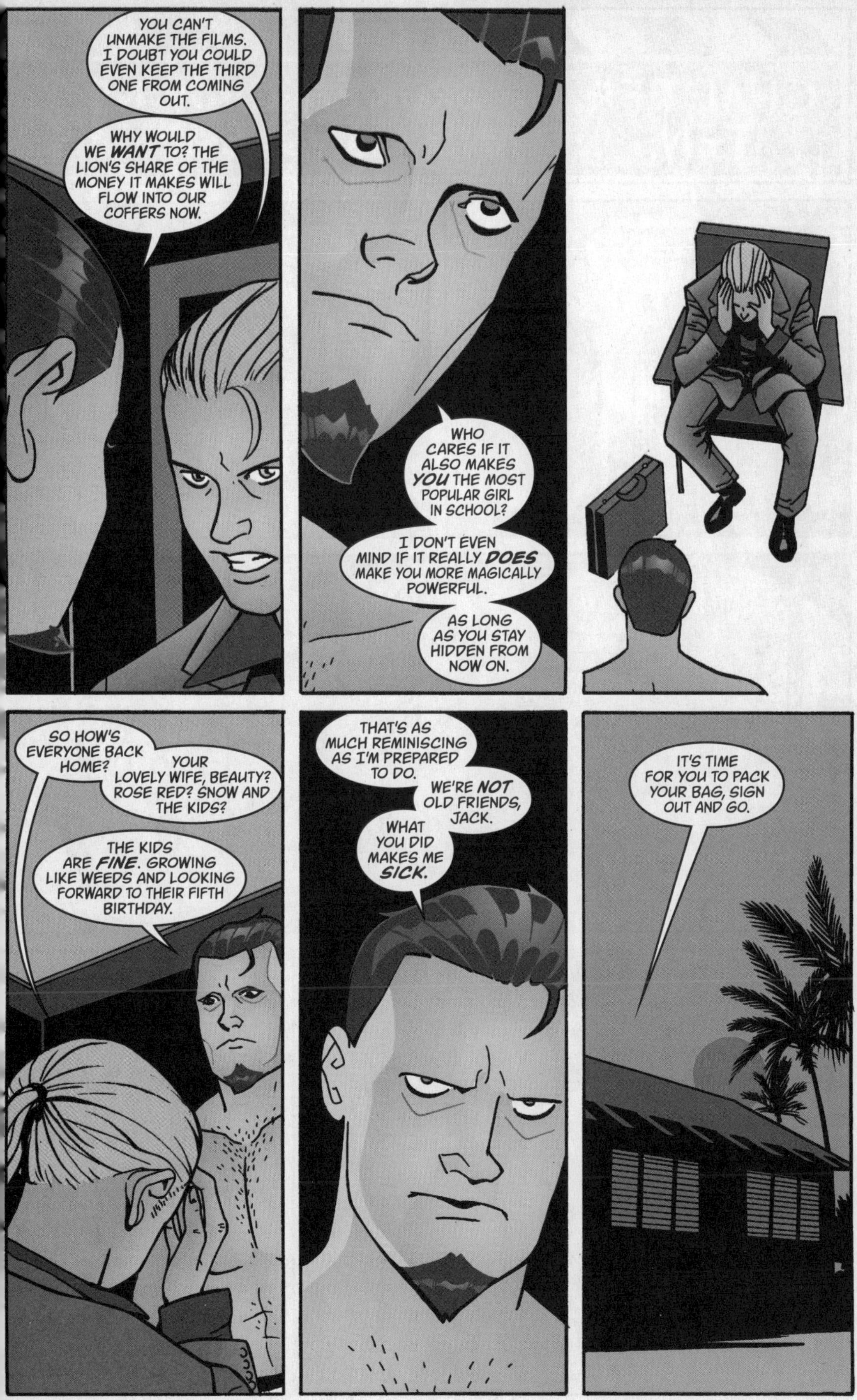

YOU CAN'T UNMAKE THE FILMS. I DOUBT YOU COULD EVEN KEEP THE THIRD ONE FROM COMING OUT.
WHY WOULD WE WANT TO? THE LION'S SHARE OF THE MONEY IT MAKES WILL FLOW INTO OUR COFFERS NOW.
WHO CARES IF IT ALSO MAKES YOU THE MOST POPULAR GIRL IN SCHOOL?
I DON'T EVEN MIND IF IT REALLY DOES MAKE YOU MORE MAGICALLY POWERFUL.
AS LONG AS YOU STAY HIDDEN FROM NOW ON.
SO HOW'S EVERYONE BACK HOME?
YOUR LOVELY WIFE, BEAUTY? ROSE RED? SNOW AND THE KIDS?
THE KIDS ARE FINE. GROWING LIKE WEEDS AND LOOKING FORWARD TO THEIR FIFTH BIRTHDAY.
THAT'S AS MUCH REMINISCING AS I'M PREPARED TO DO.
WE'RE NOT OLD FRIENDS, JACK.
WHAT YOU DID MAKES ME SICK.
IT'S TIME FOR YOU TO PACK YOUR BAG, SIGN OUT AND GO.

CHAPTER TEN: BROKEN CROWNS AND CANDLESTICKS

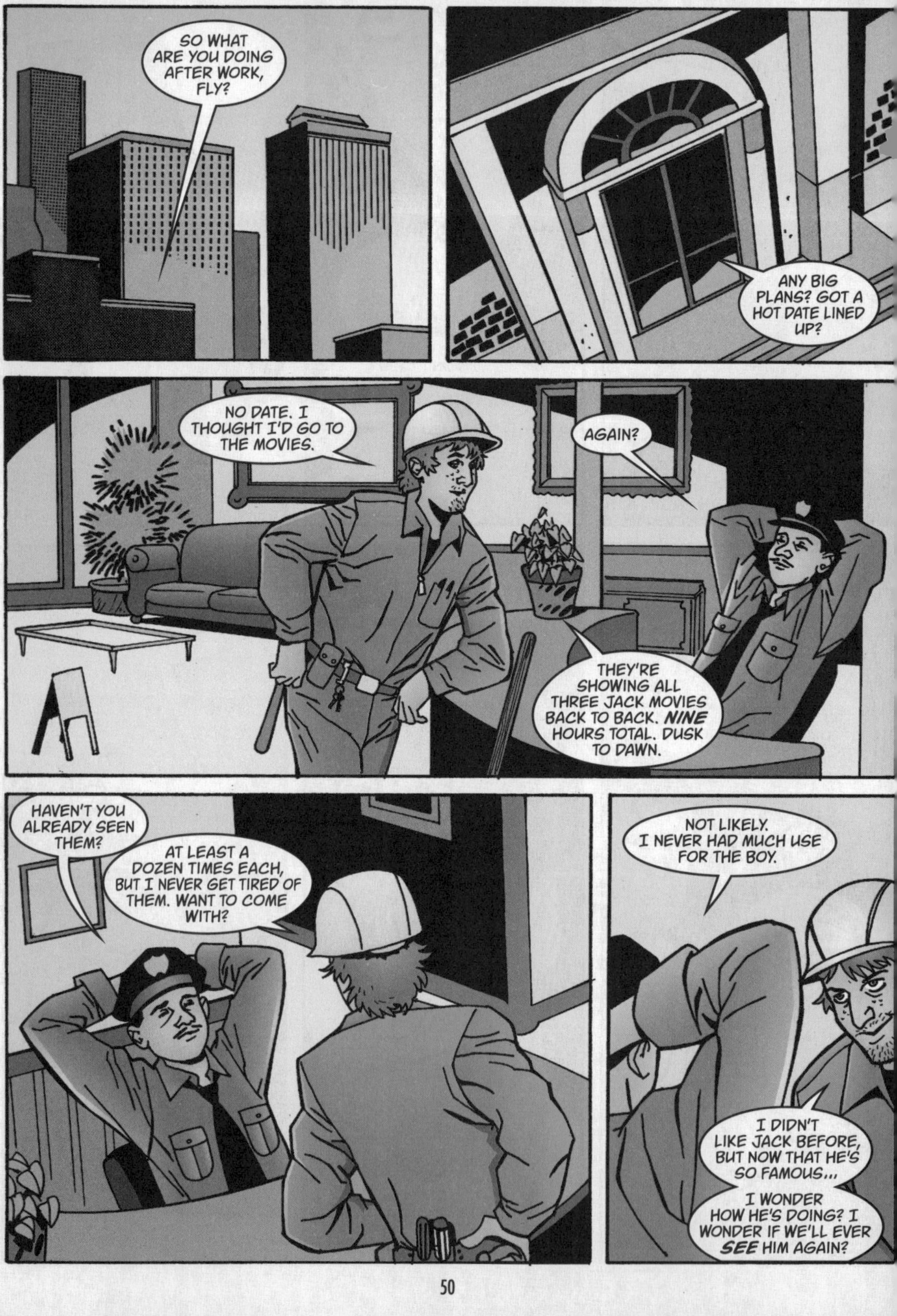

SO WHAT ARE YOU DOING AFTER WORK, FLY?
ANY BIG PLANS? GOT A HOT DATE LINED UP?
NO DATE. I THOUGHT I'D GO TO THE MOVIES.
AGAIN?
THEY'RE SHOWING ALL THREE JACK MOVIES BACK TO BACK. NINE HOURS TOTAL. DUSK TO DAWN.
HAVEN'T YOU ALREADY SEEN THEM?
AT LEAST A DOZEN TIMES EACH, BUT I NEVER GET TIRED OF THEM. WANT TO COME WITH?
NOT LIKELY. I NEVER HAD MUCH USE FOR THE BOY.
I DIDN'T LIKE JACK BEFORE, BUT NOW THAT HE'S SO FAMOUS...
I WONDER HOW HE'S DOING? I WONDER IF WE'LL EVER SEE HIM AGAIN?

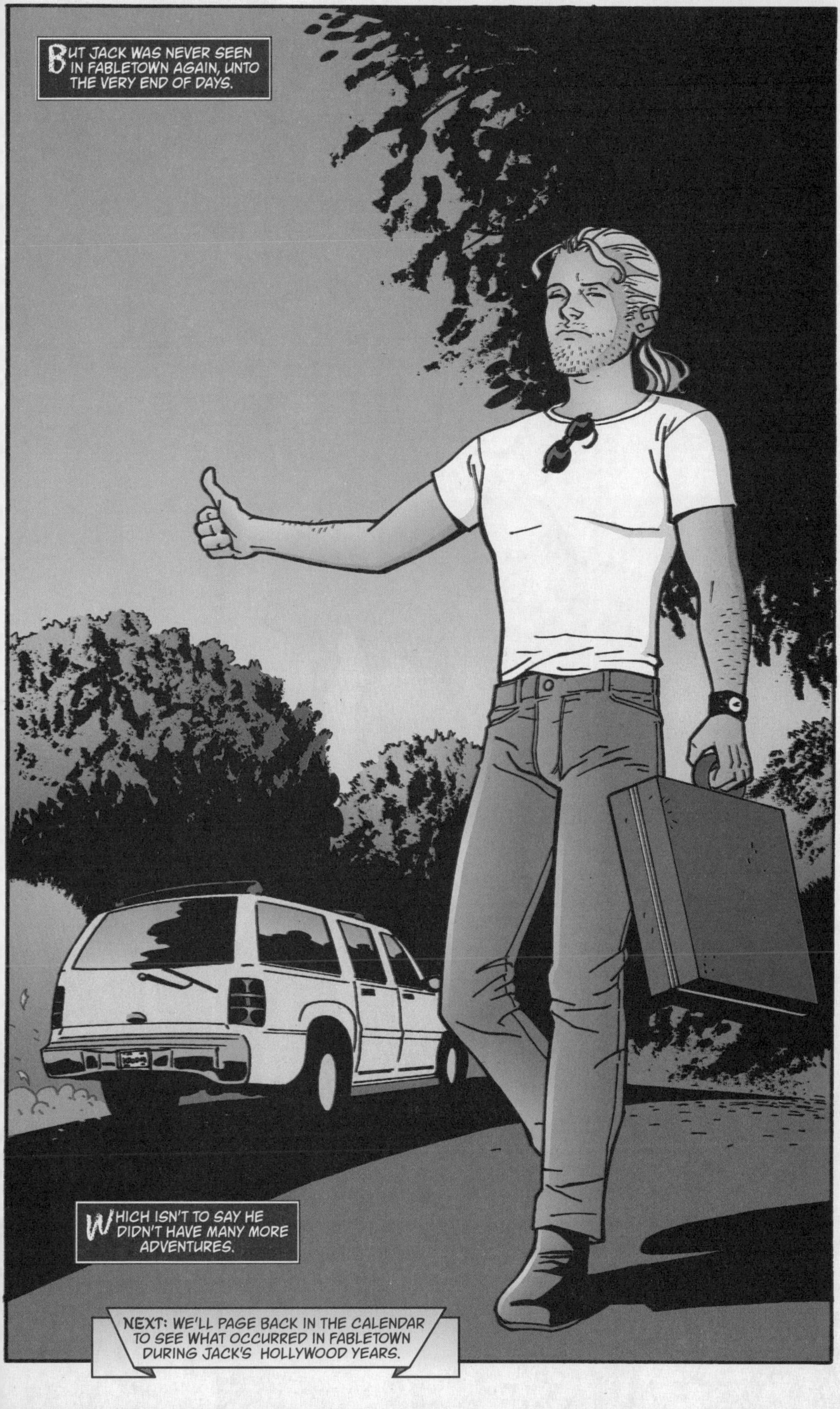
BUT JACK WAS NEVER SEEN IN FABLETOWN AGAIN, UNTO THE VERY END OF DAYS.
WHICH ISN'T TO SAY HE DIDN'T HAVE MANY MORE ADVENTURES.
NEXT: WE'LL PAGE BACK IN THE CALENDAR TO SEE WHAT OCCURRED IN FABLETOWN DURING JACK'S HOLLYWOOD YEARS.

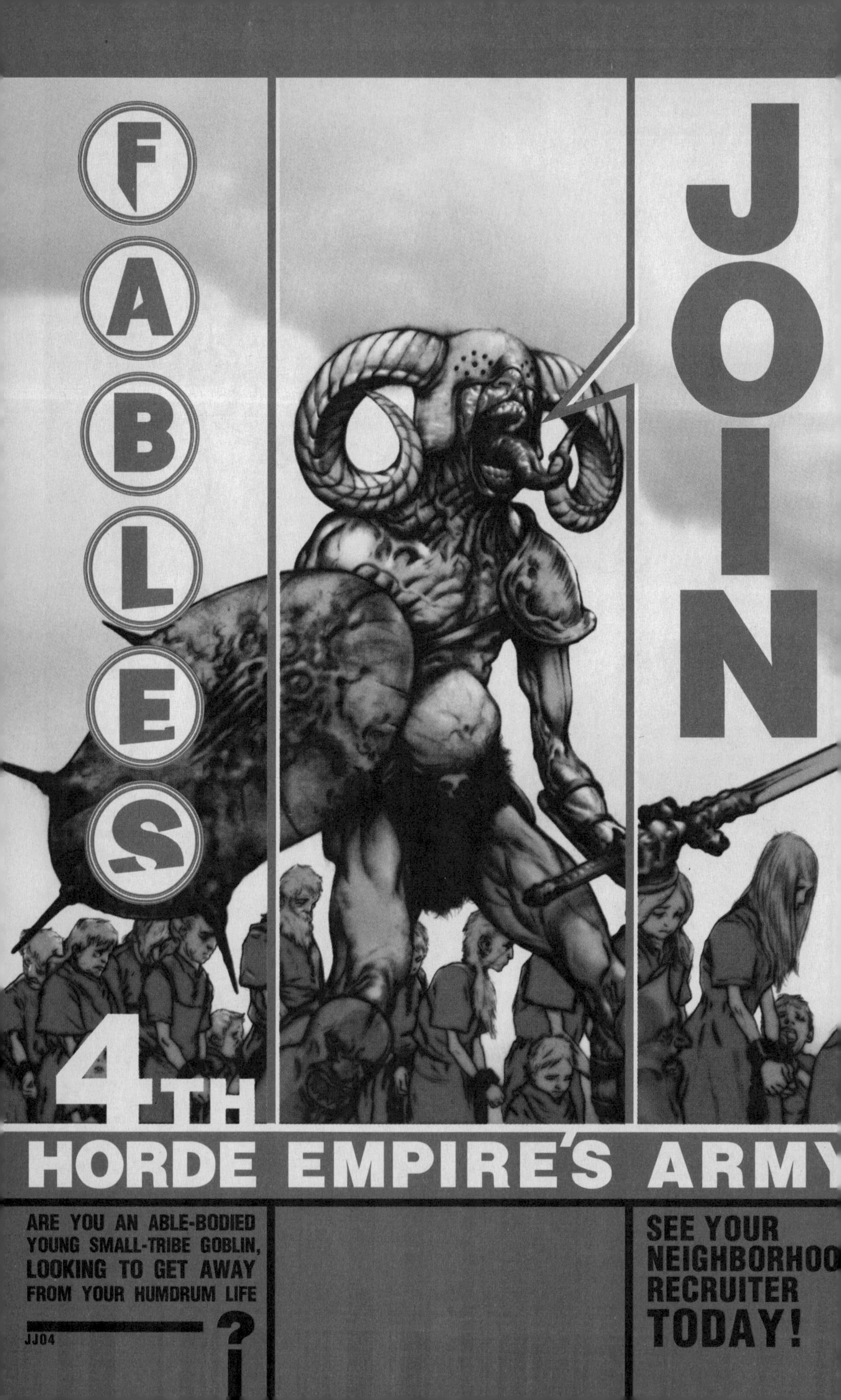
FABLES
JOIN
4TH
HORDE EMPIRE'S ARMY
ARE YOU AN ABLE-BODIED YOUNG SMALL-TRIBE GOBLIN, LOOKING TO GET AWAY FROM YOUR HUMDRUM LIFE ?
JJ04
SEE YOUR NEIGHBORHOO RECRUITER TODAY!

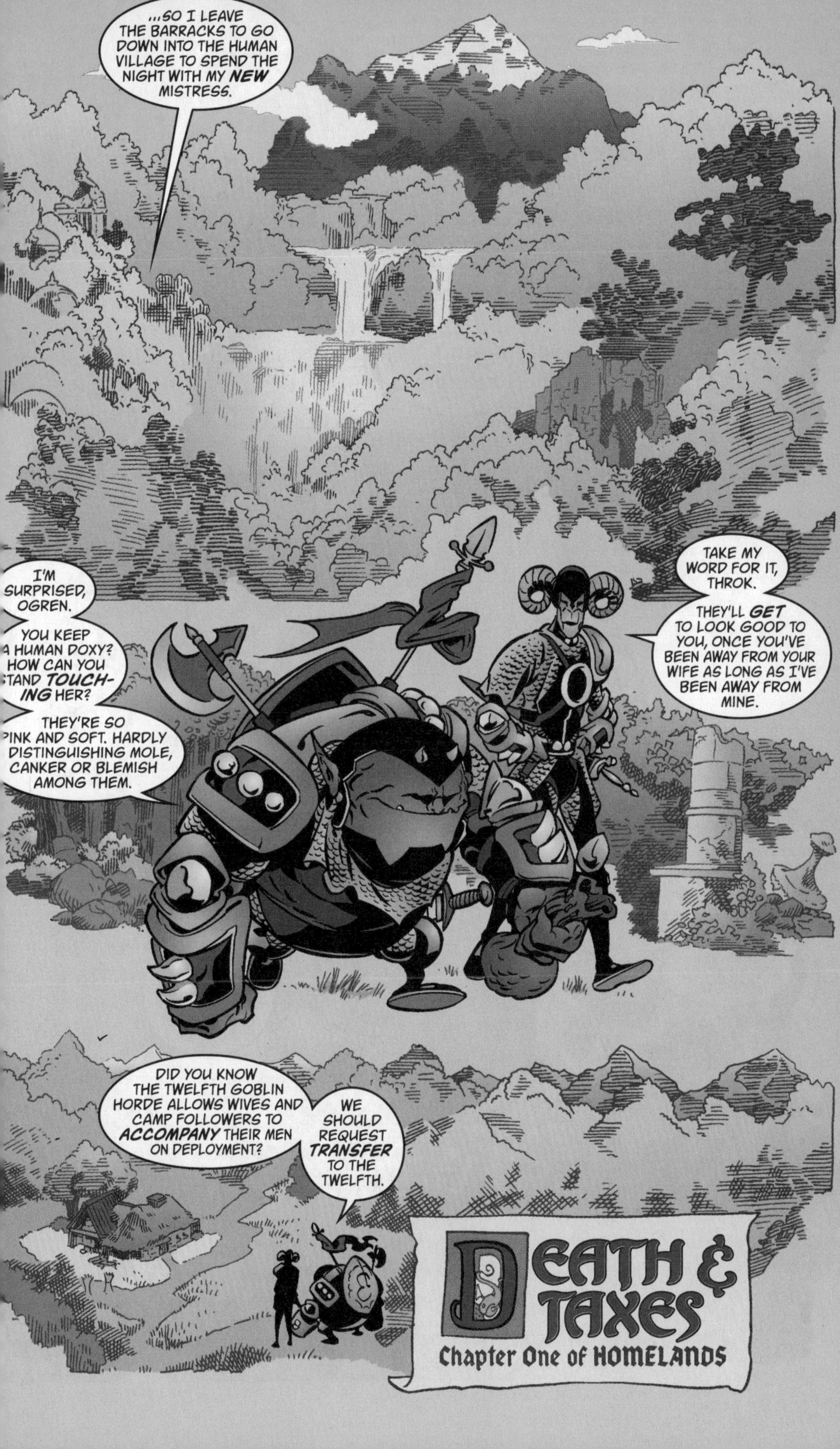
...SO I LEAVE THE BARRACKS TO GO DOWN INTO THE HUMAN VILLAGE TO SPEND THE NIGHT WITH MY NEW MISTRESS.
I'M SURPRISED, OGREN.
YOU KEEP A HUMAN DOXY? HOW CAN YOU STAND TOUCHING HER?
THEY'RE SO PINK AND SOFT. HARDLY DISTINGUISHING MOLE, CANKER OR BLEMISH AMONG THEM.
TAKE MY WORD FOR IT, THROK.
THEY'LL GET TO LOOK GOOD TO YOU, ONCE YOU'VE BEEN AWAY FROM YOUR WIFE AS LONG AS I'VE BEEN AWAY FROM MINE.
DID YOU KNOW THE TWELFTH GOBLIN HORDE ALLOWS WIVES AND CAMP FOLLOWERS TO ACCOMPANY THEIR MEN ON DEPLOYMENT?
WE SHOULD REQUEST TRANSFER TO THE TWELFTH.
DEATH & TAXES
Chapter One of HOMELANDS

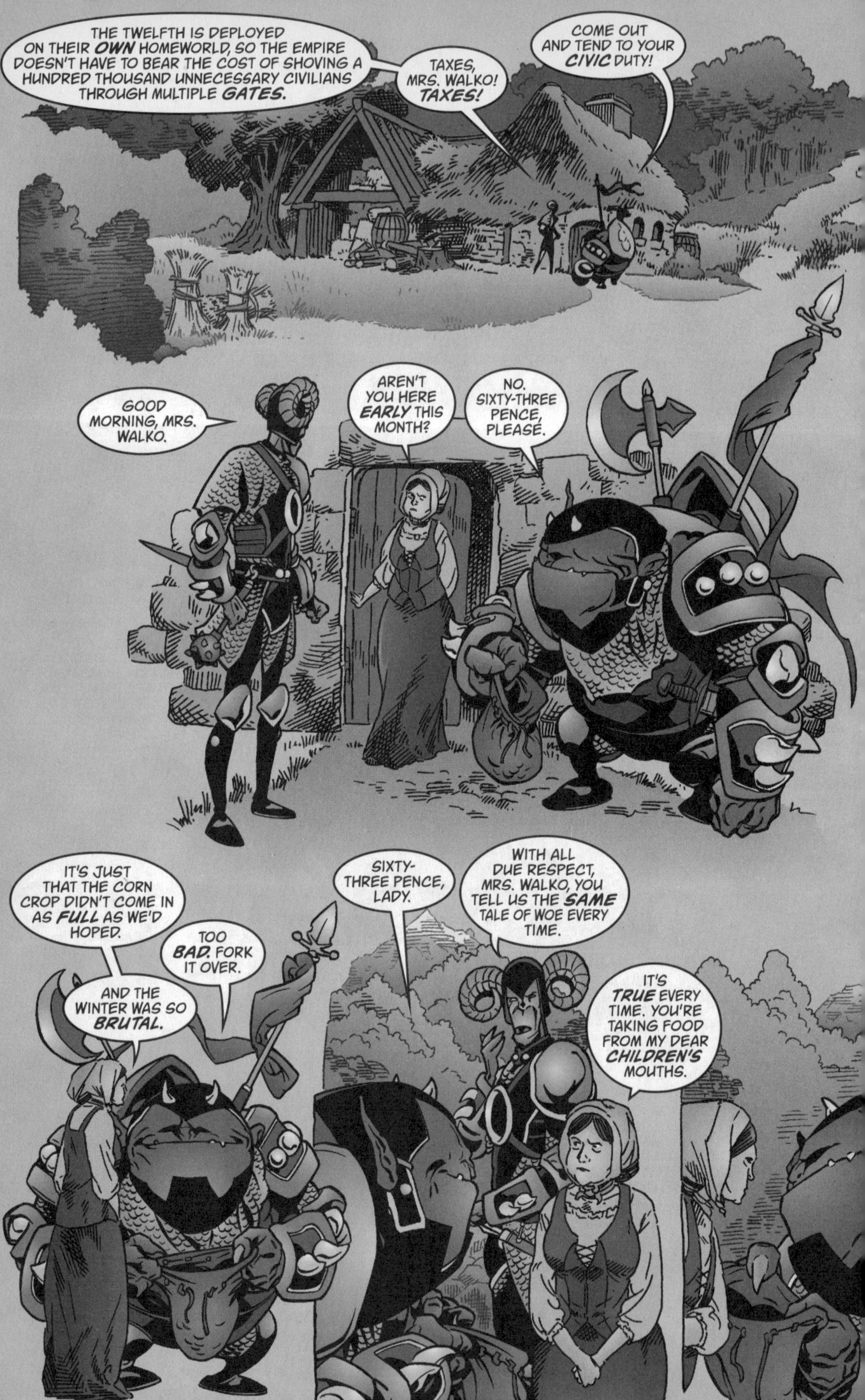
THE TWELFTH IS DEPLOYED ON THEIR OWN HOMEWORLD, SO THE EMPIRE DOESN'T HAVE TO BEAR THE COST OF SHOVING A HUNDRED THOUSAND UNNECESSARY CIVILIANS THROUGH MULTIPLE GATES.
TAXES, MRS. WALKO! TAXES!
COME OUT AND TEND TO YOUR CIVIC DUTY!
GOOD MORNING, MRS. WALKO.
AREN'T YOU HERE EARLY THIS MONTH?
NO. SIXTY-THREE PENCE, PLEASE.
IT'S JUST THAT THE CORN CROP DIDN'T COME IN AS FULL AS WE'D HOPED.
AND THE WINTER WAS SO BRUTAL.
TOO BAD. FORK IT OVER.
SIXTY-THREE PENCE, LADY.
WITH ALL DUE RESPECT, MRS. WALKO, YOU TELL US THE SAME TALE OF WOE EVERY TIME.
IT'S TRUE EVERY TIME. YOU'RE TAKING FOOD FROM MY DEAR CHILDREN'S MOUTHS.

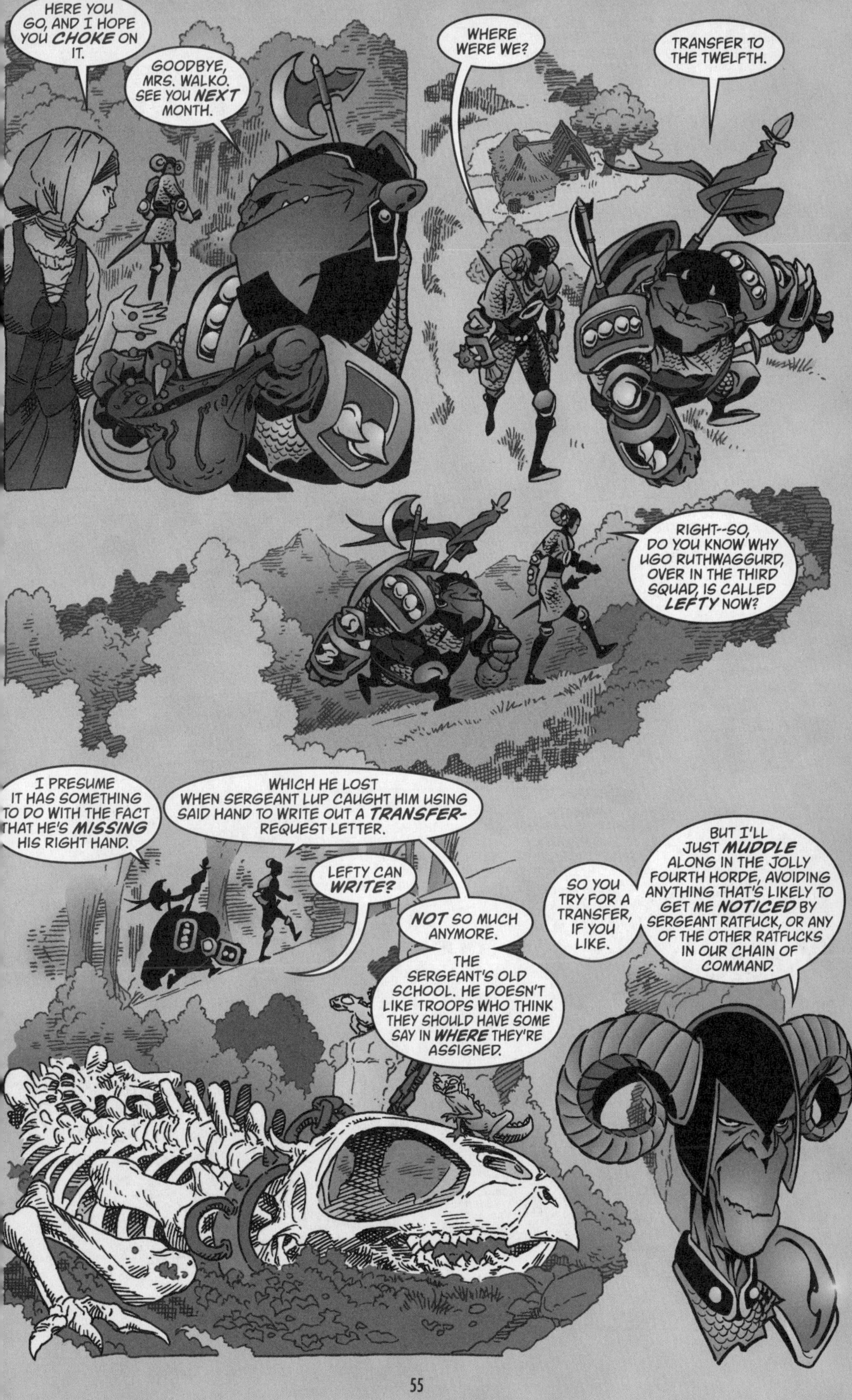
HERE YOU GO, AND I HOPE YOU CHOKE ON IT.
GOODBYE, MRS. WALKO. SEE YOU NEXT MONTH.
WHERE WERE WE?
TRANSFER TO THE TWELFTH.
RIGHT--SO, DO YOU KNOW WHY UGO RUTHWAGGURD, OVER IN THE THIRD SQUAD, IS CALLED LEFTY NOW?
I PRESUME IT HAS SOMETHING TO DO WITH THE FACT THAT HE'S MISSING HIS RIGHT HAND.
WHICH HE LOST WHEN SERGEANT LUP CAUGHT HIM USING SAID HAND TO WRITE OUT A TRANSFER-REQUEST LETTER.
LEFTY CAN WRITE?
NOT SO MUCH ANYMORE.
THE SERGEANT'S OLD SCHOOL. HE DOESN'T LIKE TROOPS WHO THINK THEY SHOULD HAVE SOME SAY IN WHERE THEY'RE ASSIGNED.
SO YOU TRY FOR A TRANSFER, IF YOU LIKE.
BUT I'LL JUST MUDDLE ALONG IN THE JOLLY FOURTH HORDE, AVOIDING ANYTHING THAT'S LIKELY TO GET ME NOTICED BY SERGEANT RATFUCK, OR ANY OF THE OTHER RATFUCKS IN OUR CHAIN OF COMMAND.

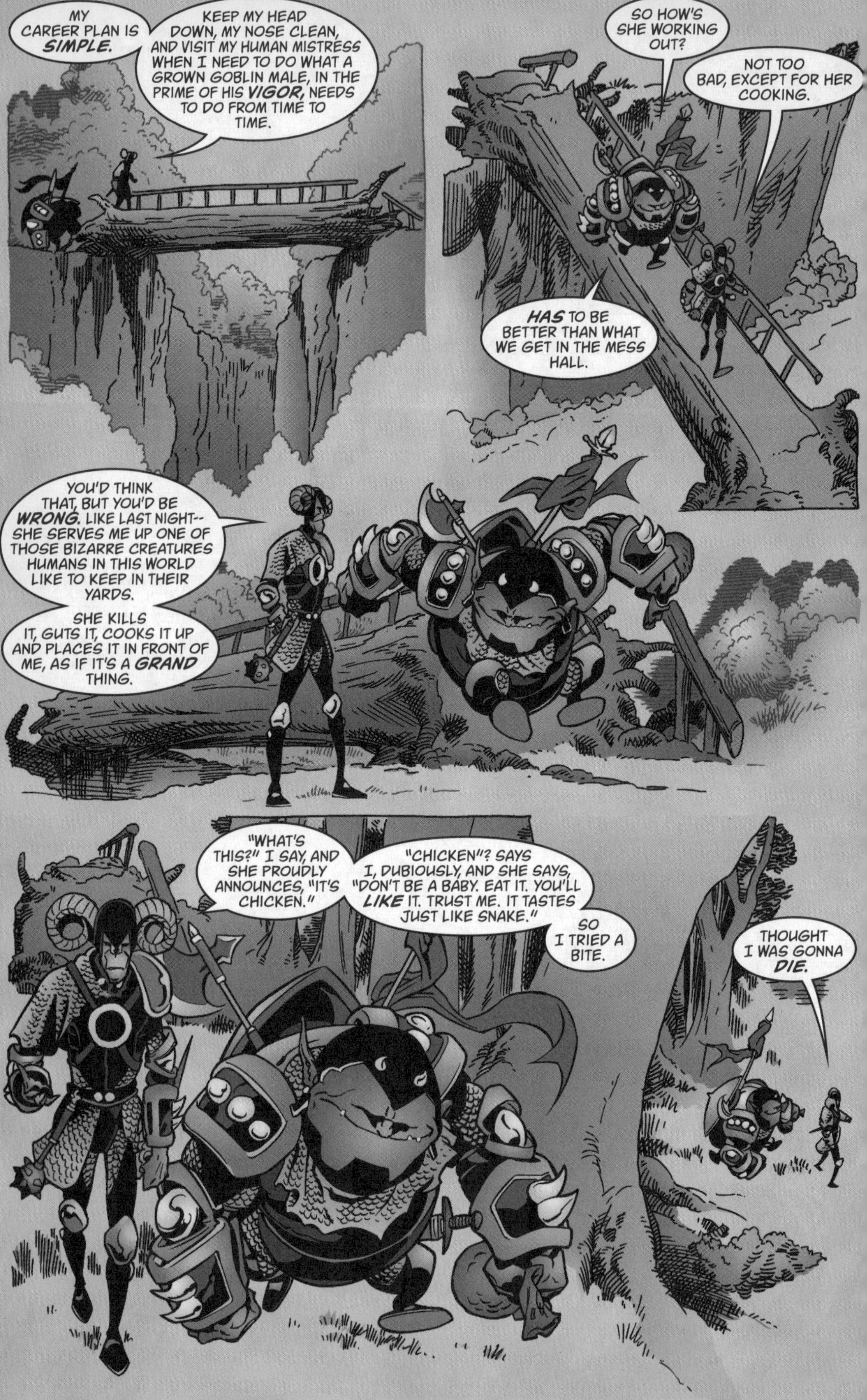

MY CAREER PLAN IS SIMPLE.
KEEP MY HEAD DOWN, MY NOSE CLEAN, AND VISIT MY HUMAN MISTRESS WHEN I NEED TO DO WHAT A GROWN GOBLIN MALE, IN THE PRIME OF HIS VIGOR, NEEDS TO DO FROM TIME TO TIME.
SO HOW'S SHE WORKING OUT?
NOT TOO BAD, EXCEPT FOR HER COOKING.
HAS TO BE BETTER THAN WHAT WE GET IN THE MESS HALL.
YOU'D THINK THAT, BUT YOU'D BE WRONG. LIKE LAST NIGHT-- SHE SERVES ME UP ONE OF THOSE BIZARRE CREATURES HUMANS IN THIS WORLD LIKE TO KEEP IN THEIR YARDS.
SHE KILLS IT, GUTS IT, COOKS IT UP AND PLACES IT IN FRONT OF ME, AS IF IT'S A GRAND THING.
"WHAT'S THIS?" I SAY, AND SHE PROUDLY ANNOUNCES, "IT'S CHICKEN."
"CHICKEN"? SAYS I, DUBIOUSLY, AND SHE SAYS, "DON'T BE A BABY. EAT IT. YOU'LL LIKE IT. TRUST ME. IT TASTES JUST LIKE SNAKE."
SO I TRIED A BITE.
THOUGHT I WAS GONNA DIE.

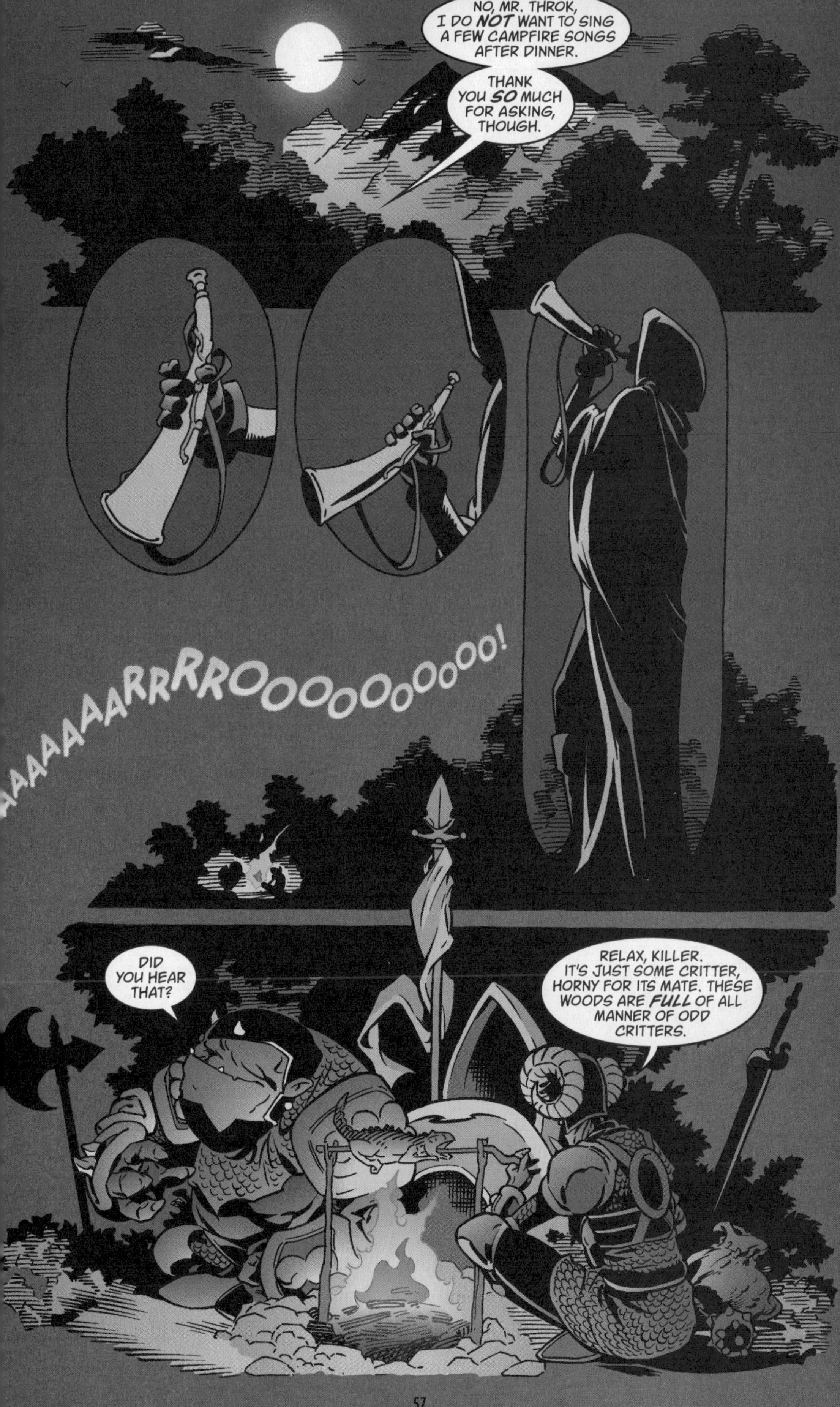
NO, MR. THROK, I DO NOT WANT TO SING A FEW CAMPFIRE SONGS AFTER DINNER.
THANK YOU SO MUCH FOR ASKING, THOUGH.
AAAAAAARRRROOOOOOOOOO!
DID YOU HEAR THAT?
RELAX, KILLER. IT'S JUST SOME CRITTER, HORNY FOR ITS MATE. THESE WOODS ARE FULL OF ALL MANNER OF ODD CRITTERS.

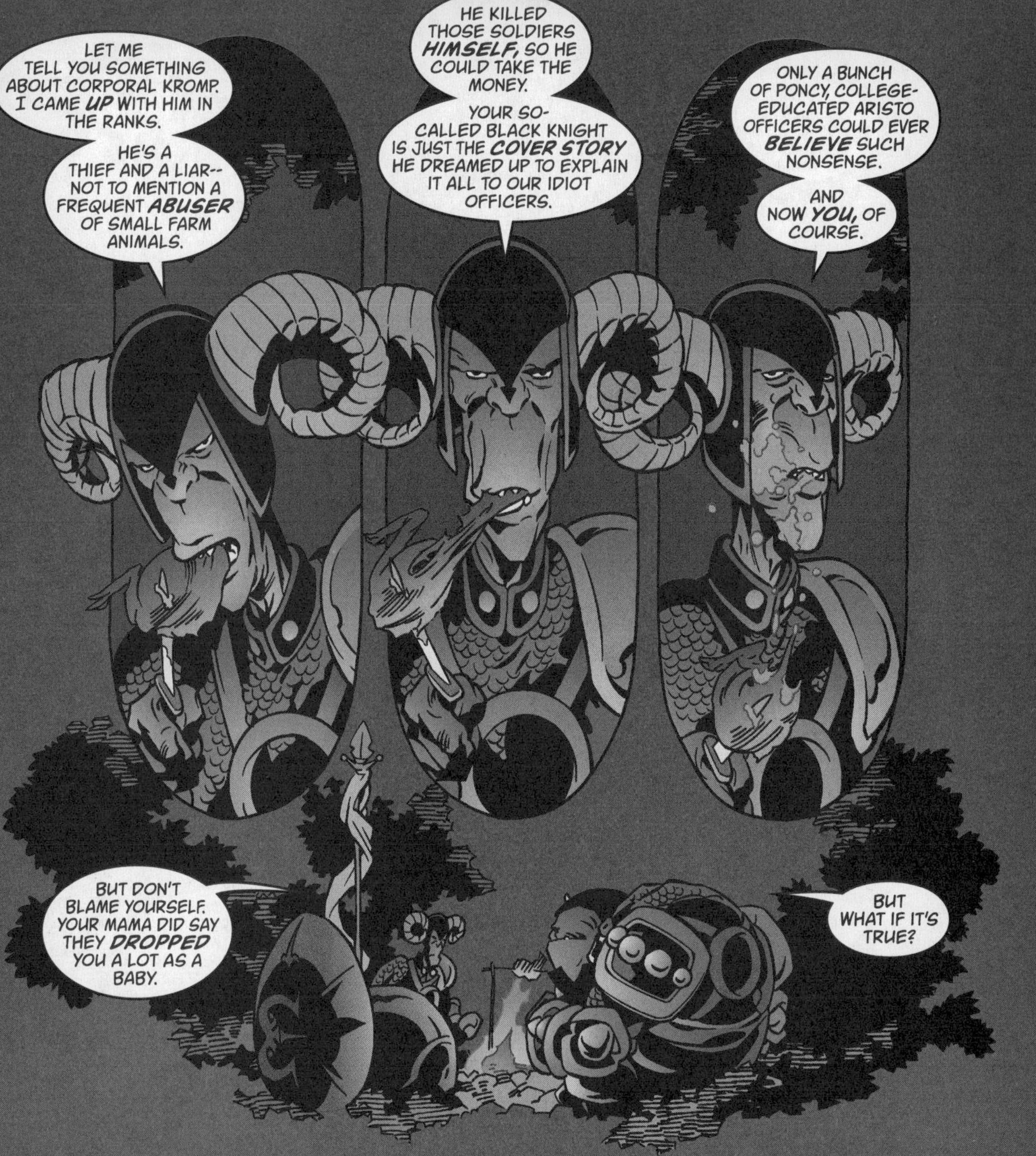
LET ME TELL YOU SOMETHING ABOUT CORPORAL KROMP. I CAME UP WITH HIM IN THE RANKS.
HE'S A THIEF AND A LIAR--NOT TO MENTION A FREQUENT ABUSER OF SMALL FARM ANIMALS.
HE KILLED THOSE SOLDIERS HIMSELF, SO HE COULD TAKE THE MONEY.
YOUR SO-CALLED BLACK KNIGHT IS JUST THE COVER STORY HE DREAMED UP TO EXPLAIN IT ALL TO OUR IDIOT OFFICERS.
ONLY A BUNCH OF PONCY, COLLEGE-EDUCATED ARISTO OFFICERS COULD EVER BELIEVE SUCH NONSENSE.
AND NOW YOU, OF COURSE.
BUT DON'T BLAME YOURSELF. YOUR MAMA DID SAY THEY DROPPED YOU A LOT AS A BABY.
BUT WHAT IF IT'S TRUE?

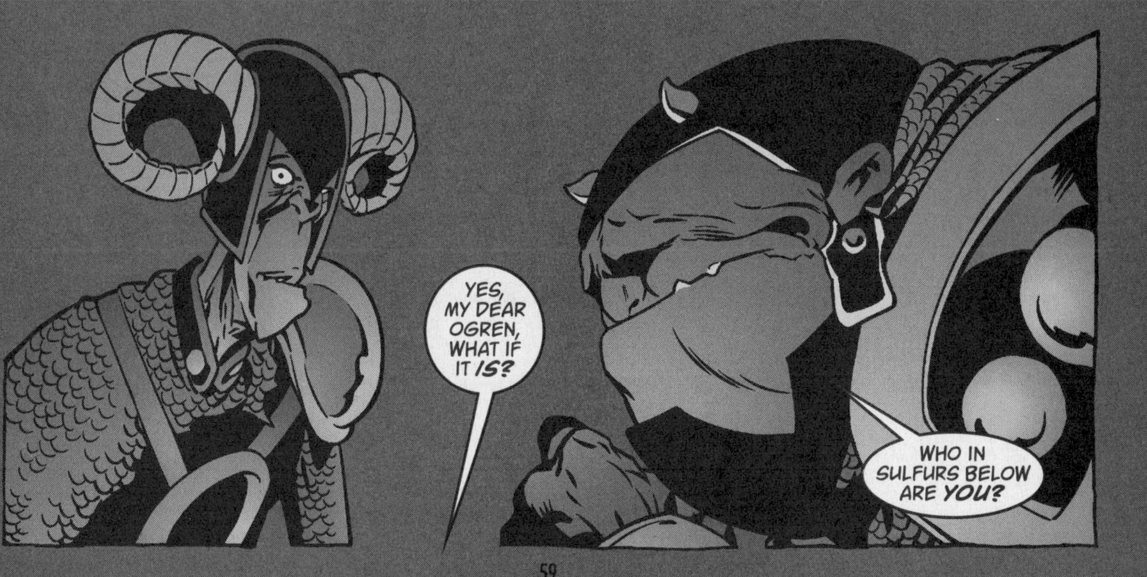
YES, MY DEAR OGREN, WHAT IF IT IS?
WHO IN SULFURS BELOW ARE YOU?

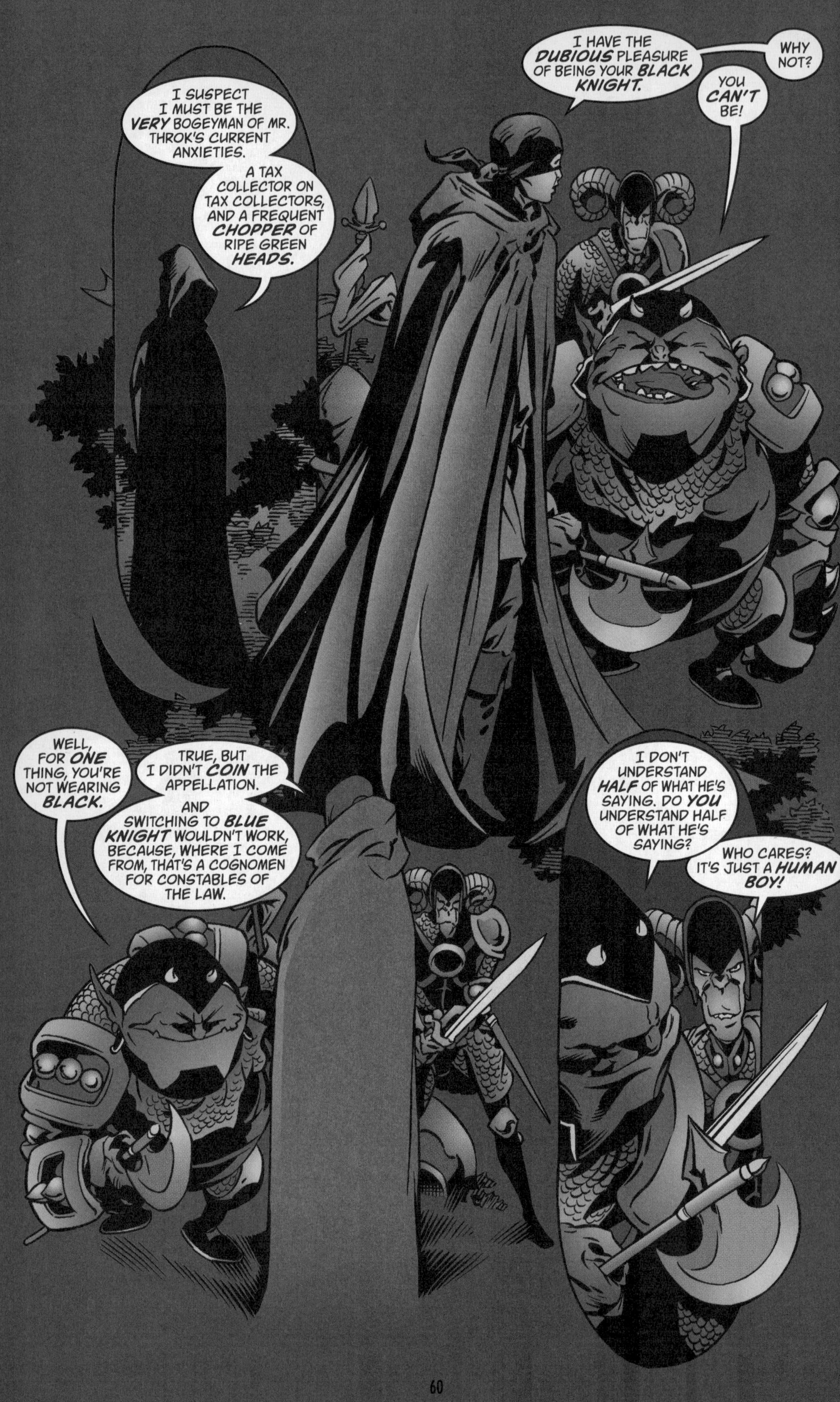
I SUSPECT I MUST BE THE VERY BOGEYMAN OF MR. THROK'S CURRENT ANXIETIES.
A TAX COLLECTOR ON TAX COLLECTORS, AND A FREQUENT CHOPPER OF RIPE GREEN HEADS.
I HAVE THE DUBIOUS PLEASURE OF BEING YOUR BLACK KNIGHT.
YOU CAN'T BE!
WHY NOT?
WELL, FOR ONE THING, YOU'RE NOT WEARING BLACK.
TRUE, BUT I DIDN'T COIN THE APPELLATION.
AND SWITCHING TO BLUE KNIGHT WOULDN'T WORK, BECAUSE, WHERE I COME FROM, THAT'S A COGNOMEN FOR CONSTABLES OF THE LAW.
I DON'T UNDERSTAND HALF OF WHAT HE'S SAYING. DO YOU UNDERSTAND HALF OF WHAT HE'S SAYING?
WHO CARES? IT'S JUST A HUMAN BOY!

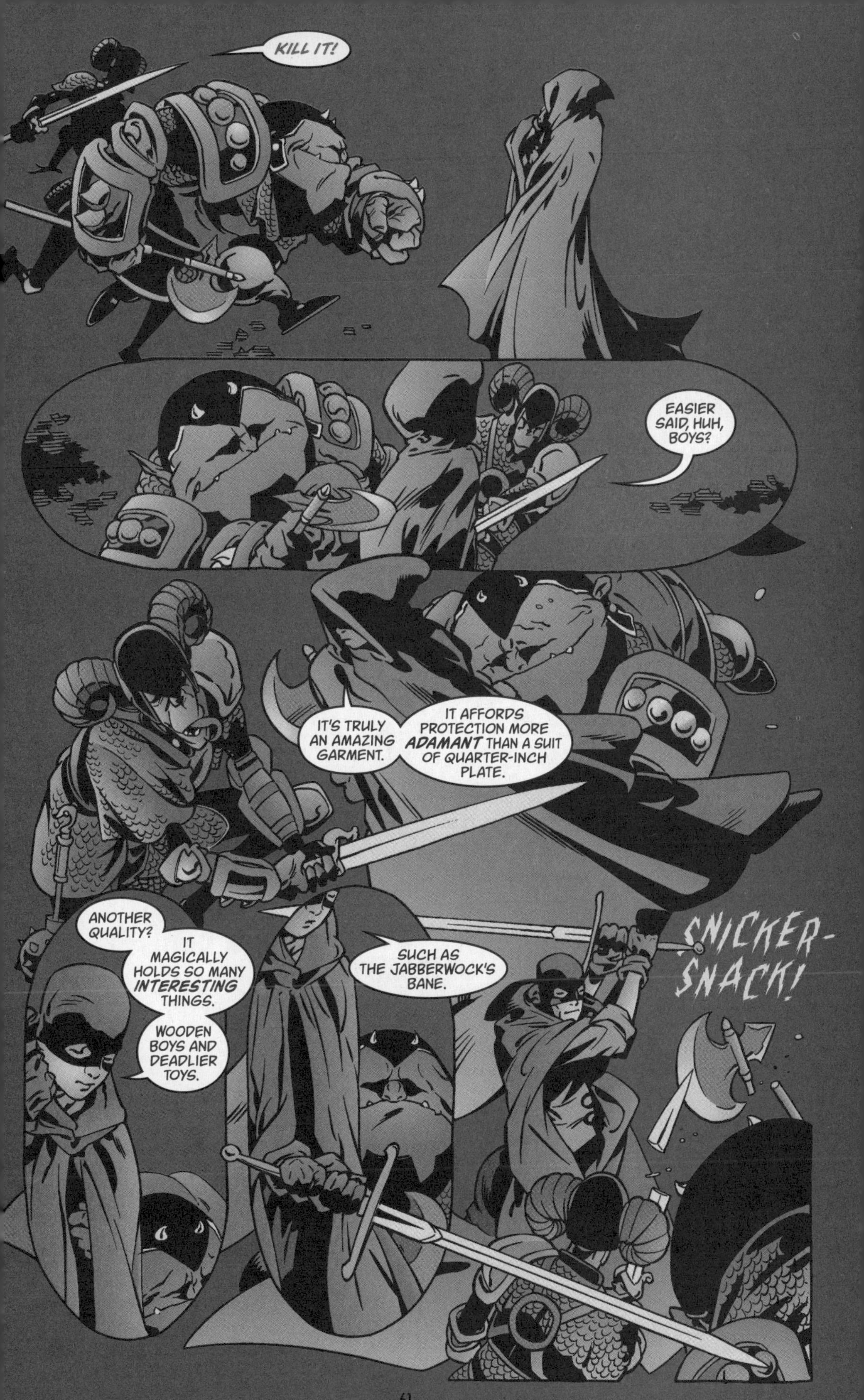

KILL IT!
EASIER SAID, HUH, BOYS?
IT'S TRULY AN AMAZING GARMENT.
IT AFFORDS PROTECTION MORE ADAMANT THAN A SUIT OF QUARTER-INCH PLATE.
ANOTHER QUALITY?
IT MAGICALLY HOLDS SO MANY INTERESTING THINGS.
WOODEN BOYS AND DEADLIER TOYS.
SUCH AS THE JABBERWOCK'S BANE.
SNICKER-SNACK!

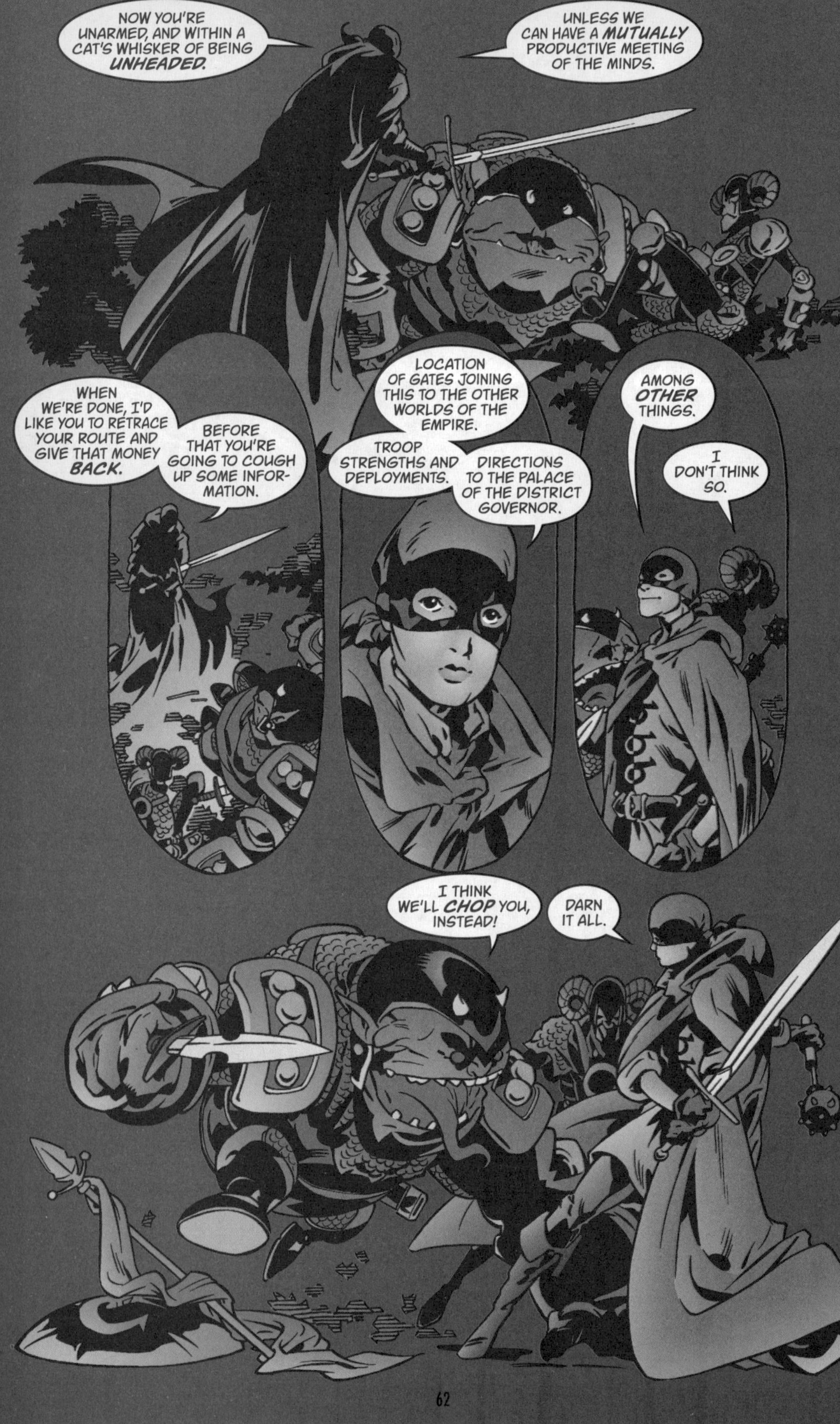
NOW YOU'RE UNARMED, AND WITHIN A CAT'S WHISKER OF BEING *UNHEADED.*
UNLESS WE CAN HAVE A *MUTUALLY* PRODUCTIVE MEETING OF THE MINDS.
WHEN WE'RE DONE, I'D LIKE YOU TO RETRACE YOUR ROUTE AND GIVE THAT MONEY *BACK.*
BEFORE THAT YOU'RE GOING TO COUGH UP SOME INFOR-MATION.
LOCATION OF GATES JOINING THIS TO THE OTHER WORLDS OF THE EMPIRE.
TROOP STRENGTHS AND DEPLOYMENTS.
DIRECTIONS TO THE PALACE OF THE DISTRICT GOVERNOR.
AMONG *OTHER* THINGS.
I DON'T THINK SO.
I THINK WE'LL *CHOP* YOU, INSTEAD!
DARN IT ALL.

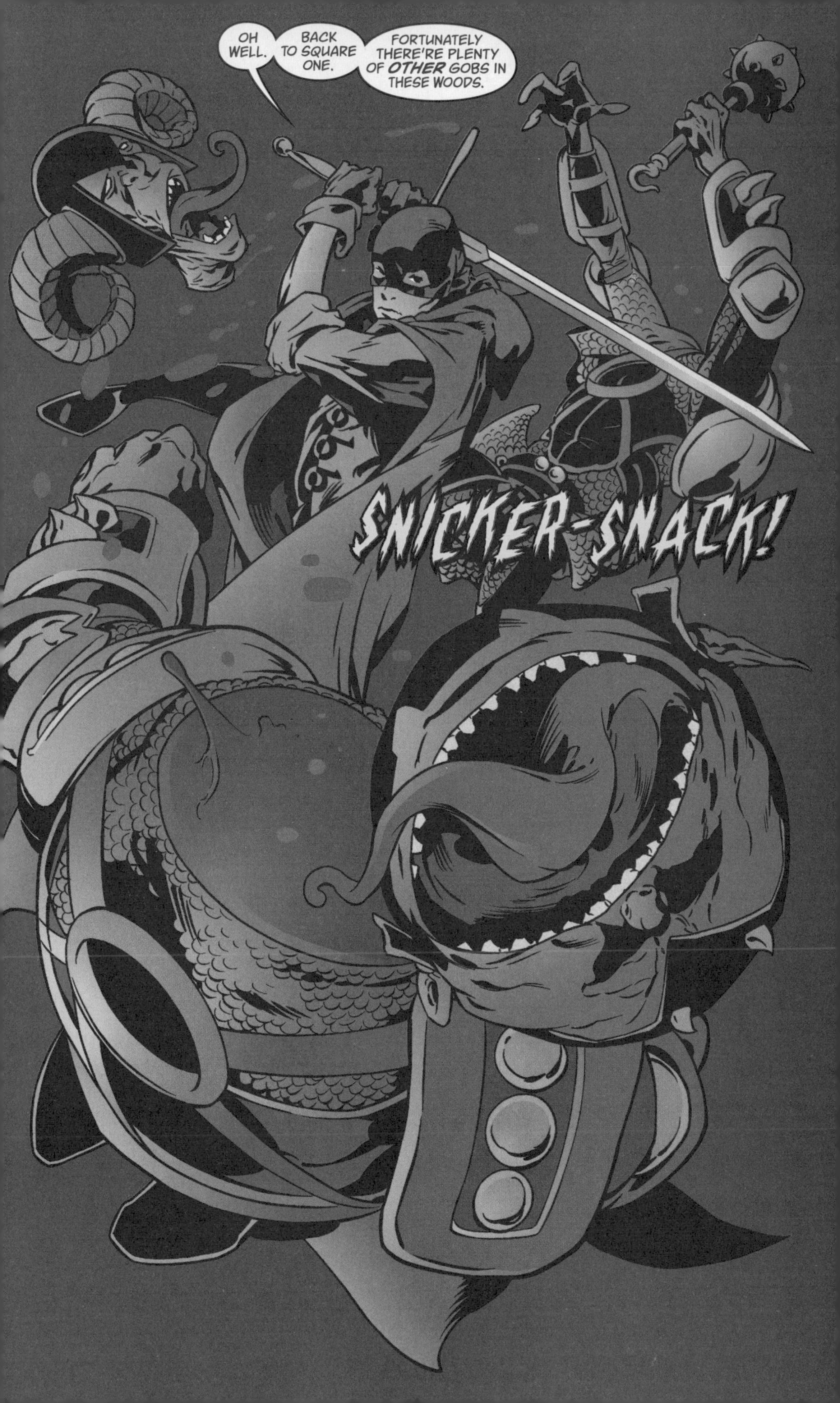
OH WELL.
BACK TO SQUARE ONE.
FORTUNATELY THERE'RE PLENTY OF OTHER GOBS IN THESE WOODS.
SNICKER-SNACK!

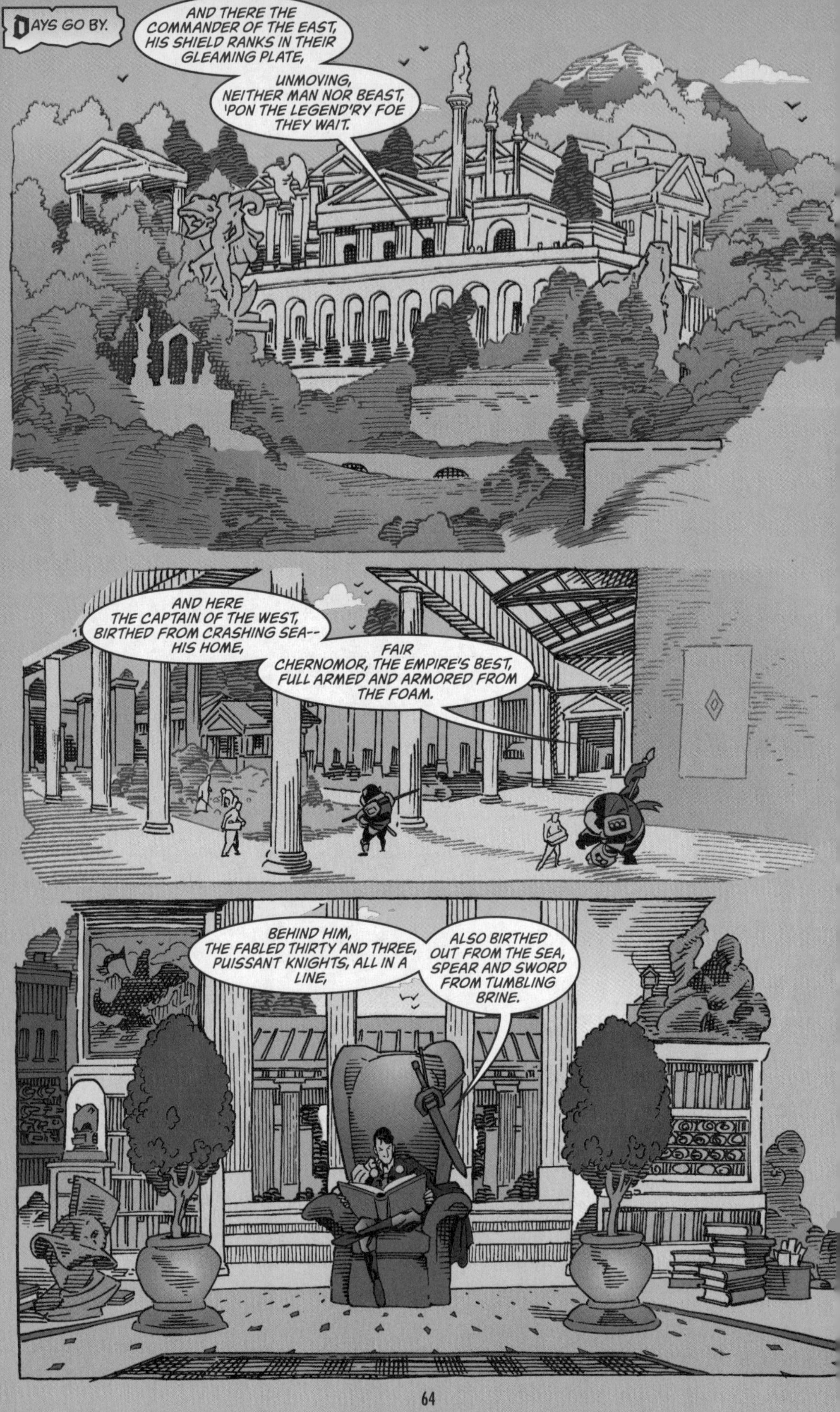
DAYS GO BY.
AND THERE THE COMMANDER OF THE EAST, HIS SHIELD RANKS IN THEIR GLEAMING PLATE,
UNMOVING, NEITHER MAN NOR BEAST, 'PON THE LEGEND'RY FOE THEY WAIT.
AND HERE THE CAPTAIN OF THE WEST, BIRTHED FROM CRASHING SEA-- HIS HOME,
FAIR CHERNOMOR, THE EMPIRE'S BEST, FULL ARMED AND ARMORED FROM THE FOAM.
BEHIND HIM, THE FABLED THIRTY AND THREE, PUISSANT KNIGHTS, ALL IN A LINE,
ALSO BIRTHED OUT FROM THE SEA, SPEAR AND SWORD FROM TUMBLING BRINE.

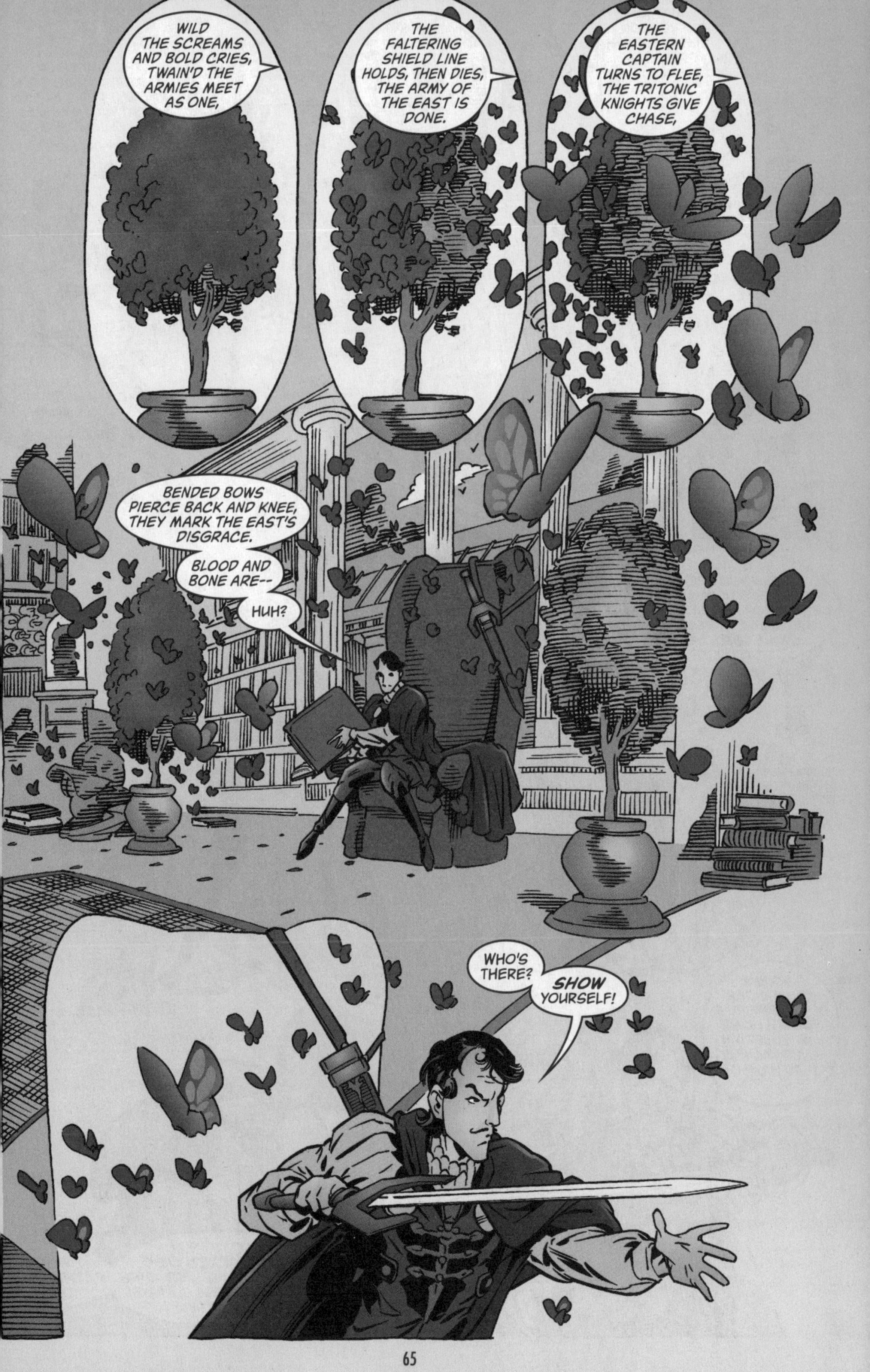
WILD THE SCREAMS AND BOLD CRIES, TWAIN'D THE ARMIES MEET AS ONE,
THE FALTERING SHIELD LINE HOLDS, THEN DIES, THE ARMY OF THE EAST IS DONE.
THE EASTERN CAPTAIN TURNS TO FLEE, THE TRITONIC KNIGHTS GIVE CHASE,
BENDED BOWS PIERCE BACK AND KNEE, THEY MARK THE EAST'S DISGRACE.
BLOOD AND BONE ARE--
HUH?
WHO'S THERE?
SHOW YOURSELF!

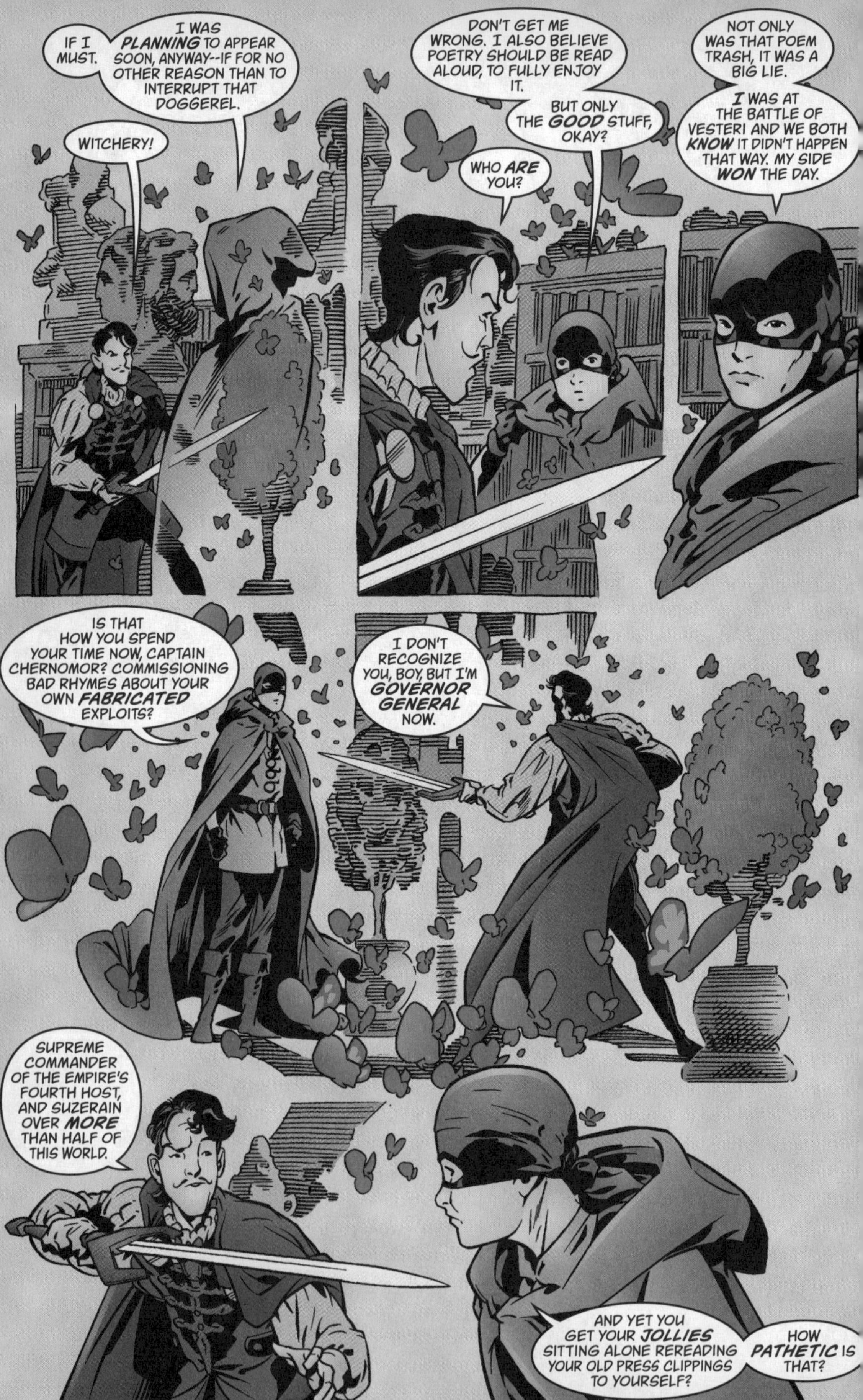
IF I MUST.
I WAS PLANNING TO APPEAR SOON, ANYWAY--IF FOR NO OTHER REASON THAN TO INTERRUPT THAT DOGGEREL.
WITCHERY!
DON'T GET ME WRONG. I ALSO BELIEVE POETRY SHOULD BE READ ALOUD, TO FULLY ENJOY IT.
BUT ONLY THE GOOD STUFF, OKAY?
WHO ARE YOU?
NOT ONLY WAS THAT POEM TRASH, IT WAS A BIG LIE.
I WAS AT THE BATTLE OF VESTERI AND WE BOTH KNOW IT DIDN'T HAPPEN THAT WAY. MY SIDE WON THE DAY.
IS THAT HOW YOU SPEND YOUR TIME NOW, CAPTAIN CHERNOMOR? COMMISSIONING BAD RHYMES ABOUT YOUR OWN FABRICATED EXPLOITS?
I DON'T RECOGNIZE YOU, BOY, BUT I'M GOVERNOR GENERAL NOW.
SUPREME COMMANDER OF THE EMPIRE'S FOURTH HOST, AND SUZERAIN OVER MORE THAN HALF OF THIS WORLD.
AND YET YOU GET YOUR JOLLIES SITTING ALONE REREADING YOUR OLD PRESS CLIPPINGS TO YOURSELF?
HOW PATHETIC IS THAT?

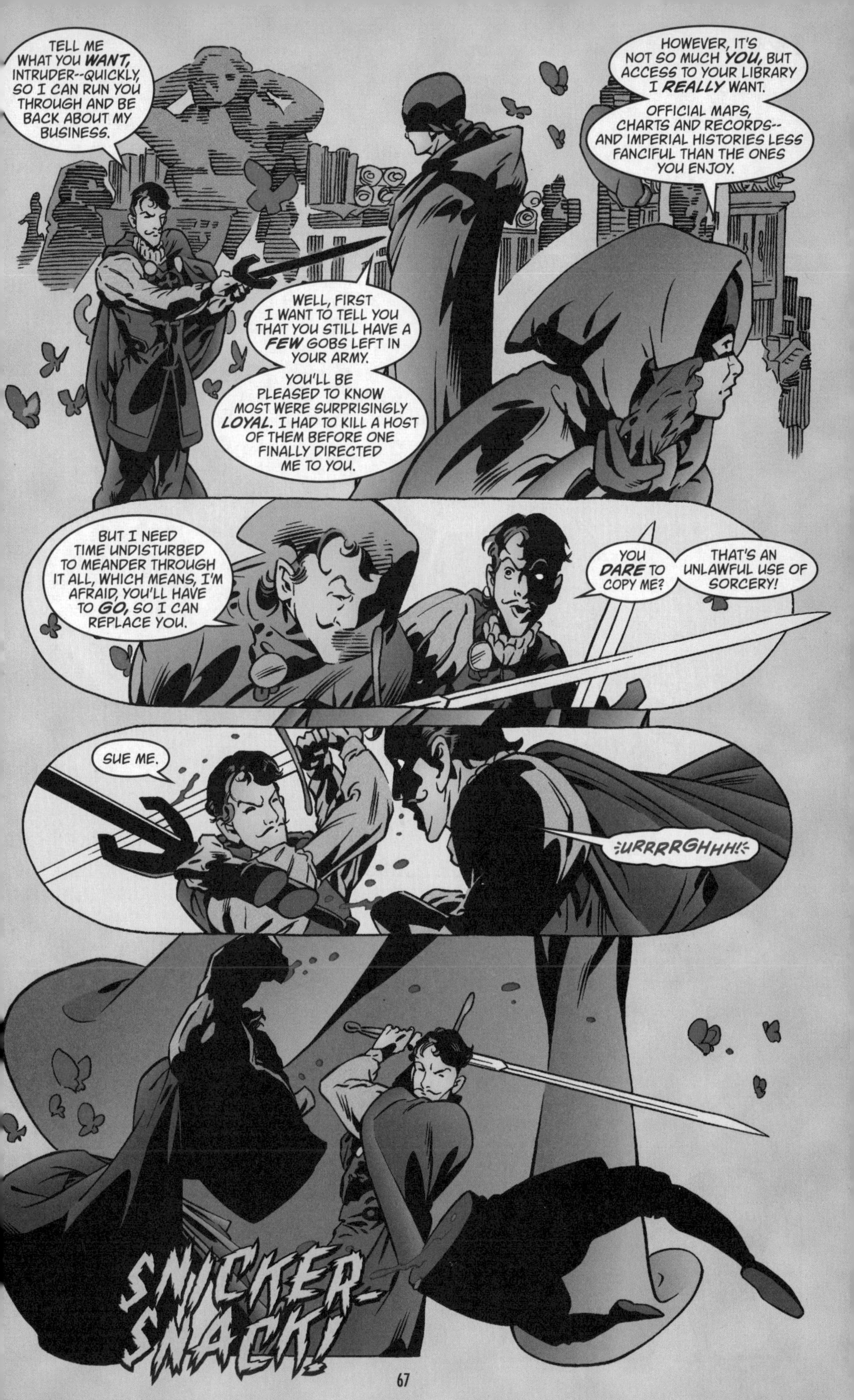

TELL ME WHAT YOU WANT, INTRUDER--QUICKLY, SO I CAN RUN YOU THROUGH AND BE BACK ABOUT MY BUSINESS.
WELL, FIRST I WANT TO TELL YOU THAT YOU STILL HAVE A FEW GOBS LEFT IN YOUR ARMY.
YOU'LL BE PLEASED TO KNOW MOST WERE SURPRISINGLY LOYAL. I HAD TO KILL A HOST OF THEM BEFORE ONE FINALLY DIRECTED ME TO YOU.
HOWEVER, IT'S NOT SO MUCH YOU, BUT ACCESS TO YOUR LIBRARY I REALLY WANT.
OFFICIAL MAPS, CHARTS AND RECORDS--AND IMPERIAL HISTORIES LESS FANCIFUL THAN THE ONES YOU ENJOY.
BUT I NEED TIME UNDISTURBED TO MEANDER THROUGH IT ALL, WHICH MEANS, I'M AFRAID, YOU'LL HAVE TO GO, SO I CAN REPLACE YOU.
YOU DARE TO COPY ME?
THAT'S AN UNLAWFUL USE OF SORCERY!
SUE ME.
URRRRGHHH!
SNICKER-SNACK!

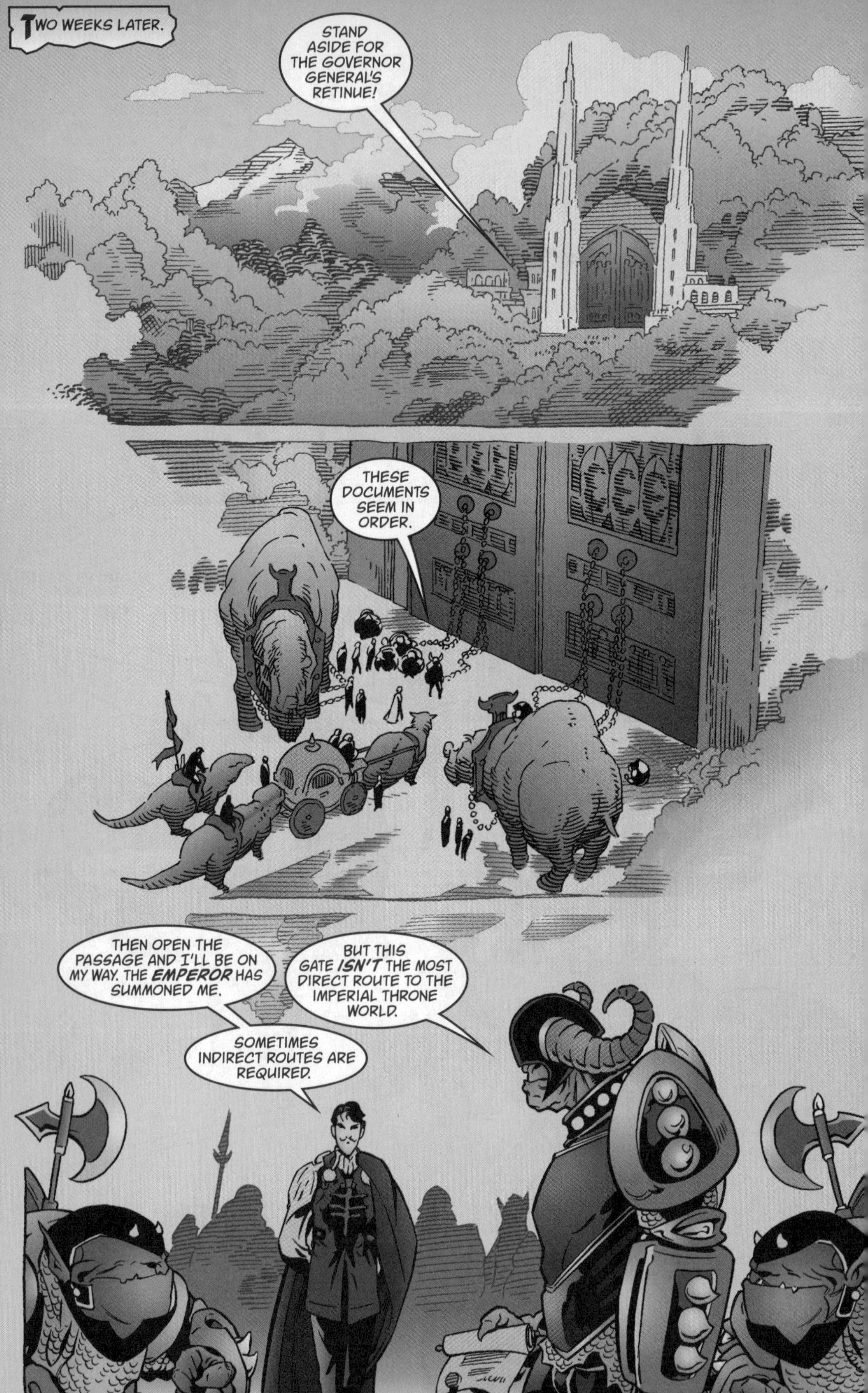
TWO WEEKS LATER.
STAND ASIDE FOR THE GOVERNOR GENERAL'S RETINUE!
THESE DOCUMENTS SEEM IN ORDER.
THEN OPEN THE PASSAGE AND I'LL BE ON MY WAY. THE EMPEROR HAS SUMMONED ME.
BUT THIS GATE ISN'T THE MOST DIRECT ROUTE TO THE IMPERIAL THRONE WORLD.
SOMETIMES INDIRECT ROUTES ARE REQUIRED.

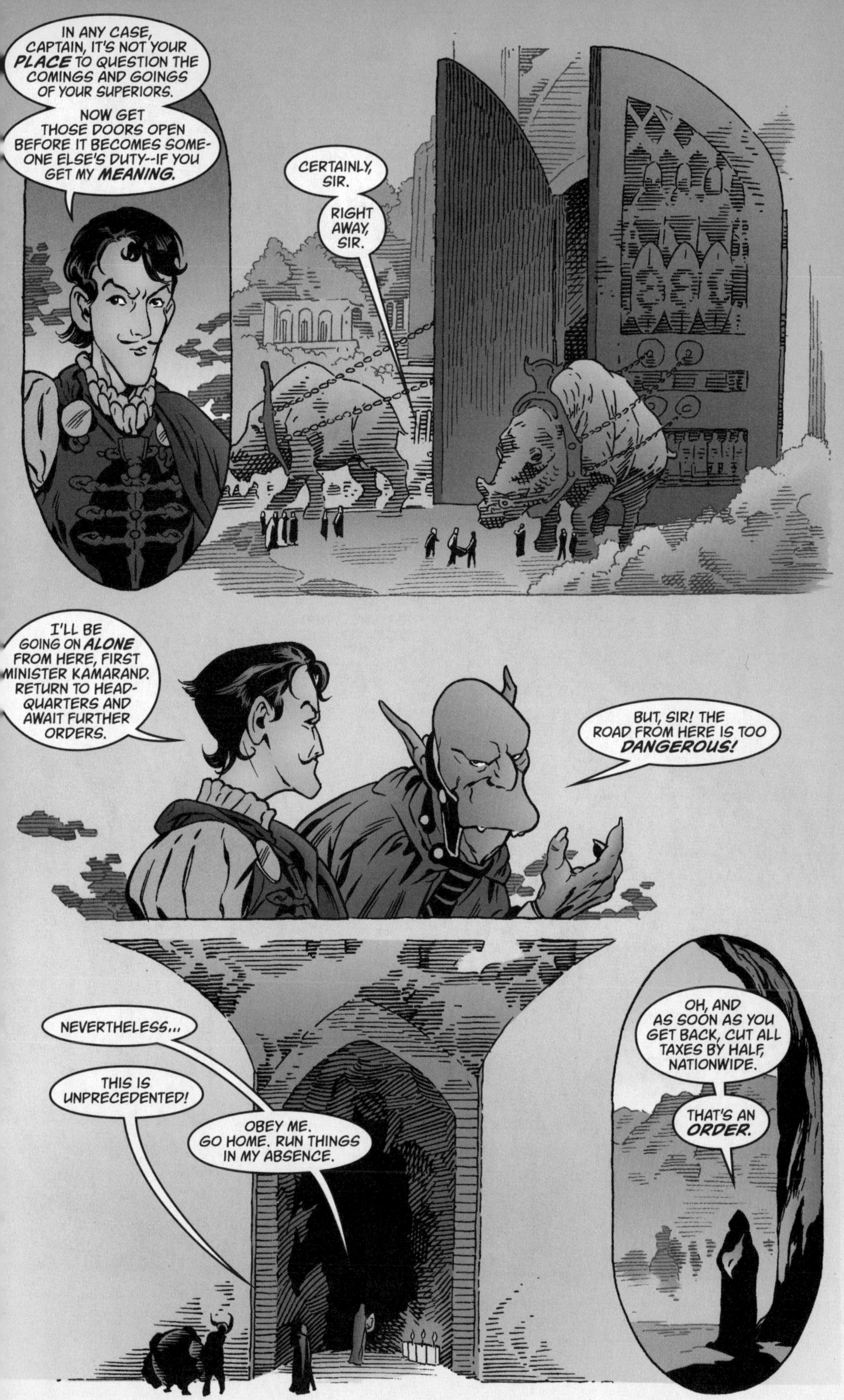
IN ANY CASE, CAPTAIN, IT'S NOT YOUR PLACE TO QUESTION THE COMINGS AND GOINGS OF YOUR SUPERIORS.
NOW GET THOSE DOORS OPEN BEFORE IT BECOMES SOME-ONE ELSE'S DUTY--IF YOU GET MY MEANING.
CERTAINLY, SIR.
RIGHT AWAY, SIR.
I'LL BE GOING ON ALONE FROM HERE, FIRST MINISTER KAMARAND. RETURN TO HEAD-QUARTERS AND AWAIT FURTHER ORDERS.
BUT, SIR! THE ROAD FROM HERE IS TOO DANGEROUS!
NEVERTHELESS...
THIS IS UNPRECEDENTED!
OBEY ME. GO HOME. RUN THINGS IN MY ABSENCE.
OH, AND AS SOON AS YOU GET BACK, CUT ALL TAXES BY HALF, NATIONWIDE.
THAT'S AN ORDER.

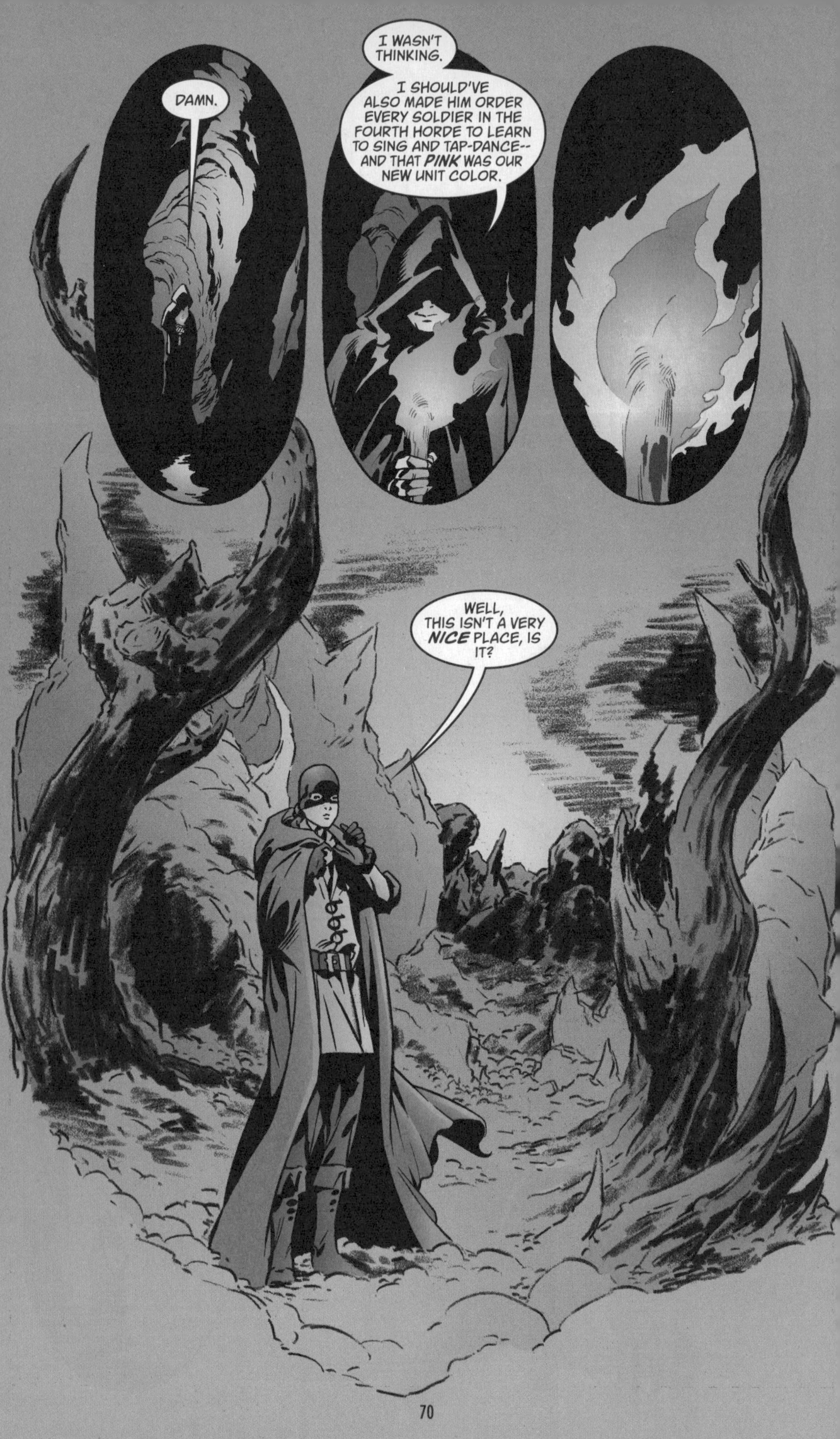
DAMN.
I WASN'T THINKING.
I SHOULD'VE ALSO MADE HIM ORDER EVERY SOLDIER IN THE FOURTH HORDE TO LEARN TO SING AND TAP-DANCE-- AND THAT PINK WAS OUR NEW UNIT COLOR.
WELL, THIS ISN'T A VERY NICE PLACE, IS IT?

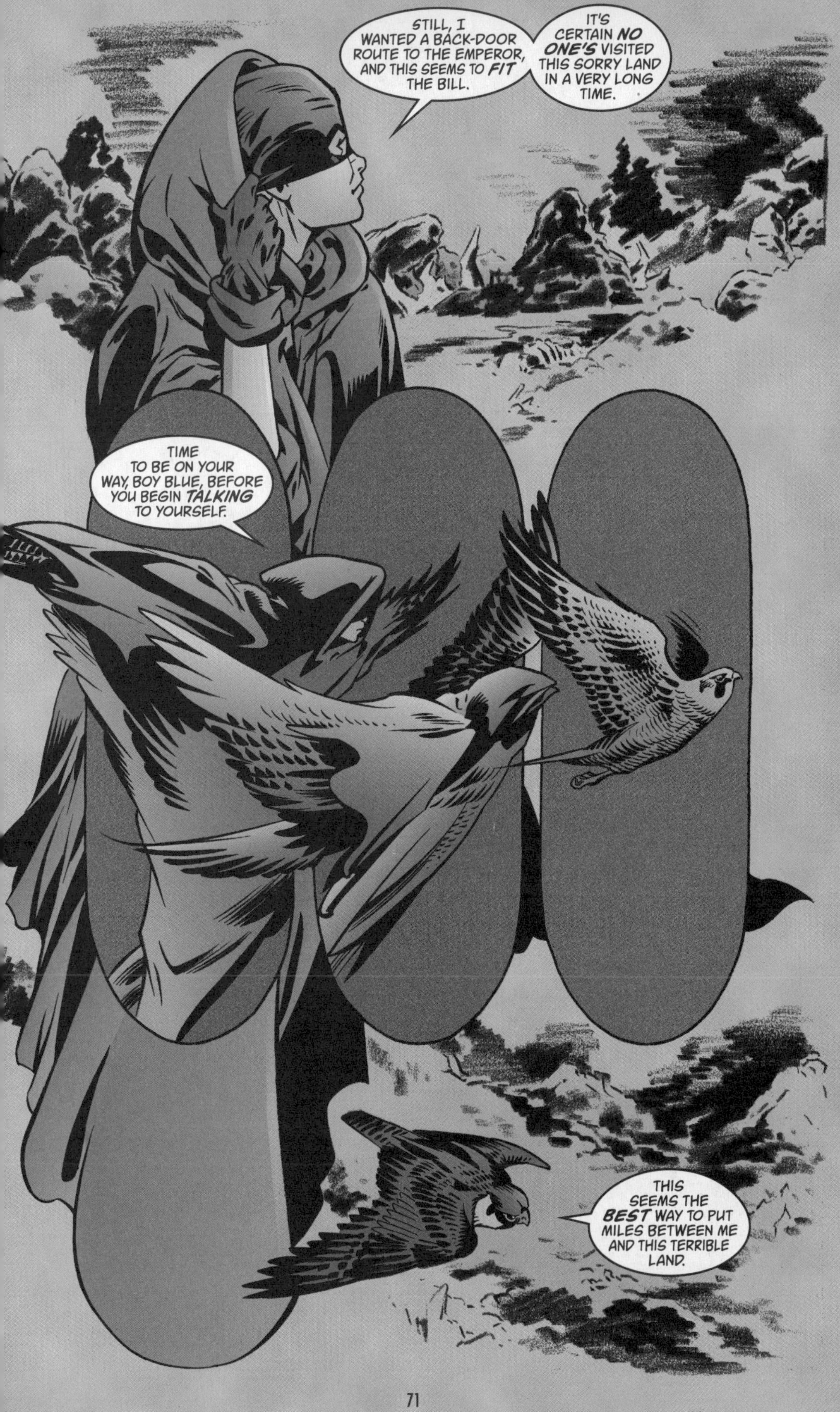
STILL, I WANTED A BACK-DOOR ROUTE TO THE EMPEROR, AND THIS SEEMS TO *FIT* THE BILL.
IT'S CERTAIN *NO ONE'S* VISITED THIS SORRY LAND IN A VERY LONG TIME.
TIME TO BE ON YOUR WAY, BOY BLUE, BEFORE YOU BEGIN *TALKING* TO YOURSELF.
THIS SEEMS THE *BEST* WAY TO PUT MILES BETWEEN ME AND THIS TERRIBLE LAND.

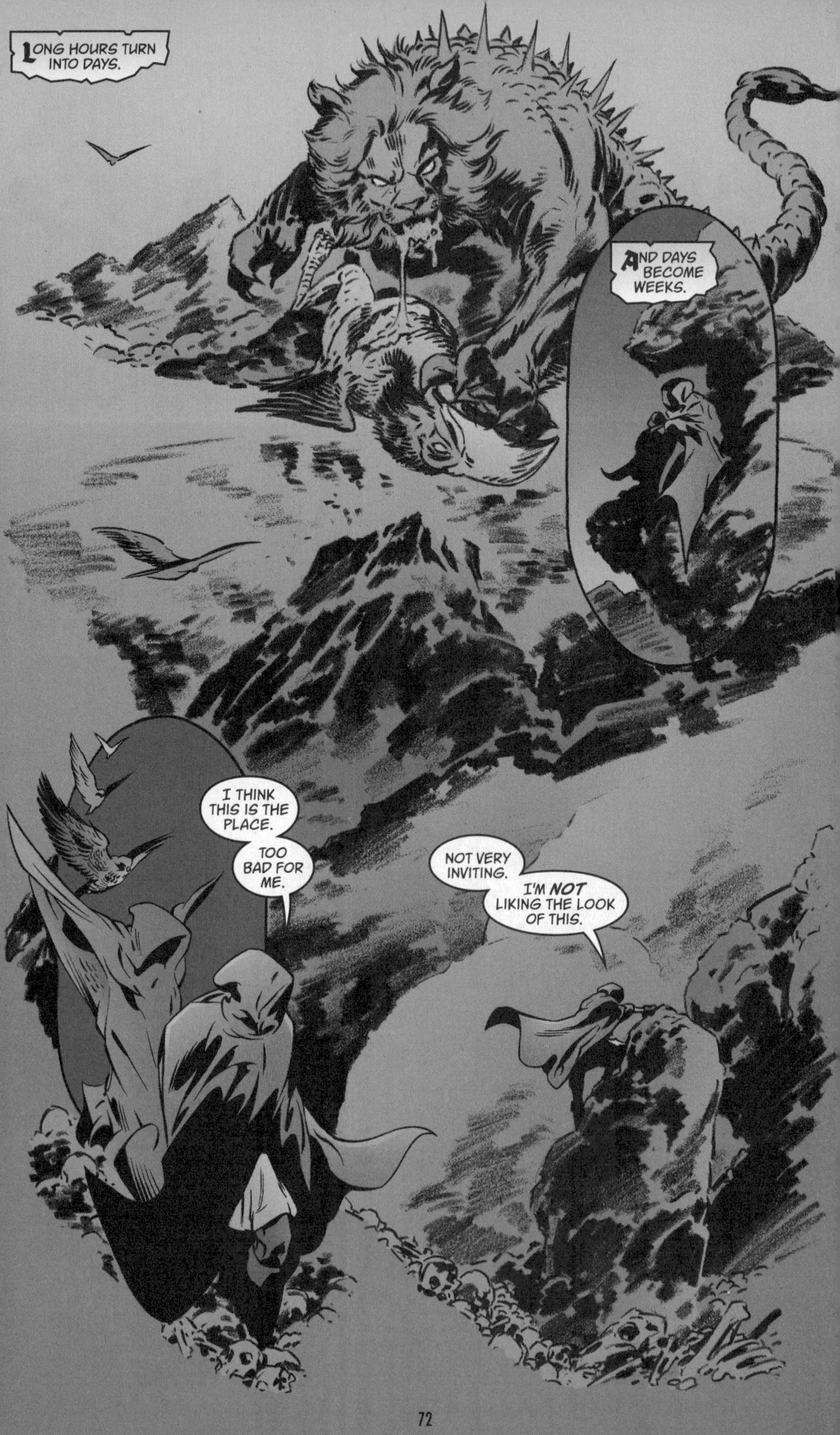

LONG HOURS TURN INTO DAYS.
AND DAYS BECOME WEEKS.
I THINK THIS IS THE PLACE.
TOO BAD FOR ME.
NOT VERY INVITING.
I'M **NOT** LIKING THE LOOK OF THIS.

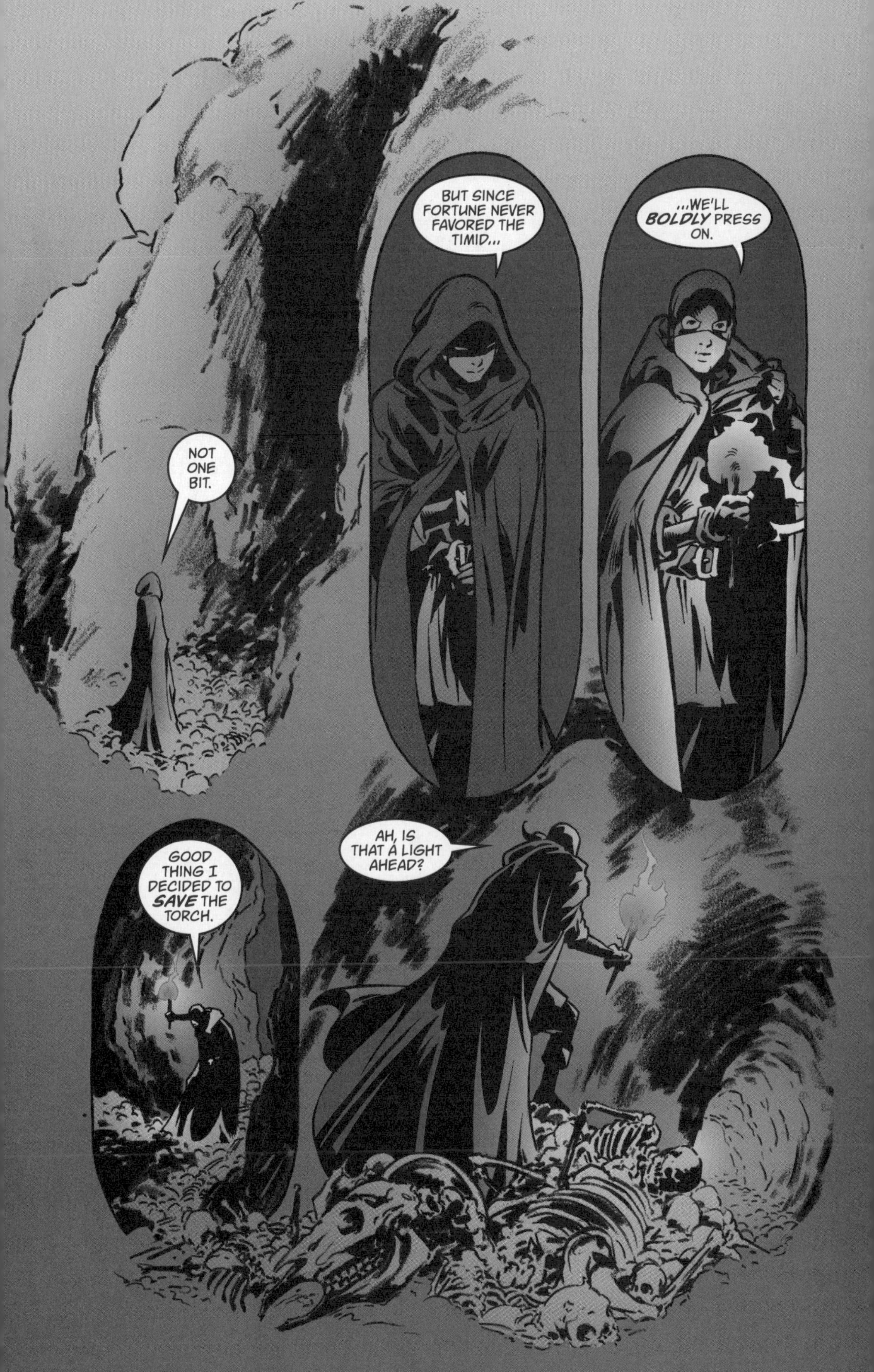
NOT ONE BIT.
BUT SINCE FORTUNE NEVER FAVORED THE TIMID...
...WE'LL BOLDLY PRESS ON.
GOOD THING I DECIDED TO SAVE THE TORCH.
AH, IS THAT A LIGHT AHEAD?

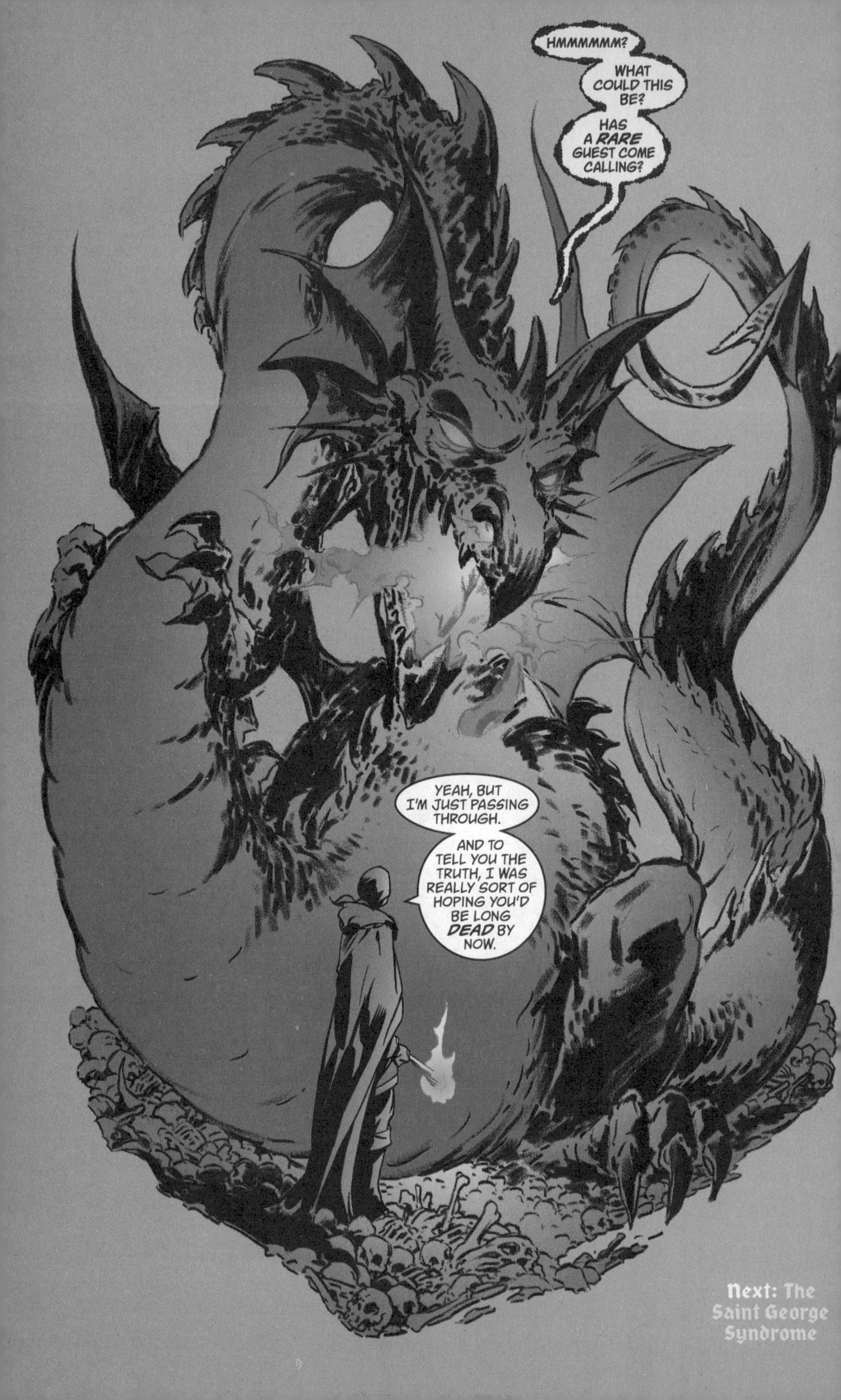
HMMMMMM?
WHAT COULD THIS BE?
HAS A RARE GUEST COME CALLING?
YEAH, BUT I'M JUST PASSING THROUGH.
AND TO TELL YOU THE TRUTH, I WAS REALLY SORT OF HOPING YOU'D BE LONG DEAD BY NOW.
Next: The Saint George Syndrome

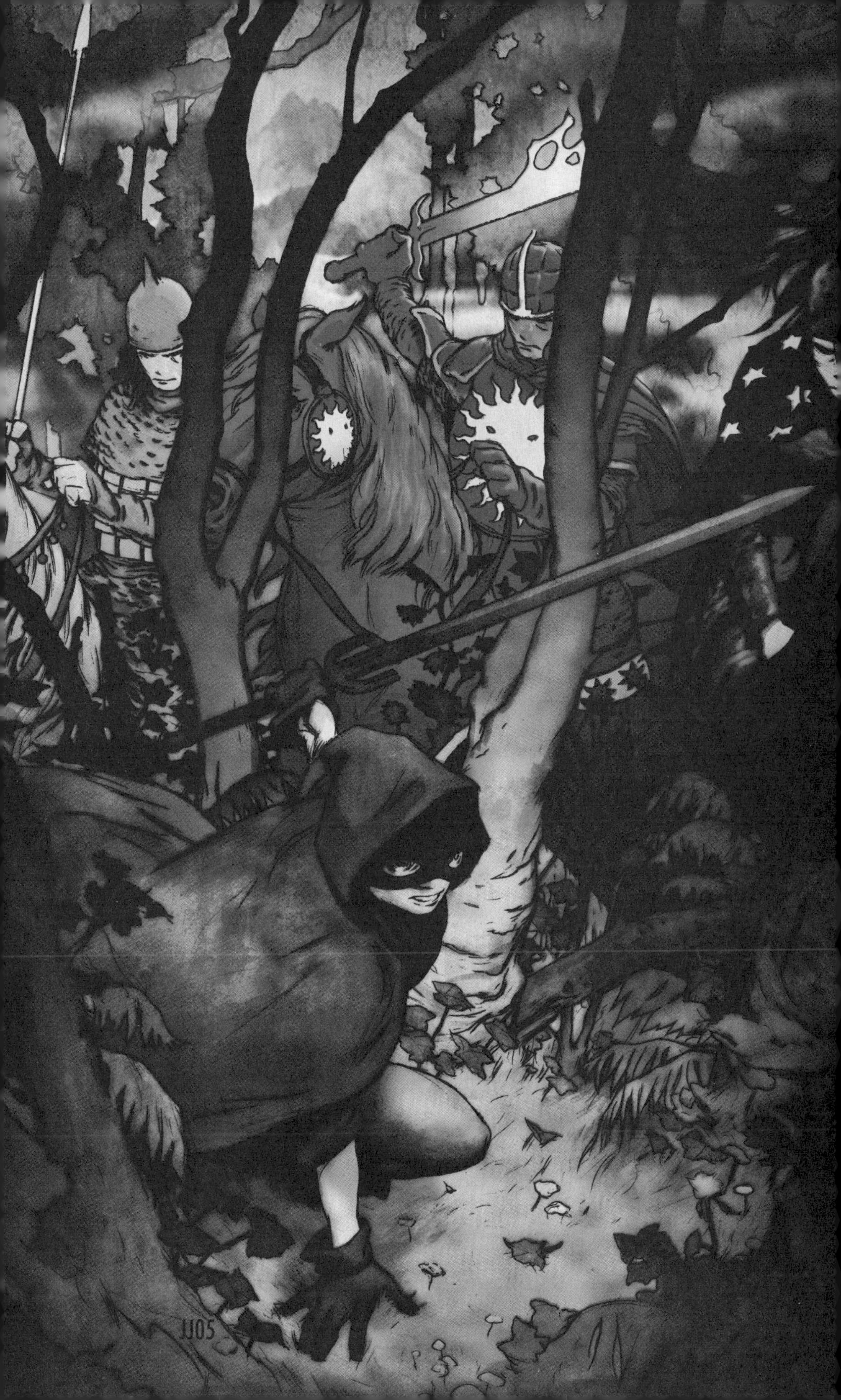

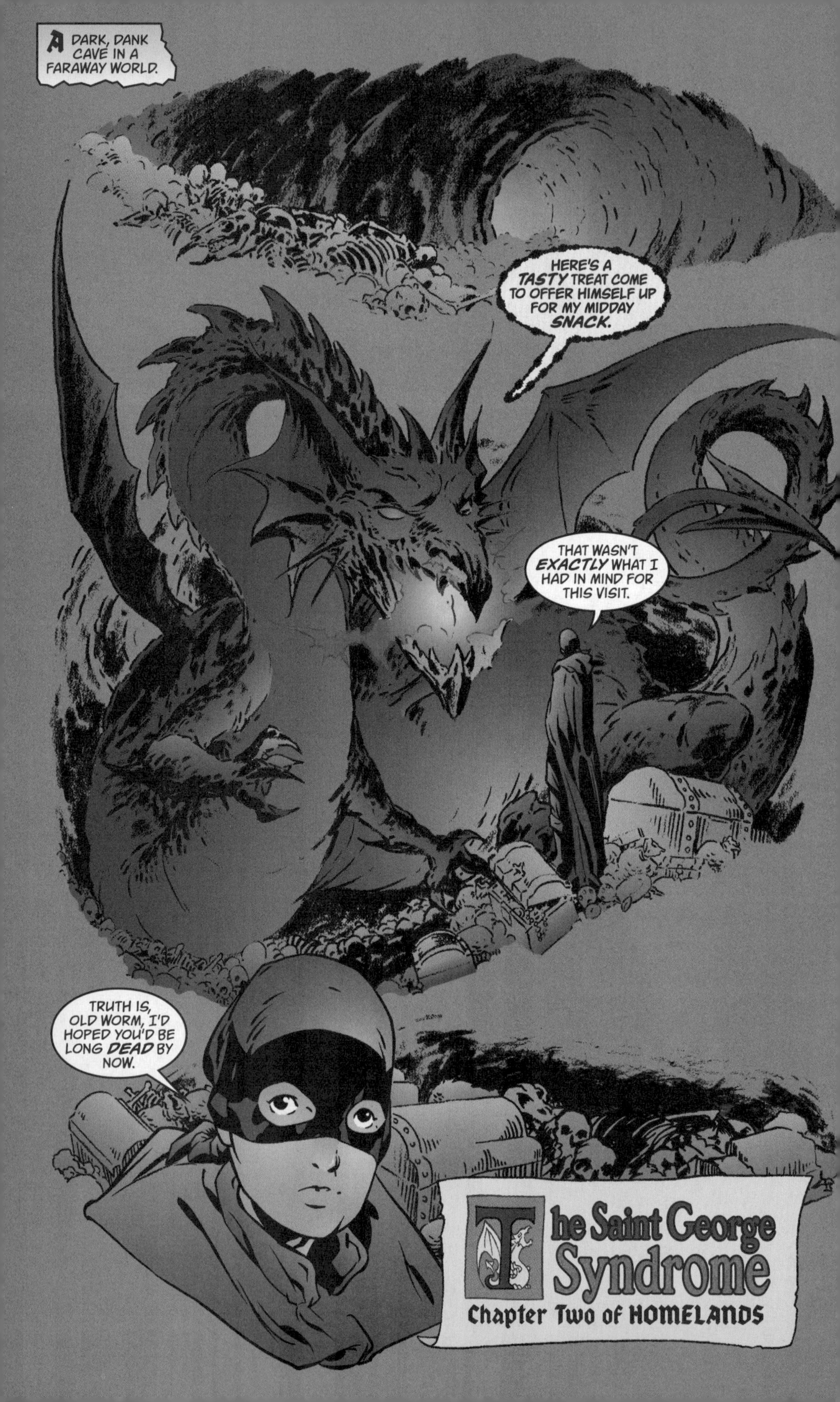
A DARK, DANK CAVE IN A FARAWAY WORLD.
HERE'S A TASTY TREAT COME TO OFFER HIMSELF UP FOR MY MIDDAY SNACK.
THAT WASN'T EXACTLY WHAT I HAD IN MIND FOR THIS VISIT.
TRUTH IS, OLD WORM, I'D HOPED YOU'D BE LONG DEAD BY NOW.
The Saint George Syndrome
Chapter Two of HOMELANDS

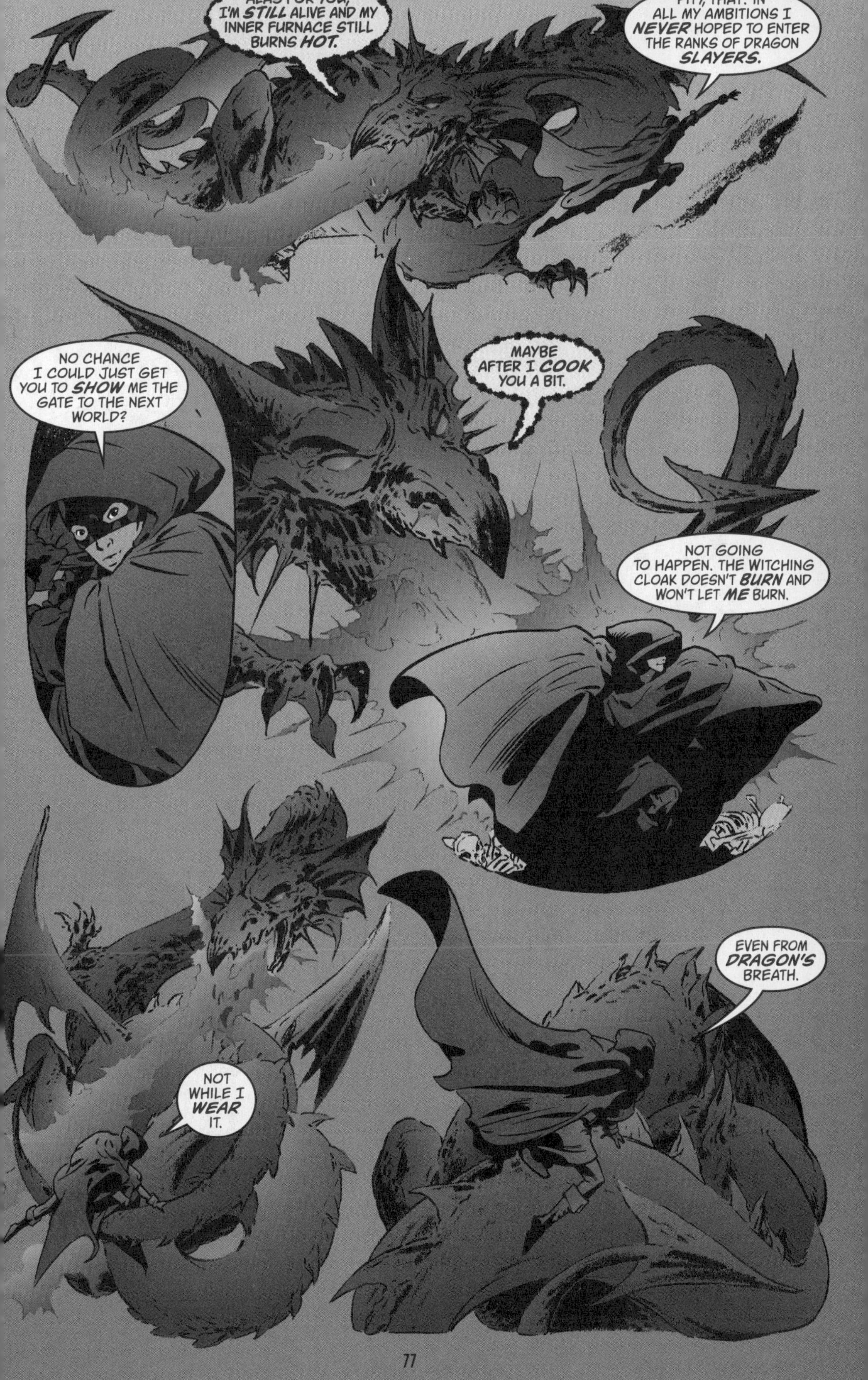
ALAS FOR YOU, I'M STILL ALIVE AND MY INNER FURNACE STILL BURNS HOT.
PITY, THAT. IN ALL MY AMBITIONS I NEVER HOPED TO ENTER THE RANKS OF DRAGON SLAYERS.
NO CHANCE I COULD JUST GET YOU TO SHOW ME THE GATE TO THE NEXT WORLD?
MAYBE AFTER I COOK YOU A BIT.
NOT GOING TO HAPPEN. THE WITCHING CLOAK DOESN'T BURN AND WON'T LET ME BURN.
NOT WHILE I WEAR IT.
EVEN FROM DRAGON'S BREATH.

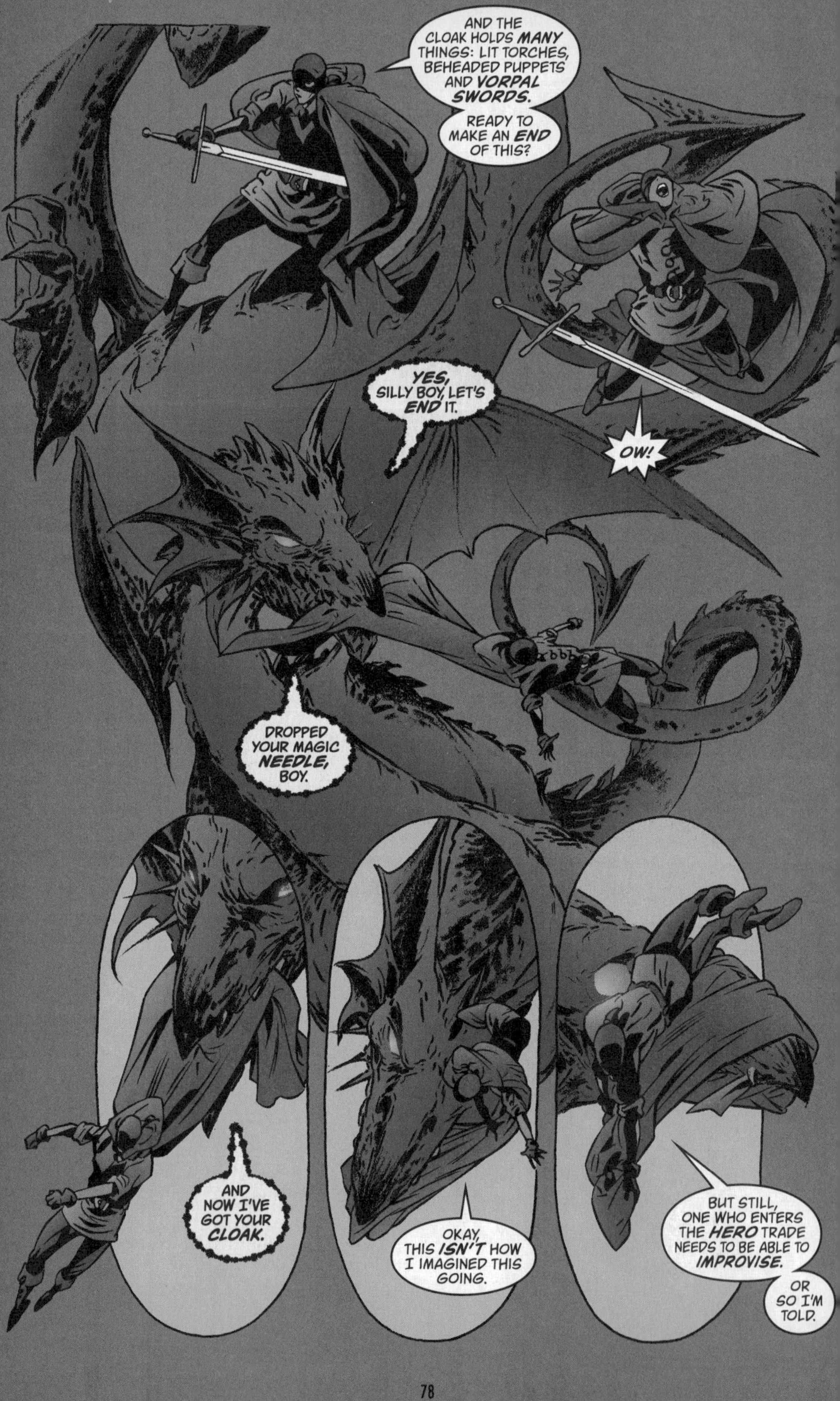
AND THE CLOAK HOLDS MANY THINGS: LIT TORCHES, BEHEADED PUPPETS AND VORPAL SWORDS.
READY TO MAKE AN END OF THIS?
YES, SILLY BOY, LET'S END IT.
OW!
DROPPED YOUR MAGIC NEEDLE, BOY.
AND NOW I'VE GOT YOUR CLOAK.
OKAY, THIS ISN'T HOW I IMAGINED THIS GOING.
BUT STILL, ONE WHO ENTERS THE HERO TRADE NEEDS TO BE ABLE TO IMPROVISE.
OR SO I'M TOLD.

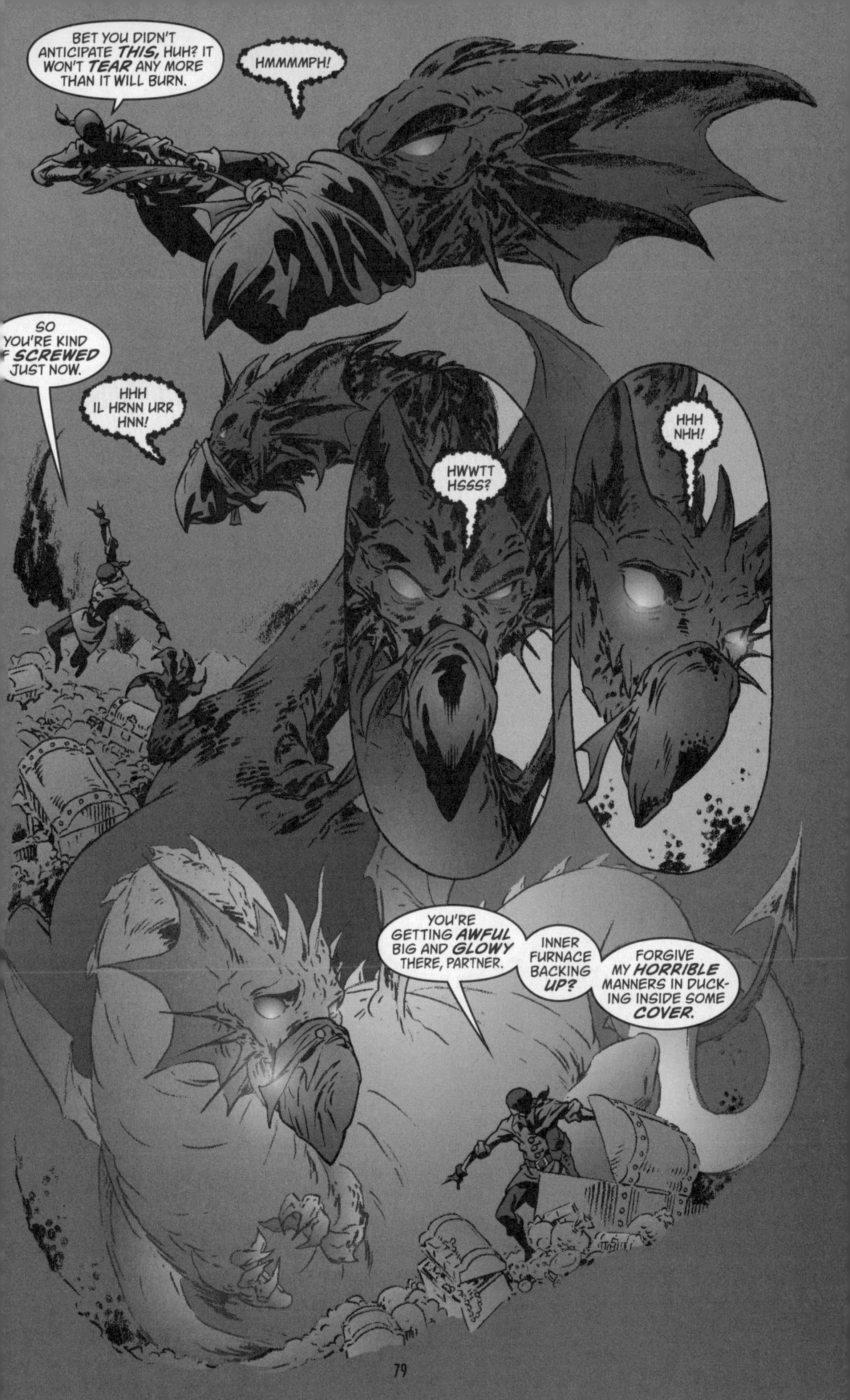
BET YOU DIDN'T ANTICIPATE THIS, HUH? IT WON'T TEAR ANY MORE THAN IT WILL BURN.
HMMMMPH!
SO YOU'RE KIND SCREWED JUST NOW.
HHH IL HRNN URR HNN!
HWWTT HSSS?
HHH NHH!
YOU'RE GETTING AWFUL BIG AND GLOWY THERE, PARTNER.
INNER FURNACE BACKING UP?
FORGIVE MY HORRIBLE MANNERS IN DUCK-ING INSIDE SOME COVER.

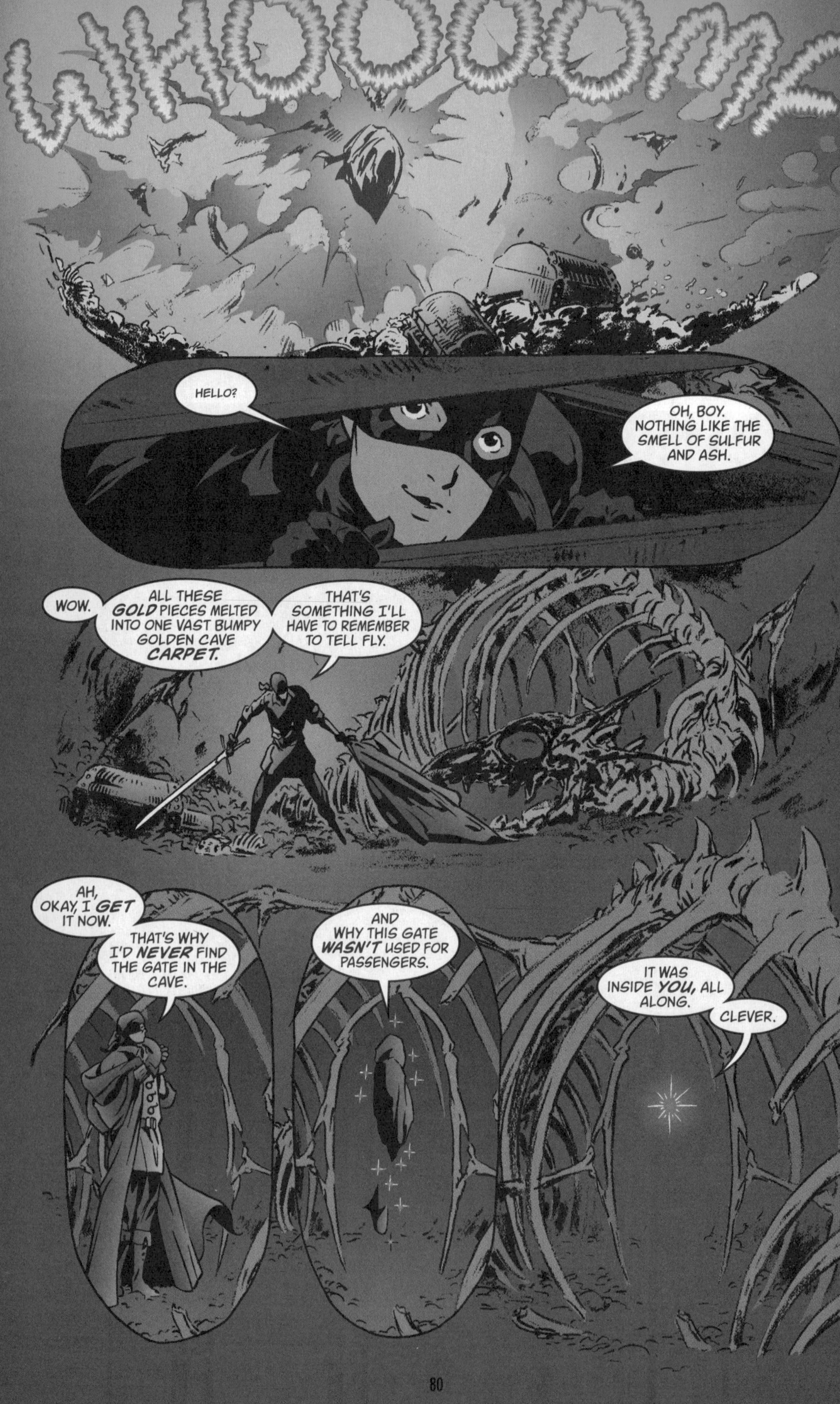
WHOOOOOMF
HELLO?
OH, BOY. NOTHING LIKE THE SMELL OF SULFUR AND ASH.
WOW.
ALL THESE GOLD PIECES MELTED INTO ONE VAST BUMPY GOLDEN CAVE CARPET.
THAT'S SOMETHING I'LL HAVE TO REMEMBER TO TELL FLY.
AH, OKAY, I GET IT NOW.
THAT'S WHY I'D NEVER FIND THE GATE IN THE CAVE.
AND WHY THIS GATE WASN'T USED FOR PASSENGERS.
IT WAS INSIDE YOU, ALL ALONG.
CLEVER.

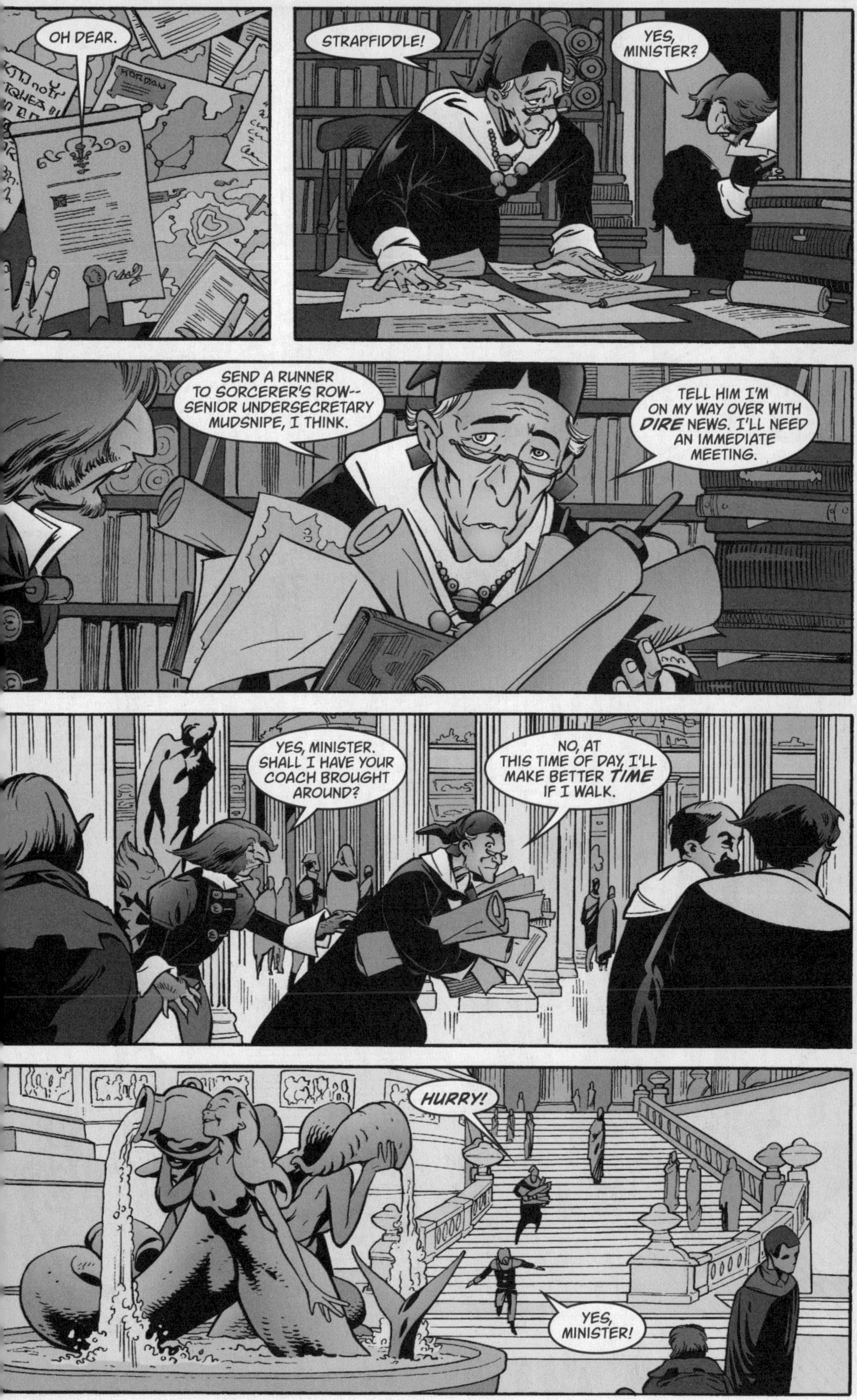
OH DEAR.
STRAPFIDDLE!
YES, MINISTER?
SEND A RUNNER TO SORCERER'S ROW-- SENIOR UNDERSECRETARY MUDSNIPE, I THINK.
TELL HIM I'M ON MY WAY OVER WITH *DIRE* NEWS. I'LL NEED AN IMMEDIATE MEETING.
YES, MINISTER. SHALL I HAVE YOUR COACH BROUGHT AROUND?
NO, AT THIS TIME OF DAY, I'LL MAKE BETTER *TIME* IF I WALK.
HURRY!
YES, MINISTER!

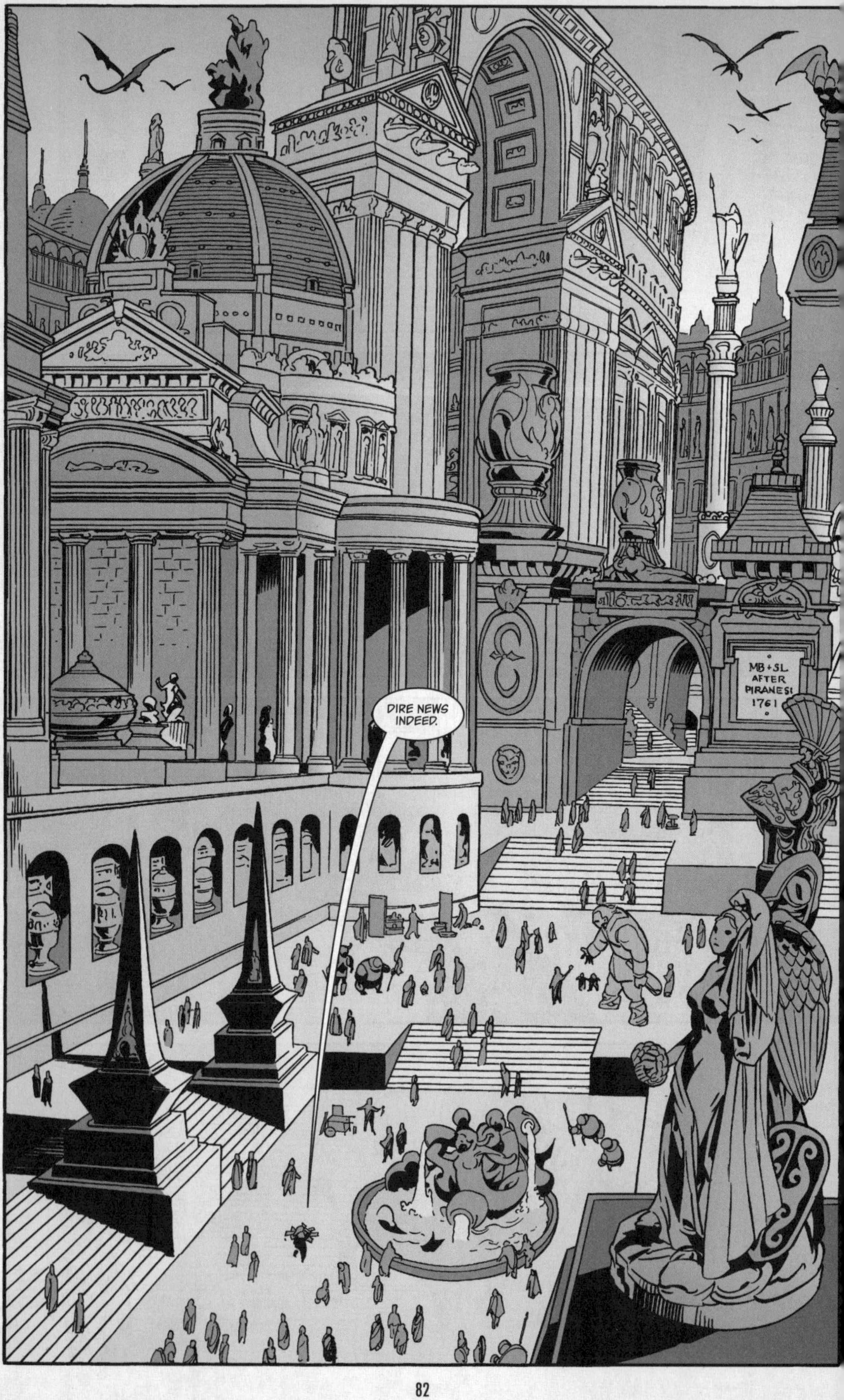
MB + SL AFTER PIRANESI 1761
DIRE NEWS INDEED.

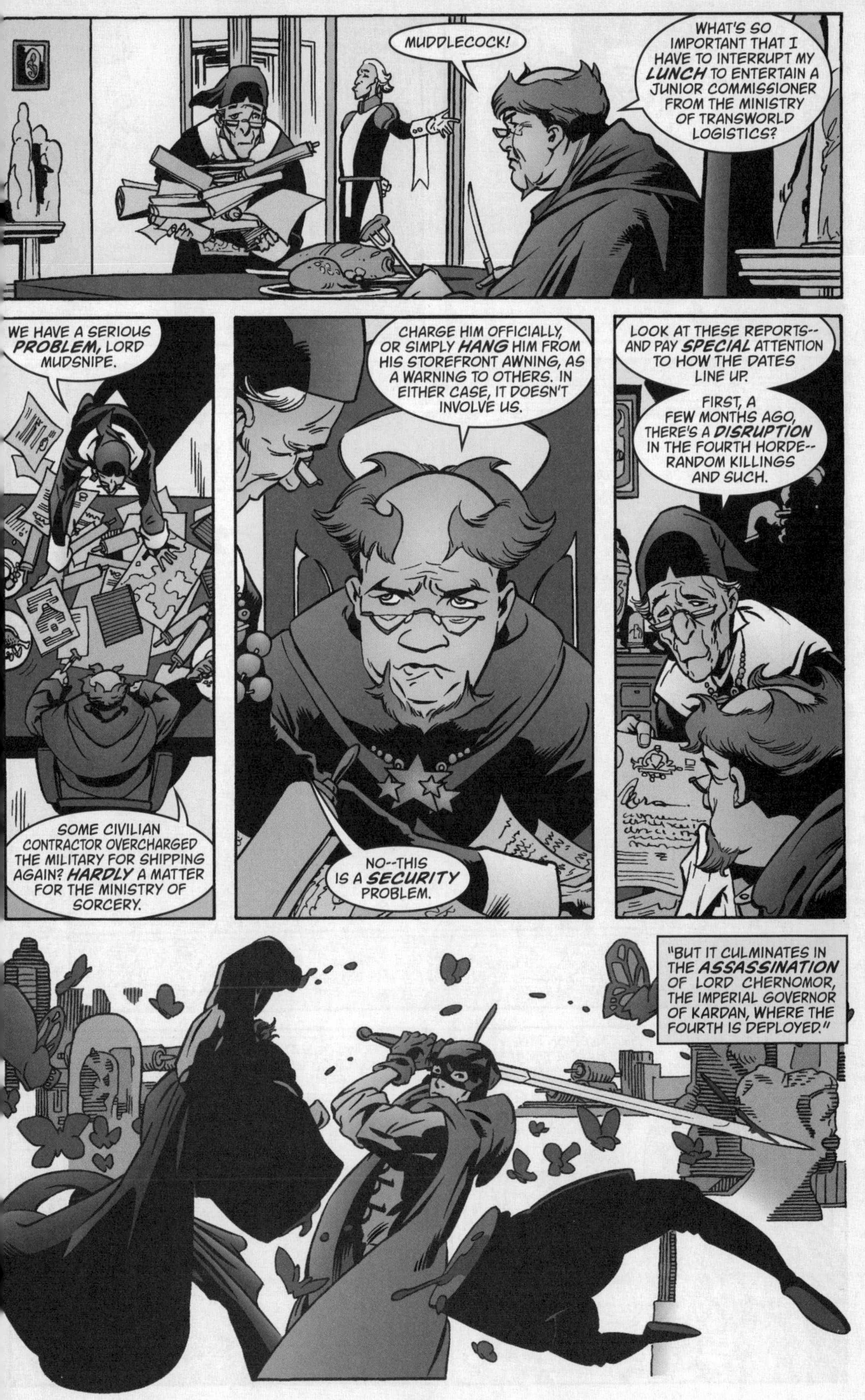
MUDDLECOCK!
WHAT'S SO IMPORTANT THAT I HAVE TO INTERRUPT MY LUNCH TO ENTERTAIN A JUNIOR COMMISSIONER FROM THE MINISTRY OF TRANSWORLD LOGISTICS?
WE HAVE A SERIOUS PROBLEM, LORD MUDSNIPE.
SOME CIVILIAN CONTRACTOR OVERCHARGED THE MILITARY FOR SHIPPING AGAIN? HARDLY A MATTER FOR THE MINISTRY OF SORCERY.
NO--THIS IS A SECURITY PROBLEM.
CHARGE HIM OFFICIALLY, OR SIMPLY HANG HIM FROM HIS STOREFRONT AWNING, AS A WARNING TO OTHERS. IN EITHER CASE, IT DOESN'T INVOLVE US.
LOOK AT THESE REPORTS-- AND PAY SPECIAL ATTENTION TO HOW THE DATES LINE UP.
FIRST, A FEW MONTHS AGO, THERE'S A DISRUPTION IN THE FOURTH HORDE-- RANDOM KILLINGS AND SUCH.
"BUT IT CULMINATES IN THE ASSASSINATION OF LORD CHERNOMOR, THE IMPERIAL GOVERNOR OF KARDAN, WHERE THE FOURTH IS DEPLOYED."

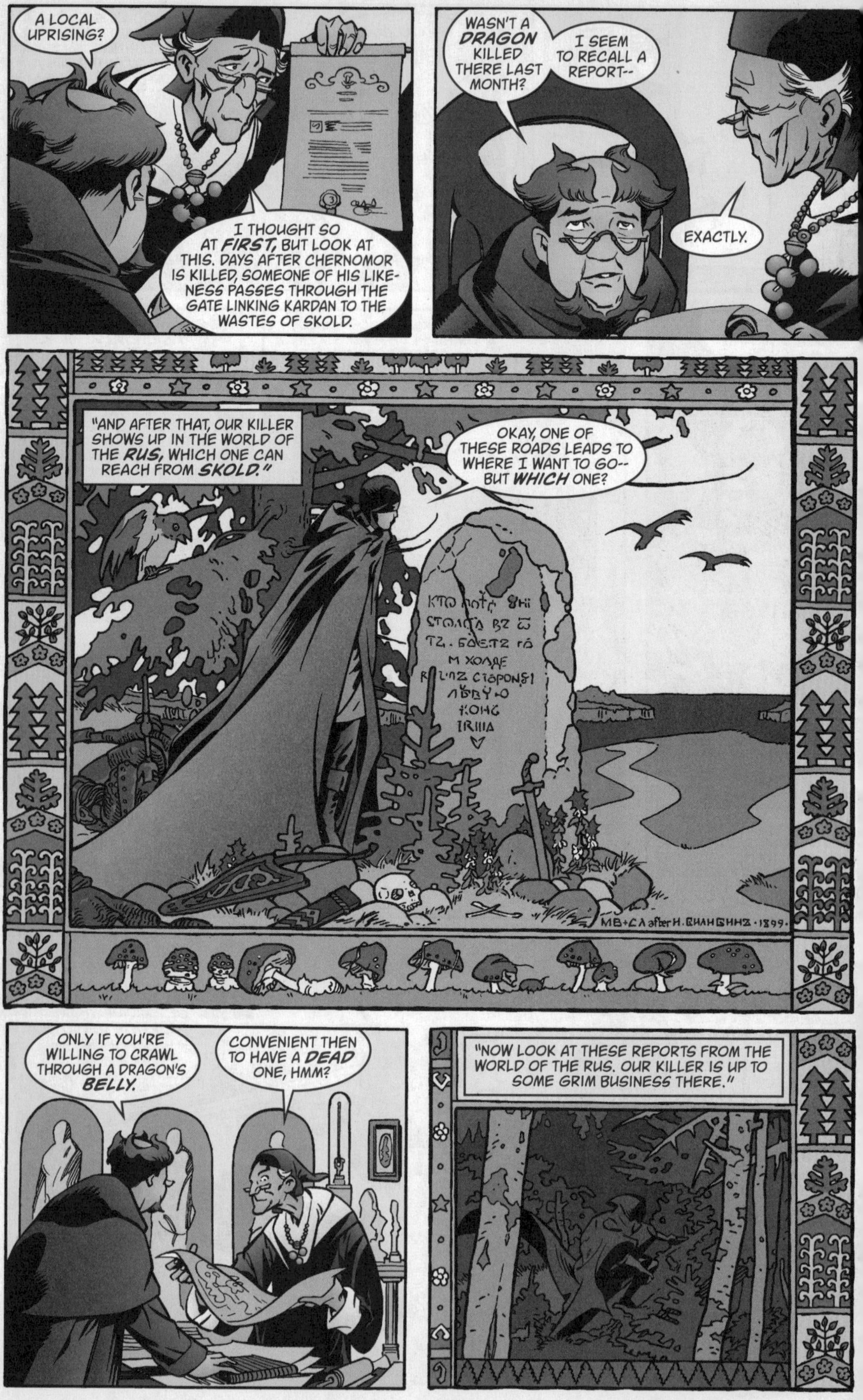

A LOCAL UPRISING?
I THOUGHT SO AT FIRST, BUT LOOK AT THIS. DAYS AFTER CHERNOMOR IS KILLED, SOMEONE OF HIS LIKENESS PASSES THROUGH THE GATE LINKING KARDAN TO THE WASTES OF SKOLD.
WASN'T A DRAGON KILLED THERE LAST MONTH?
I SEEM TO RECALL A REPORT--
EXACTLY.
"AND AFTER THAT, OUR KILLER SHOWS UP IN THE WORLD OF THE RUS, WHICH ONE CAN REACH FROM SKOLD."
OKAY, ONE OF THESE ROADS LEADS TO WHERE I WANT TO GO-- BUT WHICH ONE?
MB+CA after H. БИЛИБИН 1899.
ONLY IF YOU'RE WILLING TO CRAWL THROUGH A DRAGON'S BELLY.
CONVENIENT THEN TO HAVE A DEAD ONE, HMM?
"NOW LOOK AT THESE REPORTS FROM THE WORLD OF THE RUS. OUR KILLER IS UP TO SOME GRIM BUSINESS THERE."

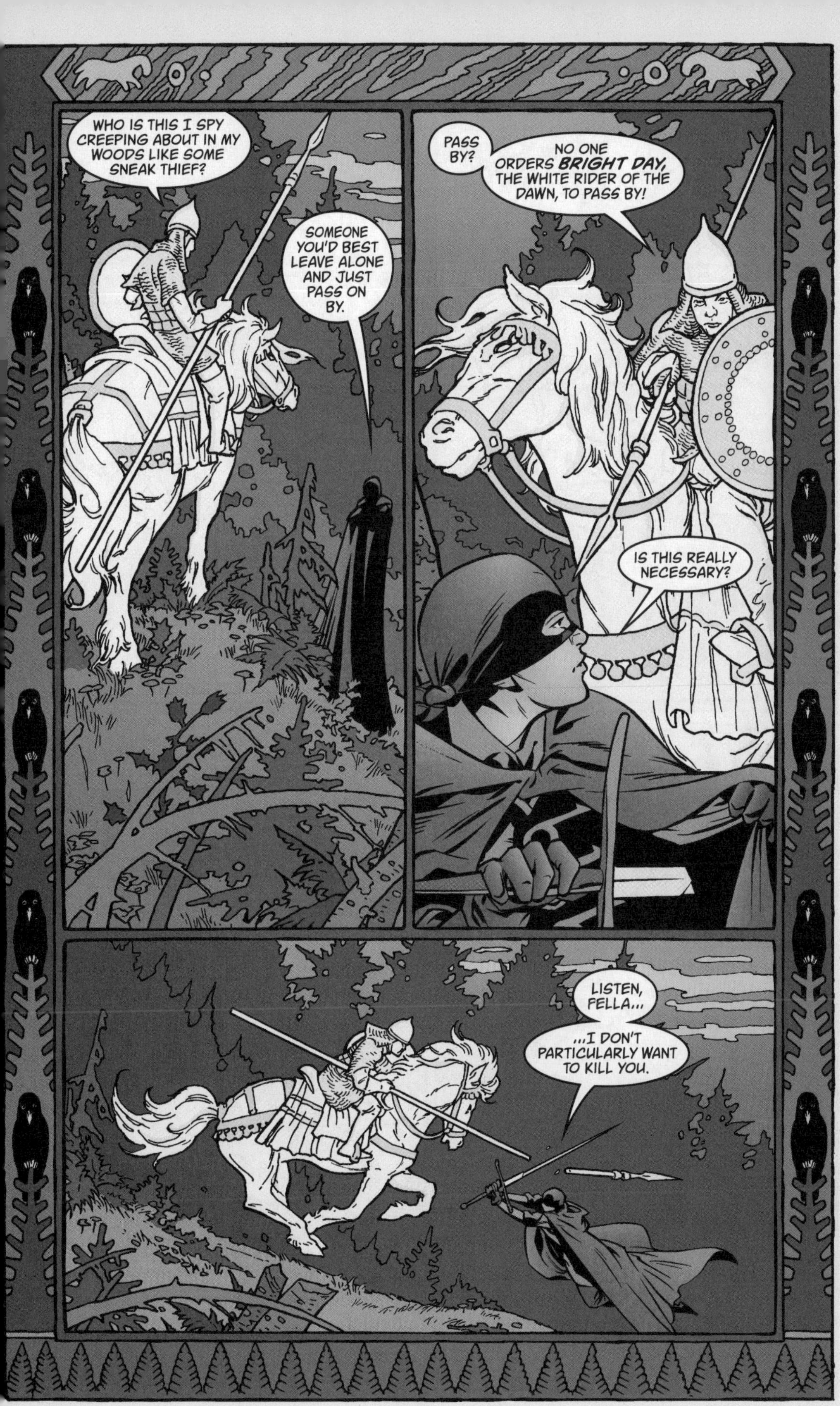
WHO IS THIS I SPY CREEPING ABOUT IN MY WOODS LIKE SOME SNEAK THIEF?
SOMEONE YOU'D BEST LEAVE ALONE AND JUST PASS ON BY.
PASS BY?
NO ONE ORDERS **BRIGHT DAY,** THE WHITE RIDER OF THE DAWN, TO PASS BY!
IS THIS REALLY NECESSARY?
LISTEN, FELLA...
...I DON'T PARTICULARLY WANT TO KILL YOU.

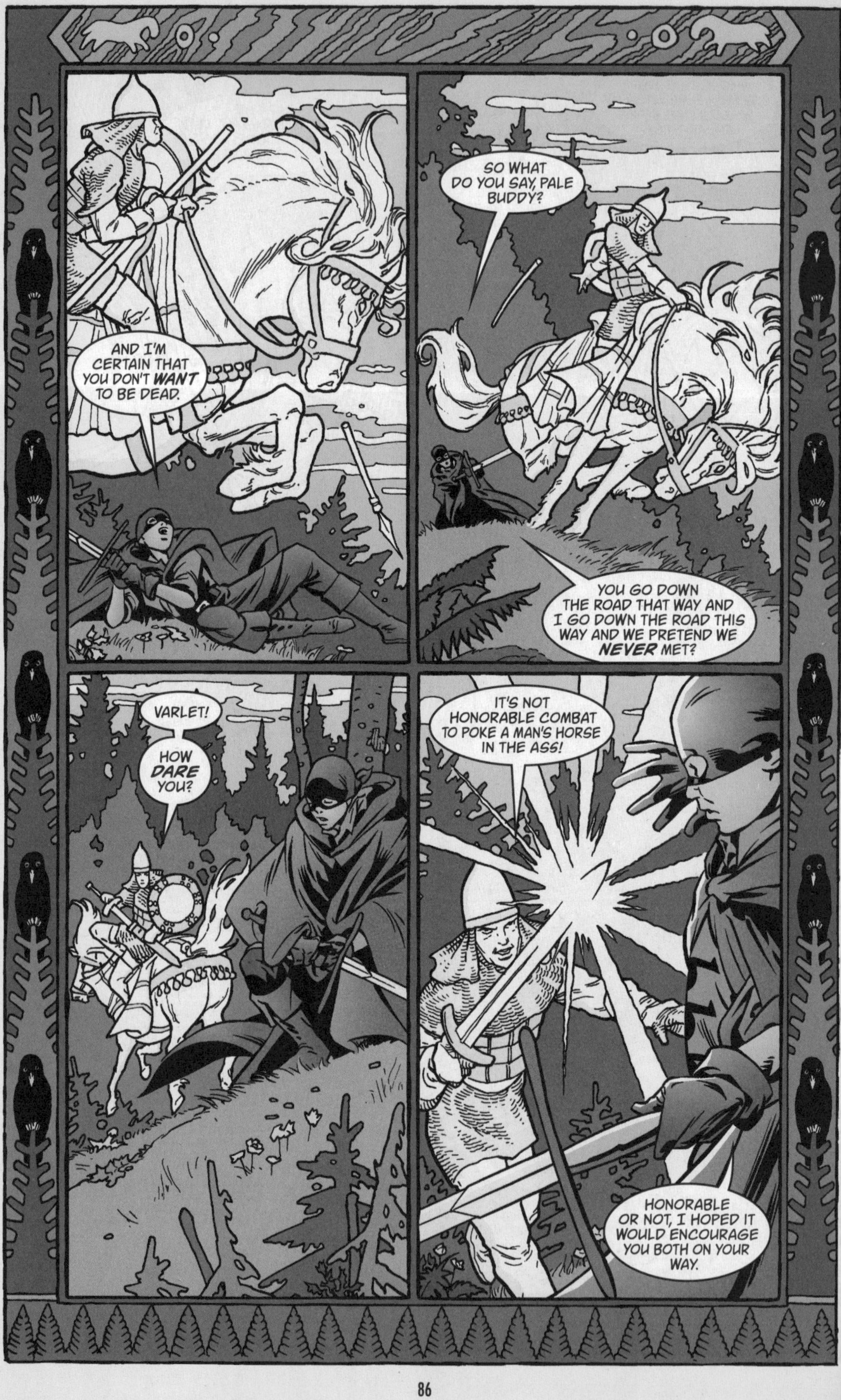
AND I'M CERTAIN THAT YOU DON'T *WANT* TO BE DEAD.
SO WHAT DO YOU SAY, PALE BUDDY?
YOU GO DOWN THE ROAD THAT WAY AND I GO DOWN THE ROAD THIS WAY AND WE PRETEND WE *NEVER* MET?
VARLET!
HOW *DARE* YOU?
IT'S NOT HONORABLE COMBAT TO POKE A MAN'S HORSE IN THE ASS!
HONORABLE OR NOT, I HOPED IT WOULD ENCOURAGE YOU BOTH ON YOUR WAY.

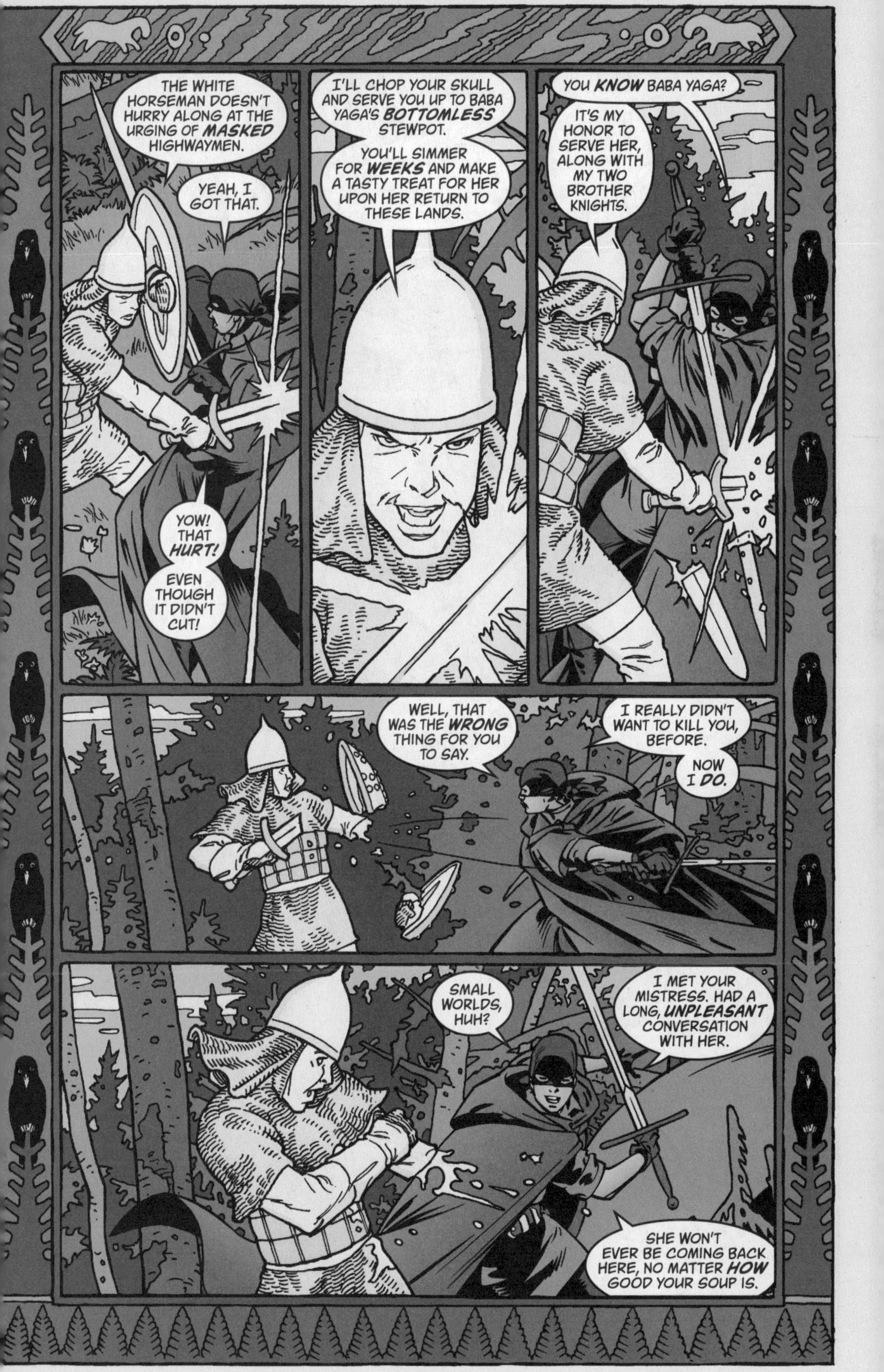

THE WHITE HORSEMAN DOESN'T HURRY ALONG AT THE URGING OF MASKED HIGHWAYMEN.
YEAH, I GOT THAT.
YOW! THAT HURT!
EVEN THOUGH IT DIDN'T CUT!
I'LL CHOP YOUR SKULL AND SERVE YOU UP TO BABA YAGA'S BOTTOMLESS STEWPOT.
YOU'LL SIMMER FOR WEEKS AND MAKE A TASTY TREAT FOR HER UPON HER RETURN TO THESE LANDS.
YOU KNOW BABA YAGA?
IT'S MY HONOR TO SERVE HER, ALONG WITH MY TWO BROTHER KNIGHTS.
WELL, THAT WAS THE WRONG THING FOR YOU TO SAY.
I REALLY DIDN'T WANT TO KILL YOU, BEFORE.
NOW I DO.
SMALL WORLDS, HUH?
I MET YOUR MISTRESS. HAD A LONG, UNPLEASANT CONVERSATION WITH HER.
SHE WON'T EVER BE COMING BACK HERE, NO MATTER HOW GOOD YOUR SOUP IS.

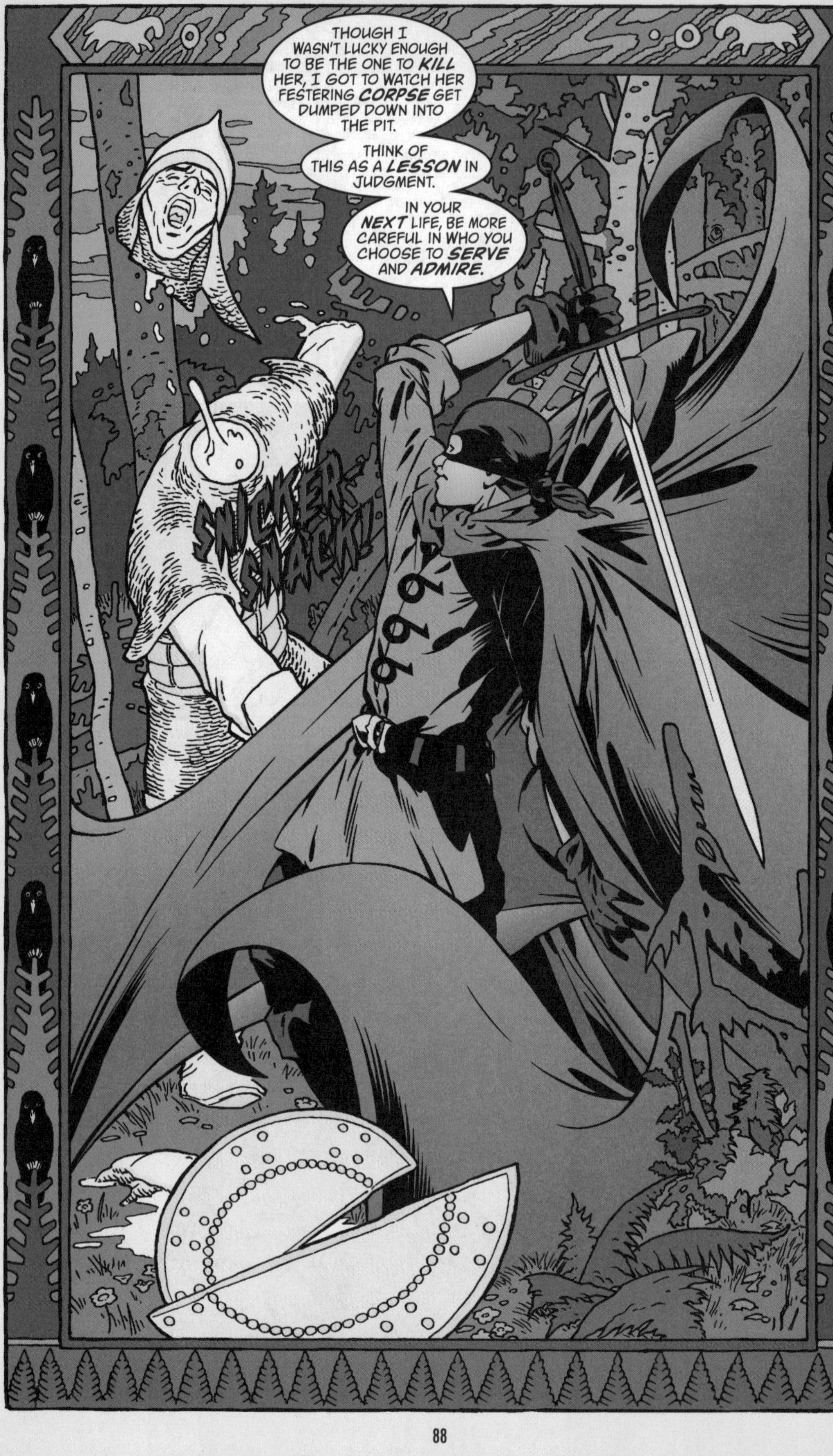
THOUGH I WASN'T LUCKY ENOUGH TO BE THE ONE TO KILL HER, I GOT TO WATCH HER FESTERING CORPSE GET DUMPED DOWN INTO THE PIT.
THINK OF THIS AS A LESSON IN JUDGMENT.
IN YOUR NEXT LIFE, BE MORE CAREFUL IN WHO YOU CHOOSE TO SERVE AND ADMIRE.
SNICKER-SNACK!

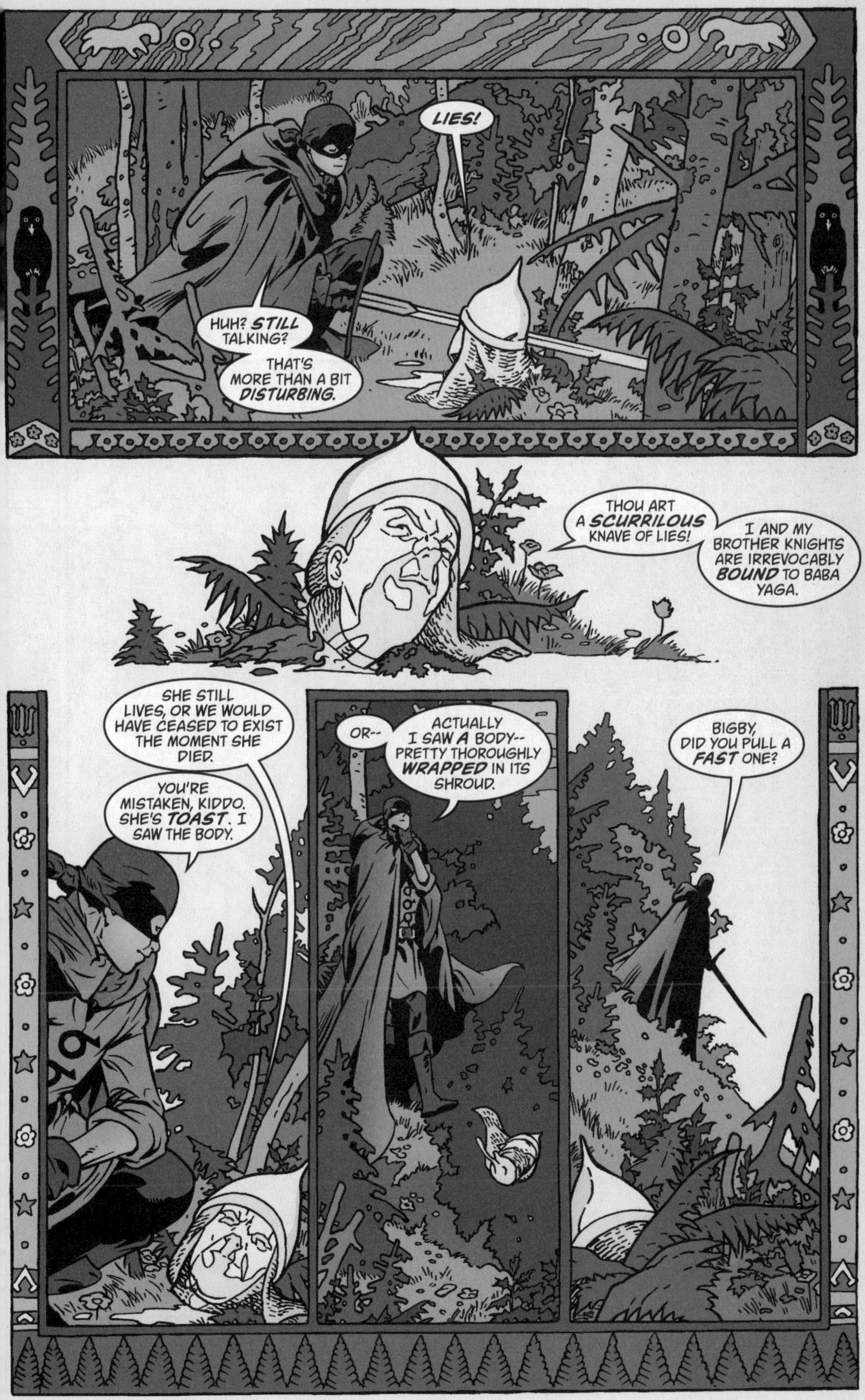

LIES!
HUH? STILL TALKING?
THAT'S MORE THAN A BIT DISTURBING.
THOU ART A SCURRILOUS KNAVE OF LIES!
I AND MY BROTHER KNIGHTS ARE IRREVOCABLY BOUND TO BABA YAGA.
SHE STILL LIVES, OR WE WOULD HAVE CEASED TO EXIST THE MOMENT SHE DIED.
YOU'RE MISTAKEN, KIDDO. SHE'S TOAST. I SAW THE BODY.
OR--
ACTUALLY I SAW A BODY-- PRETTY THOROUGHLY WRAPPED IN ITS SHROUD.
BIGBY, DID YOU PULL A FAST ONE?

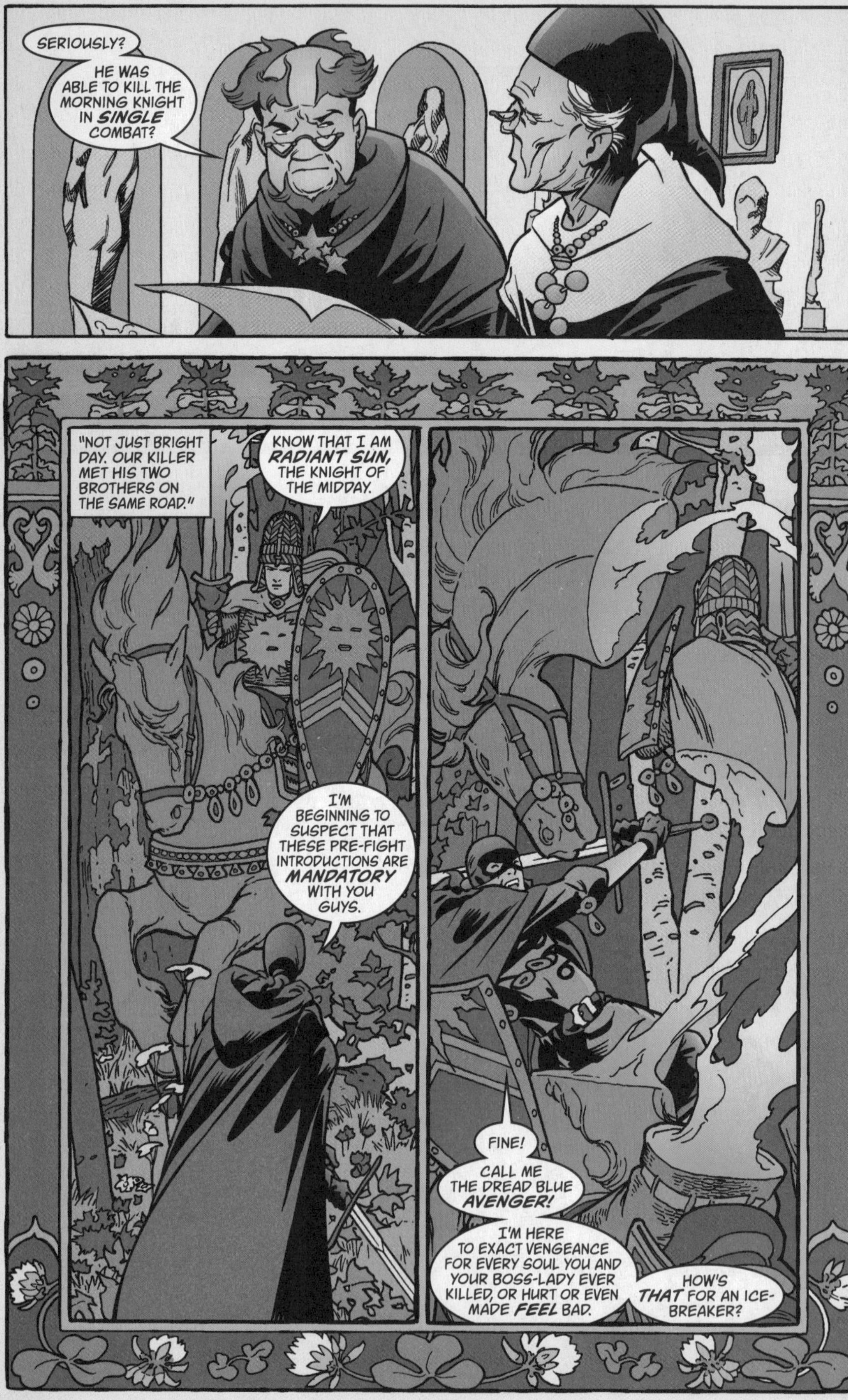

SERIOUSLY?
HE WAS ABLE TO KILL THE MORNING KNIGHT IN SINGLE COMBAT?
"NOT JUST BRIGHT DAY. OUR KILLER MET HIS TWO BROTHERS ON THE SAME ROAD."
KNOW THAT I AM RADIANT SUN, THE KNIGHT OF THE MIDDAY.
I'M BEGINNING TO SUSPECT THAT THESE PRE-FIGHT INTRODUCTIONS ARE MANDATORY WITH YOU GUYS.
FINE!
CALL ME THE DREAD BLUE AVENGER!
I'M HERE TO EXACT VENGEANCE FOR EVERY SOUL YOU AND YOUR BOSS-LADY EVER KILLED, OR HURT OR EVEN MADE FEEL BAD.
HOW'S THAT FOR AN ICE-BREAKER?

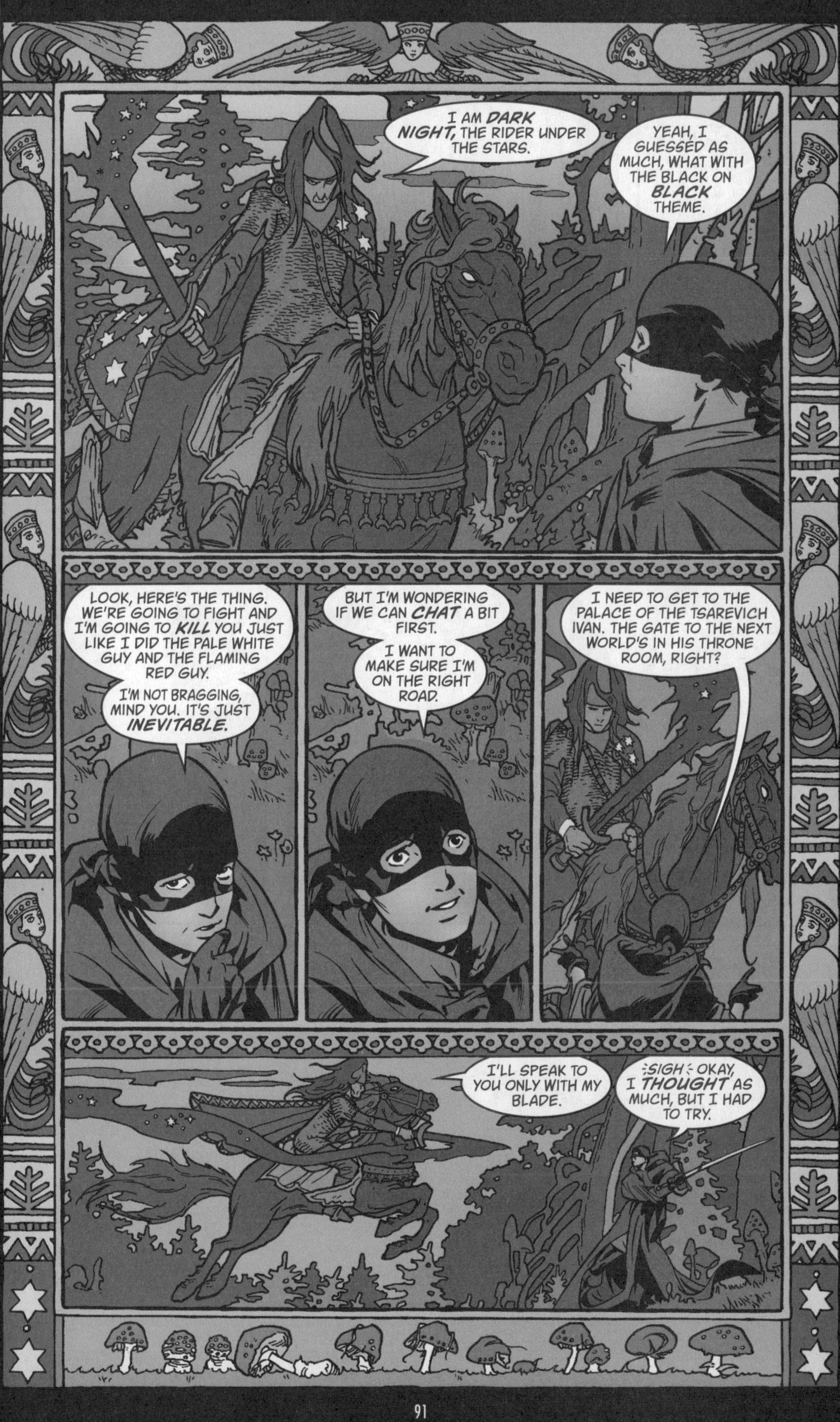
I AM DARK NIGHT, THE RIDER UNDER THE STARS.
YEAH, I GUESSED AS MUCH, WHAT WITH THE BLACK ON BLACK THEME.
LOOK, HERE'S THE THING. WE'RE GOING TO FIGHT AND I'M GOING TO KILL YOU JUST LIKE I DID THE PALE WHITE GUY AND THE FLAMING RED GUY.
I'M NOT BRAGGING, MIND YOU. IT'S JUST INEVITABLE.
BUT I'M WONDERING IF WE CAN CHAT A BIT FIRST.
I WANT TO MAKE SURE I'M ON THE RIGHT ROAD.
I NEED TO GET TO THE PALACE OF THE TSAREVICH IVAN. THE GATE TO THE NEXT WORLD'S IN HIS THRONE ROOM, RIGHT?
I'LL SPEAK TO YOU ONLY WITH MY BLADE.
SIGH OKAY, I THOUGHT AS MUCH, BUT I HAD TO TRY.

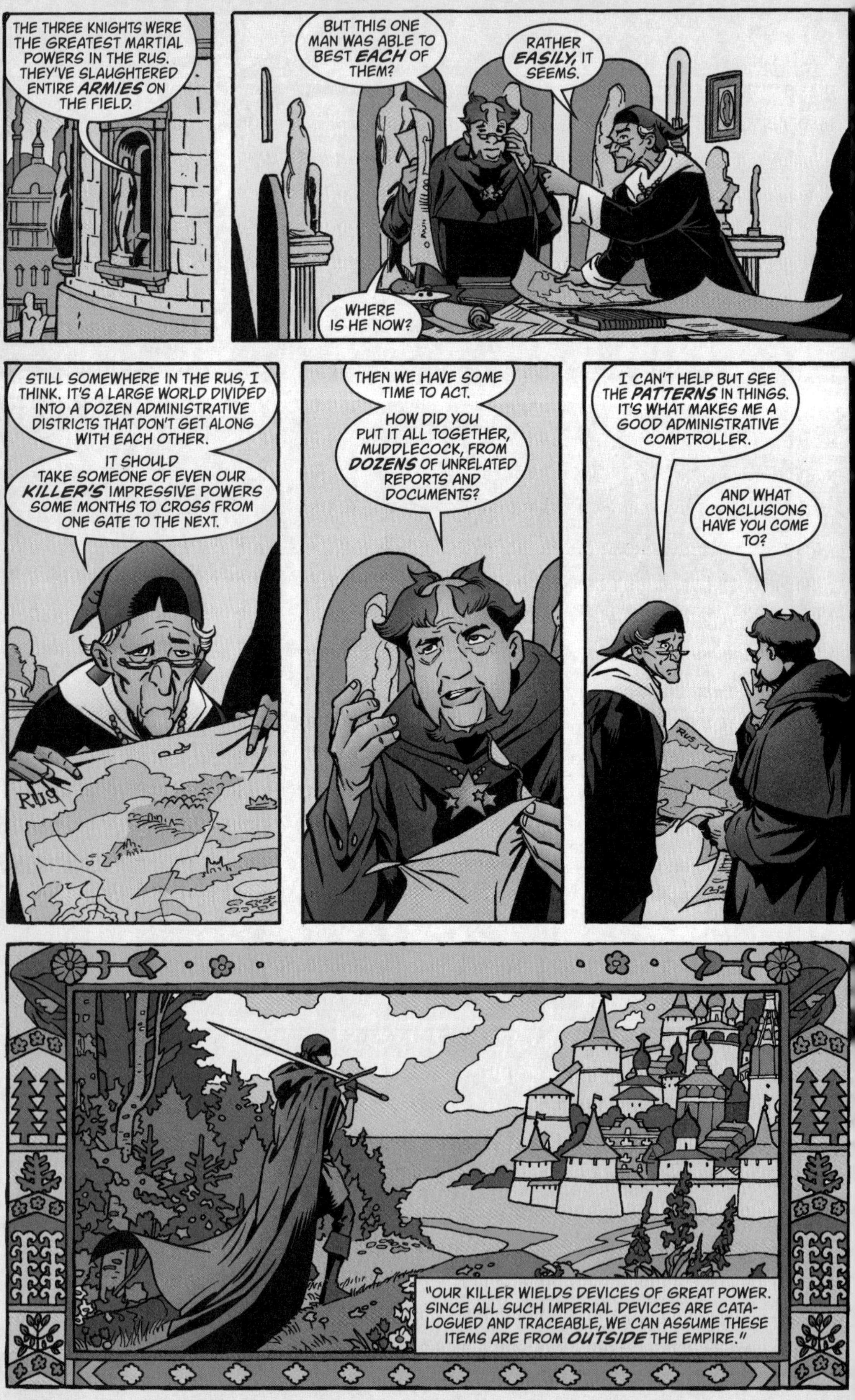

THE THREE KNIGHTS WERE THE GREATEST MARTIAL POWERS IN THE RUS. THEY'VE SLAUGHTERED ENTIRE ARMIES ON THE FIELD.
BUT THIS ONE MAN WAS ABLE TO BEST EACH OF THEM?
RATHER EASILY, IT SEEMS.
WHERE IS HE NOW?
STILL SOMEWHERE IN THE RUS, I THINK. IT'S A LARGE WORLD DIVIDED INTO A DOZEN ADMINISTRATIVE DISTRICTS THAT DON'T GET ALONG WITH EACH OTHER.
IT SHOULD TAKE SOMEONE OF EVEN OUR KILLER'S IMPRESSIVE POWERS SOME MONTHS TO CROSS FROM ONE GATE TO THE NEXT.
RUS
THEN WE HAVE SOME TIME TO ACT.
HOW DID YOU PUT IT ALL TOGETHER, MUDDLECOCK, FROM DOZENS OF UNRELATED REPORTS AND DOCUMENTS?
I CAN'T HELP BUT SEE THE PATTERNS IN THINGS. IT'S WHAT MAKES ME A GOOD ADMINISTRATIVE COMPTROLLER.
AND WHAT CONCLUSIONS HAVE YOU COME TO?
RUS
"OUR KILLER WIELDS DEVICES OF GREAT POWER. SINCE ALL SUCH IMPERIAL DEVICES ARE CATALOGUED AND TRACEABLE, WE CAN ASSUME THESE ITEMS ARE FROM OUTSIDE THE EMPIRE."

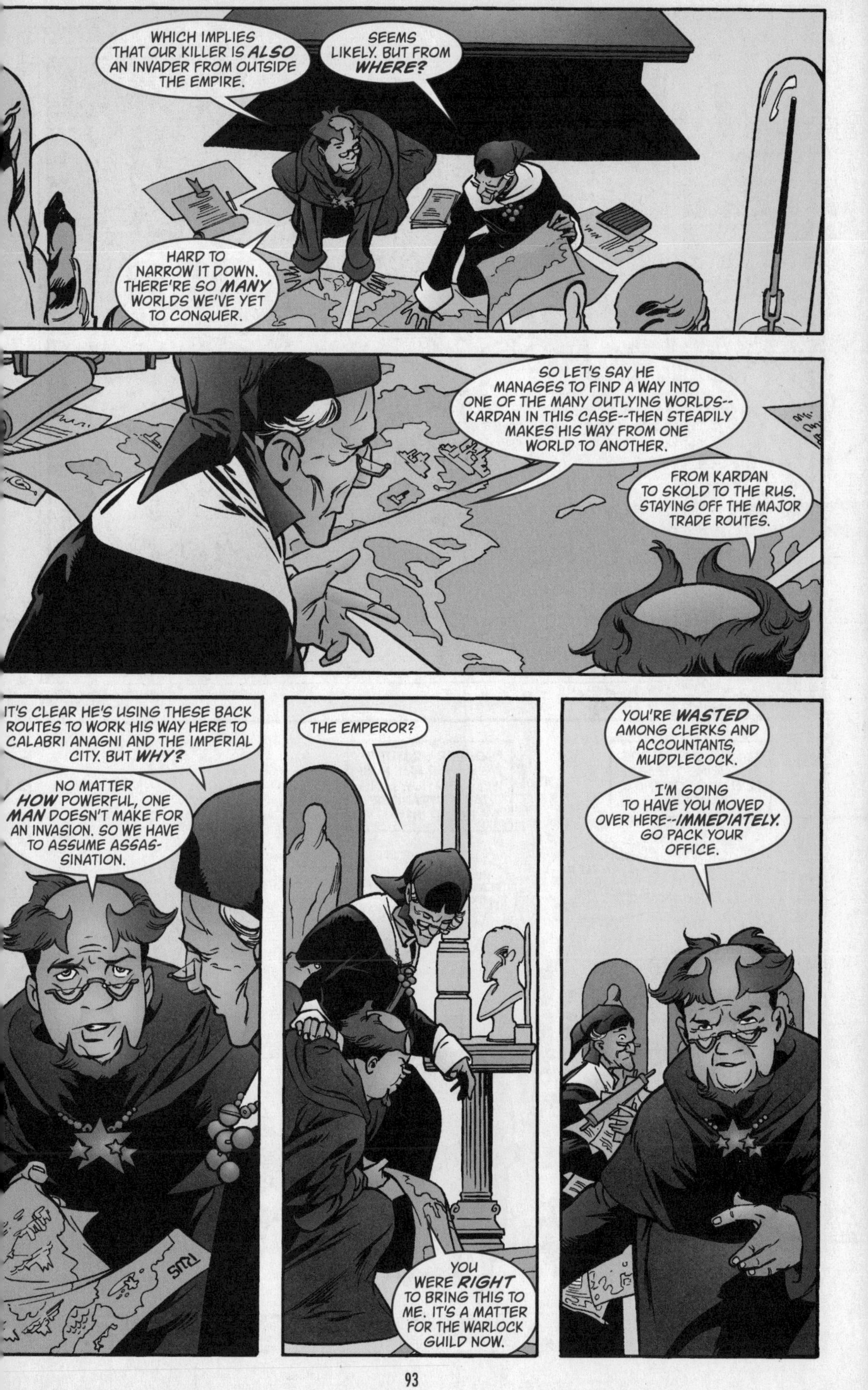
WHICH IMPLIES THAT OUR KILLER IS ALSO AN INVADER FROM OUTSIDE THE EMPIRE.
SEEMS LIKELY. BUT FROM WHERE?
HARD TO NARROW IT DOWN. THERE'RE SO MANY WORLDS WE'VE YET TO CONQUER.
SO LET'S SAY HE MANAGES TO FIND A WAY INTO ONE OF THE MANY OUTLYING WORLDS--KARDAN IN THIS CASE--THEN STEADILY MAKES HIS WAY FROM ONE WORLD TO ANOTHER.
FROM KARDAN TO SKOLD TO THE RUS. STAYING OFF THE MAJOR TRADE ROUTES.
IT'S CLEAR HE'S USING THESE BACK ROUTES TO WORK HIS WAY HERE TO CALABRI ANAGNI AND THE IMPERIAL CITY. BUT WHY?
NO MATTER HOW POWERFUL, ONE MAN DOESN'T MAKE FOR AN INVASION. SO WE HAVE TO ASSUME ASSAS-SINATION.
THE EMPEROR?
YOU WERE RIGHT TO BRING THIS TO ME. IT'S A MATTER FOR THE WARLOCK GUILD NOW.
YOU'RE WASTED AMONG CLERKS AND ACCOUNTANTS, MUDDLECOCK.
I'M GOING TO HAVE YOU MOVED OVER HERE--IMMEDIATELY. GO PACK YOUR OFFICE.

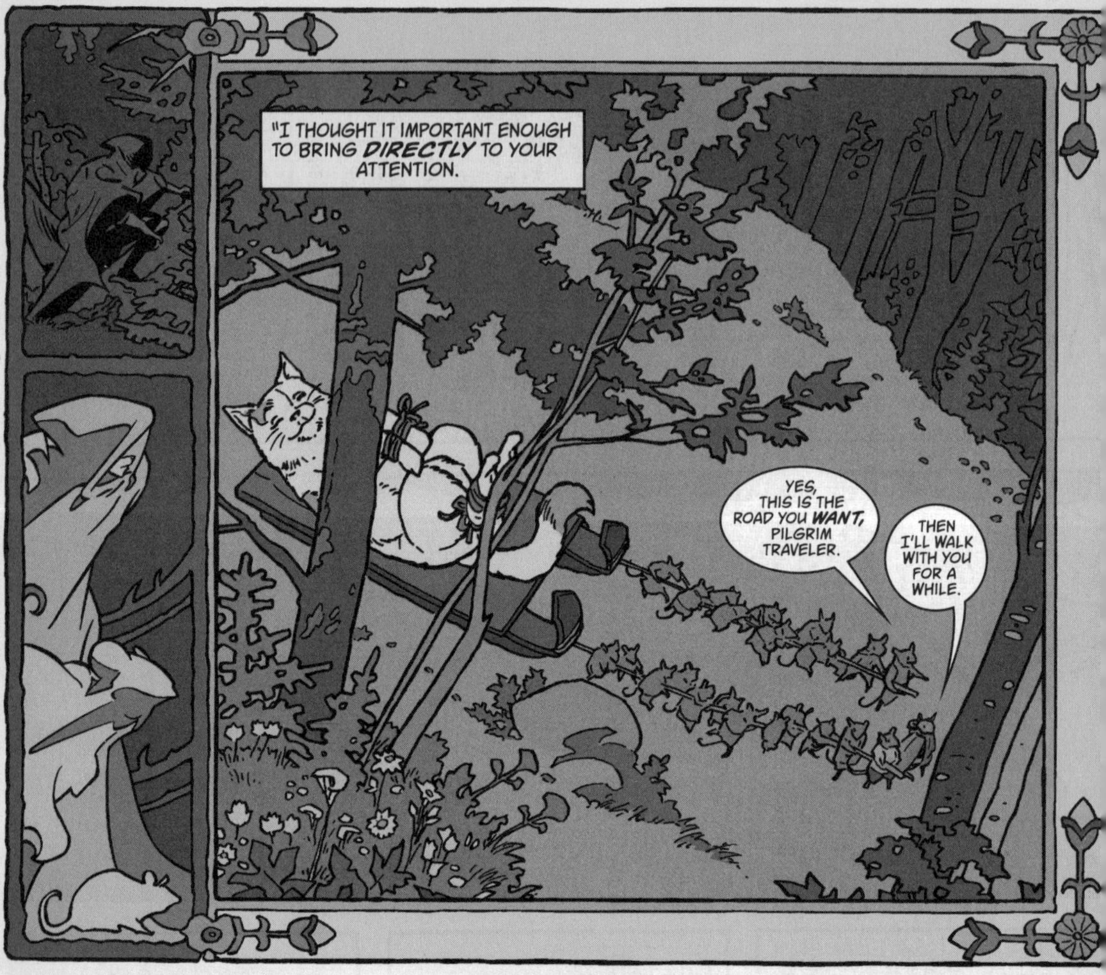

"I THOUGHT IT IMPORTANT ENOUGH TO BRING DIRECTLY TO YOUR ATTENTION.
YES, THIS IS THE ROAD YOU WANT, PILGRIM TRAVELER.
THEN I'LL WALK WITH YOU FOR A WHILE.

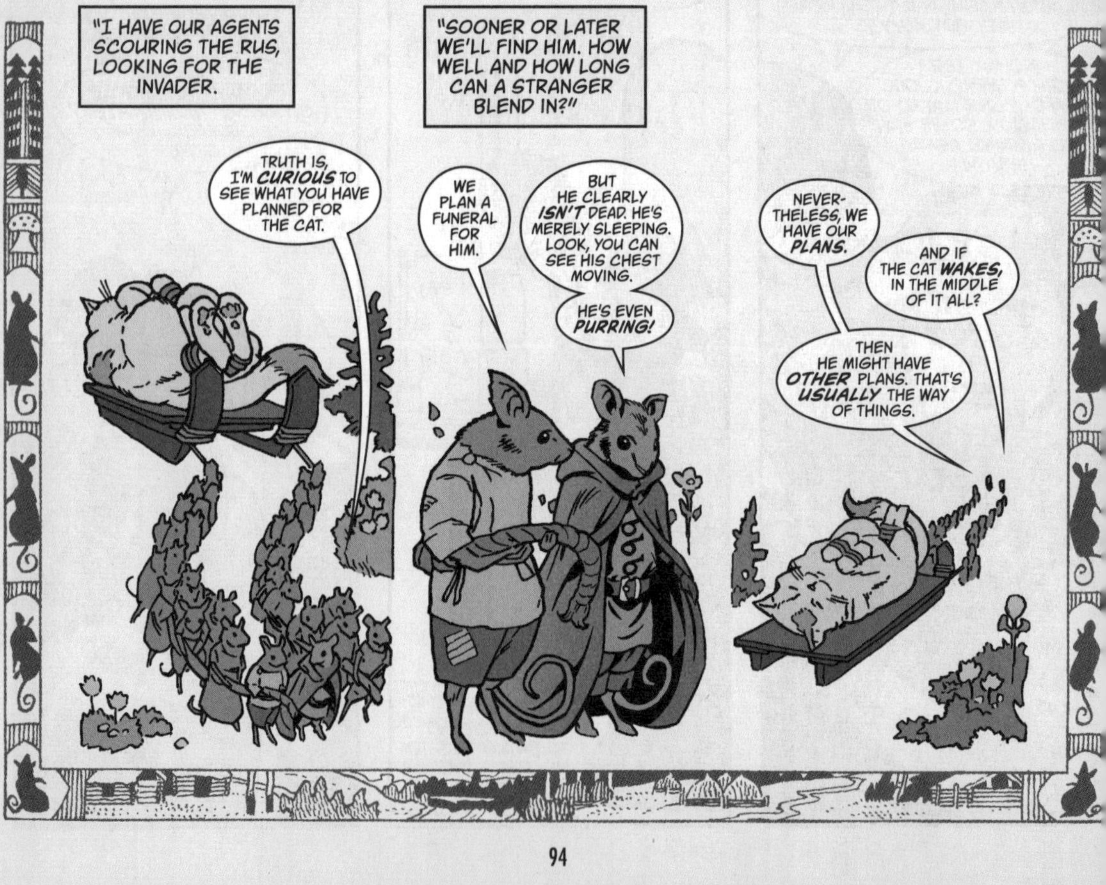

"I HAVE OUR AGENTS SCOURING THE RUS, LOOKING FOR THE INVADER.
"SOONER OR LATER WE'LL FIND HIM. HOW WELL AND HOW LONG CAN A STRANGER BLEND IN?"
TRUTH IS, I'M CURIOUS TO SEE WHAT YOU HAVE PLANNED FOR THE CAT.
WE PLAN A FUNERAL FOR HIM.
BUT HE CLEARLY ISN'T DEAD. HE'S MERELY SLEEPING. LOOK, YOU CAN SEE HIS CHEST MOVING.
HE'S EVEN PURRING!
NEVER-THELESS, WE HAVE OUR PLANS.
AND IF THE CAT WAKES, IN THE MIDDLE OF IT ALL?
THEN HE MIGHT HAVE OTHER PLANS. THAT'S USUALLY THE WAY OF THINGS.

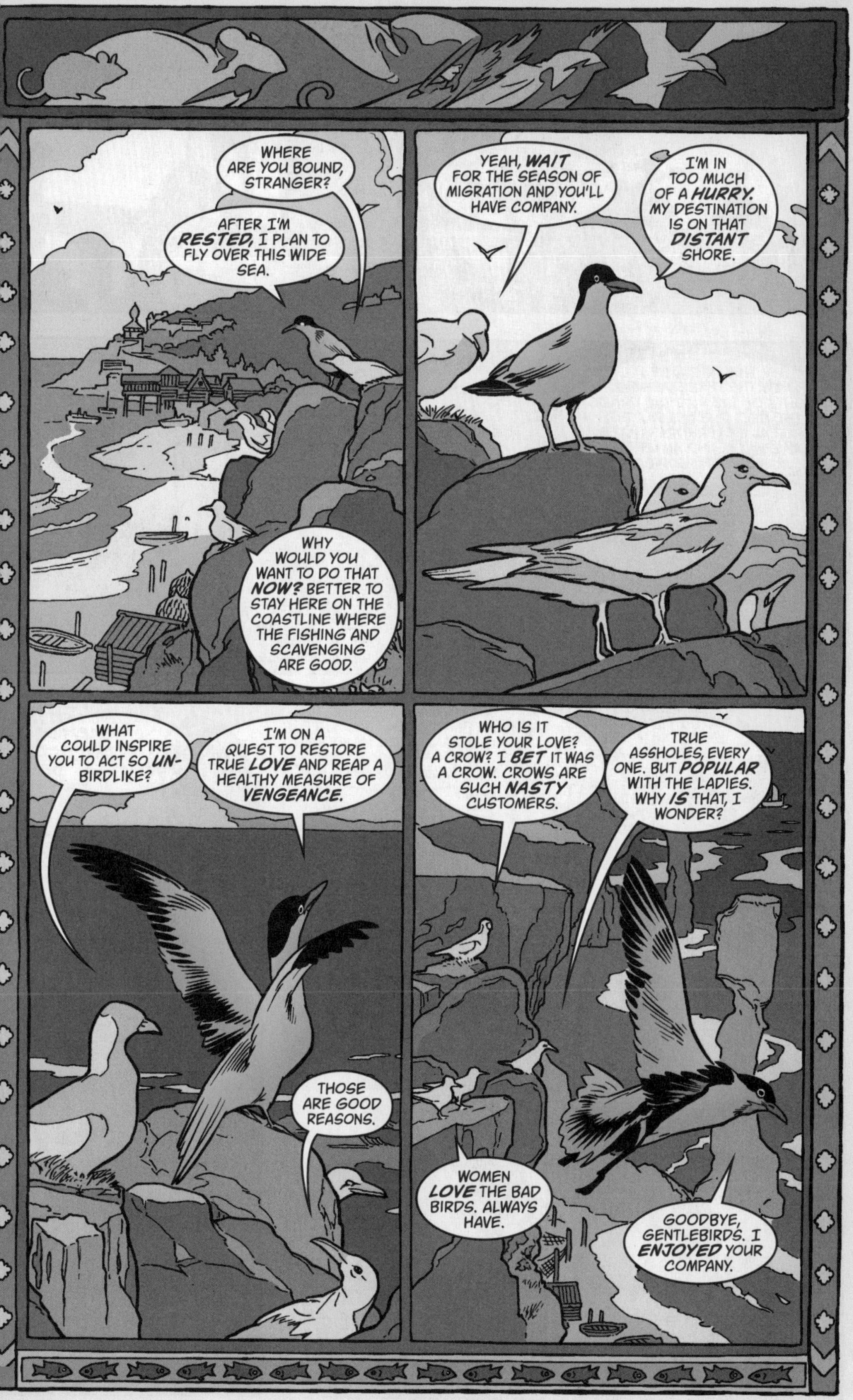

WHERE ARE YOU BOUND, STRANGER?
AFTER I'M RESTED, I PLAN TO FLY OVER THIS WIDE SEA.
WHY WOULD YOU WANT TO DO THAT NOW? BETTER TO STAY HERE ON THE COASTLINE WHERE THE FISHING AND SCAVENGING ARE GOOD.
YEAH, WAIT FOR THE SEASON OF MIGRATION AND YOU'LL HAVE COMPANY.
I'M IN TOO MUCH OF A HURRY. MY DESTINATION IS ON THAT DISTANT SHORE.
WHAT COULD INSPIRE YOU TO ACT SO UN-BIRDLIKE?
I'M ON A QUEST TO RESTORE TRUE LOVE AND REAP A HEALTHY MEASURE OF VENGEANCE.
THOSE ARE GOOD REASONS.
WHO IS IT STOLE YOUR LOVE? A CROW? I BET IT WAS A CROW. CROWS ARE SUCH NASTY CUSTOMERS.
TRUE ASSHOLES, EVERY ONE. BUT POPULAR WITH THE LADIES. WHY IS THAT, I WONDER?
WOMEN LOVE THE BAD BIRDS. ALWAYS HAVE.
GOODBYE, GENTLEBIRDS. I ENJOYED YOUR COMPANY.

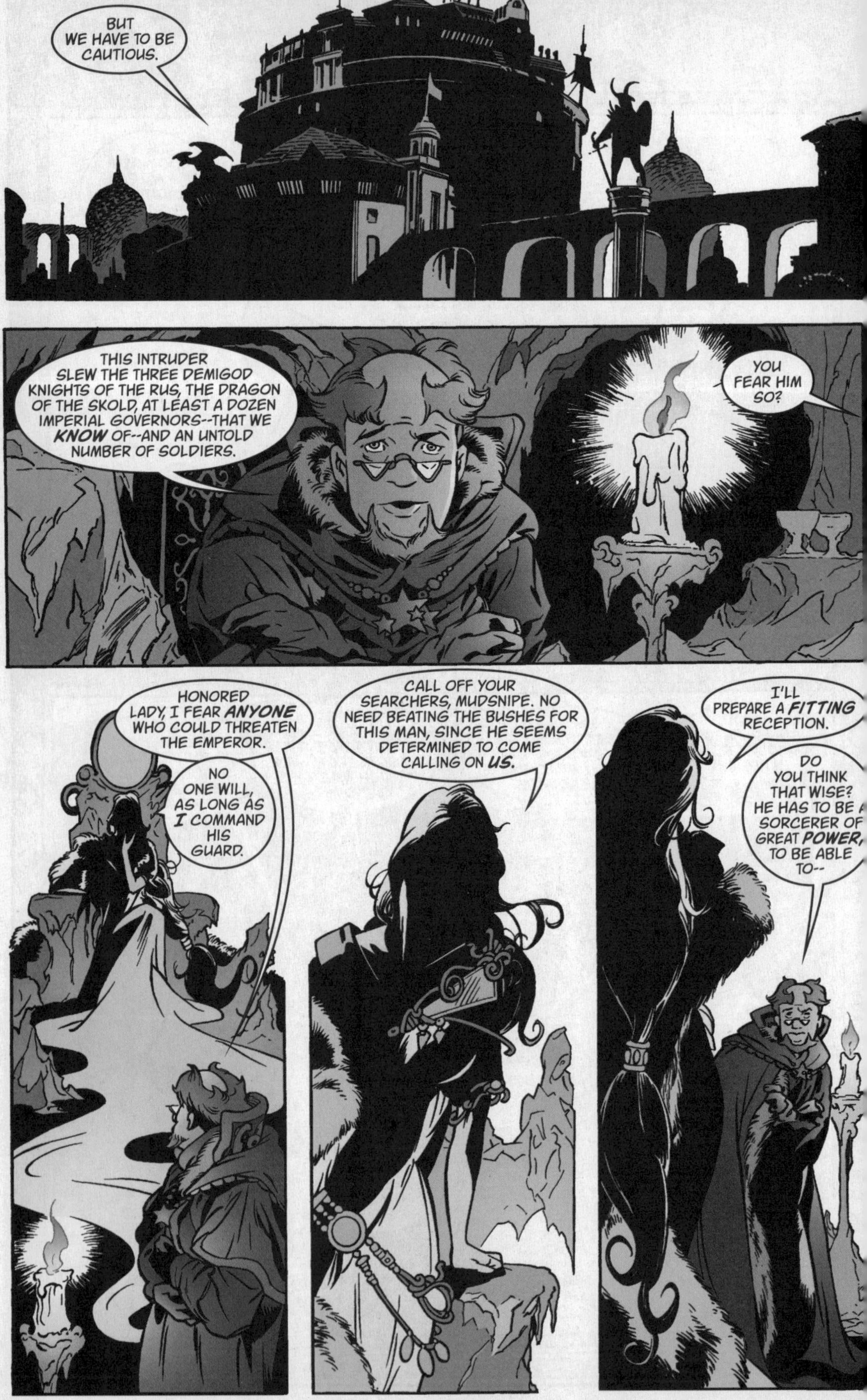
BUT WE HAVE TO BE CAUTIOUS.
THIS INTRUDER SLEW THE THREE DEMIGOD KNIGHTS OF THE RUS, THE DRAGON OF THE SKOLD, AT LEAST A DOZEN IMPERIAL GOVERNORS--THAT WE KNOW OF--AND AN UNTOLD NUMBER OF SOLDIERS.
YOU FEAR HIM SO?
HONORED LADY, I FEAR ANYONE WHO COULD THREATEN THE EMPEROR.
NO ONE WILL, AS LONG AS I COMMAND HIS GUARD.
CALL OFF YOUR SEARCHERS, MUDSNIPE. NO NEED BEATING THE BUSHES FOR THIS MAN, SINCE HE SEEMS DETERMINED TO COME CALLING ON US.
I'LL PREPARE A FITTING RECEPTION.
DO YOU THINK THAT WISE? HE HAS TO BE A SORCERER OF GREAT POWER, TO BE ABLE TO--

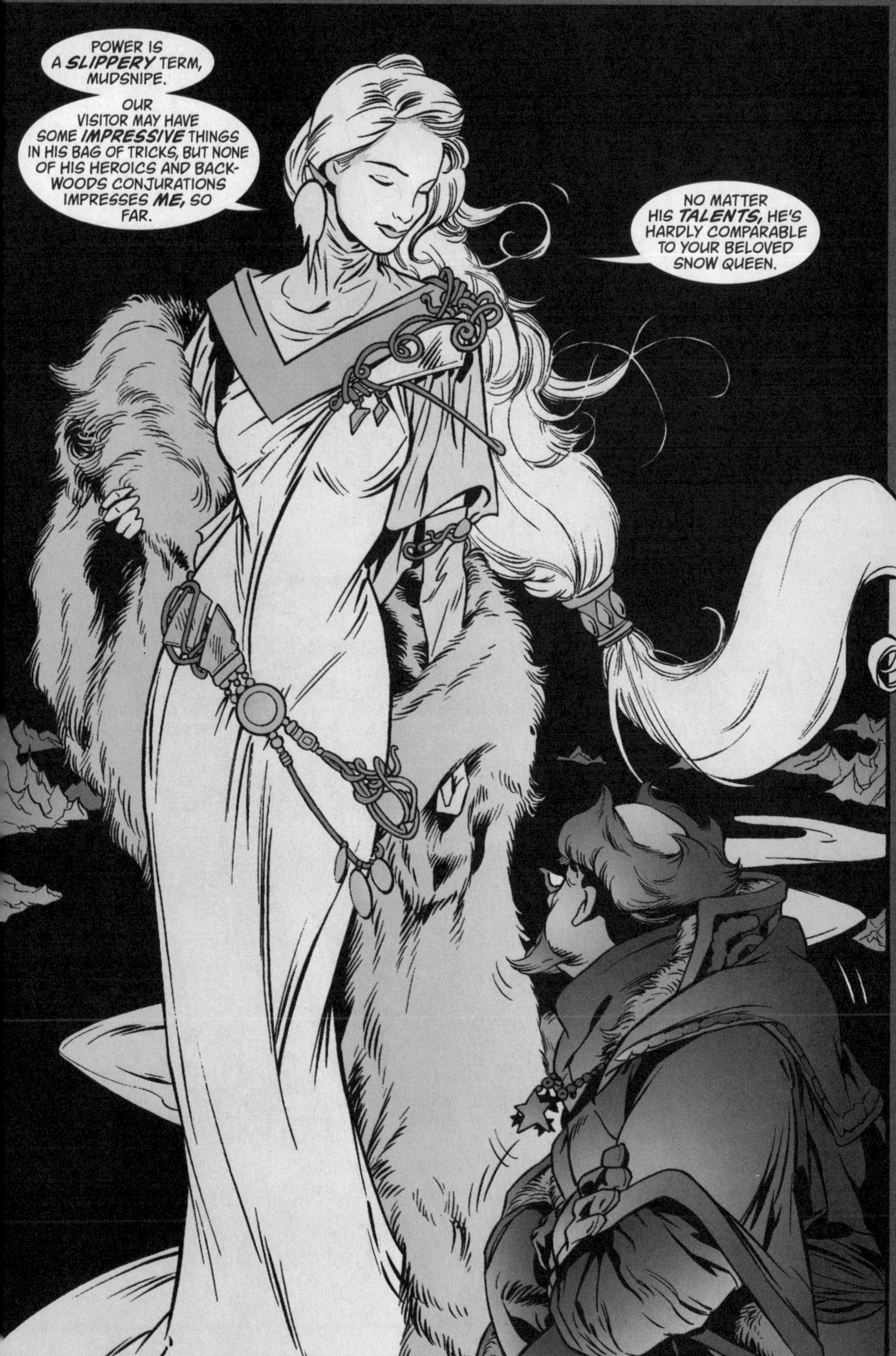
POWER IS A SLIPPERY TERM, MUDSNIPE.
OUR VISITOR MAY HAVE SOME IMPRESSIVE THINGS IN HIS BAG OF TRICKS, BUT NONE OF HIS HEROICS AND BACK-WOODS CONJURATIONS IMPRESSES ME, SO FAR.
NO MATTER HIS TALENTS, HE'S HARDLY COMPARABLE TO YOUR BELOVED SNOW QUEEN.

NEXT: THE ADVERSARY!

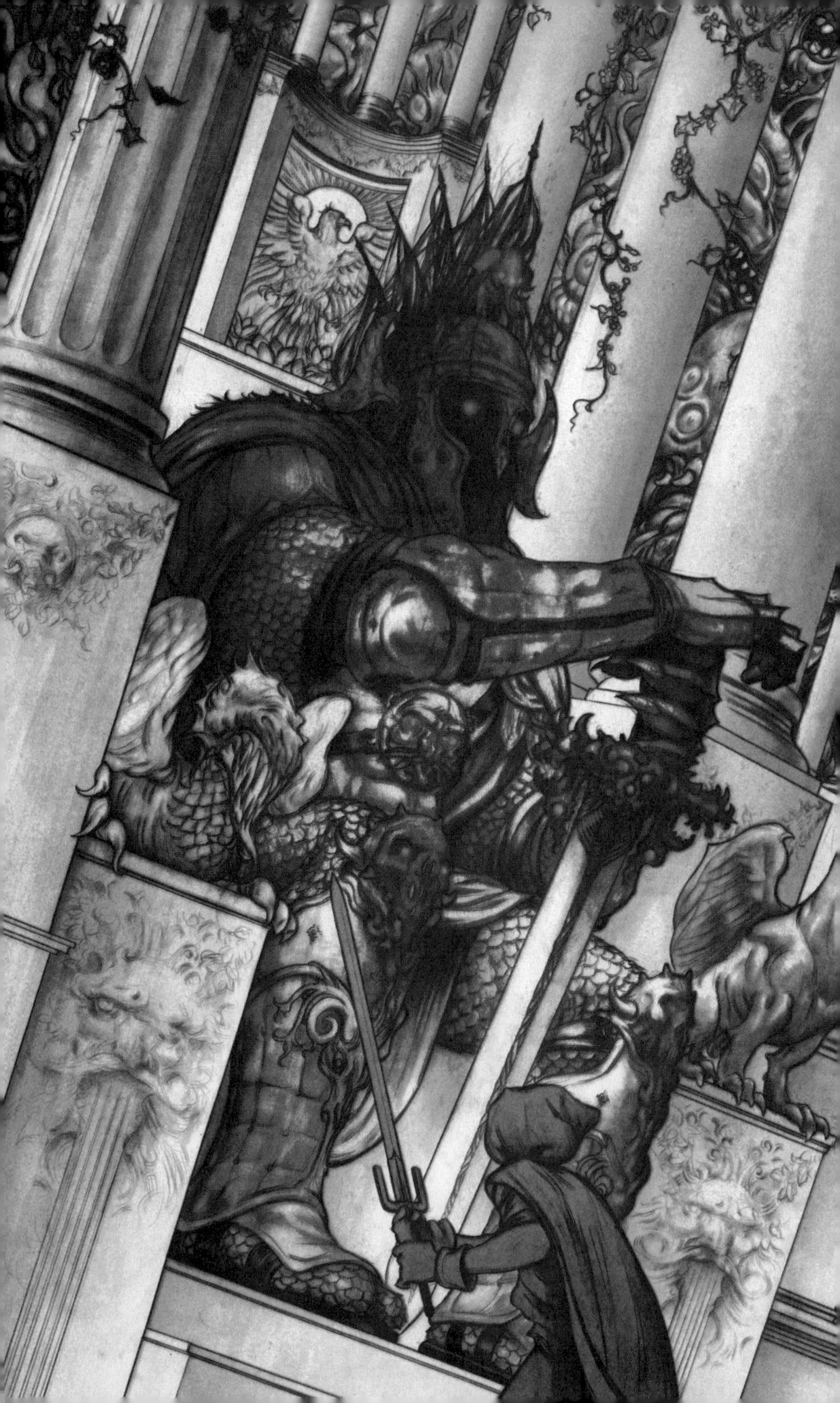

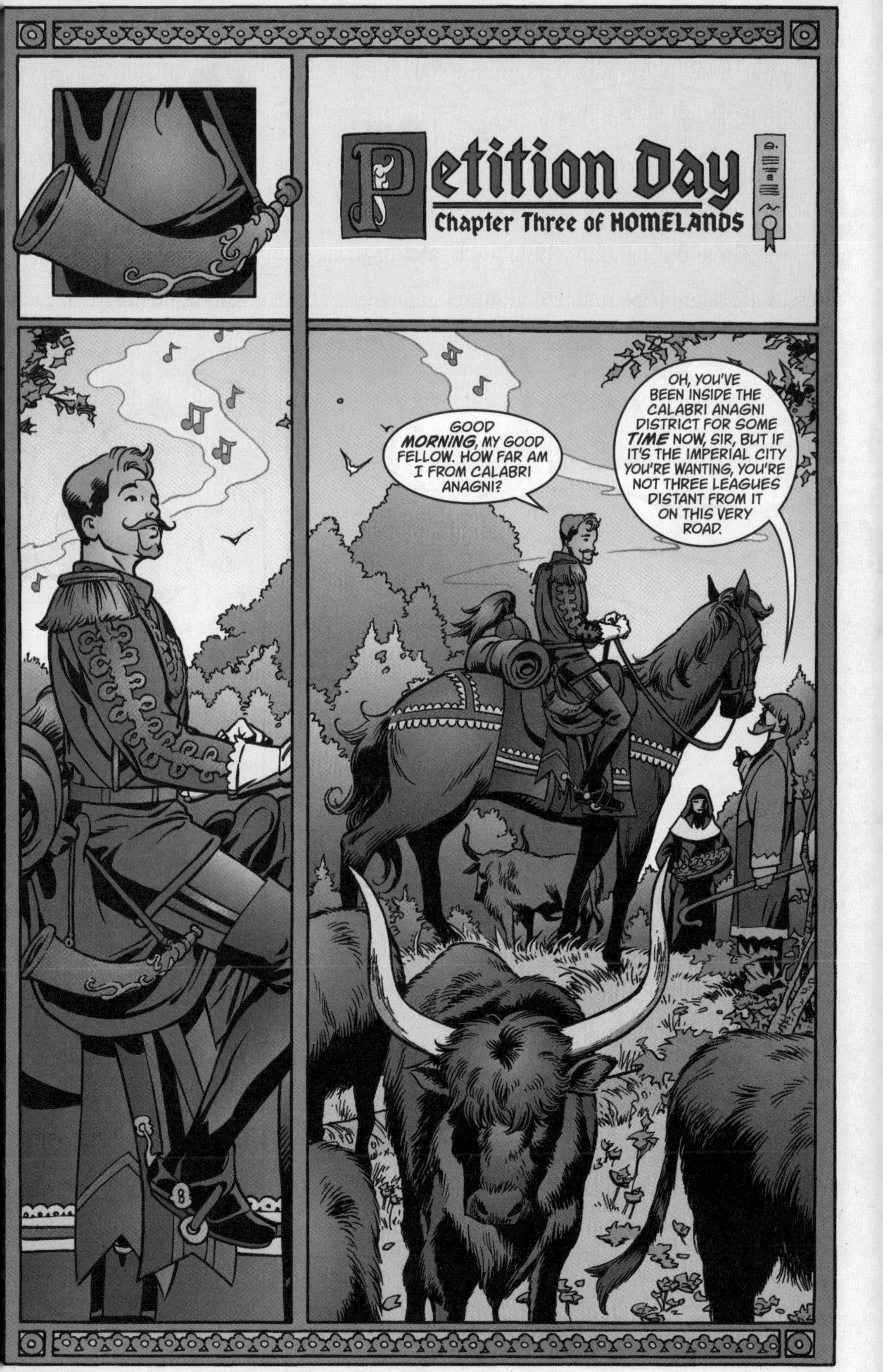

Petition Day
Chapter Three of HOMELANDS
GOOD MORNING, MY GOOD FELLOW. HOW FAR AM I FROM CALABRI ANAGNI?
OH, YOU'VE BEEN INSIDE THE CALABRI ANAGNI DISTRICT FOR SOME TIME NOW, SIR, BUT IF IT'S THE IMPERIAL CITY YOU'RE WANTING, YOU'RE NOT THREE LEAGUES DISTANT FROM IT ON THIS VERY ROAD.

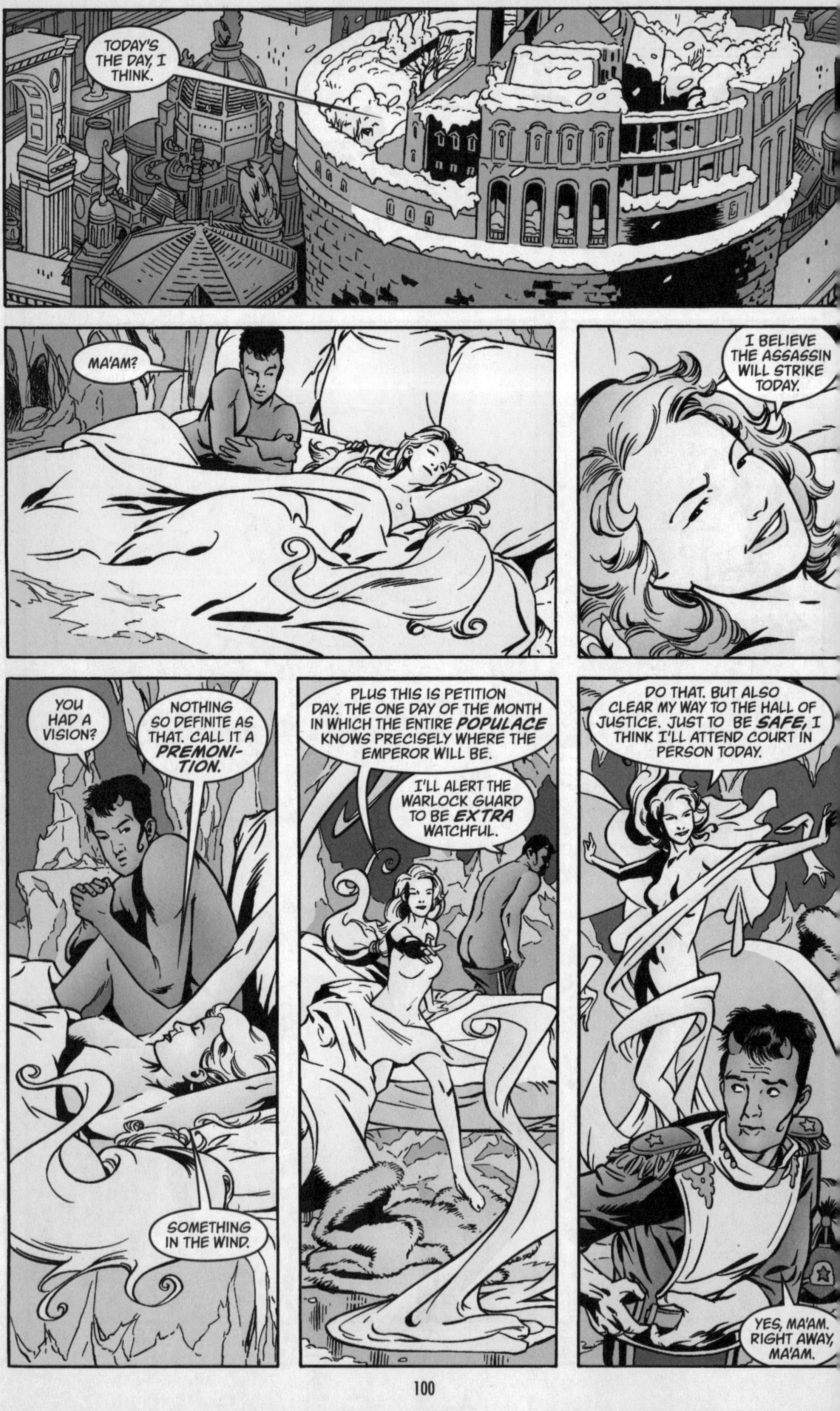

TODAY'S THE DAY, I THINK.
MA'AM?
I BELIEVE THE ASSASSIN WILL STRIKE TODAY.
YOU HAD A VISION?
NOTHING SO DEFINITE AS THAT. CALL IT A *PREMONITION.*
SOMETHING IN THE WIND.
PLUS THIS IS PETITION DAY. THE ONE DAY OF THE MONTH IN WHICH THE ENTIRE *POPULACE* KNOWS PRECISELY WHERE THE EMPEROR WILL BE.
I'LL ALERT THE WARLOCK GUARD TO BE *EXTRA* WATCHFUL.
DO THAT. BUT ALSO CLEAR MY WAY TO THE HALL OF JUSTICE. JUST TO BE *SAFE,* I THINK I'LL ATTEND COURT IN PERSON TODAY.
YES, MA'AM. RIGHT AWAY, MA'AM.

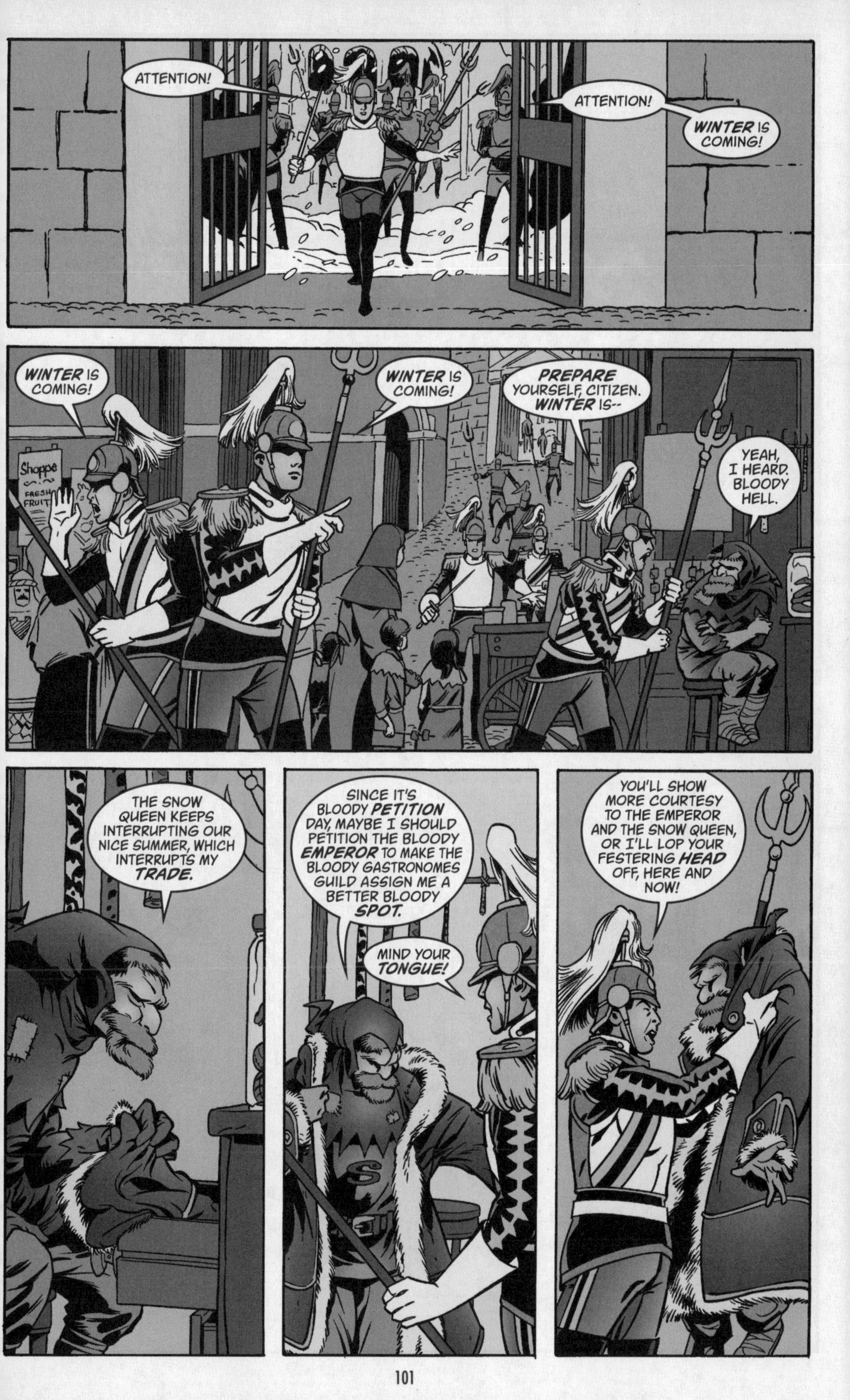
ATTENTION!
ATTENTION!
WINTER IS COMING!
WINTER IS COMING!
WINTER IS COMING!
PREPARE YOURSELF, CITIZEN. WINTER IS--
YEAH, I HEARD. BLOODY HELL.
Shoppe
FRESH FRUIT
THE SNOW QUEEN KEEPS INTERRUPTING OUR NICE SUMMER, WHICH INTERRUPTS MY TRADE.
SINCE IT'S BLOODY PETITION DAY, MAYBE I SHOULD PETITION THE BLOODY EMPEROR TO MAKE THE BLOODY GASTRONOMES GUILD ASSIGN ME A BETTER BLOODY SPOT.
MIND YOUR TONGUE!
YOU'LL SHOW MORE COURTESY TO THE EMPEROR AND THE SNOW QUEEN, OR I'LL LOP YOUR FESTERING HEAD OFF, HERE AND NOW!

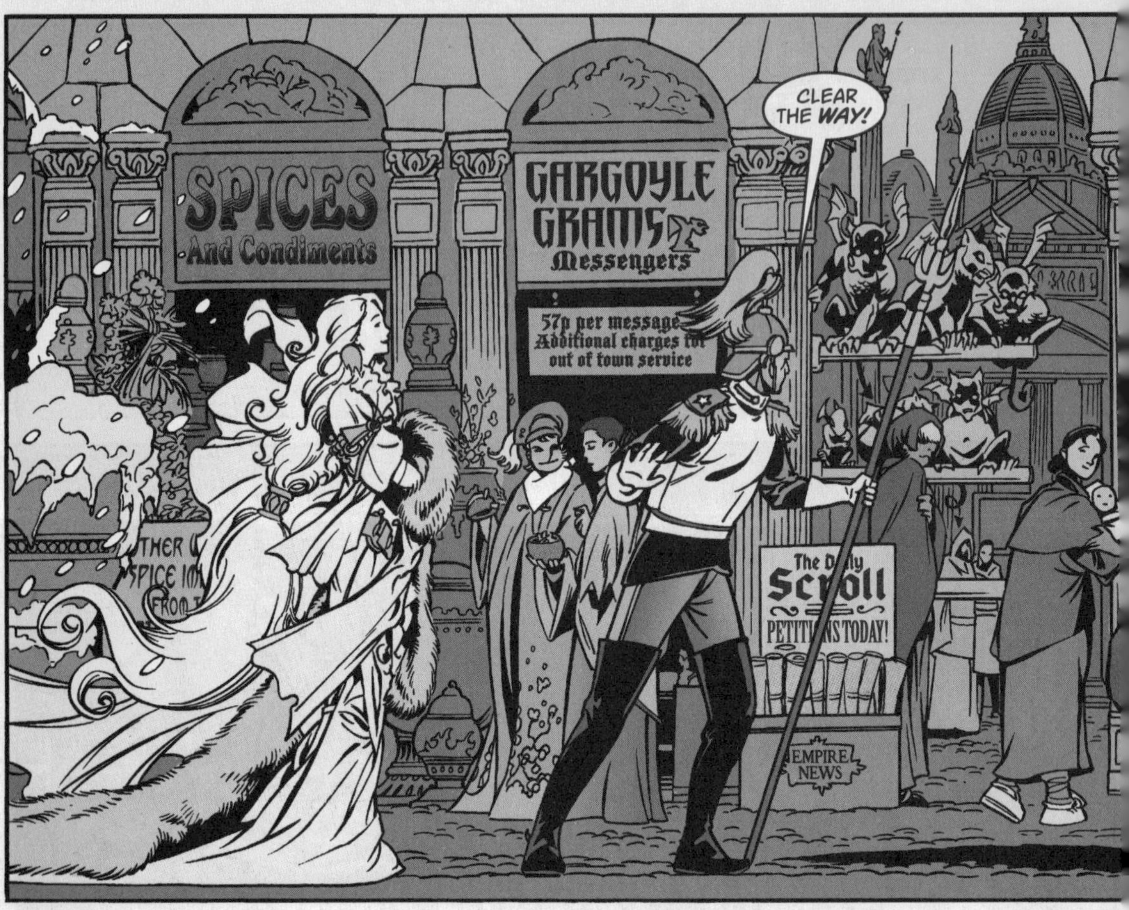
SPICES
And Condiments
GARGOYLE GRAMS
Messengers
57p per message. Additional charges for out of town service
CLEAR THE WAY!
The Daily Scroll
PETITIONS TODAY!
EMPIRE NEWS

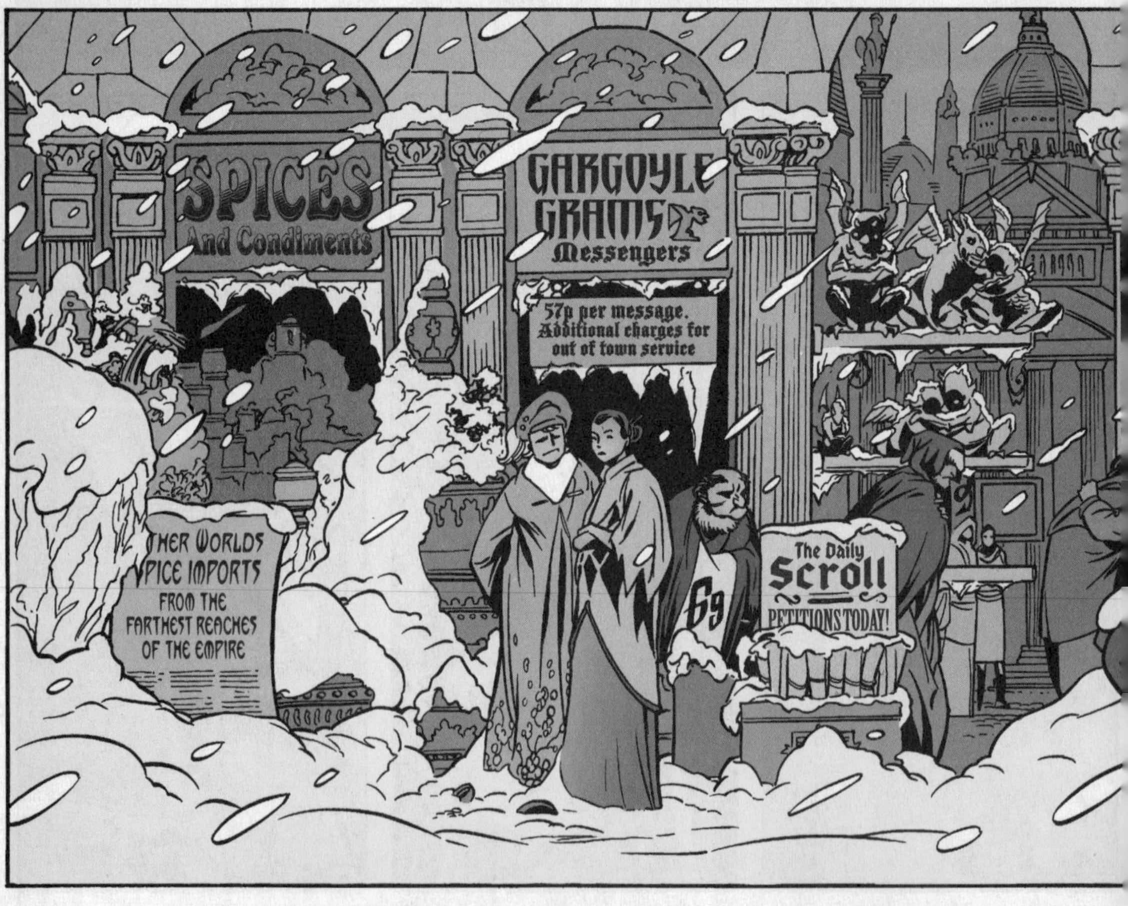
SPICES
And Condiments
GARGOYLE GRAMS
Messengers
57p per message. Additional charges for out of town service
THER WORLDS
PICE IMPORTS
FROM THE FARTHEST REACHES OF THE EMPIRE
The Daily Scroll
PETITIONS TODAY!

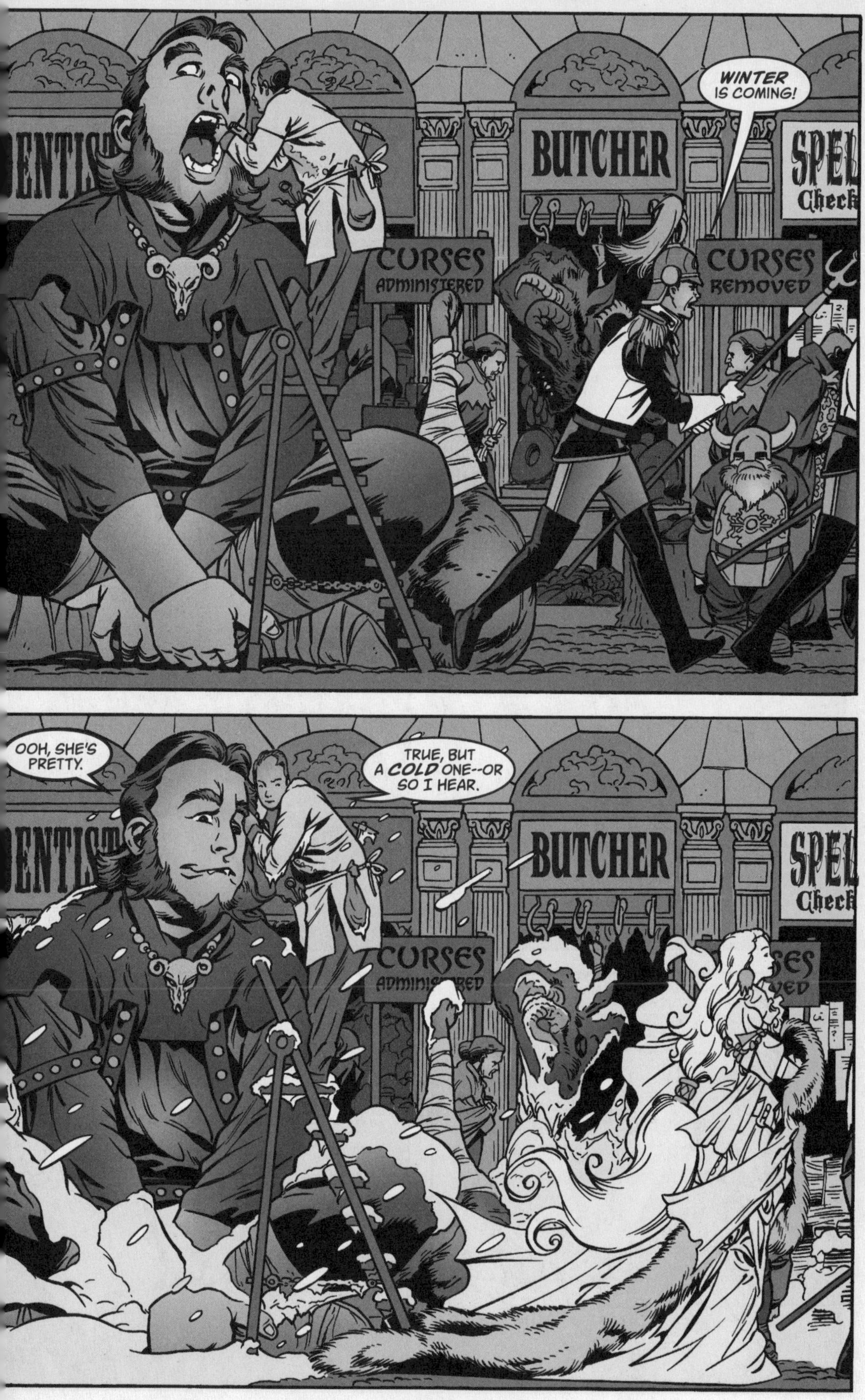
DENTIST
BUTCHER
SPEL
Check
CURSES ADMINISTERED
CURSES REMOVED
WINTER IS COMING!
OOH, SHE'S PRETTY.
TRUE, BUT A COLD ONE--OR SO I HEAR.

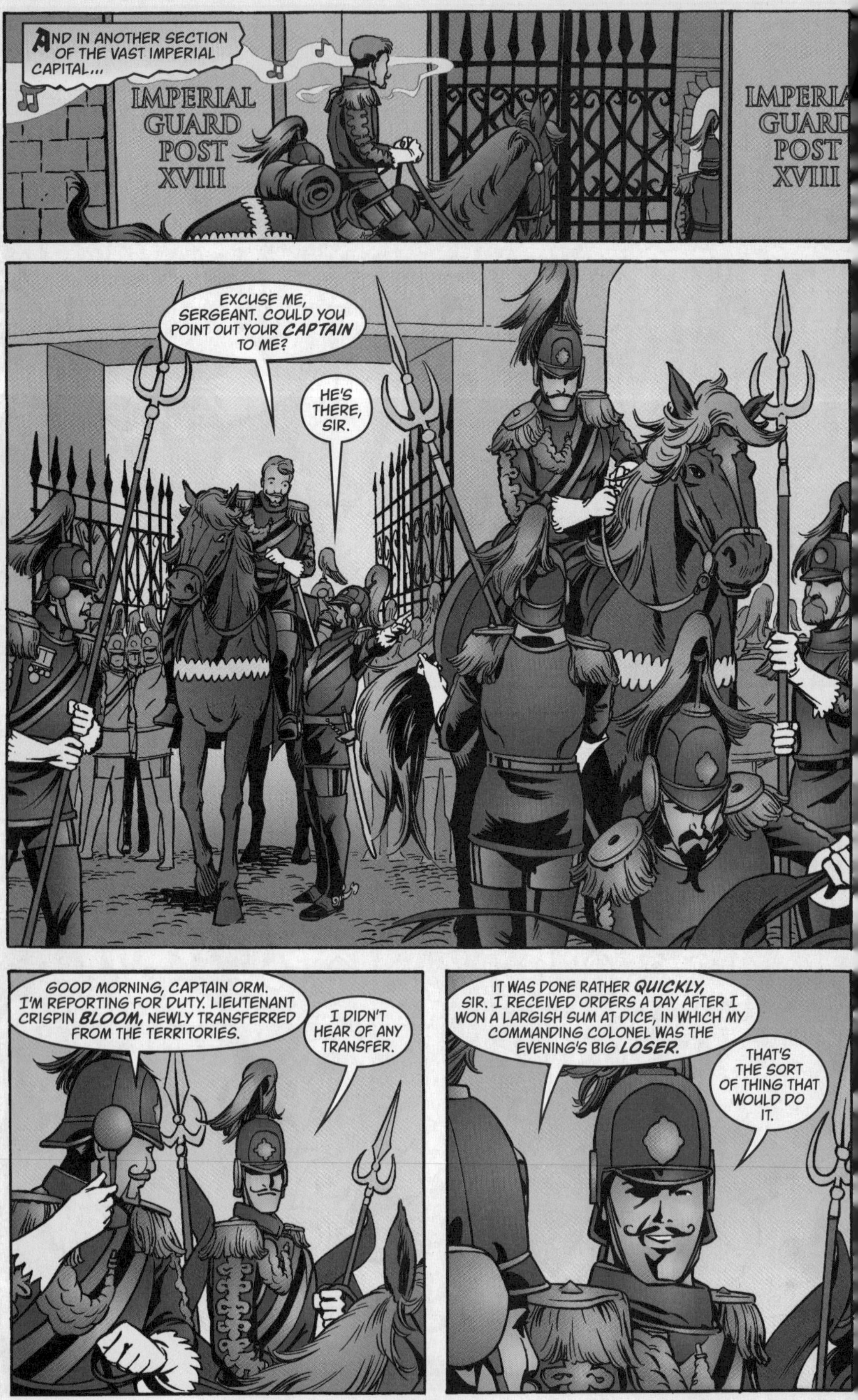
AND IN ANOTHER SECTION OF THE VAST IMPERIAL CAPITAL...
IMPERIAL GUARD POST XVIII
IMPERIAL GUARD POST XVIII
EXCUSE ME, SERGEANT. COULD YOU POINT OUT YOUR CAPTAIN TO ME?
HE'S THERE, SIR.
GOOD MORNING, CAPTAIN ORM. I'M REPORTING FOR DUTY. LIEUTENANT CRISPIN BLOOM, NEWLY TRANSFERRED FROM THE TERRITORIES.
I DIDN'T HEAR OF ANY TRANSFER.
IT WAS DONE RATHER QUICKLY, SIR. I RECEIVED ORDERS A DAY AFTER I WON A LARGISH SUM AT DICE, IN WHICH MY COMMANDING COLONEL WAS THE EVENING'S BIG LOSER.
THAT'S THE SORT OF THING THAT WOULD DO IT.

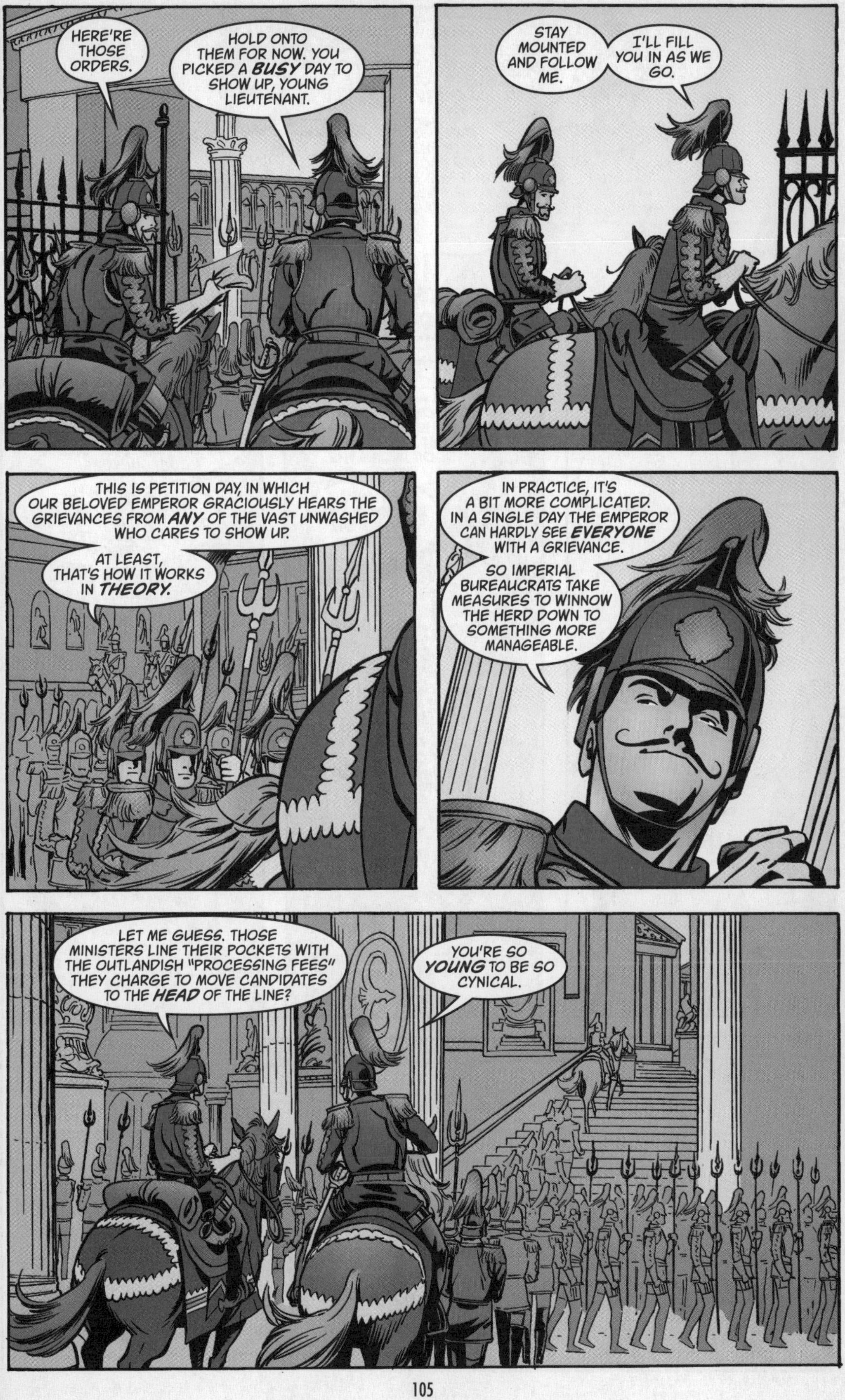
HERE'RE THOSE ORDERS.
HOLD ONTO THEM FOR NOW. YOU PICKED A **BUSY** DAY TO SHOW UP, YOUNG LIEUTENANT.
STAY MOUNTED AND FOLLOW ME.
I'LL FILL YOU IN AS WE GO.
THIS IS PETITION DAY, IN WHICH OUR BELOVED EMPEROR GRACIOUSLY HEARS THE GRIEVANCES FROM **ANY** OF THE VAST UNWASHED WHO CARES TO SHOW UP.
AT LEAST, THAT'S HOW IT WORKS IN **THEORY.**
IN PRACTICE, IT'S A BIT MORE COMPLICATED. IN A SINGLE DAY THE EMPEROR CAN HARDLY SEE **EVERYONE** WITH A GRIEVANCE.
SO IMPERIAL BUREAUCRATS TAKE MEASURES TO WINNOW THE HERD DOWN TO SOMETHING MORE MANAGEABLE.
LET ME GUESS. THOSE MINISTERS LINE THEIR POCKETS WITH THE OUTLANDISH "PROCESSING FEES" THEY CHARGE TO MOVE CANDIDATES TO THE **HEAD** OF THE LINE?
YOU'RE SO **YOUNG** TO BE SO CYNICAL.

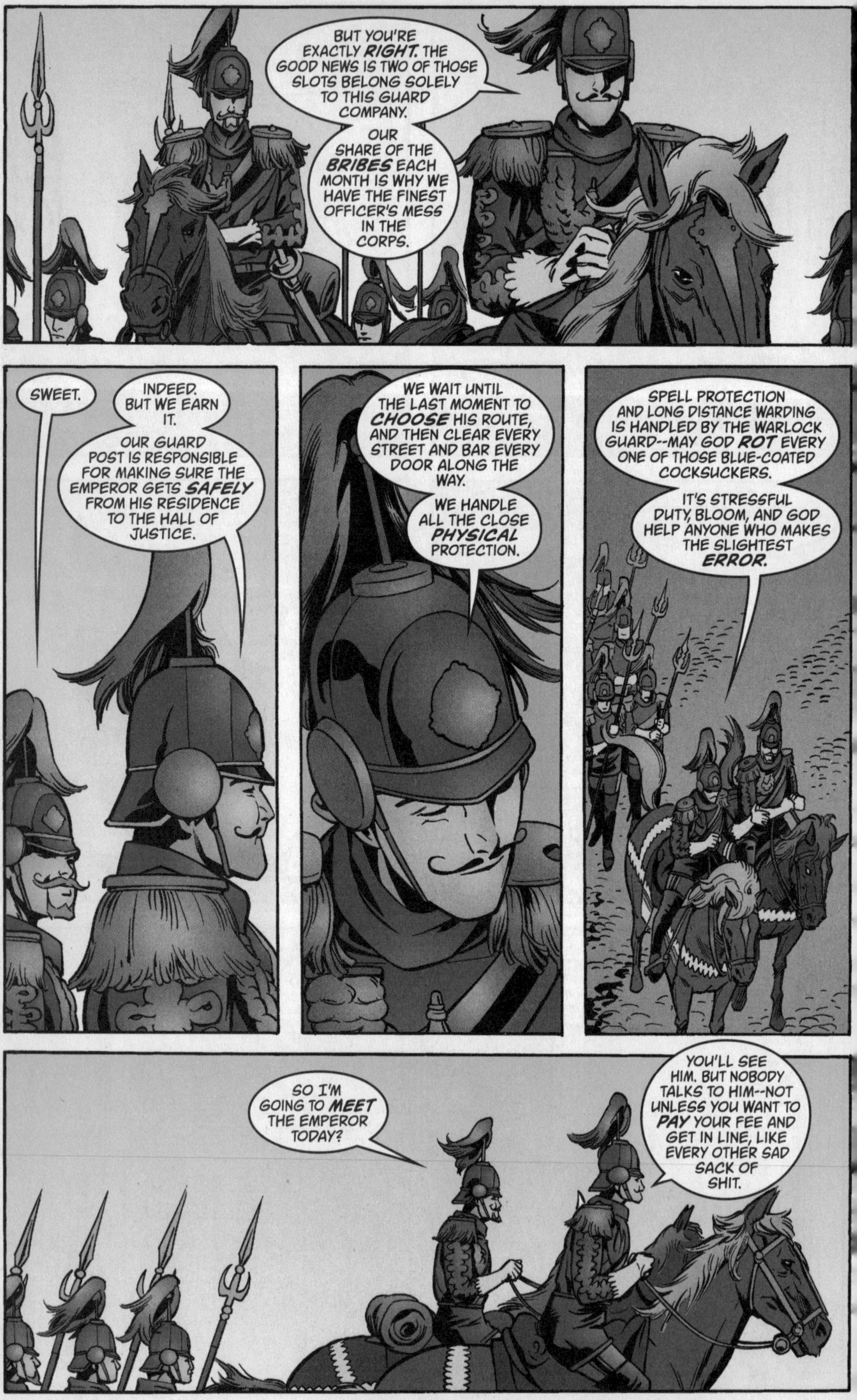
BUT YOU'RE EXACTLY RIGHT. THE GOOD NEWS IS TWO OF THOSE SLOTS BELONG SOLELY TO THIS GUARD COMPANY.
OUR SHARE OF THE BRIBES EACH MONTH IS WHY WE HAVE THE FINEST OFFICER'S MESS IN THE CORPS.
SWEET.
INDEED. BUT WE EARN IT.
OUR GUARD POST IS RESPONSIBLE FOR MAKING SURE THE EMPEROR GETS SAFELY FROM HIS RESIDENCE TO THE HALL OF JUSTICE.
WE WAIT UNTIL THE LAST MOMENT TO CHOOSE HIS ROUTE, AND THEN CLEAR EVERY STREET AND BAR EVERY DOOR ALONG THE WAY.
WE HANDLE ALL THE CLOSE PHYSICAL PROTECTION.
SPELL PROTECTION AND LONG DISTANCE WARDING IS HANDLED BY THE WARLOCK GUARD--MAY GOD ROT EVERY ONE OF THOSE BLUE-COATED COCKSUCKERS.
IT'S STRESSFUL DUTY, BLOOM, AND GOD HELP ANYONE WHO MAKES THE SLIGHTEST ERROR.
SO I'M GOING TO MEET THE EMPEROR TODAY?
YOU'LL SEE HIM. BUT NOBODY TALKS TO HIM--NOT UNLESS YOU WANT TO PAY YOUR FEE AND GET IN LINE, LIKE EVERY OTHER SAD SACK OF SHIT.

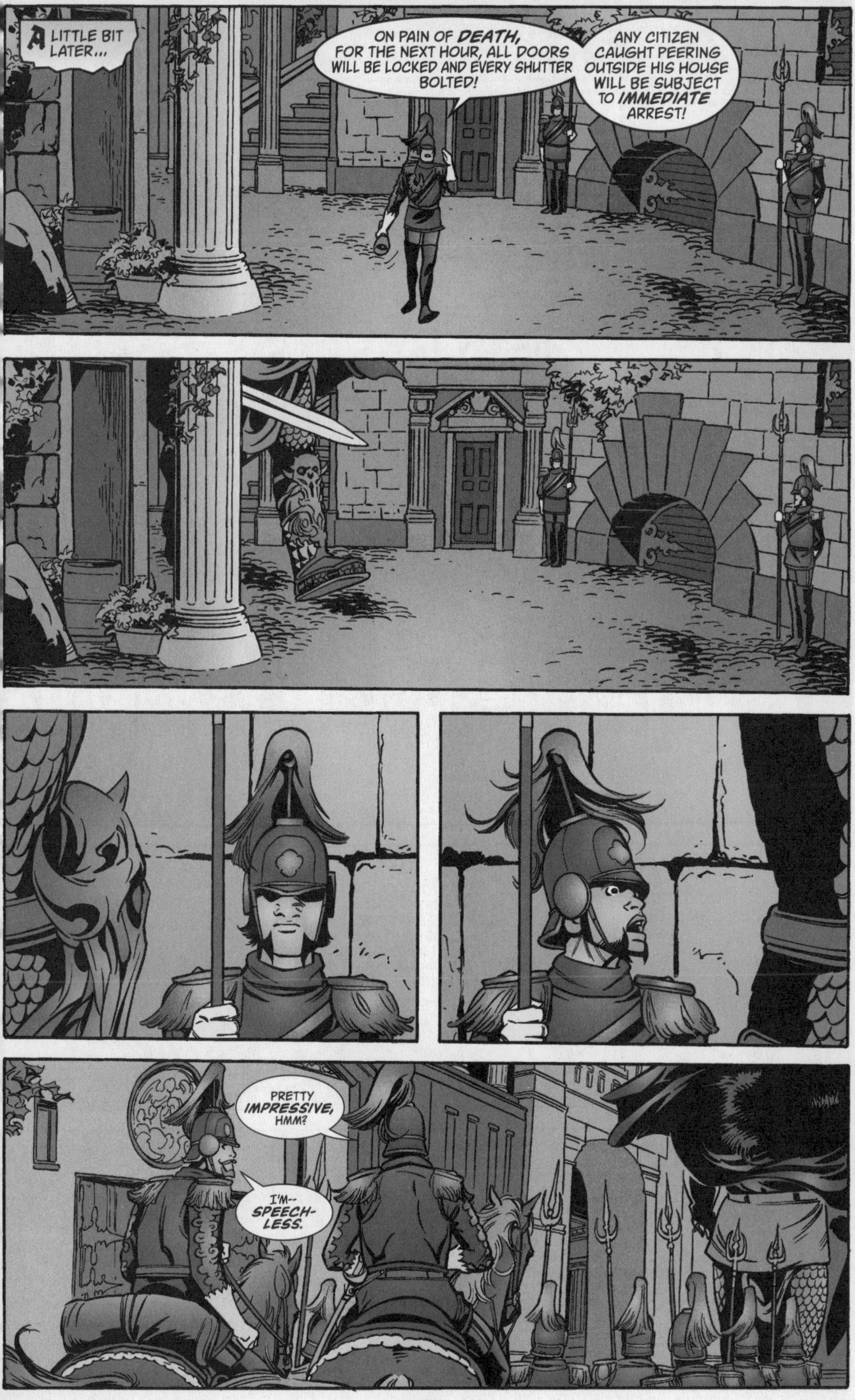
A LITTLE BIT LATER...
ON PAIN OF *DEATH,* FOR THE NEXT HOUR, ALL DOORS WILL BE LOCKED AND EVERY SHUTTER BOLTED!
ANY CITIZEN CAUGHT PEERING OUTSIDE HIS HOUSE WILL BE SUBJECT TO *IMMEDIATE* ARREST!
PRETTY *IMPRESSIVE,* HMM?
I'M-- *SPEECH-LESS.*

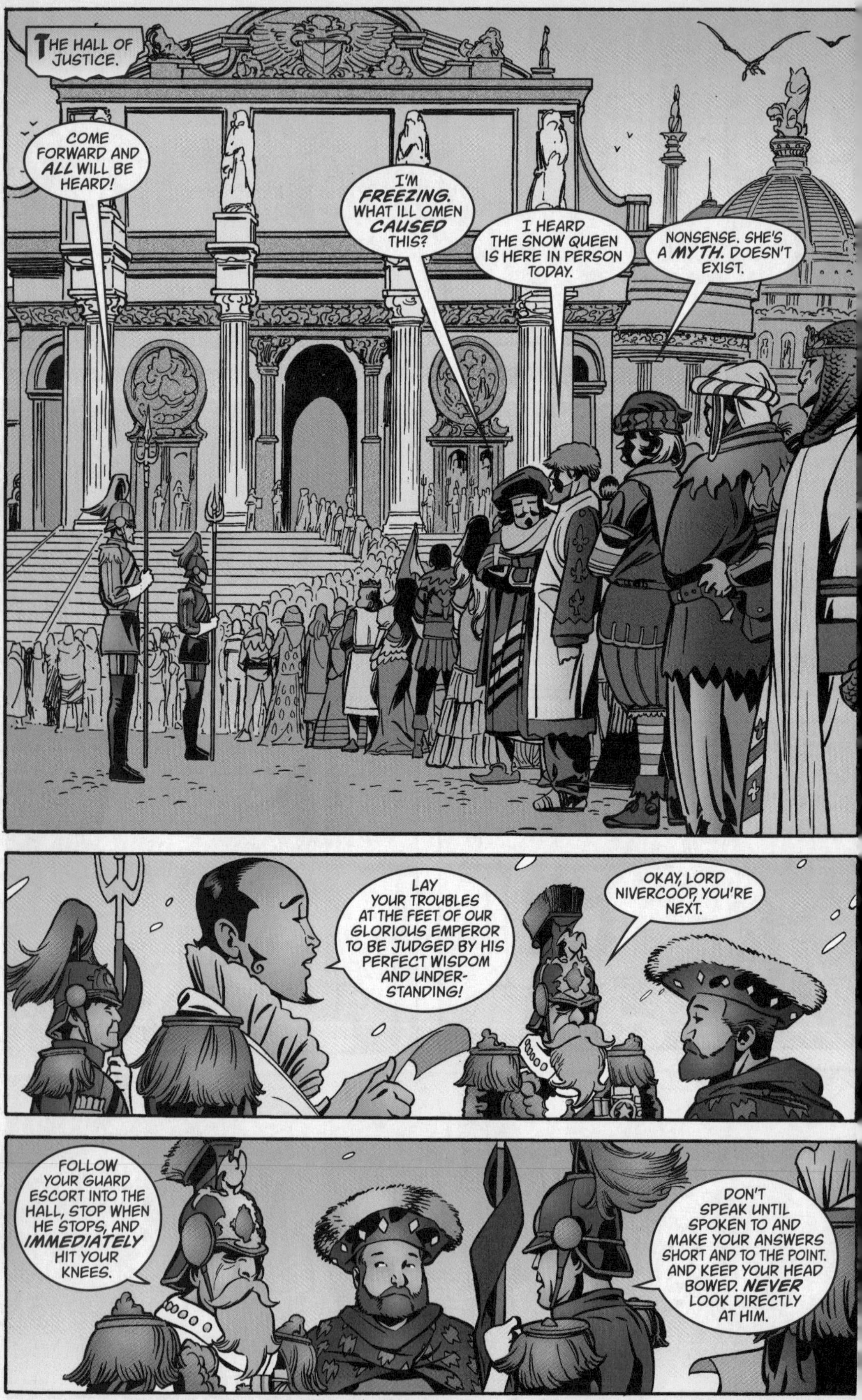
THE HALL OF JUSTICE.
COME FORWARD AND ALL WILL BE HEARD!
I'M FREEZING. WHAT ILL OMEN CAUSED THIS?
I HEARD THE SNOW QUEEN IS HERE IN PERSON TODAY.
NONSENSE. SHE'S A MYTH. DOESN'T EXIST.
LAY YOUR TROUBLES AT THE FEET OF OUR GLORIOUS EMPEROR TO BE JUDGED BY HIS PERFECT WISDOM AND UNDER-STANDING!
OKAY, LORD NIVERCOOP, YOU'RE NEXT.
FOLLOW YOUR GUARD ESCORT INTO THE HALL, STOP WHEN HE STOPS, AND IMMEDIATELY HIT YOUR KNEES.
DON'T SPEAK UNTIL SPOKEN TO AND MAKE YOUR ANSWERS SHORT AND TO THE POINT. AND KEEP YOUR HEAD BOWED. NEVER LOOK DIRECTLY AT HIM.

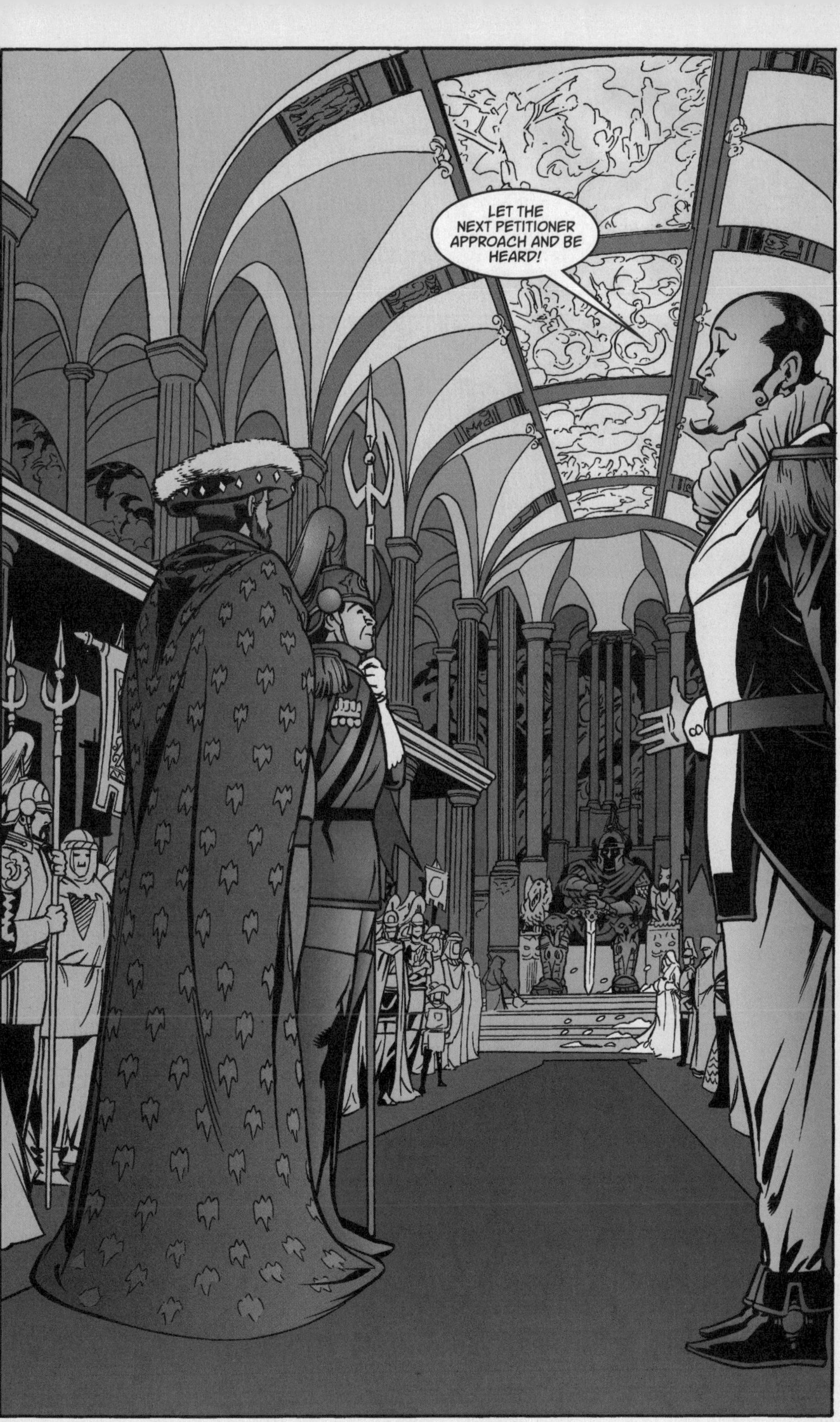
LET THE NEXT PETITIONER APPROACH AND BE HEARD!

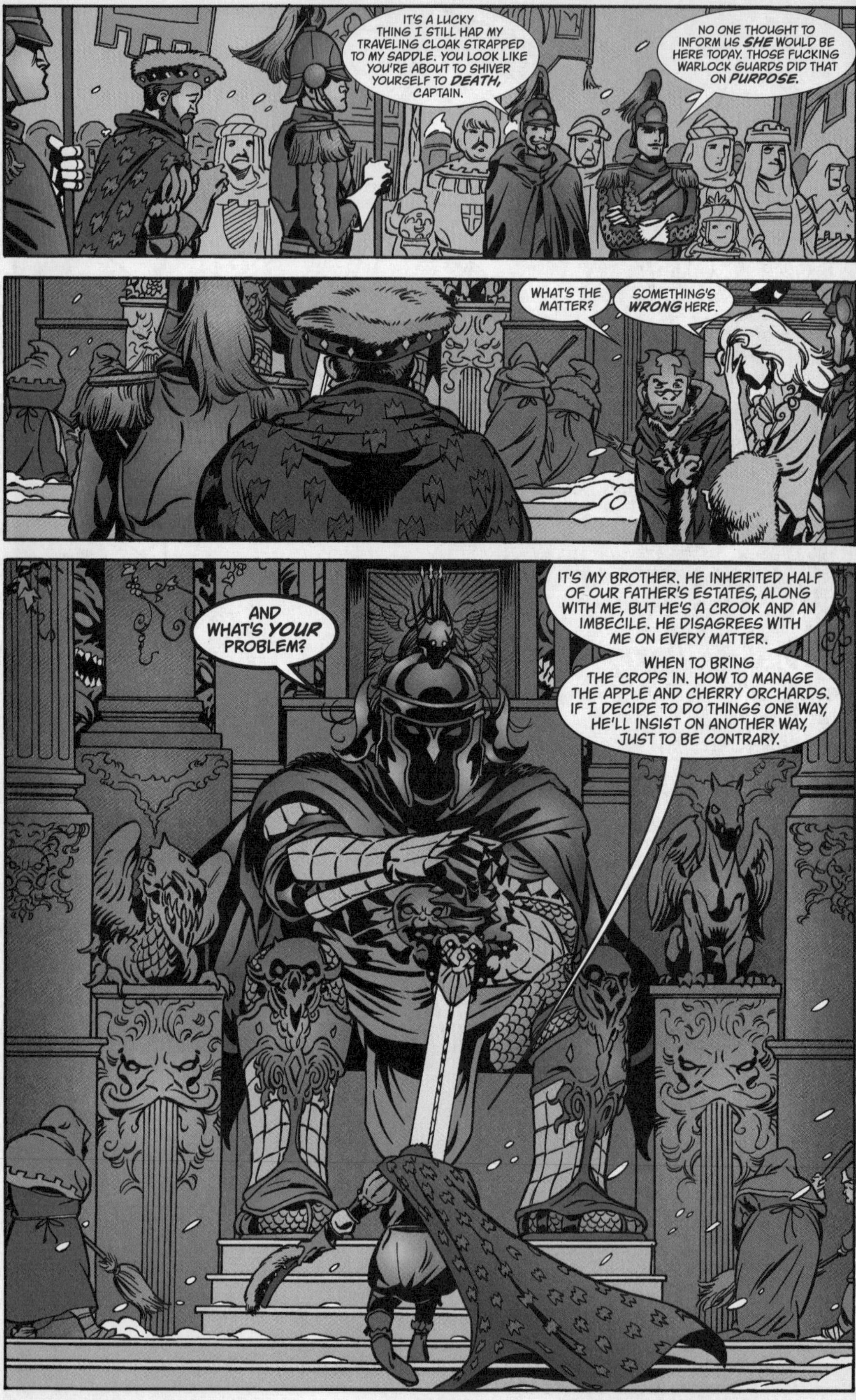
IT'S A LUCKY THING I STILL HAD MY TRAVELING CLOAK STRAPPED TO MY SADDLE. YOU LOOK LIKE YOU'RE ABOUT TO SHIVER YOURSELF TO DEATH, CAPTAIN.
NO ONE THOUGHT TO INFORM US SHE WOULD BE HERE TODAY. THOSE FUCKING WARLOCK GUARDS DID THAT ON PURPOSE.
WHAT'S THE MATTER?
SOMETHING'S WRONG HERE.
AND WHAT'S YOUR PROBLEM?
IT'S MY BROTHER. HE INHERITED HALF OF OUR FATHER'S ESTATES, ALONG WITH ME, BUT HE'S A CROOK AND AN IMBECILE. HE DISAGREES WITH ME ON EVERY MATTER.
WHEN TO BRING THE CROPS IN. HOW TO MANAGE THE APPLE AND CHERRY ORCHARDS. IF I DECIDE TO DO THINGS ONE WAY, HE'LL INSIST ON ANOTHER WAY, JUST TO BE CONTRARY.

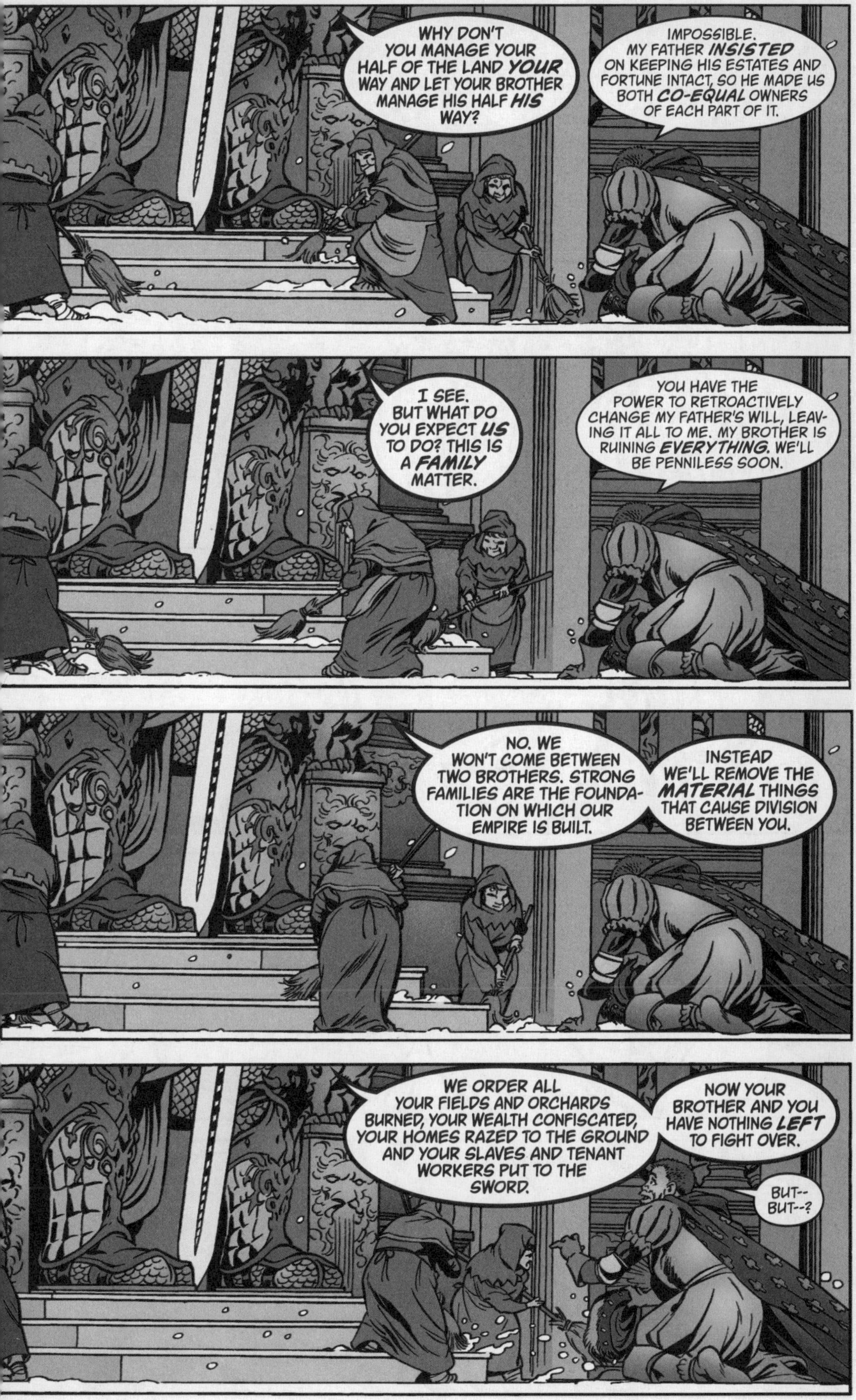
WHY DON'T YOU MANAGE YOUR HALF OF THE LAND YOUR WAY AND LET YOUR BROTHER MANAGE HIS HALF HIS WAY?
IMPOSSIBLE. MY FATHER INSISTED ON KEEPING HIS ESTATES AND FORTUNE INTACT, SO HE MADE US BOTH CO-EQUAL OWNERS OF EACH PART OF IT.
I SEE. BUT WHAT DO YOU EXPECT US TO DO? THIS IS A FAMILY MATTER.
YOU HAVE THE POWER TO RETROACTIVELY CHANGE MY FATHER'S WILL, LEAVING IT ALL TO ME. MY BROTHER IS RUINING EVERYTHING. WE'LL BE PENNILESS SOON.
NO. WE WON'T COME BETWEEN TWO BROTHERS. STRONG FAMILIES ARE THE FOUNDATION ON WHICH OUR EMPIRE IS BUILT.
INSTEAD WE'LL REMOVE THE MATERIAL THINGS THAT CAUSE DIVISION BETWEEN YOU.
WE ORDER ALL YOUR FIELDS AND ORCHARDS BURNED, YOUR WEALTH CONFISCATED, YOUR HOMES RAZED TO THE GROUND AND YOUR SLAVES AND TENANT WORKERS PUT TO THE SWORD.
NOW YOUR BROTHER AND YOU HAVE NOTHING LEFT TO FIGHT OVER.
BUT-- BUT--?

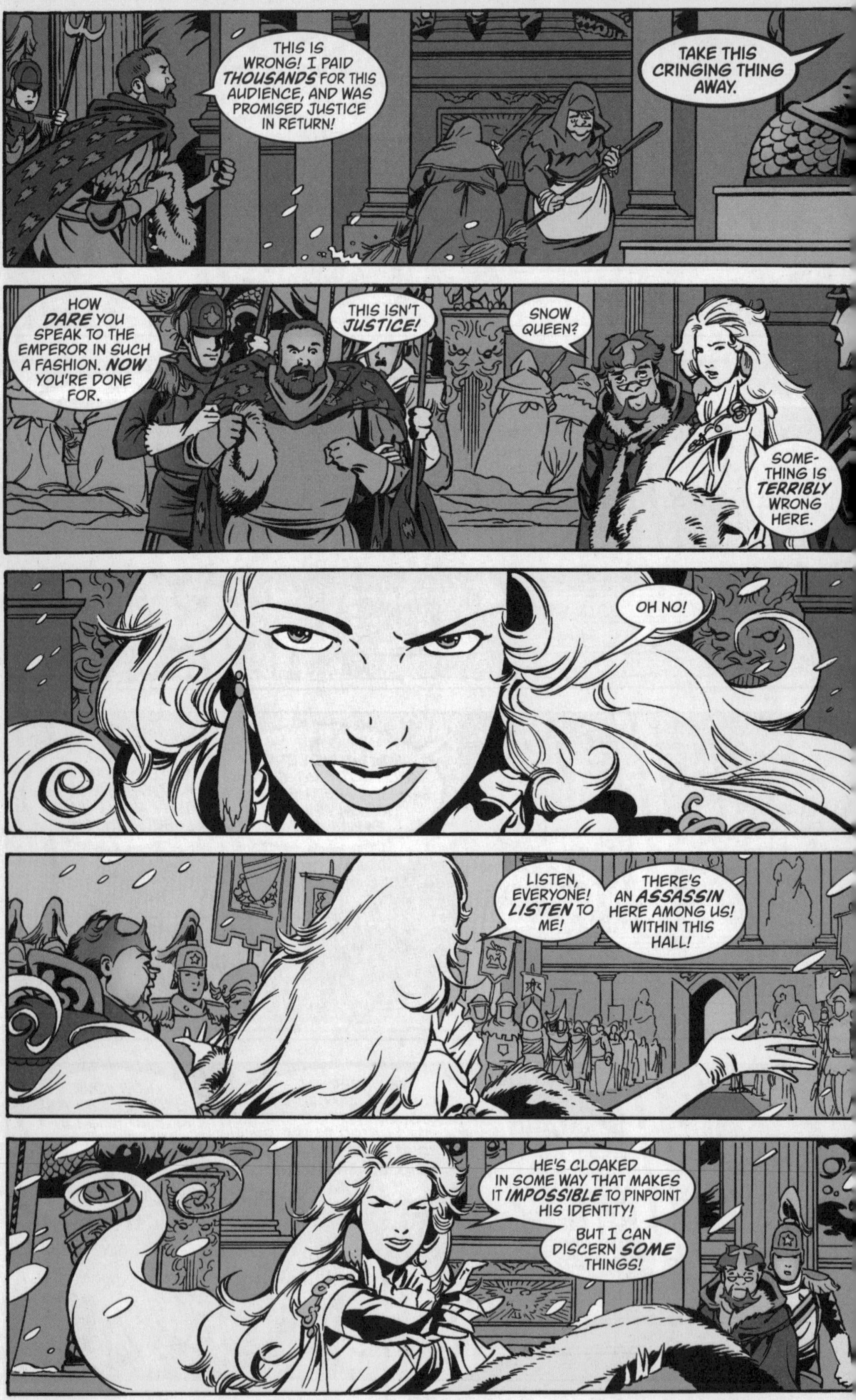
THIS IS WRONG! I PAID THOUSANDS FOR THIS AUDIENCE, AND WAS PROMISED JUSTICE IN RETURN!
TAKE THIS CRINGING THING AWAY.
HOW DARE YOU SPEAK TO THE EMPEROR IN SUCH A FASHION. NOW YOU'RE DONE FOR.
THIS ISN'T JUSTICE!
SNOW QUEEN?
SOMETHING IS TERRIBLY WRONG HERE.
OH NO!
LISTEN, EVERYONE! LISTEN TO ME!
THERE'S AN ASSASSIN HERE AMONG US! WITHIN THIS HALL!
HE'S CLOAKED IN SOME WAY THAT MAKES IT IMPOSSIBLE TO PINPOINT HIS IDENTITY!
BUT I CAN DISCERN SOME THINGS!

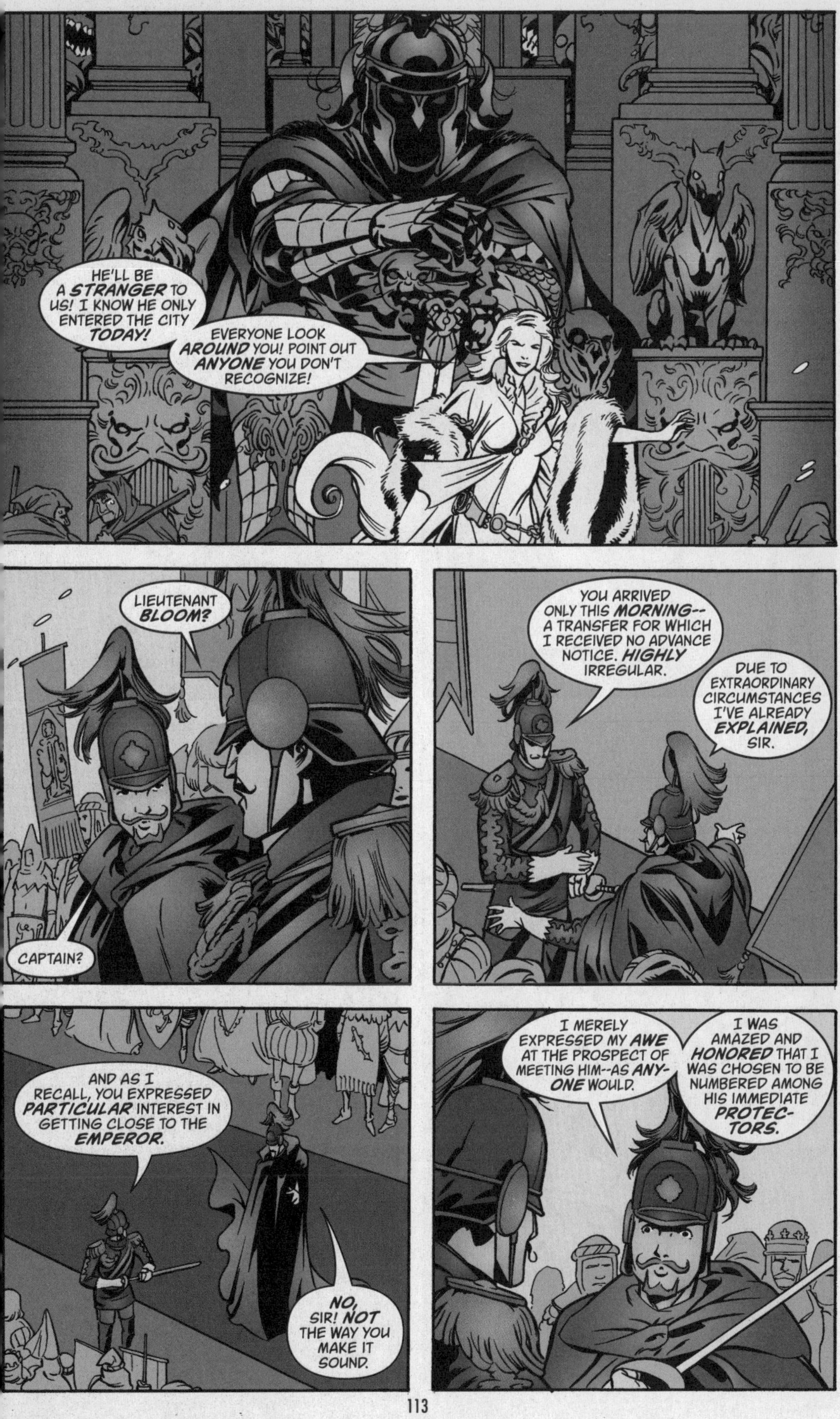

HE'LL BE A STRANGER TO US! I KNOW HE ONLY ENTERED THE CITY TODAY!
EVERYONE LOOK AROUND YOU! POINT OUT ANYONE YOU DON'T RECOGNIZE!
LIEUTENANT BLOOM?
CAPTAIN?
YOU ARRIVED ONLY THIS MORNING-- A TRANSFER FOR WHICH I RECEIVED NO ADVANCE NOTICE. HIGHLY IRREGULAR.
DUE TO EXTRAORDINARY CIRCUMSTANCES I'VE ALREADY EXPLAINED, SIR.
AND AS I RECALL, YOU EXPRESSED PARTICULAR INTEREST IN GETTING CLOSE TO THE EMPEROR.
NO, SIR! NOT THE WAY YOU MAKE IT SOUND.
I MERELY EXPRESSED MY AWE AT THE PROSPECT OF MEETING HIM--AS ANY-ONE WOULD.
I WAS AMAZED AND HONORED THAT I WAS CHOSEN TO BE NUMBERED AMONG HIS IMMEDIATE PROTEC-TORS.

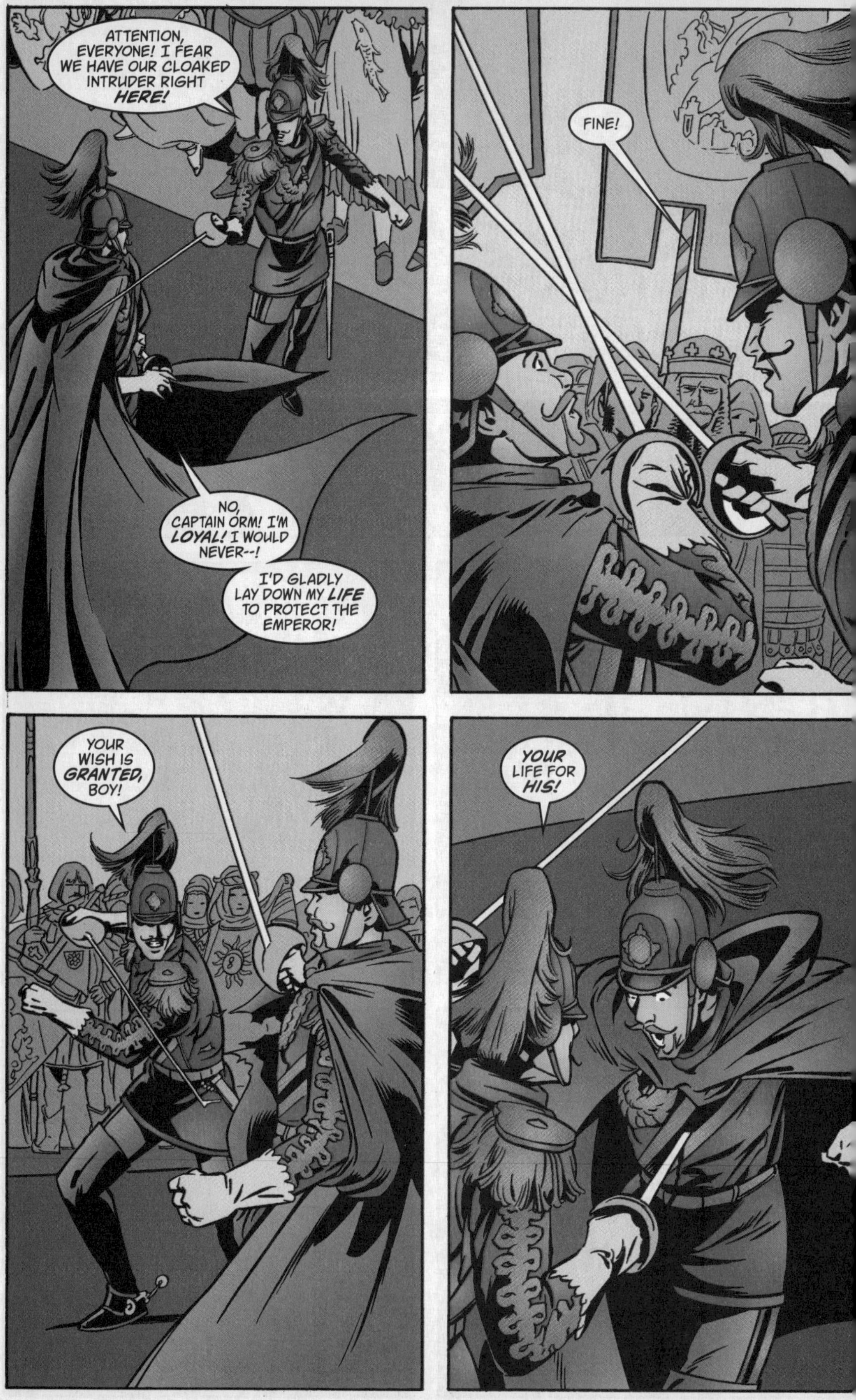
ATTENTION, EVERYONE! I FEAR WE HAVE OUR CLOAKED INTRUDER RIGHT HERE!
NO, CAPTAIN ORM! I'M LOYAL! I WOULD NEVER--!
I'D GLADLY LAY DOWN MY LIFE TO PROTECT THE EMPEROR!
FINE!
YOUR WISH IS GRANTED, BOY!
YOUR LIFE FOR HIS!

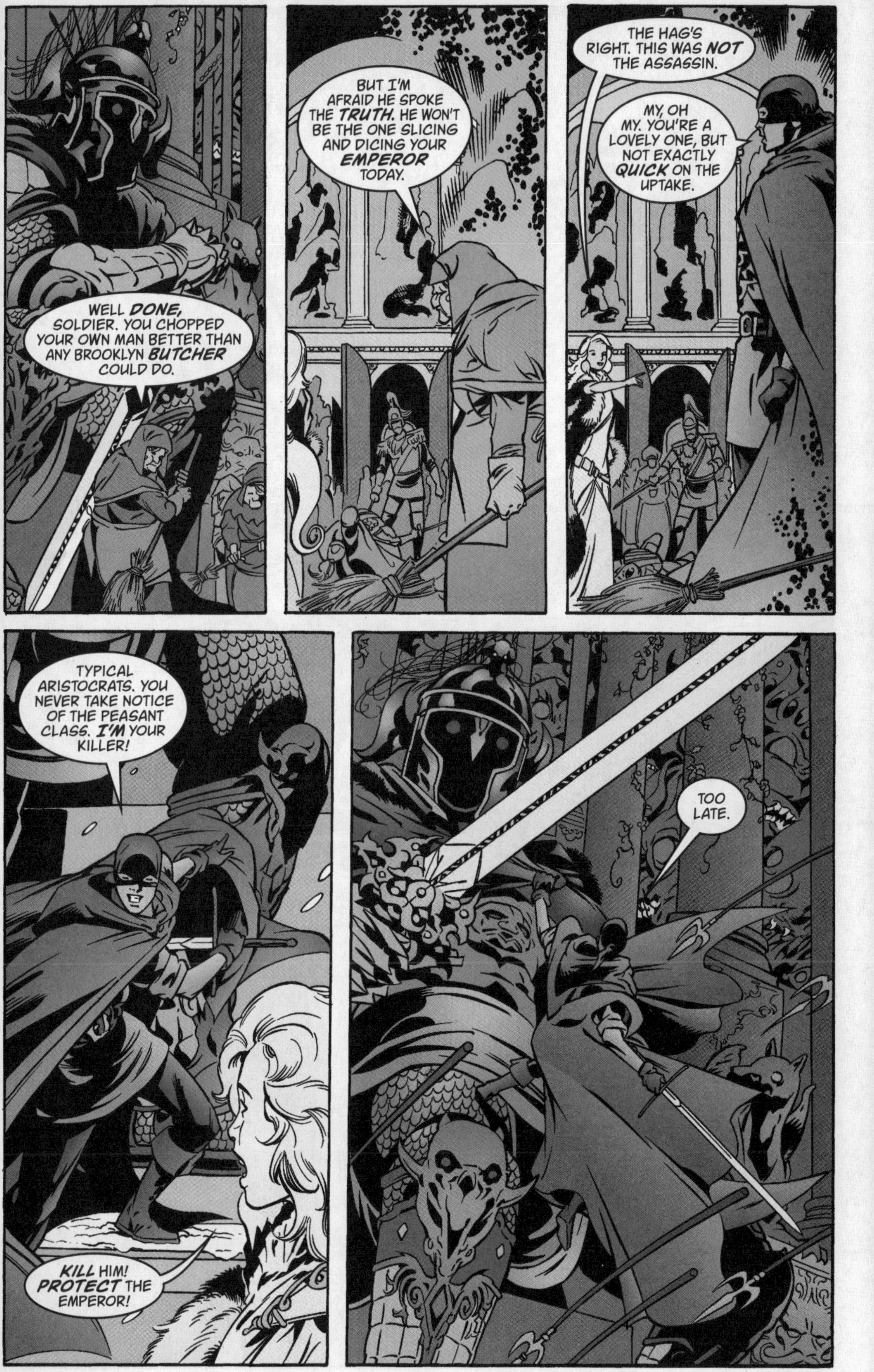
WELL DONE, SOLDIER. YOU CHOPPED YOUR OWN MAN BETTER THAN ANY BROOKLYN BUTCHER COULD DO.
BUT I'M AFRAID HE SPOKE THE TRUTH. HE WON'T BE THE ONE SLICING AND DICING YOUR EMPEROR TODAY.
THE HAG'S RIGHT. THIS WAS NOT THE ASSASSIN.
MY, OH MY. YOU'RE A LOVELY ONE, BUT NOT EXACTLY QUICK ON THE UPTAKE.
TYPICAL ARISTOCRATS. YOU NEVER TAKE NOTICE OF THE PEASANT CLASS. I'M YOUR KILLER!
KILL HIM! PROTECT THE EMPEROR!
TOO LATE.

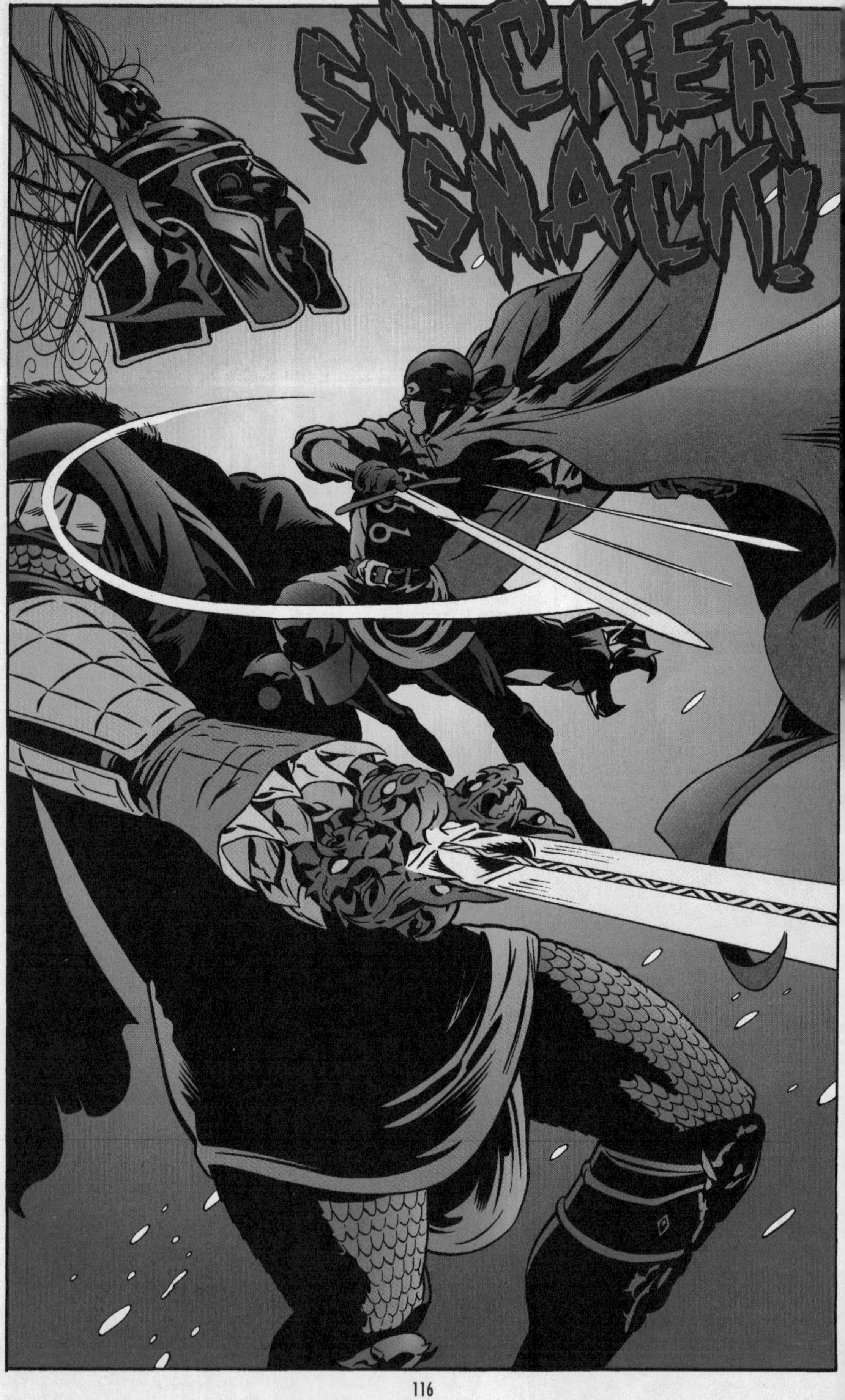
SNICKER-SNACK!!

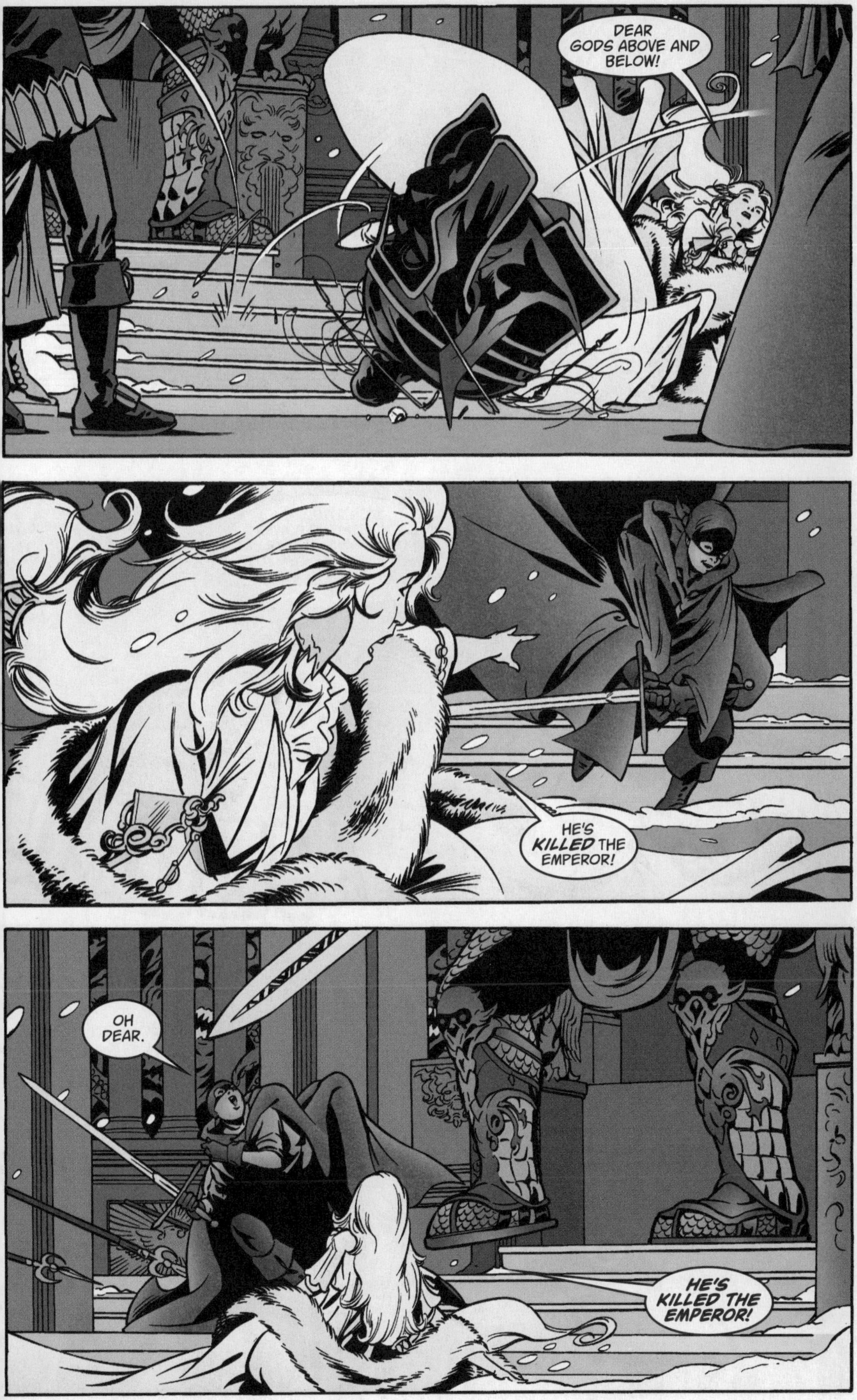
DEAR GODS ABOVE AND BELOW!
HE'S KILLED THE EMPEROR!
OH DEAR.
HE'S KILLED THE EMPEROR!

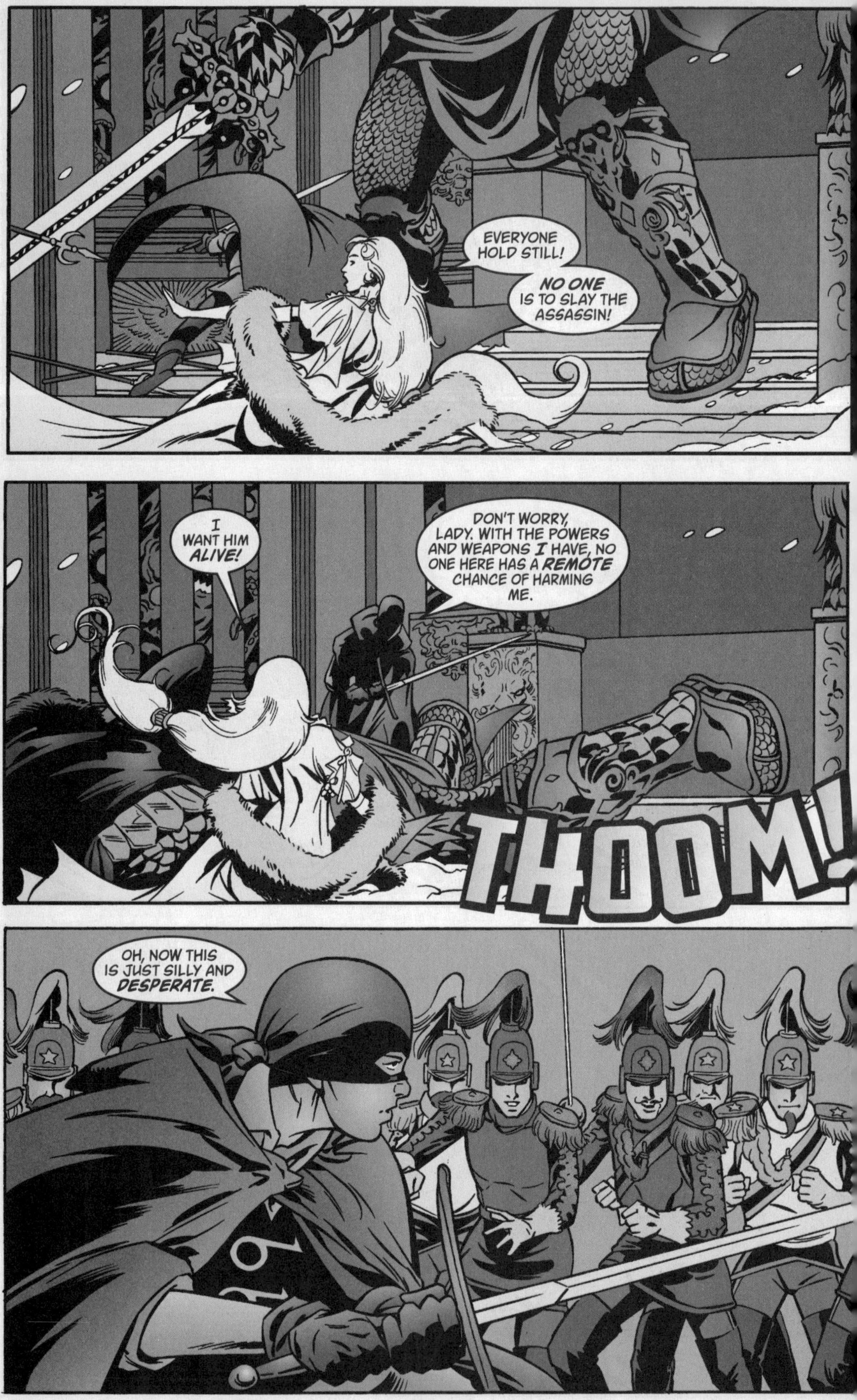
EVERYONE HOLD STILL!
NO ONE IS TO SLAY THE ASSASSIN!
I WANT HIM ALIVE!
DON'T WORRY, LADY. WITH THE POWERS AND WEAPONS I HAVE, NO ONE HERE HAS A REMOTE CHANCE OF HARMING ME.
THOOM!
OH, NOW THIS IS JUST SILLY AND DESPERATE.

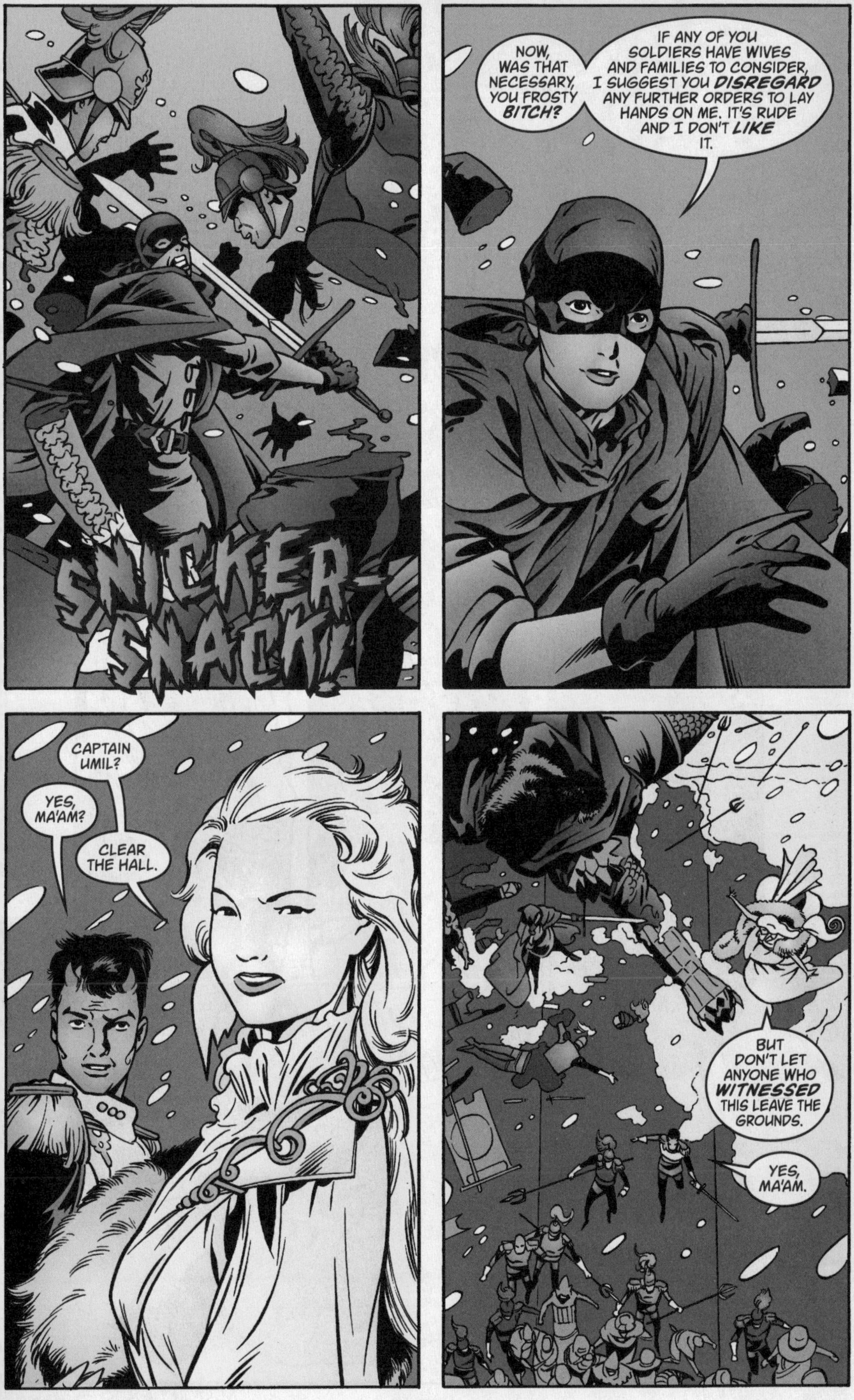
SNICKER-SNACK!
NOW, WAS THAT NECESSARY, YOU FROSTY BITCH?
IF ANY OF YOU SOLDIERS HAVE WIVES AND FAMILIES TO CONSIDER, I SUGGEST YOU DISREGARD ANY FURTHER ORDERS TO LAY HANDS ON ME. IT'S RUDE AND I DON'T LIKE IT.
CAPTAIN UMIL?
YES, MA'AM?
CLEAR THE HALL.
BUT DON'T LET ANYONE WHO WITNESSED THIS LEAVE THE GROUNDS.
YES, MA'AM.

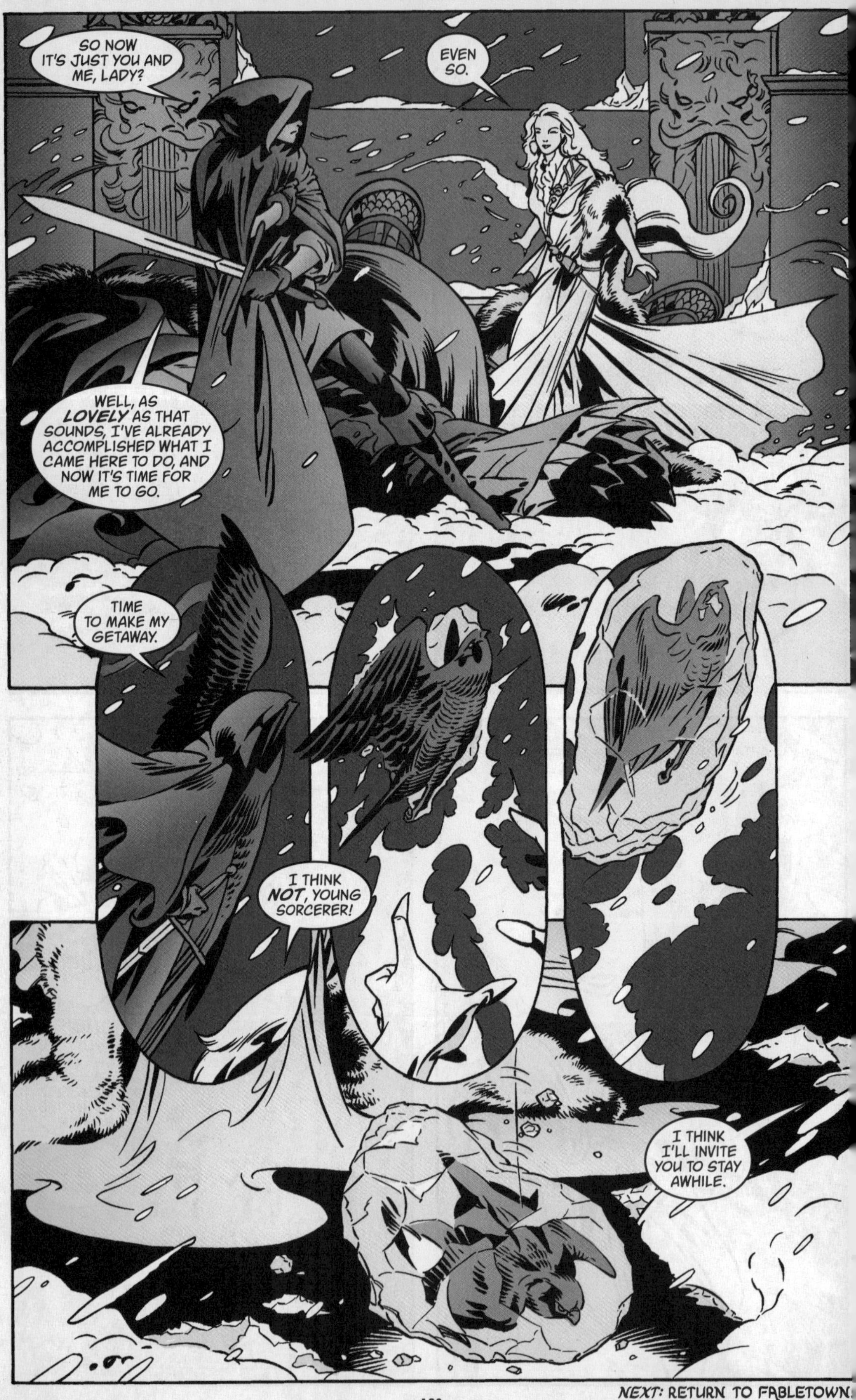

SO NOW IT'S JUST YOU AND ME, LADY?
EVEN SO.
WELL, AS *LOVELY* AS THAT SOUNDS, I'VE ALREADY ACCOMPLISHED WHAT I CAME HERE TO DO, AND NOW IT'S TIME FOR ME TO GO.
TIME TO MAKE MY GETAWAY.
I THINK *NOT*, YOUNG SORCERER!
I THINK I'LL INVITE YOU TO STAY AWHILE.

NEXT: RETURN TO FABLETOWN!

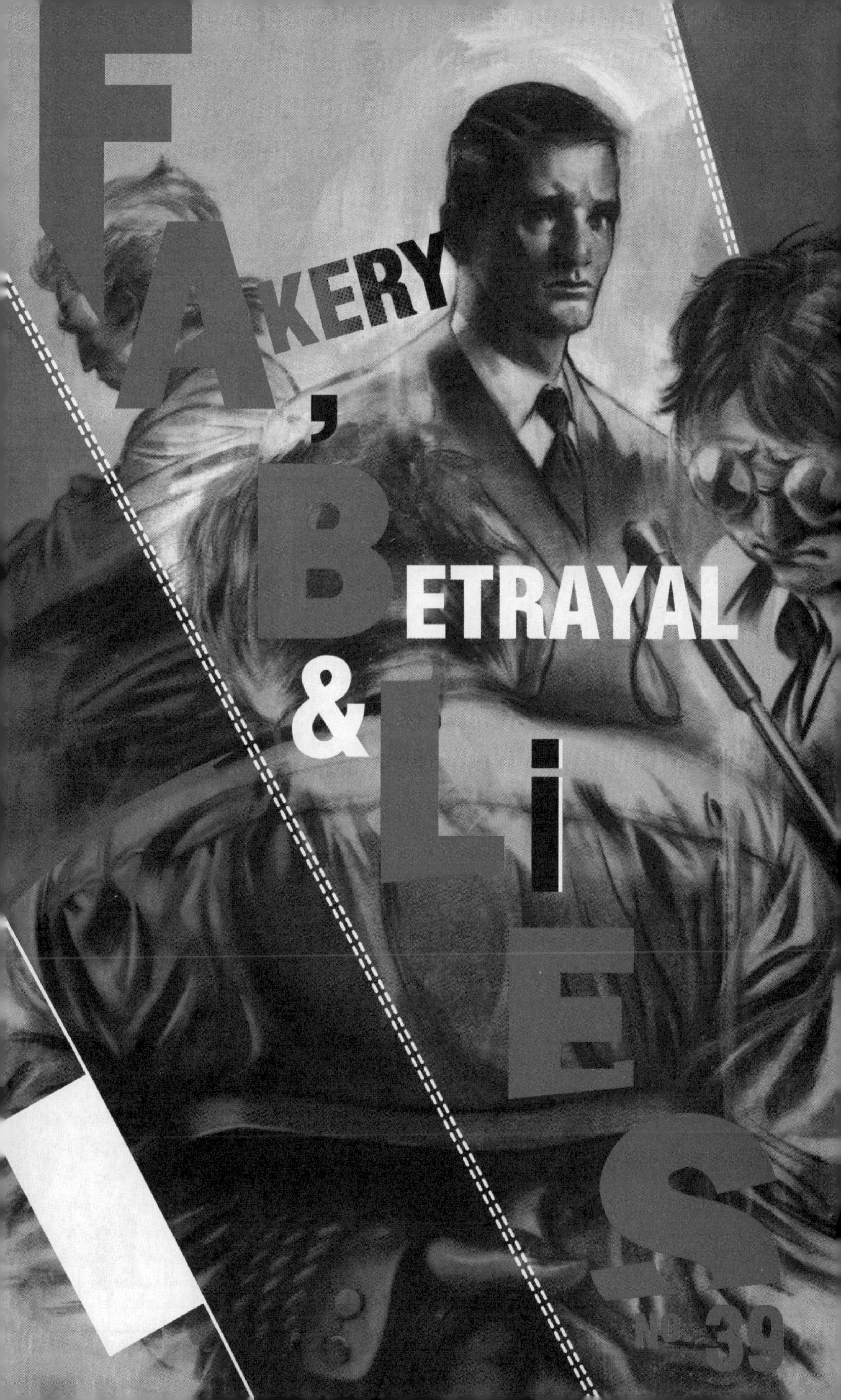
FAKERY,
BETRAYAL
&
LIES
No. 39

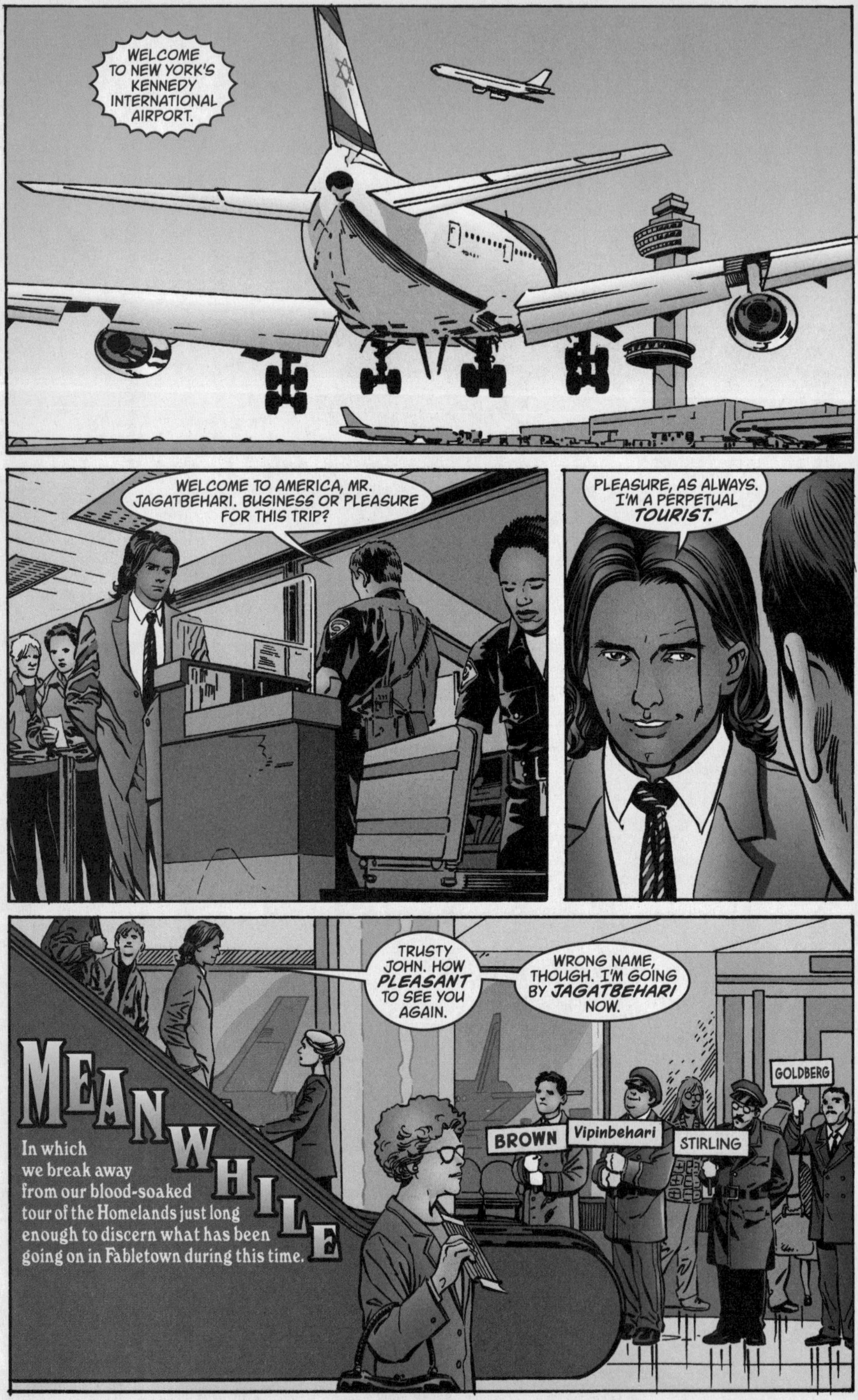
WELCOME TO NEW YORK'S KENNEDY INTERNATIONAL AIRPORT.
WELCOME TO AMERICA, MR. JAGATBEHARI. BUSINESS OR PLEASURE FOR THIS TRIP?
PLEASURE, AS ALWAYS. I'M A PERPETUAL *TOURIST.*
MEANWHILE
In which we break away from our blood-soaked tour of the Homelands just long enough to discern what has been going on in Fabletown during this time.
TRUSTY JOHN. HOW *PLEASANT* TO SEE YOU AGAIN.
WRONG NAME, THOUGH. I'M GOING BY *JAGATBEHARI* NOW.
BROWN
Vipinbehari
STIRLING
GOLDBERG

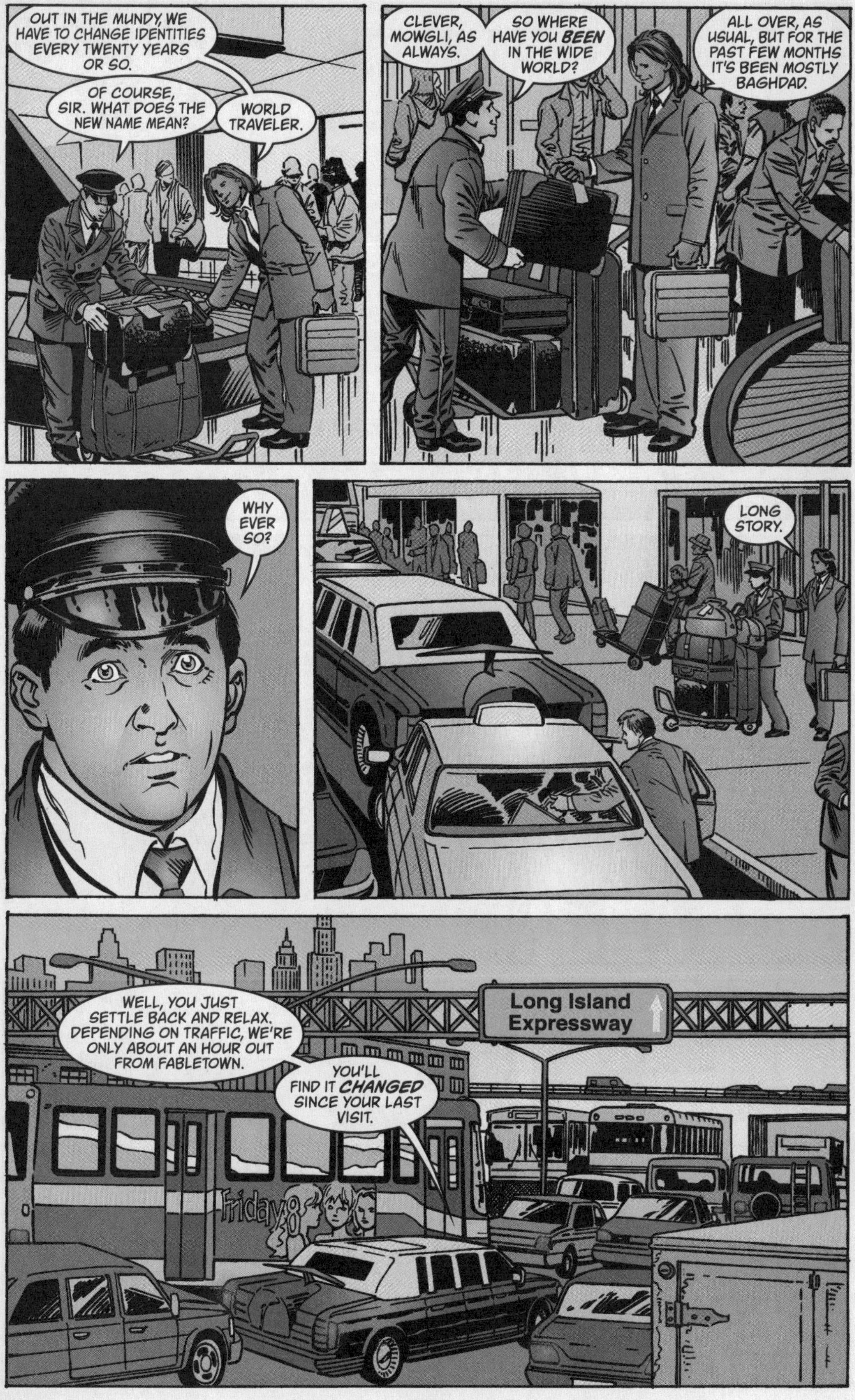
OUT IN THE MUNDY, WE HAVE TO CHANGE IDENTITIES EVERY TWENTY YEARS OR SO.
OF COURSE, SIR. WHAT DOES THE NEW NAME MEAN?
WORLD TRAVELER.
CLEVER, MOWGLI, AS ALWAYS.
SO WHERE HAVE YOU BEEN IN THE WIDE WORLD?
ALL OVER, AS USUAL, BUT FOR THE PAST FEW MONTHS IT'S BEEN MOSTLY BAGHDAD.
WHY EVER SO?
LONG STORY.
WELL, YOU JUST SETTLE BACK AND RELAX. DEPENDING ON TRAFFIC, WE'RE ONLY ABOUT AN HOUR OUT FROM FABLETOWN.
YOU'LL FIND IT CHANGED SINCE YOUR LAST VISIT.
Long Island Expressway
Friday 8

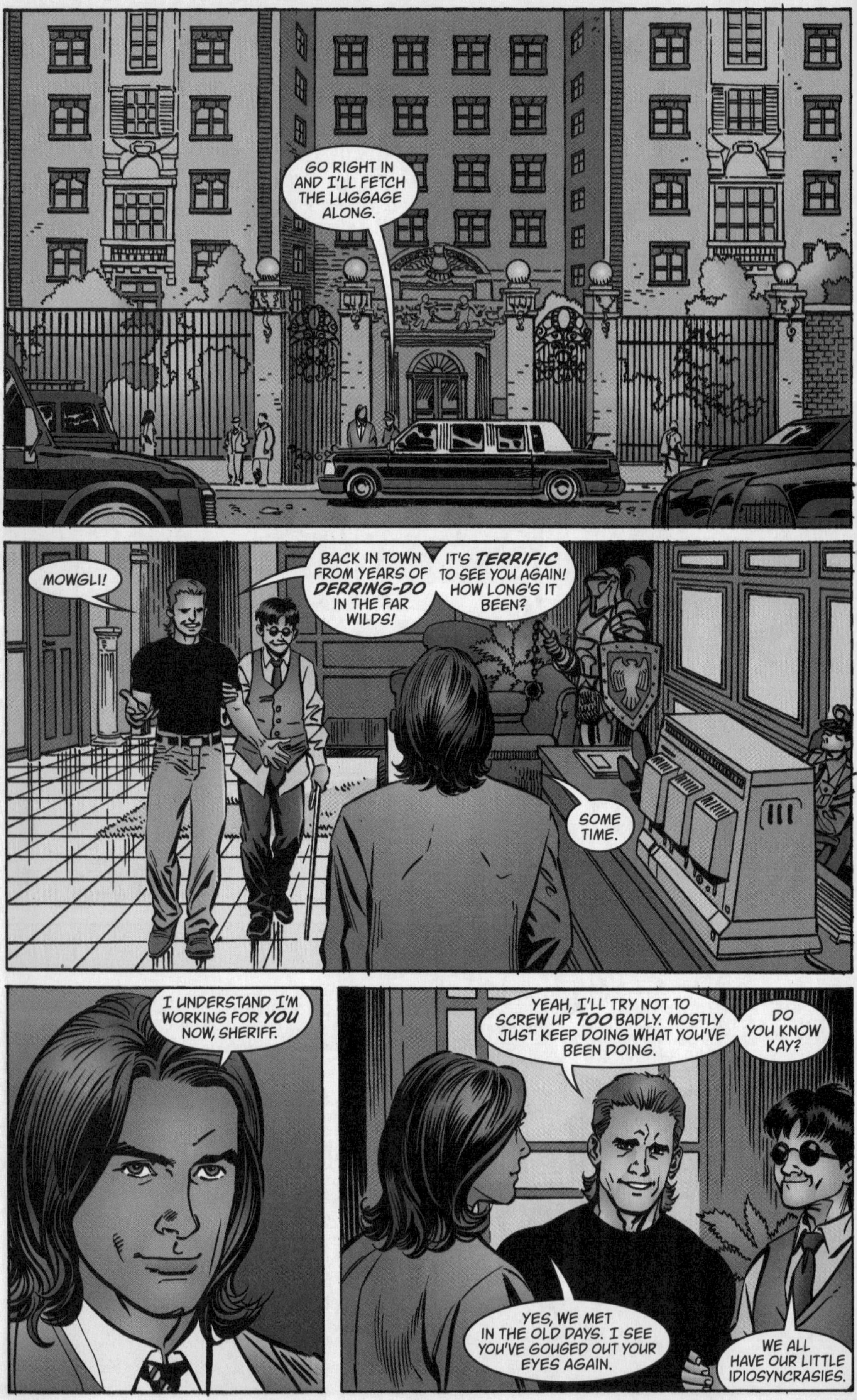
GO RIGHT IN AND I'LL FETCH THE LUGGAGE ALONG.
MOWGLI!
BACK IN TOWN FROM YEARS OF DERRING-DO IN THE FAR WILDS!
IT'S TERRIFIC TO SEE YOU AGAIN! HOW LONG'S IT BEEN?
SOME TIME.
I UNDERSTAND I'M WORKING FOR YOU NOW, SHERIFF.
YEAH, I'LL TRY NOT TO SCREW UP TOO BADLY. MOSTLY JUST KEEP DOING WHAT YOU'VE BEEN DOING.
DO YOU KNOW KAY?
YES, WE MET IN THE OLD DAYS. I SEE YOU'VE GOUGED OUT YOUR EYES AGAIN.
WE ALL HAVE OUR LITTLE IDIOSYNCRASIES.

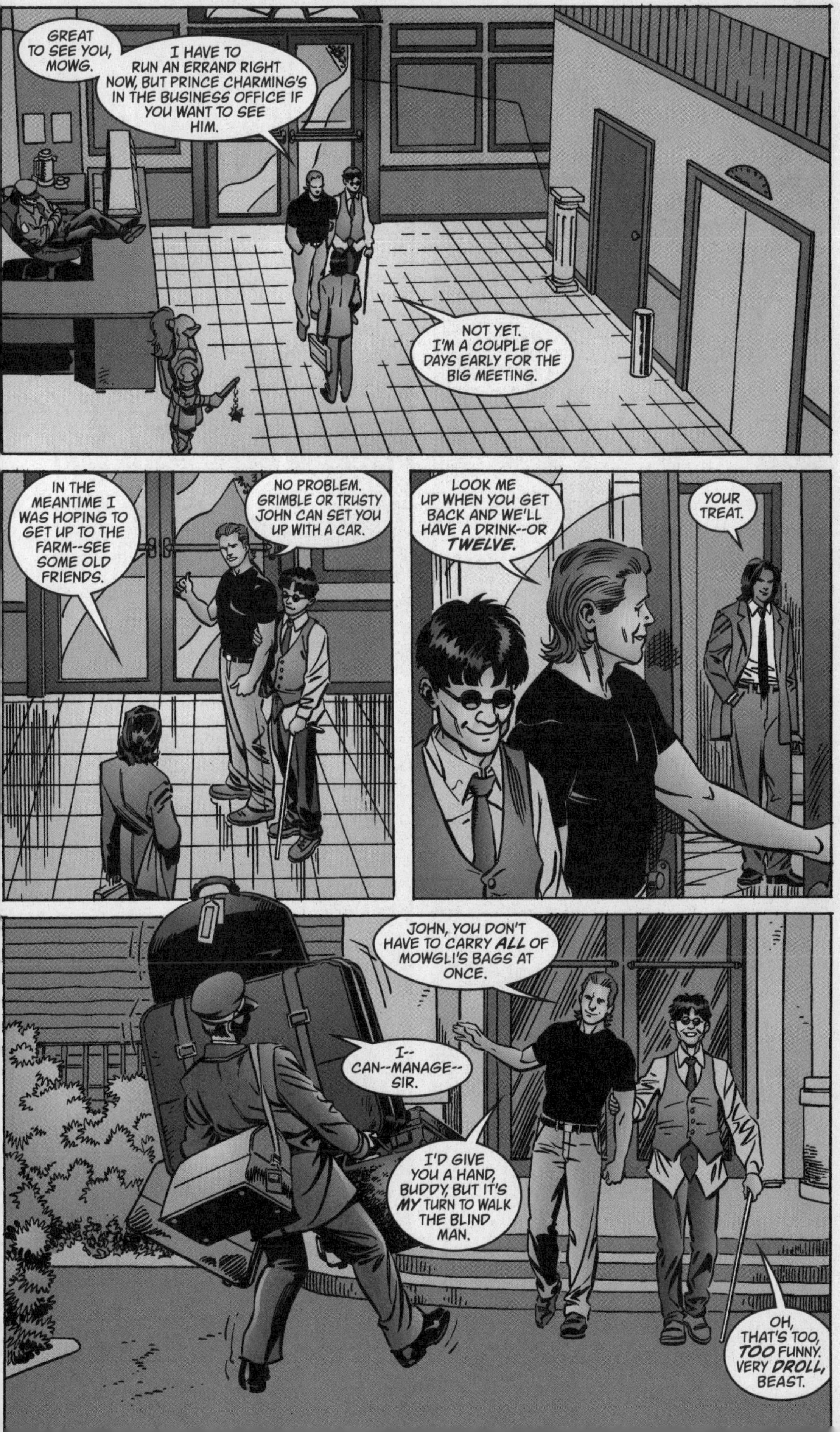

GREAT TO SEE YOU, MOWG.
I HAVE TO RUN AN ERRAND RIGHT NOW, BUT PRINCE CHARMING'S IN THE BUSINESS OFFICE IF YOU WANT TO SEE HIM.
NOT YET. I'M A COUPLE OF DAYS EARLY FOR THE BIG MEETING.
IN THE MEANTIME I WAS HOPING TO GET UP TO THE FARM--SEE SOME OLD FRIENDS.
NO PROBLEM. GRIMBLE OR TRUSTY JOHN CAN SET YOU UP WITH A CAR.
LOOK ME UP WHEN YOU GET BACK AND WE'LL HAVE A DRINK--OR **TWELVE.**
YOUR TREAT.
JOHN, YOU DON'T HAVE TO CARRY **ALL** OF MOWGLI'S BAGS AT ONCE.
I--CAN--MANAGE--SIR.
I'D GIVE YOU A HAND, BUDDY, BUT IT'S **MY** TURN TO WALK THE BLIND MAN.
OH, THAT'S TOO, **TOO** FUNNY. VERY **DROLL,** BEAST.

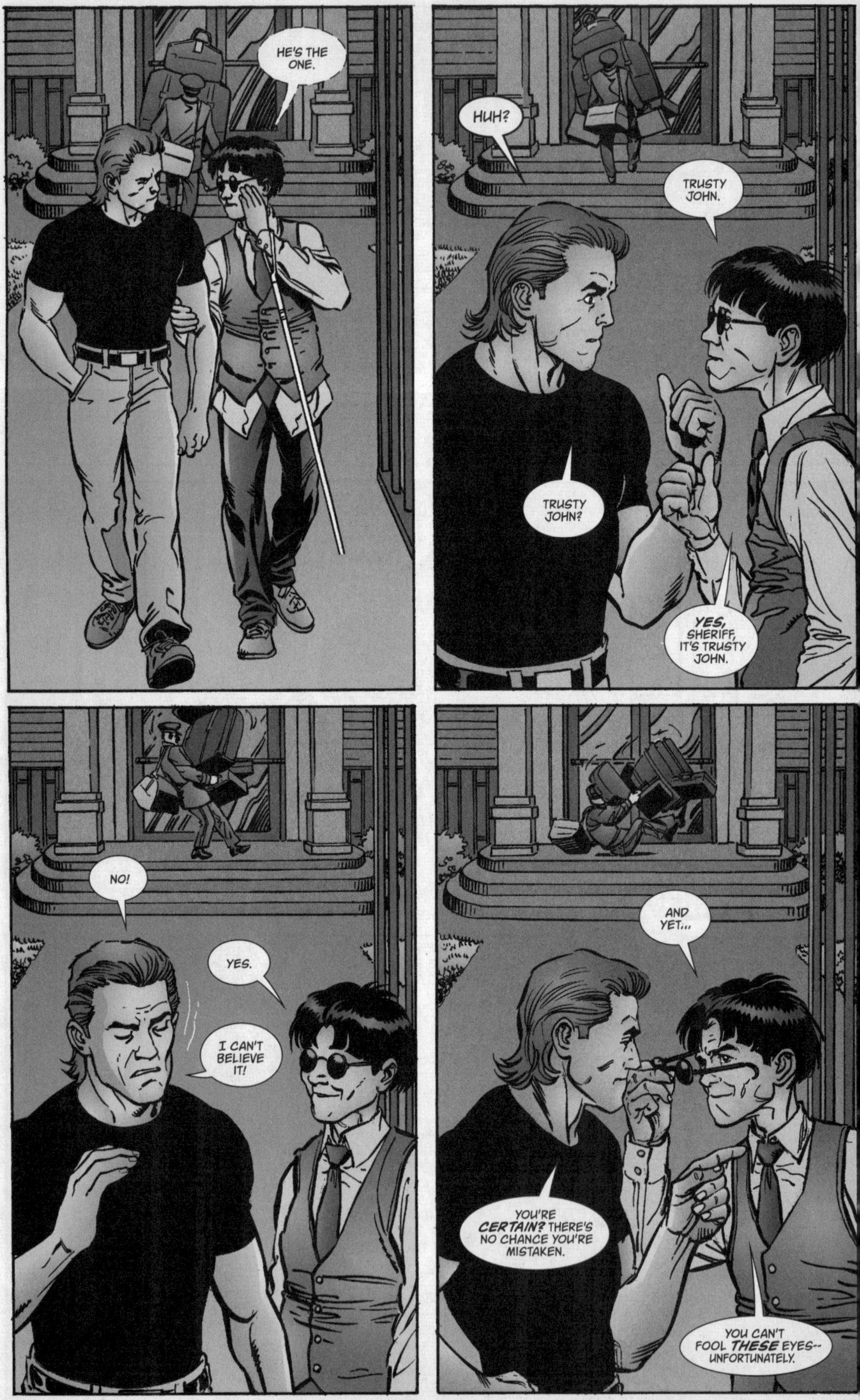
HE'S THE ONE.
HUH?
TRUSTY JOHN.
TRUSTY JOHN?
YES, SHERIFF, IT'S TRUSTY JOHN.
NO!
YES.
I CAN'T BELIEVE IT!
AND YET...
YOU'RE CERTAIN? THERE'S NO CHANCE YOU'RE MISTAKEN.
YOU CAN'T FOOL THESE EYES-- UNFORTUNATELY.

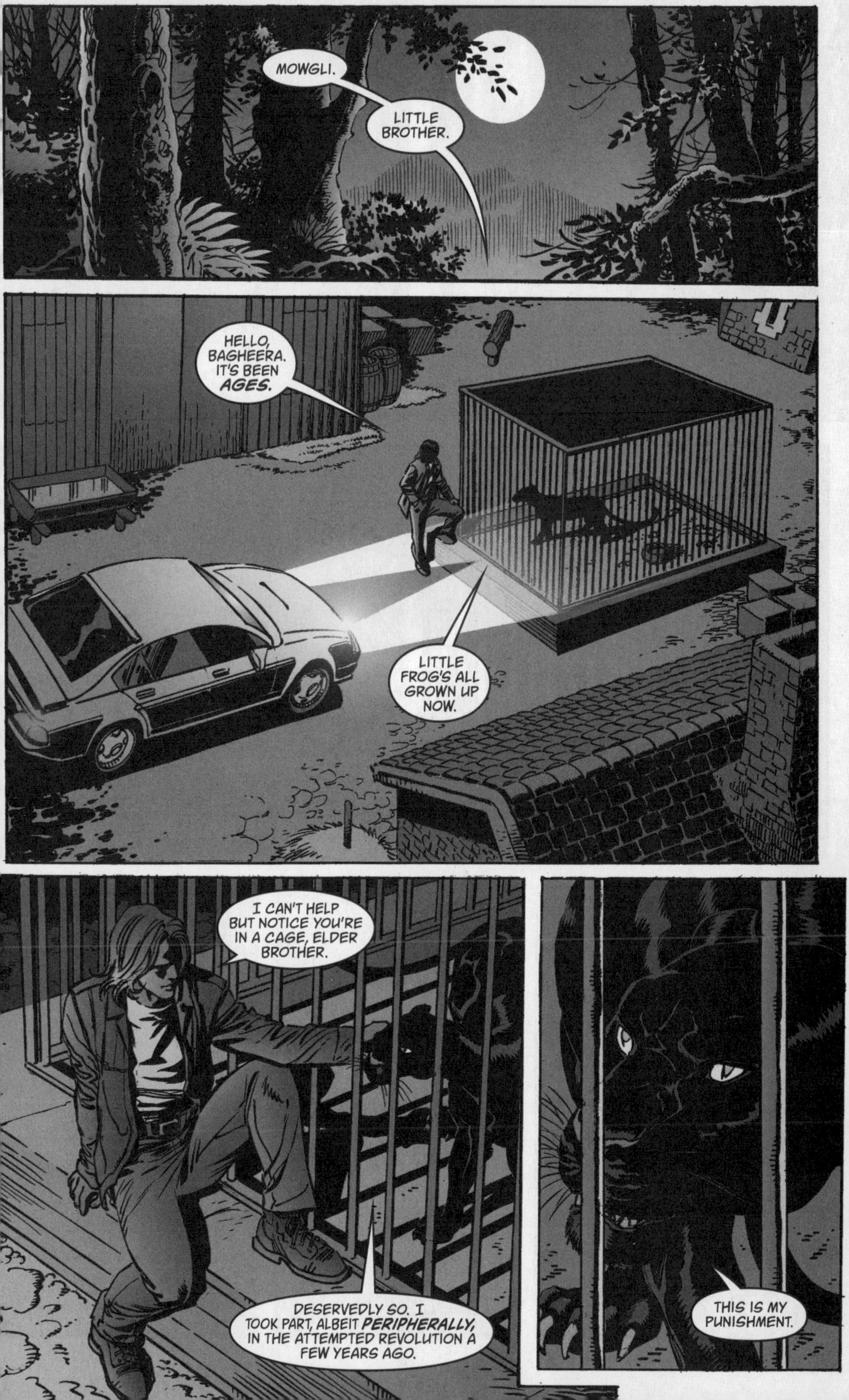
MOWGLI.
LITTLE BROTHER.
HELLO, BAGHEERA. IT'S BEEN AGES.
LITTLE FROG'S ALL GROWN UP NOW.
I CAN'T HELP BUT NOTICE YOU'RE IN A CAGE, ELDER BROTHER.
DESERVEDLY SO. I TOOK PART, ALBEIT PERIPHERALLY, IN THE ATTEMPTED REVOLUTION A FEW YEARS AGO.
THIS IS MY PUNISHMENT.

YOU *ALONE?* WHY DID THEY SINGLE YOU OUT?

NO ONE DID. THE RING-LEADERS WERE EXECUTED. THE REST WERE GIVEN A CHOICE OF HARD LABOR OR JAIL TIME.

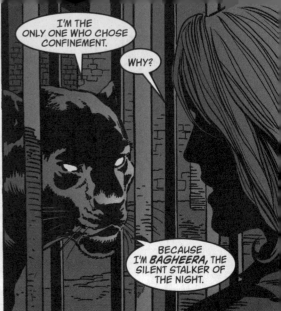

I'M THE ONLY ONE WHO CHOSE CONFINEMENT.

WHY?

BECAUSE I'M *BAGHEERA*, THE SILENT STALKER OF THE NIGHT.

I'M NO LOWLY OX OR PLOW-HORSE. I *REFUSE* TO LABOR IN THE FIELDS, LIKE SOME COMMON *DRAFT* ANIMAL.

HMMM.

WELL, I'M HERE TO SPRING YOU.

HOW DO YOU PROPOSE TO DO *THAT?*

I'M NOT SURE.

BUT I'LL FIGURE SOMETHING OUT. I OWE YOU A *BLOOD* DEBT. YOU RANSOMED MY LIFE AMONG THE SEEONEE WOLF PACK.

I KILLED A FAT BULL TO BRIBE THEM INTO *ACCEPTING* YOU.

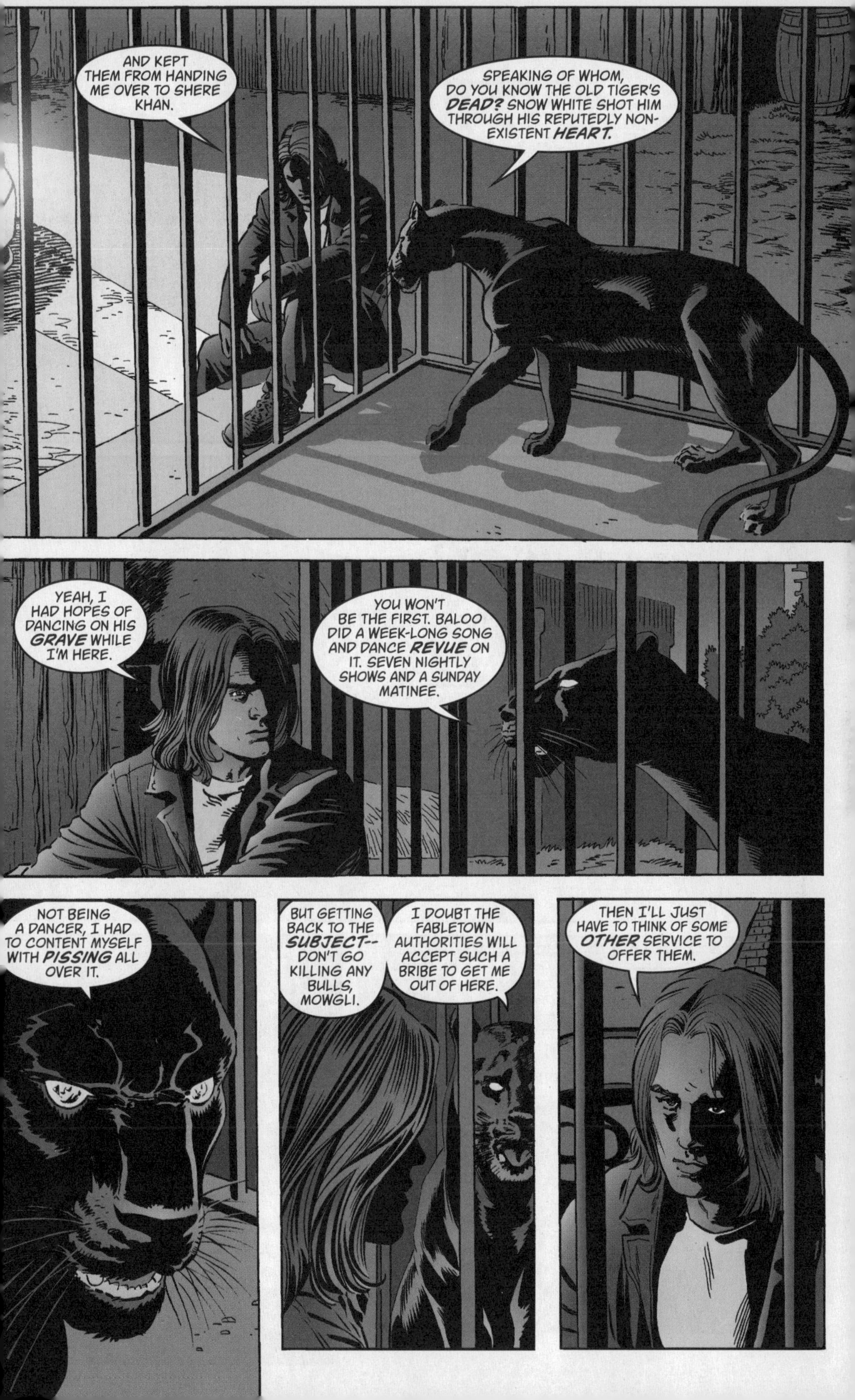
AND KEPT THEM FROM HANDING ME OVER TO SHERE KHAN.
SPEAKING OF WHOM, DO YOU KNOW THE OLD TIGER'S **DEAD?** SNOW WHITE SHOT HIM THROUGH HIS REPUTEDLY NON-EXISTENT **HEART.**
YEAH, I HAD HOPES OF DANCING ON HIS **GRAVE** WHILE I'M HERE.
YOU WON'T BE THE FIRST. BALOO DID A WEEK-LONG SONG AND DANCE **REVUE** ON IT. SEVEN NIGHTLY SHOWS AND A SUNDAY MATINEE.
NOT BEING A DANCER, I HAD TO CONTENT MYSELF WITH **PISSING** ALL OVER IT.
BUT GETTING BACK TO THE **SUBJECT--** DON'T GO KILLING ANY BULLS, MOWGLI.
I DOUBT THE FABLETOWN AUTHORITIES WILL ACCEPT SUCH A BRIBE TO GET ME OUT OF HERE.
THEN I'LL JUST HAVE TO THINK OF SOME **OTHER** SERVICE TO OFFER THEM.

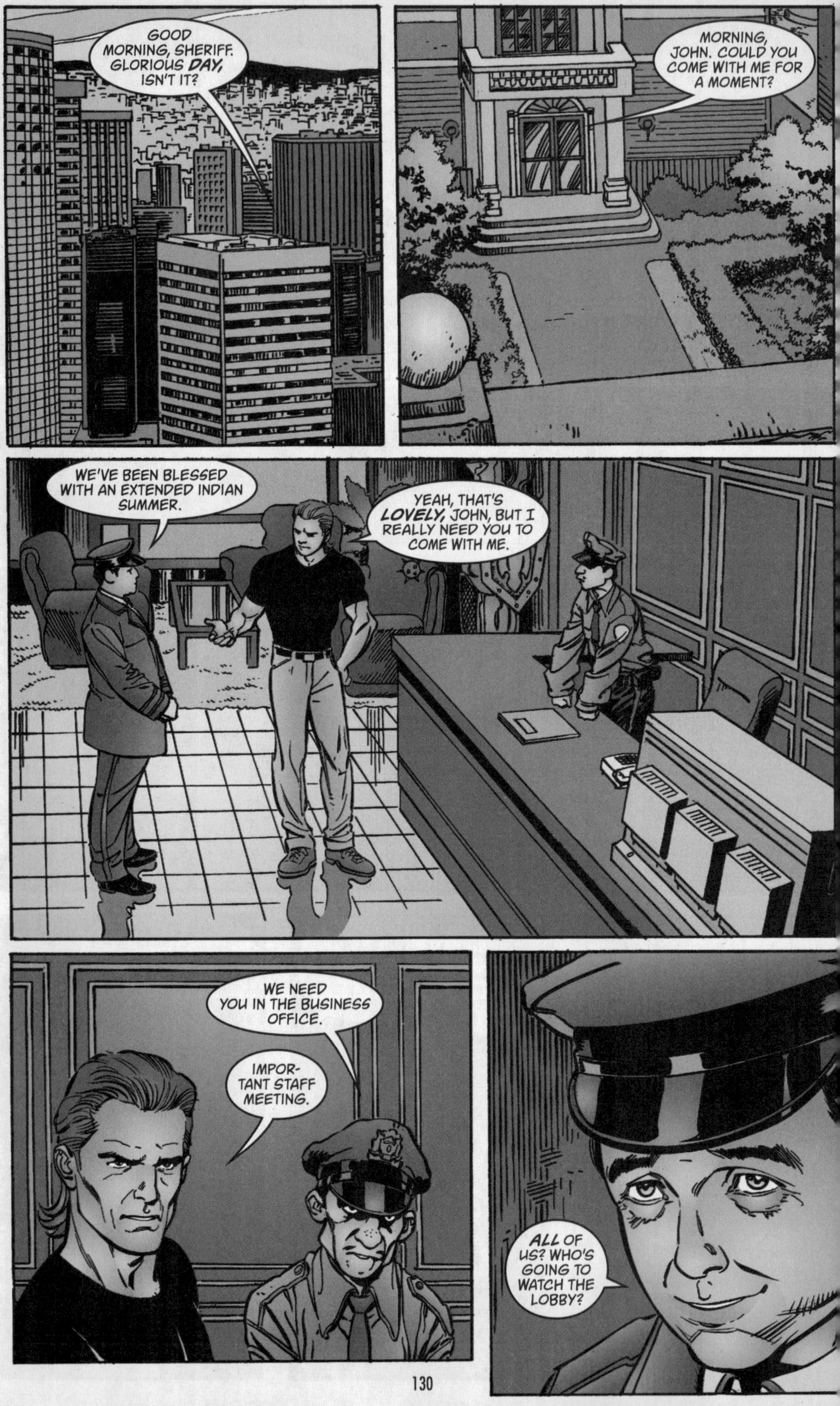
GOOD MORNING, SHERIFF. GLORIOUS DAY, ISN'T IT?
MORNING, JOHN. COULD YOU COME WITH ME FOR A MOMENT?
WE'VE BEEN BLESSED WITH AN EXTENDED INDIAN SUMMER.
YEAH, THAT'S LOVELY, JOHN, BUT I REALLY NEED YOU TO COME WITH ME.
WE NEED YOU IN THE BUSINESS OFFICE.
IMPORTANT STAFF MEETING.
ALL OF US? WHO'S GOING TO WATCH THE LOBBY?

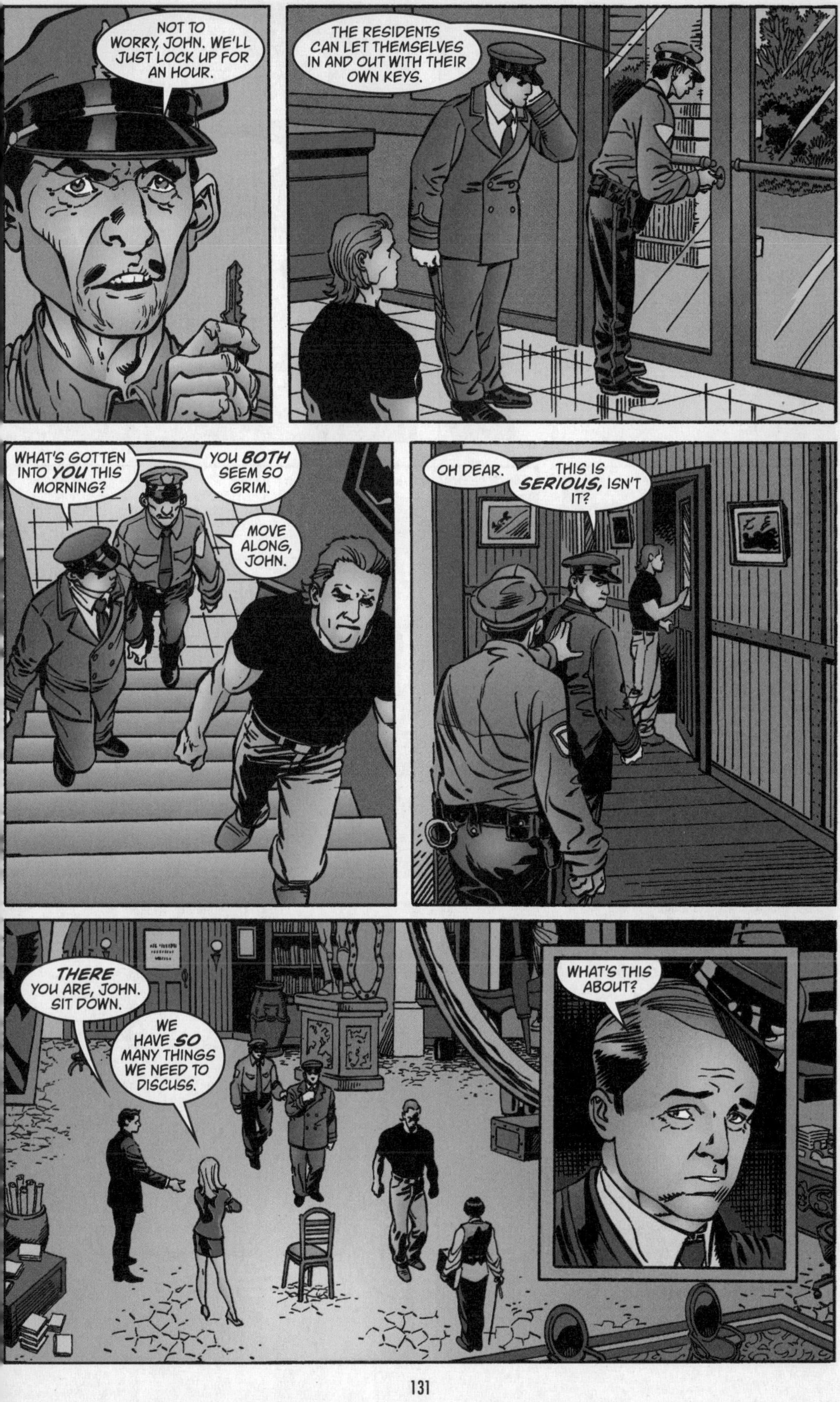
NOT TO WORRY, JOHN. WE'LL JUST LOCK UP FOR AN HOUR.
THE RESIDENTS CAN LET THEMSELVES IN AND OUT WITH THEIR OWN KEYS.
WHAT'S GOTTEN INTO YOU THIS MORNING?
YOU BOTH SEEM SO GRIM.
MOVE ALONG, JOHN.
OH DEAR.
THIS IS SERIOUS, ISN'T IT?
THERE YOU ARE, JOHN. SIT DOWN.
WE HAVE SO MANY THINGS WE NEED TO DISCUSS.
WHAT'S THIS ABOUT?

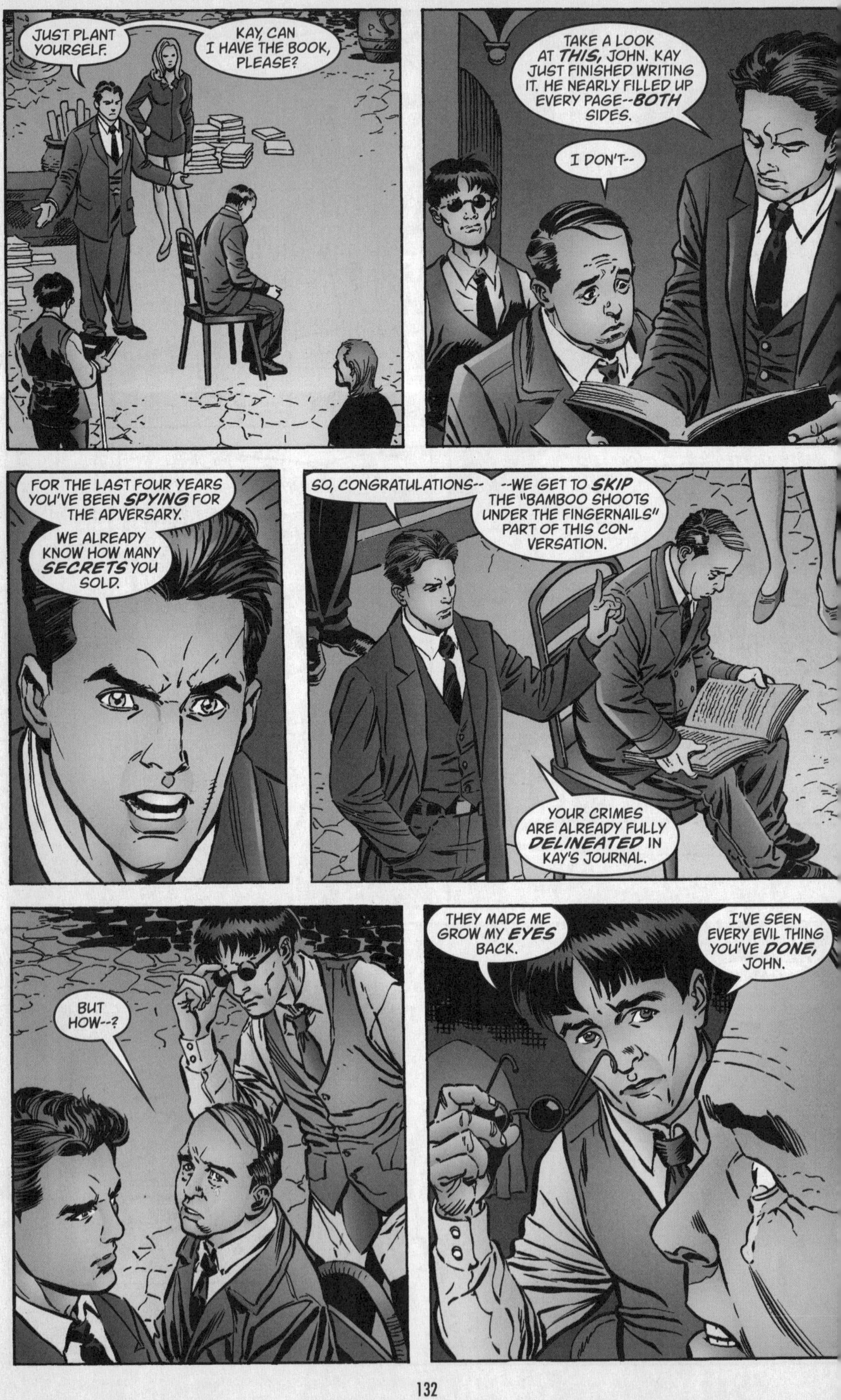
JUST PLANT YOURSELF.
KAY, CAN I HAVE THE BOOK, PLEASE?
TAKE A LOOK AT THIS, JOHN. KAY JUST FINISHED WRITING IT. HE NEARLY FILLED UP EVERY PAGE--BOTH SIDES.
I DON'T--
FOR THE LAST FOUR YEARS YOU'VE BEEN SPYING FOR THE ADVERSARY.
WE ALREADY KNOW HOW MANY SECRETS YOU SOLD.
SO, CONGRATULATIONS--
--WE GET TO SKIP THE "BAMBOO SHOOTS UNDER THE FINGERNAILS" PART OF THIS CONVERSATION.
YOUR CRIMES ARE ALREADY FULLY DELINEATED IN KAY'S JOURNAL.
BUT HOW--?
THEY MADE ME GROW MY EYES BACK.
I'VE SEEN EVERY EVIL THING YOU'VE DONE, JOHN.

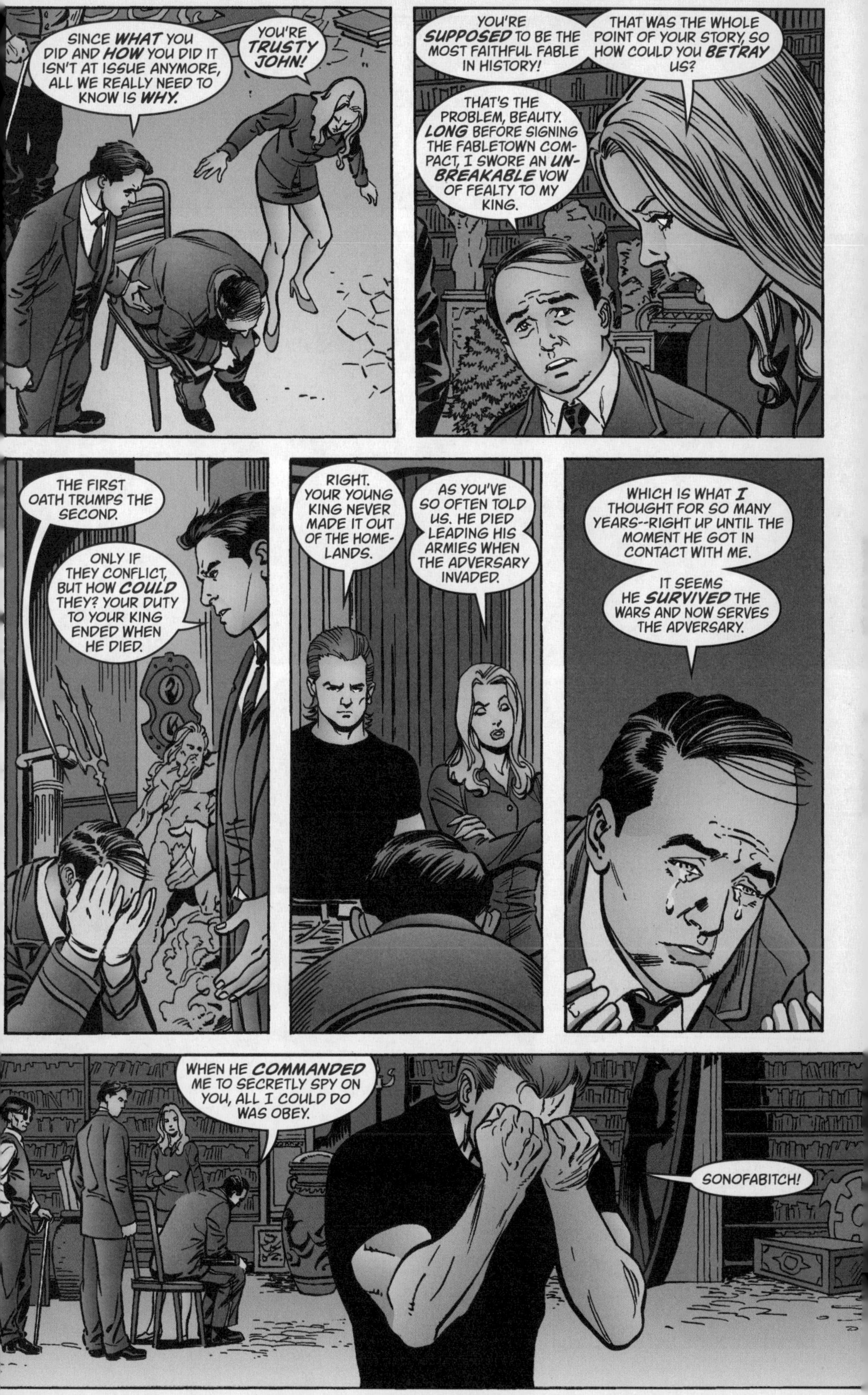
SINCE WHAT YOU DID AND HOW YOU DID IT ISN'T AT ISSUE ANYMORE, ALL WE REALLY NEED TO KNOW IS WHY.
YOU'RE TRUSTY JOHN!
YOU'RE SUPPOSED TO BE THE MOST FAITHFUL FABLE IN HISTORY!
THAT WAS THE WHOLE POINT OF YOUR STORY, SO HOW COULD YOU BETRAY US?
THAT'S THE PROBLEM, BEAUTY. LONG BEFORE SIGNING THE FABLETOWN COMPACT, I SWORE AN UNBREAKABLE VOW OF FEALTY TO MY KING.
THE FIRST OATH TRUMPS THE SECOND.
ONLY IF THEY CONFLICT, BUT HOW COULD THEY? YOUR DUTY TO YOUR KING ENDED WHEN HE DIED.
RIGHT. YOUR YOUNG KING NEVER MADE IT OUT OF THE HOMELANDS.
AS YOU'VE SO OFTEN TOLD US. HE DIED LEADING HIS ARMIES WHEN THE ADVERSARY INVADED.
WHICH IS WHAT I THOUGHT FOR SO MANY YEARS--RIGHT UP UNTIL THE MOMENT HE GOT IN CONTACT WITH ME.
IT SEEMS HE SURVIVED THE WARS AND NOW SERVES THE ADVERSARY.
WHEN HE COMMANDED ME TO SECRETLY SPY ON YOU, ALL I COULD DO WAS OBEY.
SONOFABITCH!

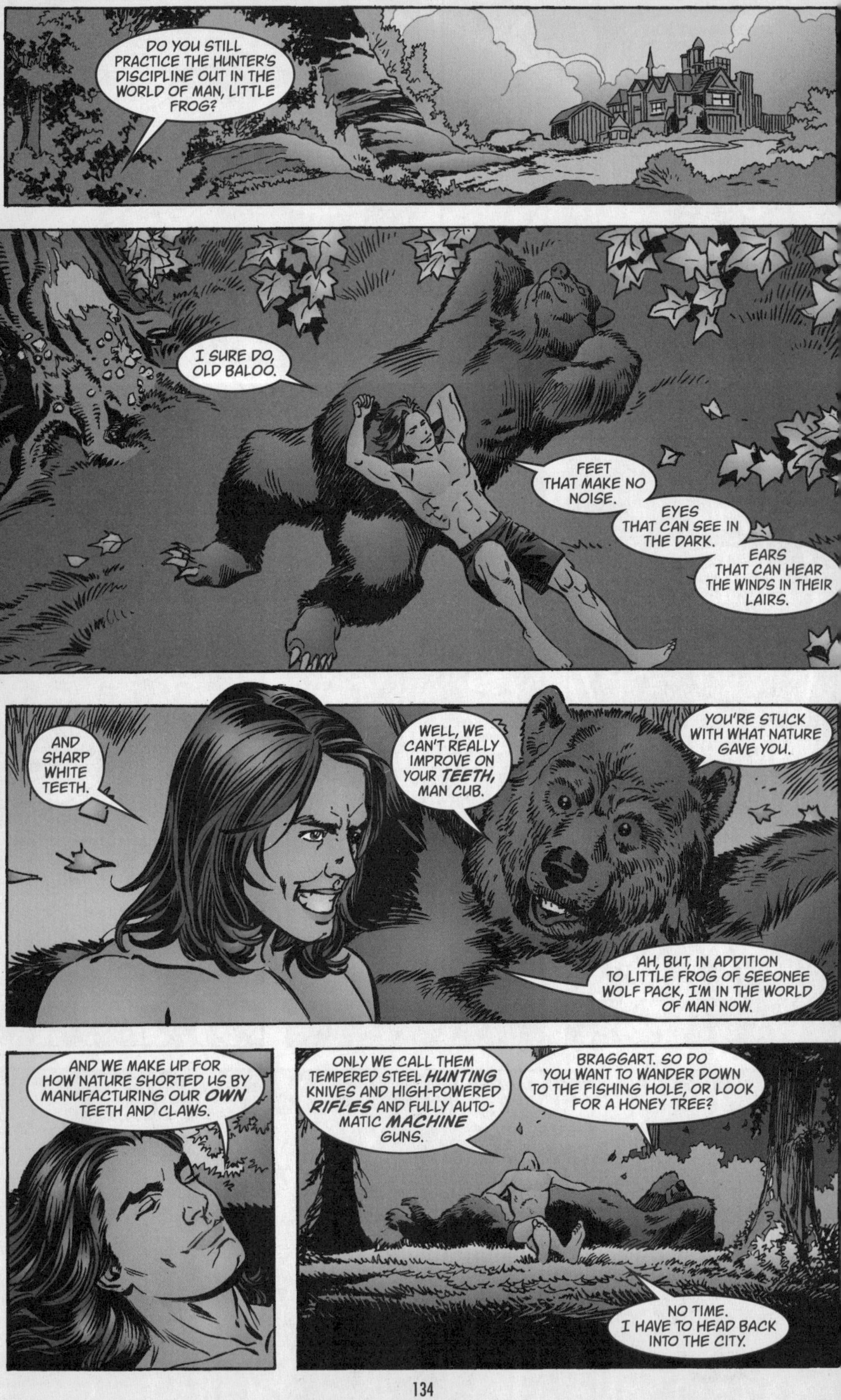
DO YOU STILL PRACTICE THE HUNTER'S DISCIPLINE OUT IN THE WORLD OF MAN, LITTLE FROG?
I SURE DO, OLD BALOO.
FEET THAT MAKE NO NOISE.
EYES THAT CAN SEE IN THE DARK.
EARS THAT CAN HEAR THE WINDS IN THEIR LAIRS.
AND SHARP WHITE TEETH.
WELL, WE CAN'T REALLY IMPROVE ON YOUR TEETH, MAN CUB.
YOU'RE STUCK WITH WHAT NATURE GAVE YOU.
AH, BUT, IN ADDITION TO LITTLE FROG OF SEEONEE WOLF PACK, I'M IN THE WORLD OF MAN NOW.
AND WE MAKE UP FOR HOW NATURE SHORTED US BY MANUFACTURING OUR OWN TEETH AND CLAWS.
ONLY WE CALL THEM TEMPERED STEEL HUNTING KNIVES AND HIGH-POWERED RIFLES AND FULLY AUTO-MATIC MACHINE GUNS.
BRAGGART. SO DO YOU WANT TO WANDER DOWN TO THE FISHING HOLE, OR LOOK FOR A HONEY TREE?
NO TIME. I HAVE TO HEAD BACK INTO THE CITY.

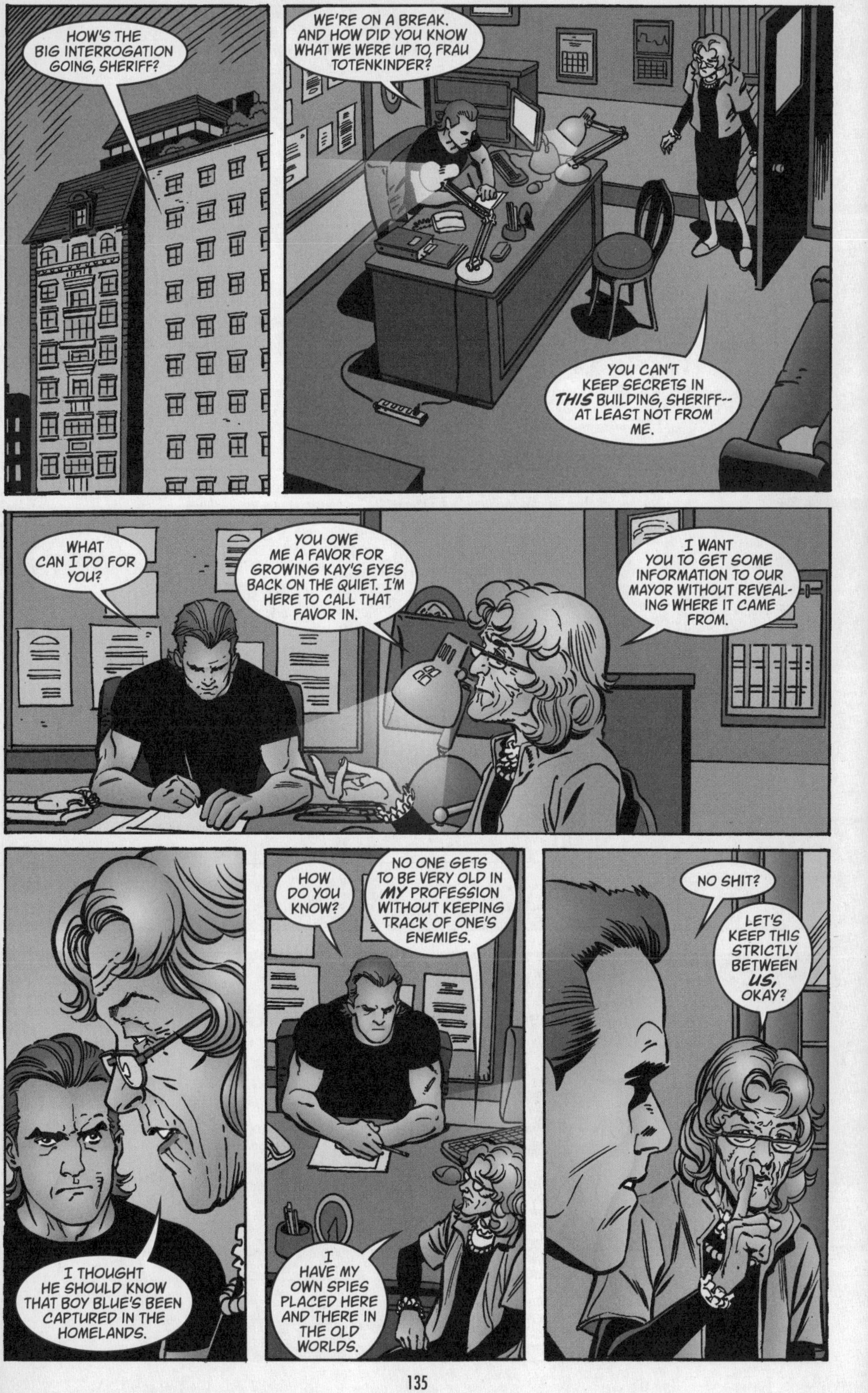
HOW'S THE BIG INTERROGATION GOING, SHERIFF?
WE'RE ON A BREAK. AND HOW DID YOU KNOW WHAT WE WERE UP TO, FRAU TOTENKINDER?
YOU CAN'T KEEP SECRETS IN THIS BUILDING, SHERIFF-- AT LEAST NOT FROM ME.
WHAT CAN I DO FOR YOU?
YOU OWE ME A FAVOR FOR GROWING KAY'S EYES BACK ON THE QUIET. I'M HERE TO CALL THAT FAVOR IN.
I WANT YOU TO GET SOME INFORMATION TO OUR MAYOR WITHOUT REVEALING WHERE IT CAME FROM.
I THOUGHT HE SHOULD KNOW THAT BOY BLUE'S BEEN CAPTURED IN THE HOMELANDS.
HOW DO YOU KNOW?
I HAVE MY OWN SPIES PLACED HERE AND THERE IN THE OLD WORLDS.
NO ONE GETS TO BE VERY OLD IN MY PROFESSION WITHOUT KEEPING TRACK OF ONE'S ENEMIES.
NO SHIT?
LET'S KEEP THIS STRICTLY BETWEEN US, OKAY?

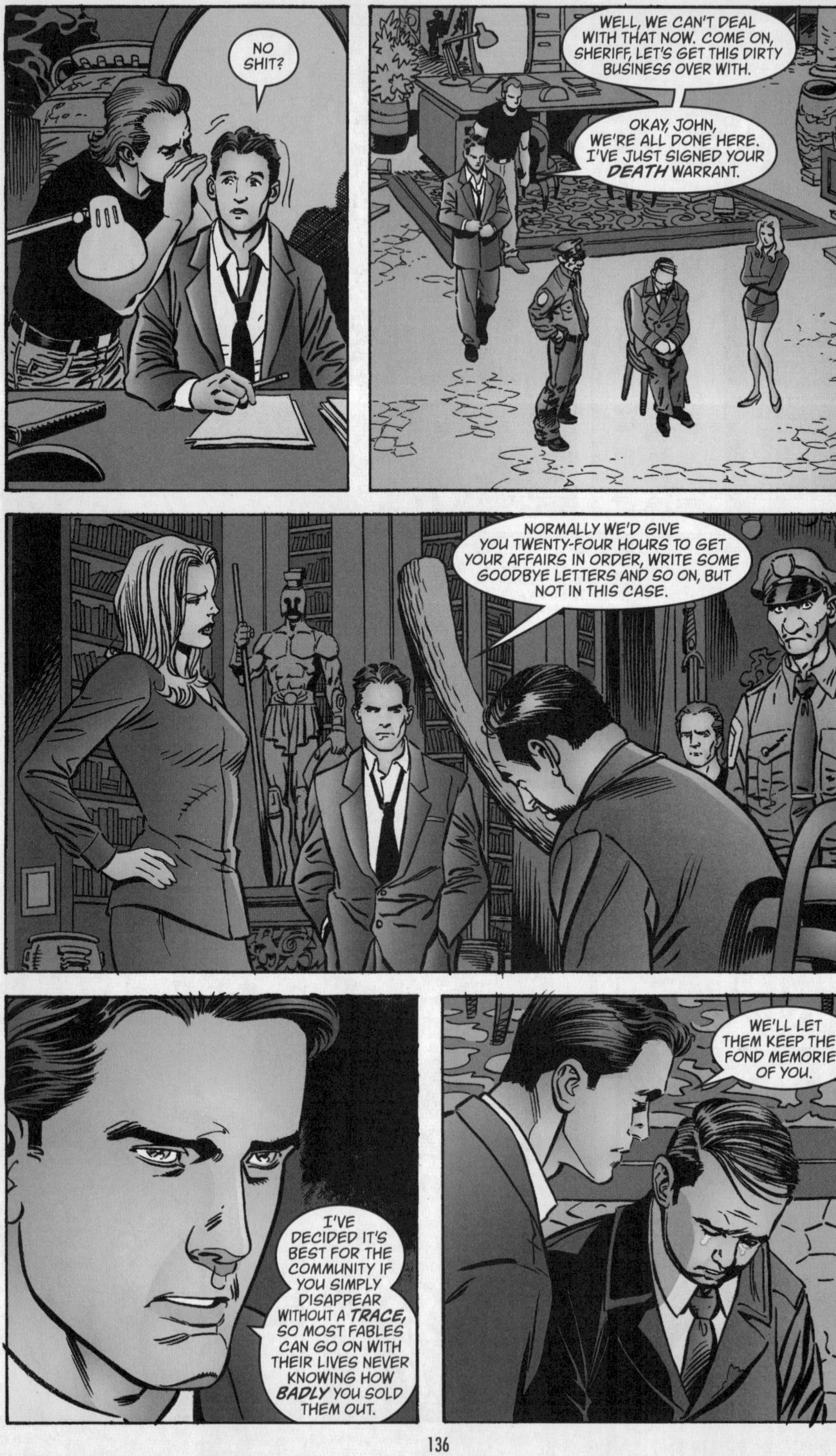
NO SHIT?
WELL, WE CAN'T DEAL WITH THAT NOW. COME ON, SHERIFF, LET'S GET THIS DIRTY BUSINESS OVER WITH.
OKAY, JOHN, WE'RE ALL DONE HERE. I'VE JUST SIGNED YOUR DEATH WARRANT.
NORMALLY WE'D GIVE YOU TWENTY-FOUR HOURS TO GET YOUR AFFAIRS IN ORDER, WRITE SOME GOODBYE LETTERS AND SO ON, BUT NOT IN THIS CASE.
I'VE DECIDED IT'S BEST FOR THE COMMUNITY IF YOU SIMPLY DISAPPEAR WITHOUT A TRACE, SO MOST FABLES CAN GO ON WITH THEIR LIVES NEVER KNOWING HOW BADLY YOU SOLD THEM OUT.
WE'LL LET THEM KEEP THEIR FOND MEMORIES OF YOU.

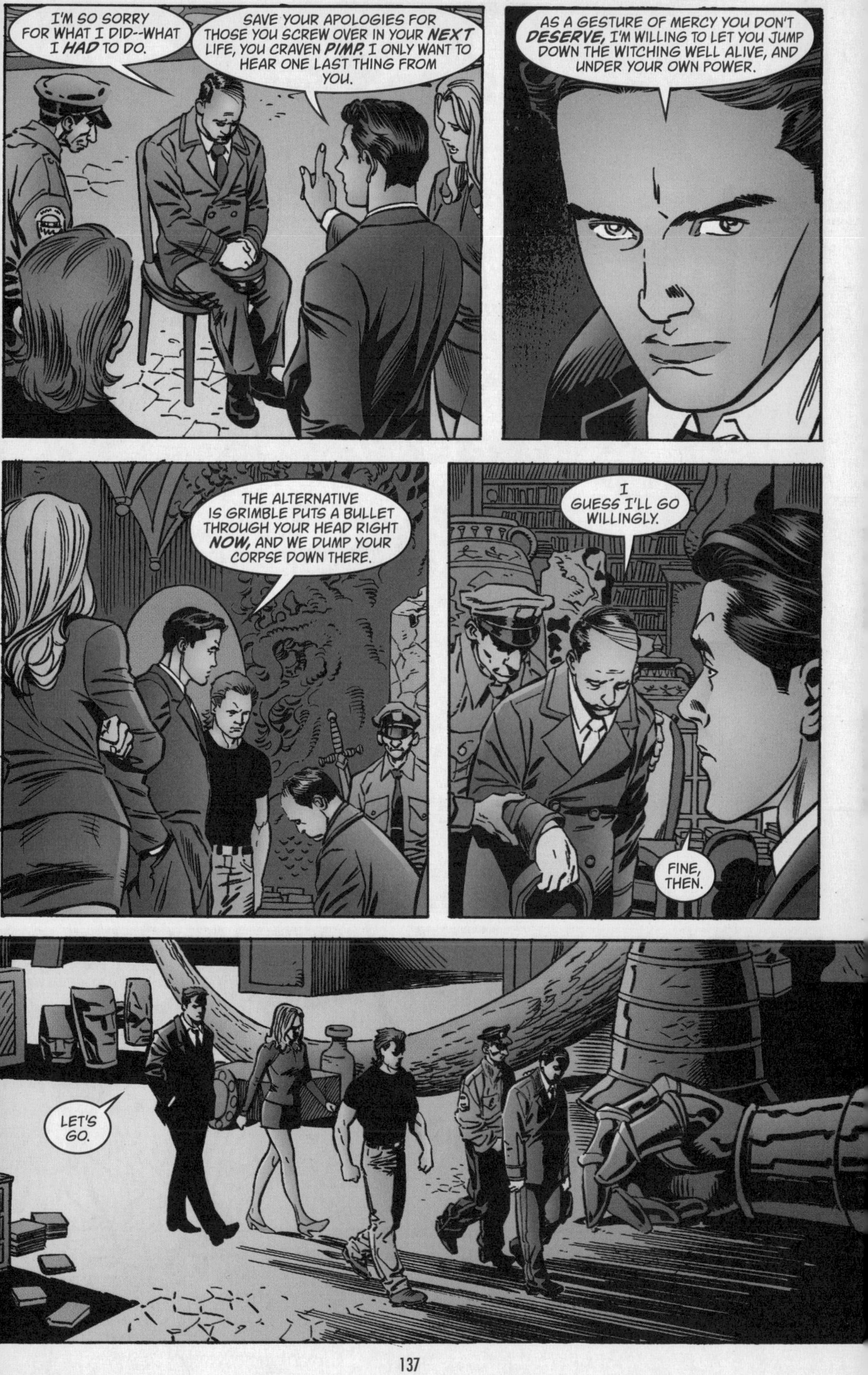

I'M SO SORRY FOR WHAT I DID--WHAT I *HAD* TO DO.
SAVE YOUR APOLOGIES FOR THOSE YOU SCREW OVER IN YOUR *NEXT* LIFE, YOU CRAVEN *PIMP*. I ONLY WANT TO HEAR ONE LAST THING FROM YOU.
AS A GESTURE OF MERCY YOU DON'T *DESERVE*, I'M WILLING TO LET YOU JUMP DOWN THE WITCHING WELL ALIVE, AND UNDER YOUR OWN POWER.
THE ALTERNATIVE IS GRIMBLE PUTS A BULLET THROUGH YOUR HEAD RIGHT *NOW*, AND WE DUMP YOUR CORPSE DOWN THERE.
I GUESS I'LL GO WILLINGLY.
FINE, THEN.
LET'S GO.

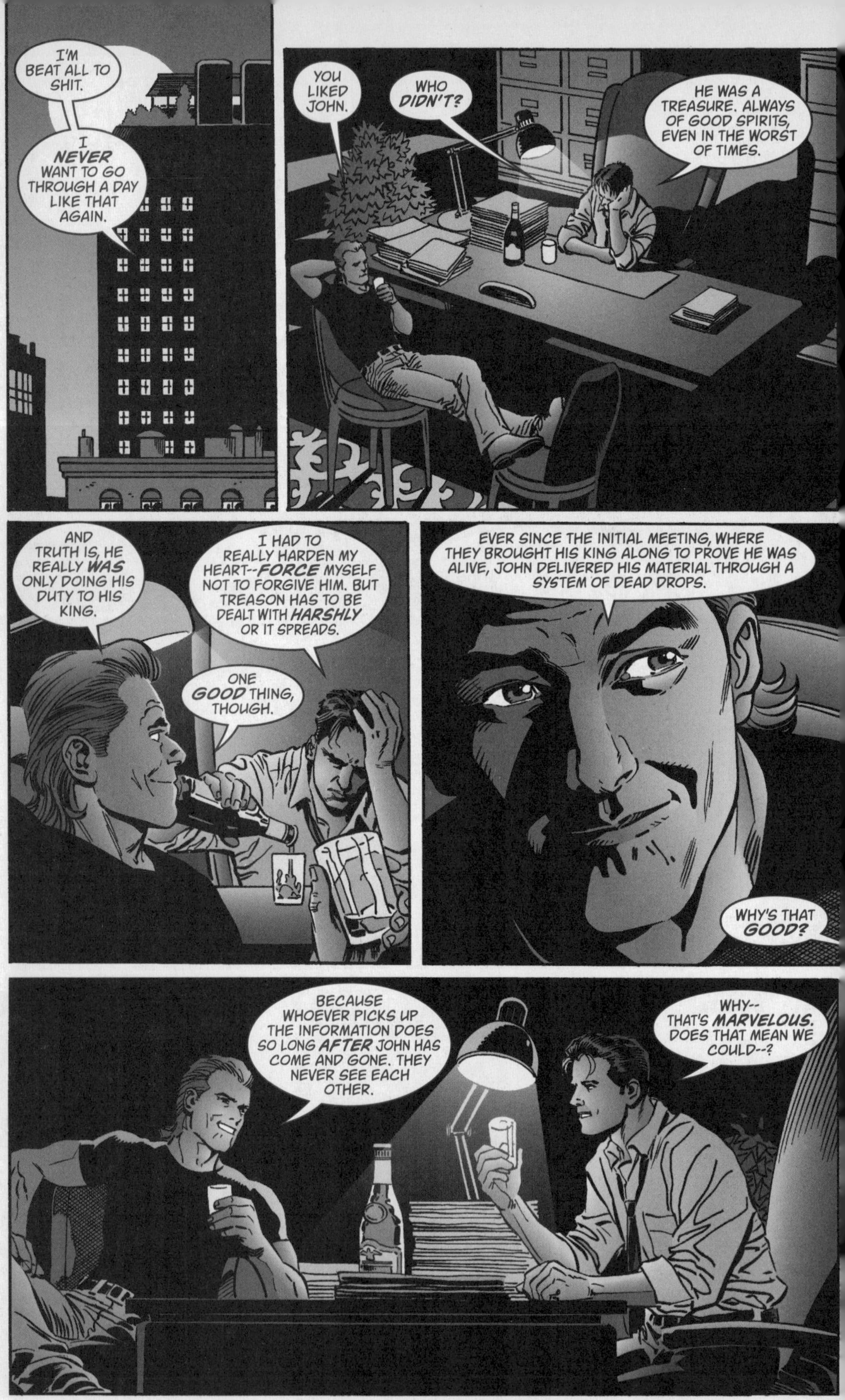
I'M BEAT ALL TO SHIT.
I NEVER WANT TO GO THROUGH A DAY LIKE THAT AGAIN.
YOU LIKED JOHN.
WHO DIDN'T?
HE WAS A TREASURE. ALWAYS OF GOOD SPIRITS, EVEN IN THE WORST OF TIMES.
AND TRUTH IS, HE REALLY WAS ONLY DOING HIS DUTY TO HIS KING.
I HAD TO REALLY HARDEN MY HEART--FORCE MYSELF NOT TO FORGIVE HIM. BUT TREASON HAS TO BE DEALT WITH HARSHLY OR IT SPREADS.
ONE GOOD THING, THOUGH.
EVER SINCE THE INITIAL MEETING, WHERE THEY BROUGHT HIS KING ALONG TO PROVE HE WAS ALIVE, JOHN DELIVERED HIS MATERIAL THROUGH A SYSTEM OF DEAD DROPS.
WHY'S THAT GOOD?
BECAUSE WHOEVER PICKS UP THE INFORMATION DOES SO LONG AFTER JOHN HAS COME AND GONE. THEY NEVER SEE EACH OTHER.
WHY--THAT'S MARVELOUS. DOES THAT MEAN WE COULD--?

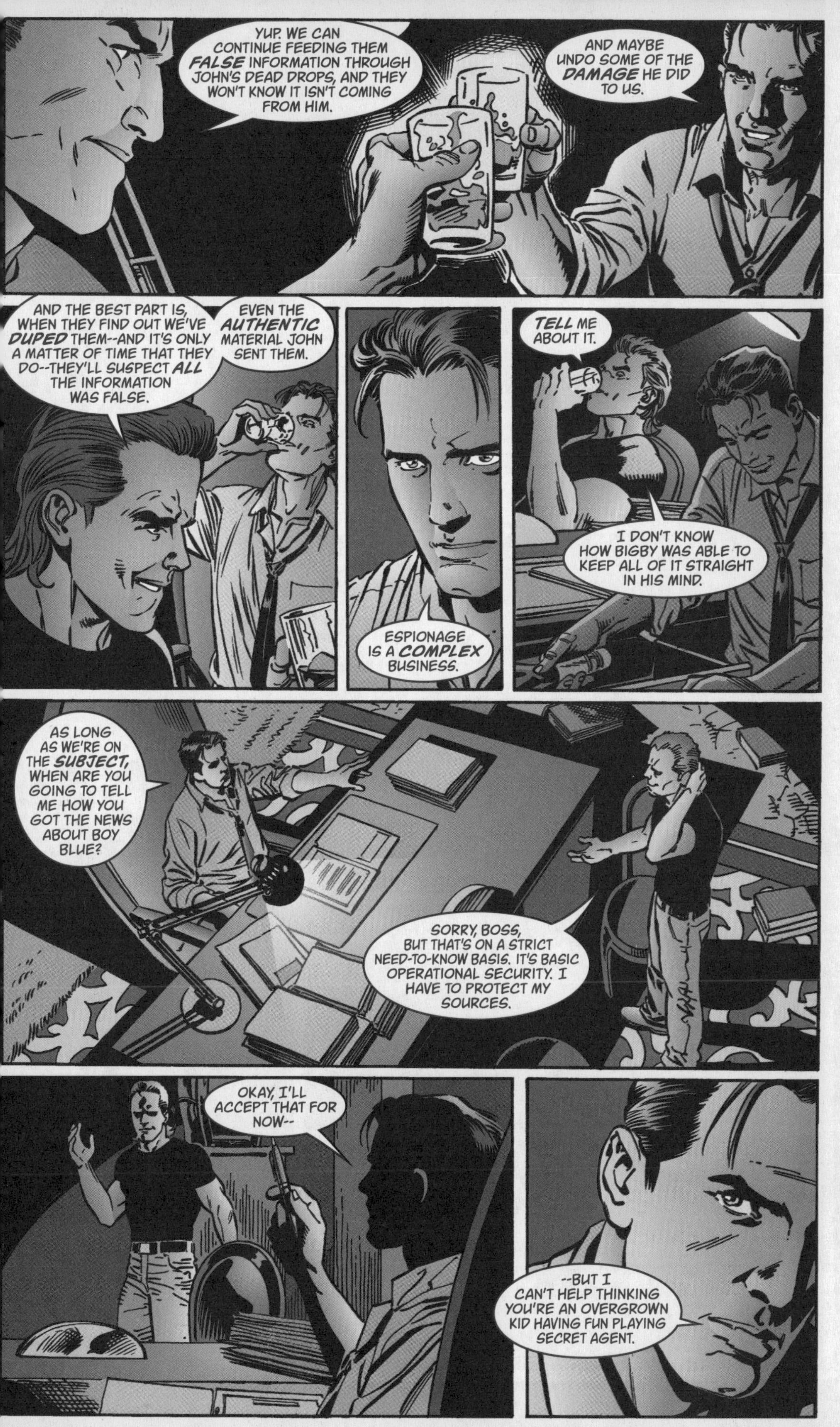
YUP. WE CAN CONTINUE FEEDING THEM FALSE INFORMATION THROUGH JOHN'S DEAD DROPS, AND THEY WON'T KNOW IT ISN'T COMING FROM HIM.
AND MAYBE UNDO SOME OF THE DAMAGE HE DID TO US.
AND THE BEST PART IS, WHEN THEY FIND OUT WE'VE DUPED THEM--AND IT'S ONLY A MATTER OF TIME THAT THEY DO--THEY'LL SUSPECT ALL THE INFORMATION WAS FALSE.
EVEN THE AUTHENTIC MATERIAL JOHN SENT THEM.
ESPIONAGE IS A COMPLEX BUSINESS.
TELL ME ABOUT IT.
I DON'T KNOW HOW BIGBY WAS ABLE TO KEEP ALL OF IT STRAIGHT IN HIS MIND.
AS LONG AS WE'RE ON THE SUBJECT, WHEN ARE YOU GOING TO TELL ME HOW YOU GOT THE NEWS ABOUT BOY BLUE?
SORRY, BOSS, BUT THAT'S ON A STRICT NEED-TO-KNOW BASIS. IT'S BASIC OPERATIONAL SECURITY. I HAVE TO PROTECT MY SOURCES.
OKAY, I'LL ACCEPT THAT FOR NOW--
--BUT I CAN'T HELP THINKING YOU'RE AN OVERGROWN KID HAVING FUN PLAYING SECRET AGENT.

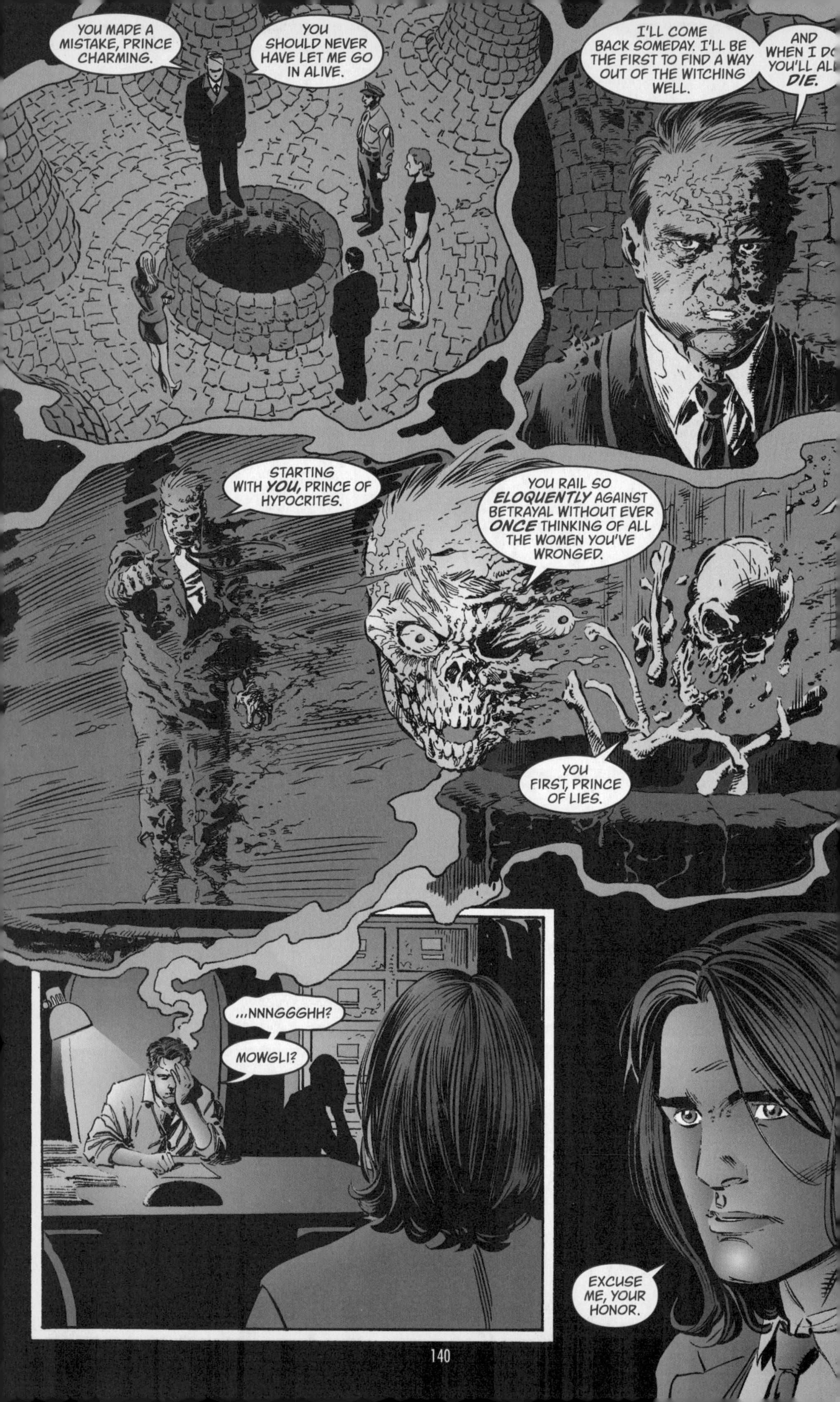
YOU MADE A MISTAKE, PRINCE CHARMING.
YOU SHOULD NEVER HAVE LET ME GO IN ALIVE.
I'LL COME BACK SOMEDAY. I'LL BE THE FIRST TO FIND A WAY OUT OF THE WITCHING WELL.
AND WHEN I DO YOU'LL ALL DIE.
STARTING WITH YOU, PRINCE OF HYPOCRITES.
YOU RAIL SO ELOQUENTLY AGAINST BETRAYAL WITHOUT EVER ONCE THINKING OF ALL THE WOMEN YOU'VE WRONGED.
YOU FIRST, PRINCE OF LIES.
...NNNGGGHH?
MOWGLI?
EXCUSE ME, YOUR HONOR.

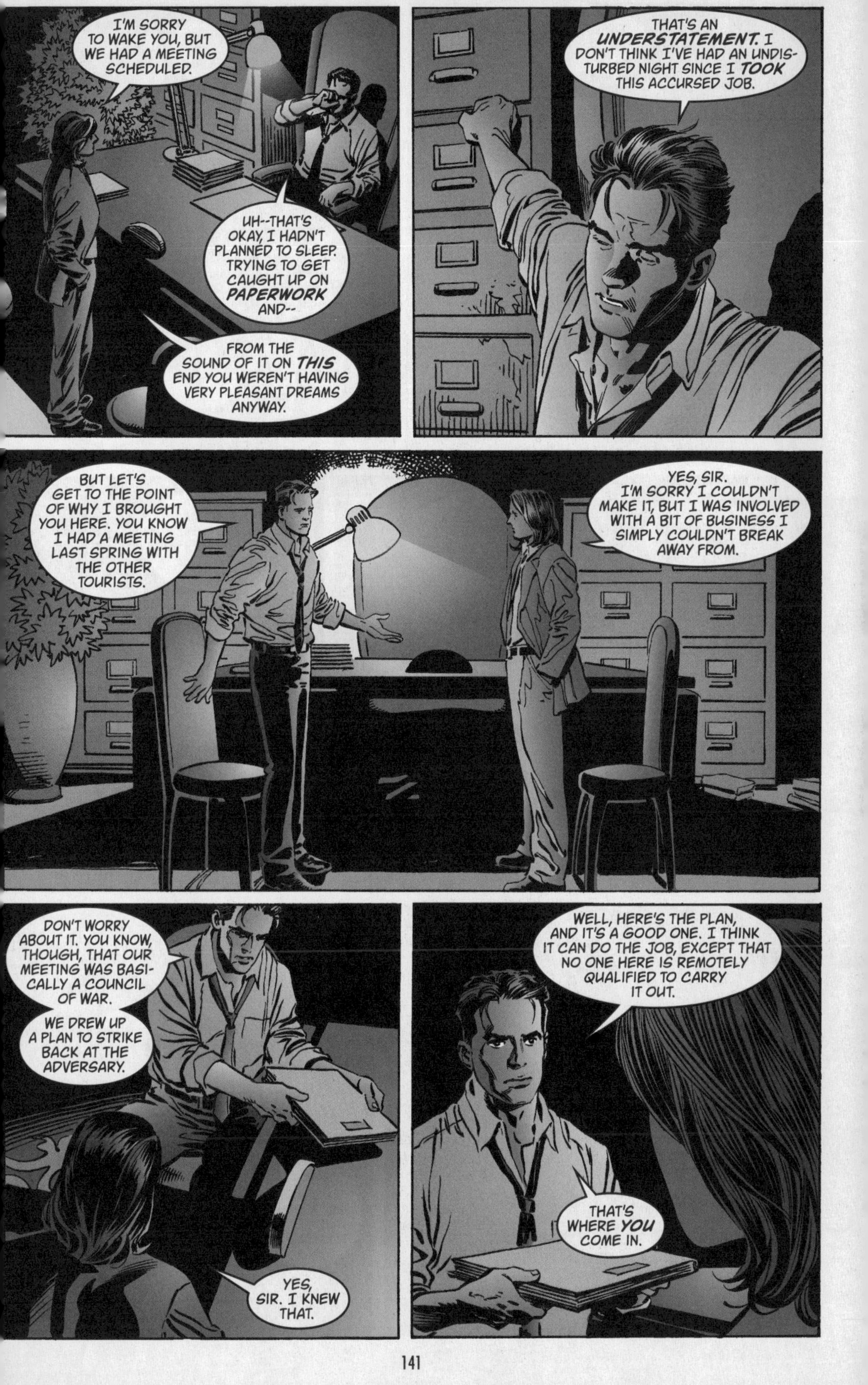
I'M SORRY TO WAKE YOU, BUT WE HAD A MEETING SCHEDULED.
UH--THAT'S OKAY, I HADN'T PLANNED TO SLEEP. TRYING TO GET CAUGHT UP ON PAPERWORK AND--
FROM THE SOUND OF IT ON THIS END YOU WEREN'T HAVING VERY PLEASANT DREAMS ANYWAY.
THAT'S AN UNDERSTATEMENT. I DON'T THINK I'VE HAD AN UNDISTURBED NIGHT SINCE I TOOK THIS ACCURSED JOB.
BUT LET'S GET TO THE POINT OF WHY I BROUGHT YOU HERE. YOU KNOW I HAD A MEETING LAST SPRING WITH THE OTHER TOURISTS.
YES, SIR. I'M SORRY I COULDN'T MAKE IT, BUT I WAS INVOLVED WITH A BIT OF BUSINESS I SIMPLY COULDN'T BREAK AWAY FROM.
DON'T WORRY ABOUT IT. YOU KNOW, THOUGH, THAT OUR MEETING WAS BASICALLY A COUNCIL OF WAR.
WE DREW UP A PLAN TO STRIKE BACK AT THE ADVERSARY.
YES, SIR. I KNEW THAT.
WELL, HERE'S THE PLAN, AND IT'S A GOOD ONE. I THINK IT CAN DO THE JOB, EXCEPT THAT NO ONE HERE IS REMOTELY QUALIFIED TO CARRY IT OUT.
THAT'S WHERE YOU COME IN.

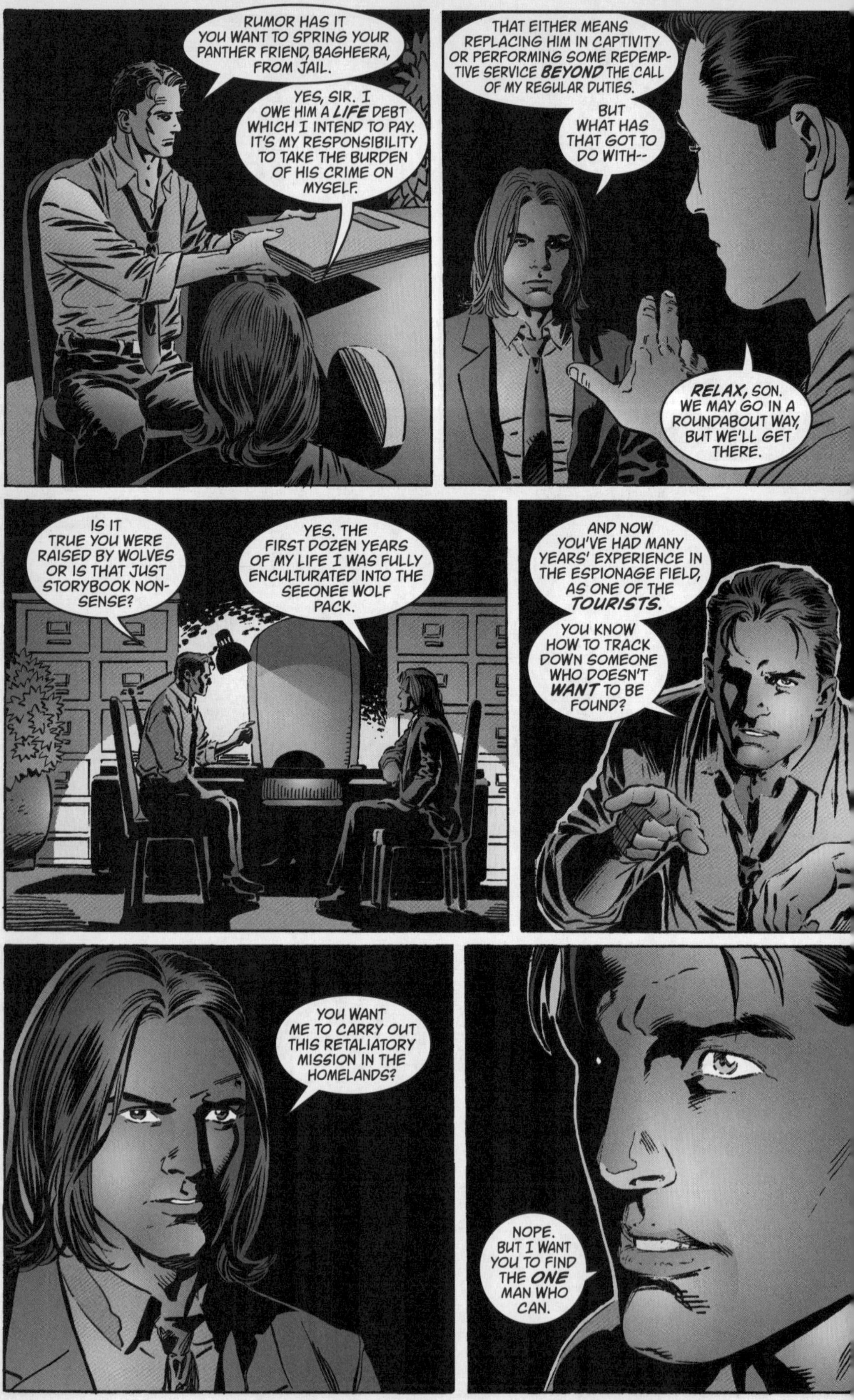
RUMOR HAS IT YOU WANT TO SPRING YOUR PANTHER FRIEND, BAGHEERA, FROM JAIL.
YES, SIR. I OWE HIM A LIFE DEBT WHICH I INTEND TO PAY. IT'S MY RESPONSIBILITY TO TAKE THE BURDEN OF HIS CRIME ON MYSELF.
THAT EITHER MEANS REPLACING HIM IN CAPTIVITY OR PERFORMING SOME REDEMP- TIVE SERVICE BEYOND THE CALL OF MY REGULAR DUTIES.
BUT WHAT HAS THAT GOT TO DO WITH--
RELAX, SON. WE MAY GO IN A ROUNDABOUT WAY, BUT WE'LL GET THERE.
IS IT TRUE YOU WERE RAISED BY WOLVES OR IS THAT JUST STORYBOOK NON- SENSE?
YES. THE FIRST DOZEN YEARS OF MY LIFE I WAS FULLY ENCULTURATED INTO THE SEEONEE WOLF PACK.
AND NOW YOU'VE HAD MANY YEARS' EXPERIENCE IN THE ESPIONAGE FIELD, AS ONE OF THE TOURISTS.
YOU KNOW HOW TO TRACK DOWN SOMEONE WHO DOESN'T WANT TO BE FOUND?
YOU WANT ME TO CARRY OUT THIS RETALIATORY MISSION IN THE HOMELANDS?
NOPE. BUT I WANT YOU TO FIND THE ONE MAN WHO CAN.

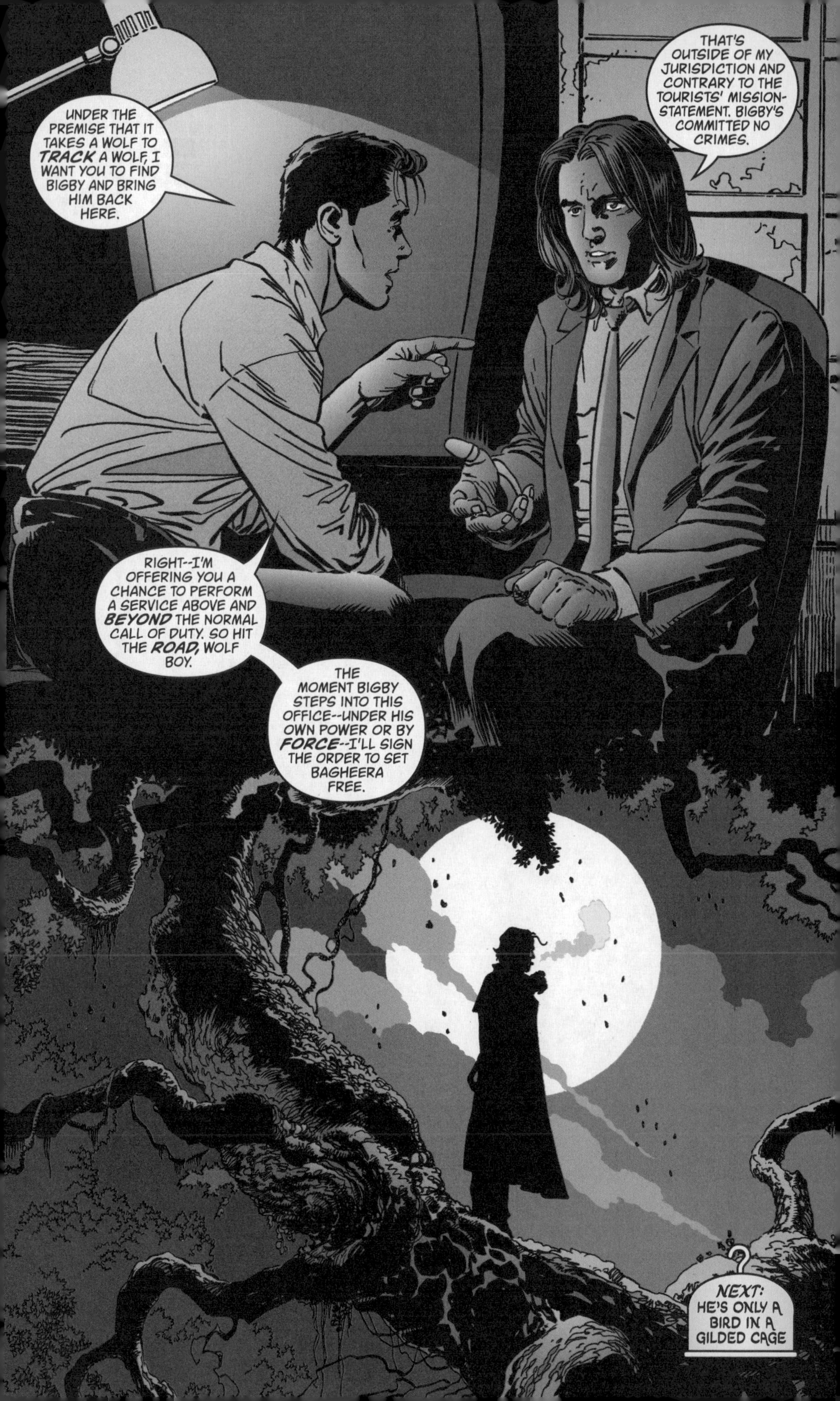
UNDER THE PREMISE THAT IT TAKES A WOLF TO TRACK A WOLF, I WANT YOU TO FIND BIGBY AND BRING HIM BACK HERE.
THAT'S OUTSIDE OF MY JURISDICTION AND CONTRARY TO THE TOURISTS' MISSION-STATEMENT. BIGBY'S COMMITTED NO CRIMES.
RIGHT--I'M OFFERING YOU A CHANCE TO PERFORM A SERVICE ABOVE AND BEYOND THE NORMAL CALL OF DUTY. SO HIT THE ROAD, WOLF BOY.
THE MOMENT BIGBY STEPS INTO THIS OFFICE--UNDER HIS OWN POWER OR BY FORCE--I'LL SIGN THE ORDER TO SET BAGHEERA FREE.
NEXT: HE'S ONLY A BIRD IN A GILDED CAGE

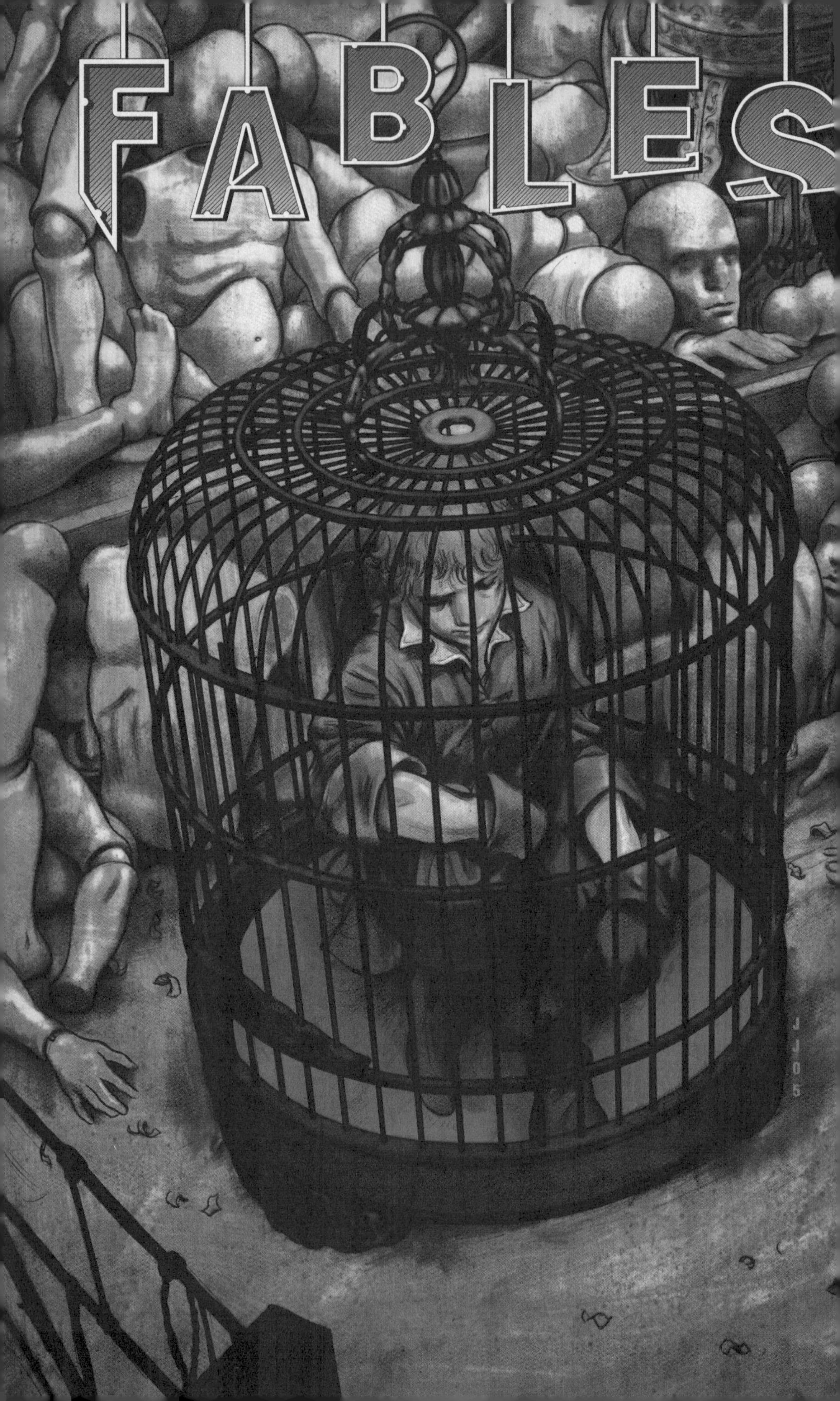
FABLES

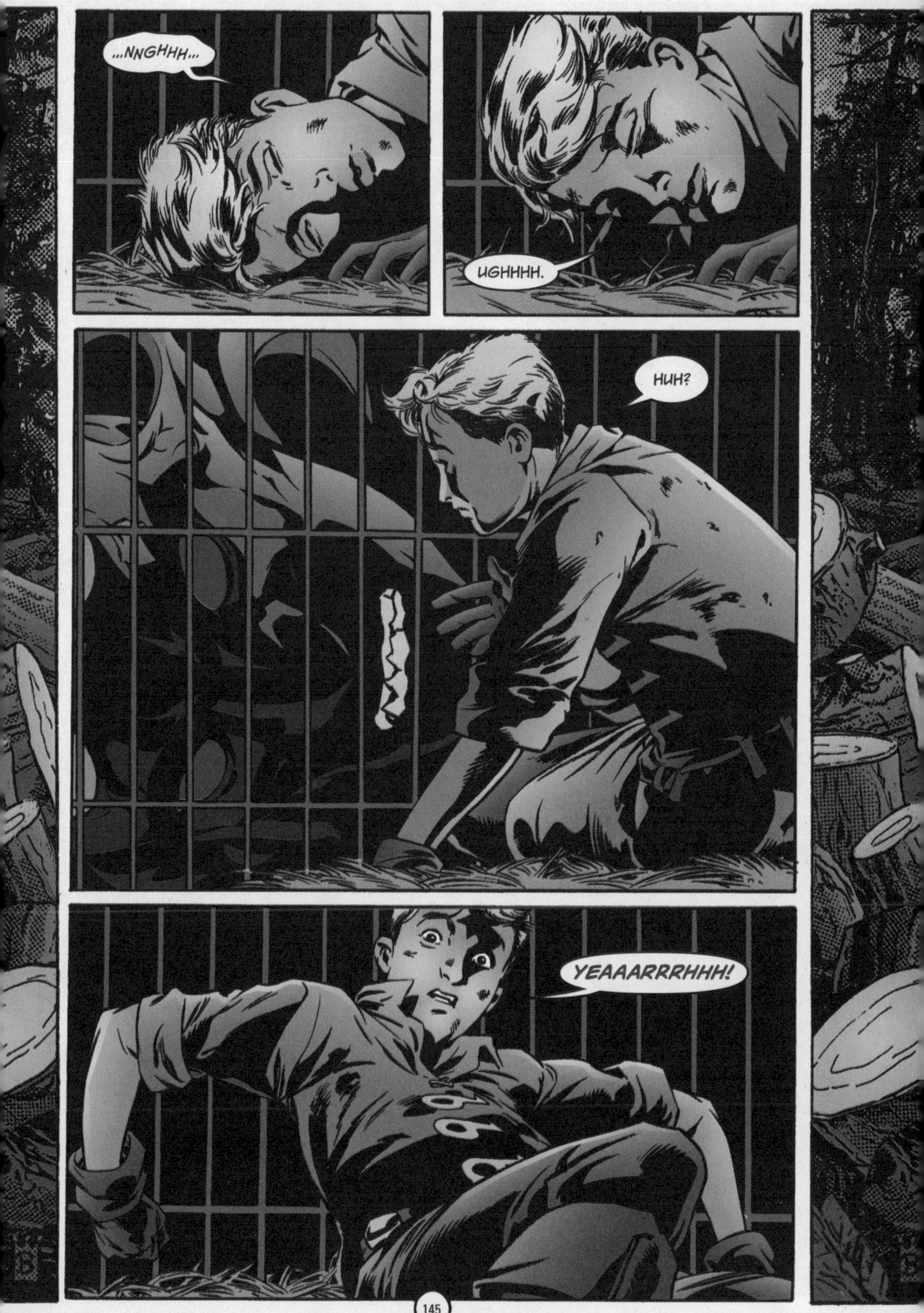
...NNGHHH...
UGHHHH.
HUH?
YEAAARRRHHH!

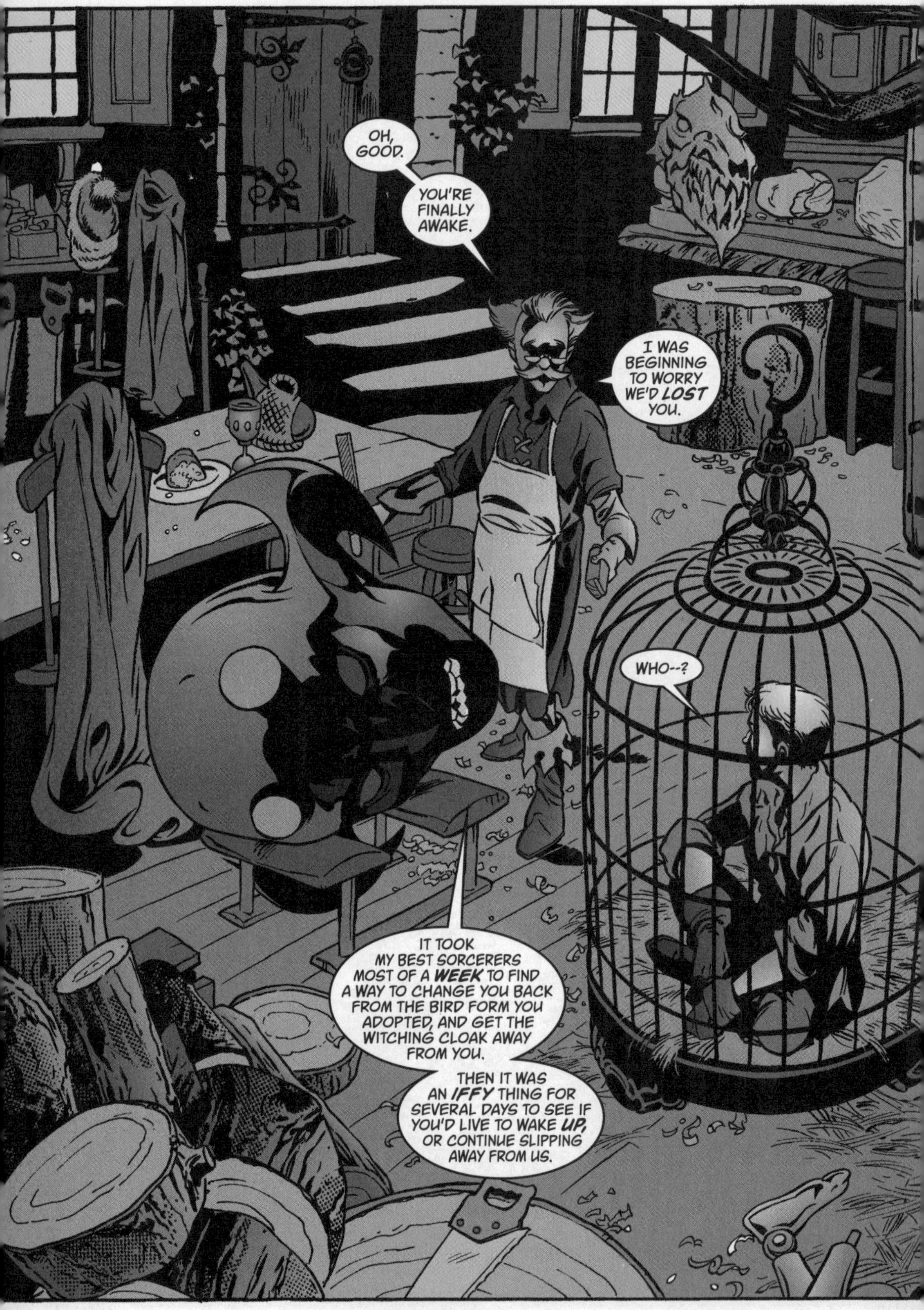
OH, GOOD.
YOU'RE FINALLY AWAKE.
I WAS BEGINNING TO WORRY WE'D LOST YOU.
WHO--?
IT TOOK MY BEST SORCERERS MOST OF A WEEK TO FIND A WAY TO CHANGE YOU BACK FROM THE BIRD FORM YOU ADOPTED, AND GET THE WITCHING CLOAK AWAY FROM YOU.
THEN IT WAS AN IFFY THING FOR SEVERAL DAYS TO SEE IF YOU'D LIVE TO WAKE UP, OR CONTINUE SLIPPING AWAY FROM US.

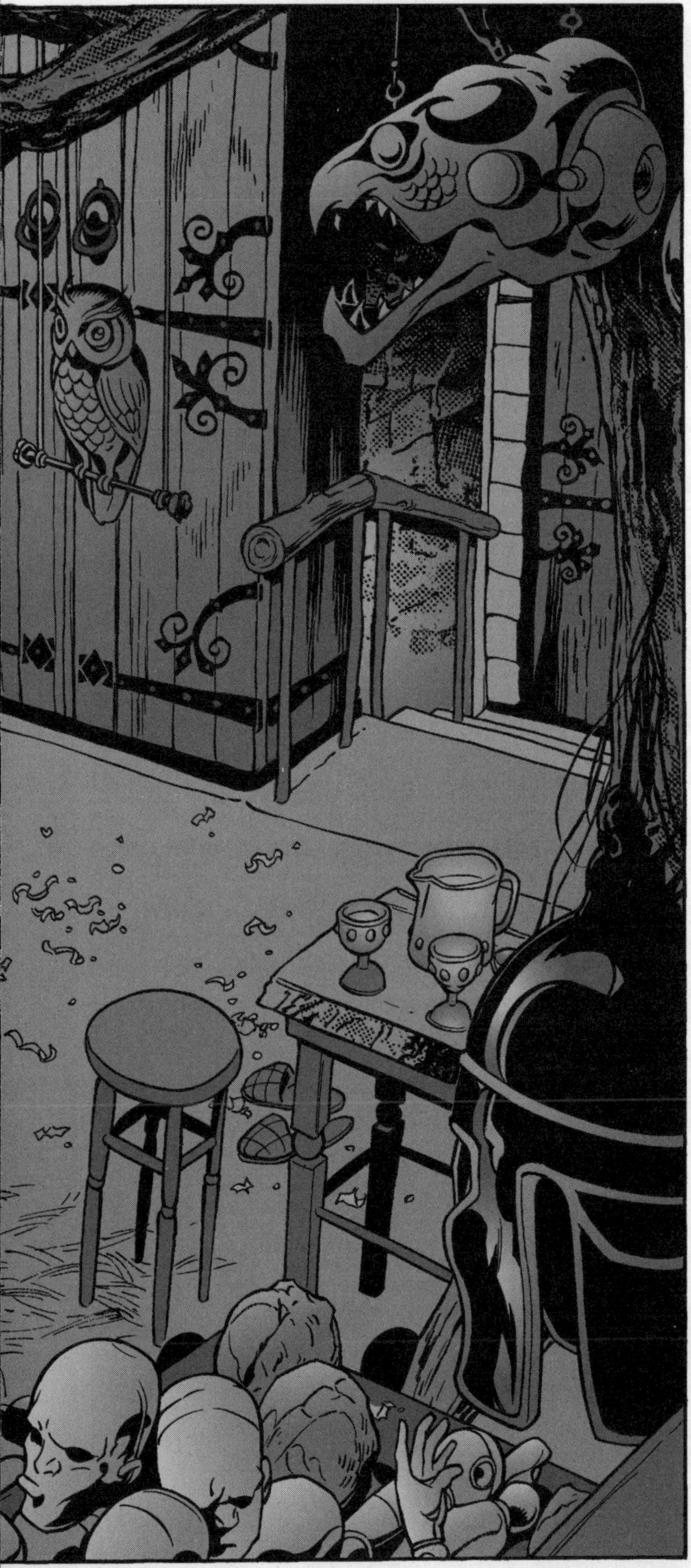

He's Only a Bird in a Gilded Cage

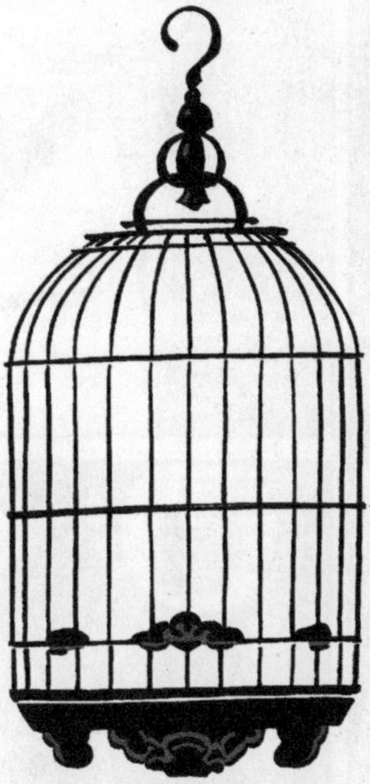

Chapter Four of
HOMELANDS

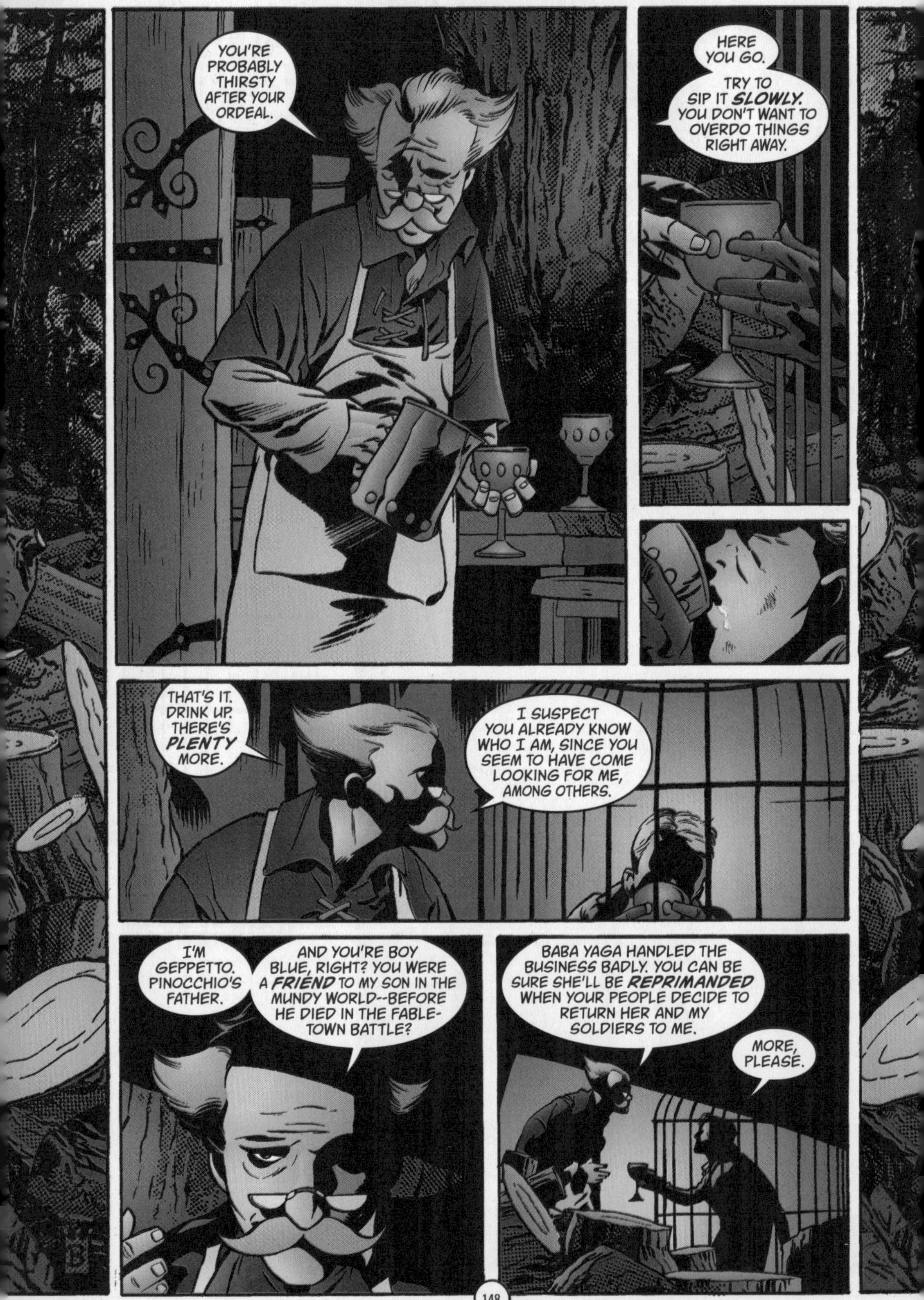
YOU'RE PROBABLY THIRSTY AFTER YOUR ORDEAL.
HERE YOU GO.
TRY TO SIP IT SLOWLY. YOU DON'T WANT TO OVERDO THINGS RIGHT AWAY.
THAT'S IT. DRINK UP. THERE'S PLENTY MORE.
I SUSPECT YOU ALREADY KNOW WHO I AM, SINCE YOU SEEM TO HAVE COME LOOKING FOR ME, AMONG OTHERS.
I'M GEPPETTO. PINOCCHIO'S FATHER.
AND YOU'RE BOY BLUE, RIGHT? YOU WERE A FRIEND TO MY SON IN THE MUNDY WORLD--BEFORE HE DIED IN THE FABLE-TOWN BATTLE?
BABA YAGA HANDLED THE BUSINESS BADLY. YOU CAN BE SURE SHE'LL BE REPRIMANDED WHEN YOUR PEOPLE DECIDE TO RETURN HER AND MY SOLDIERS TO ME.
MORE, PLEASE.

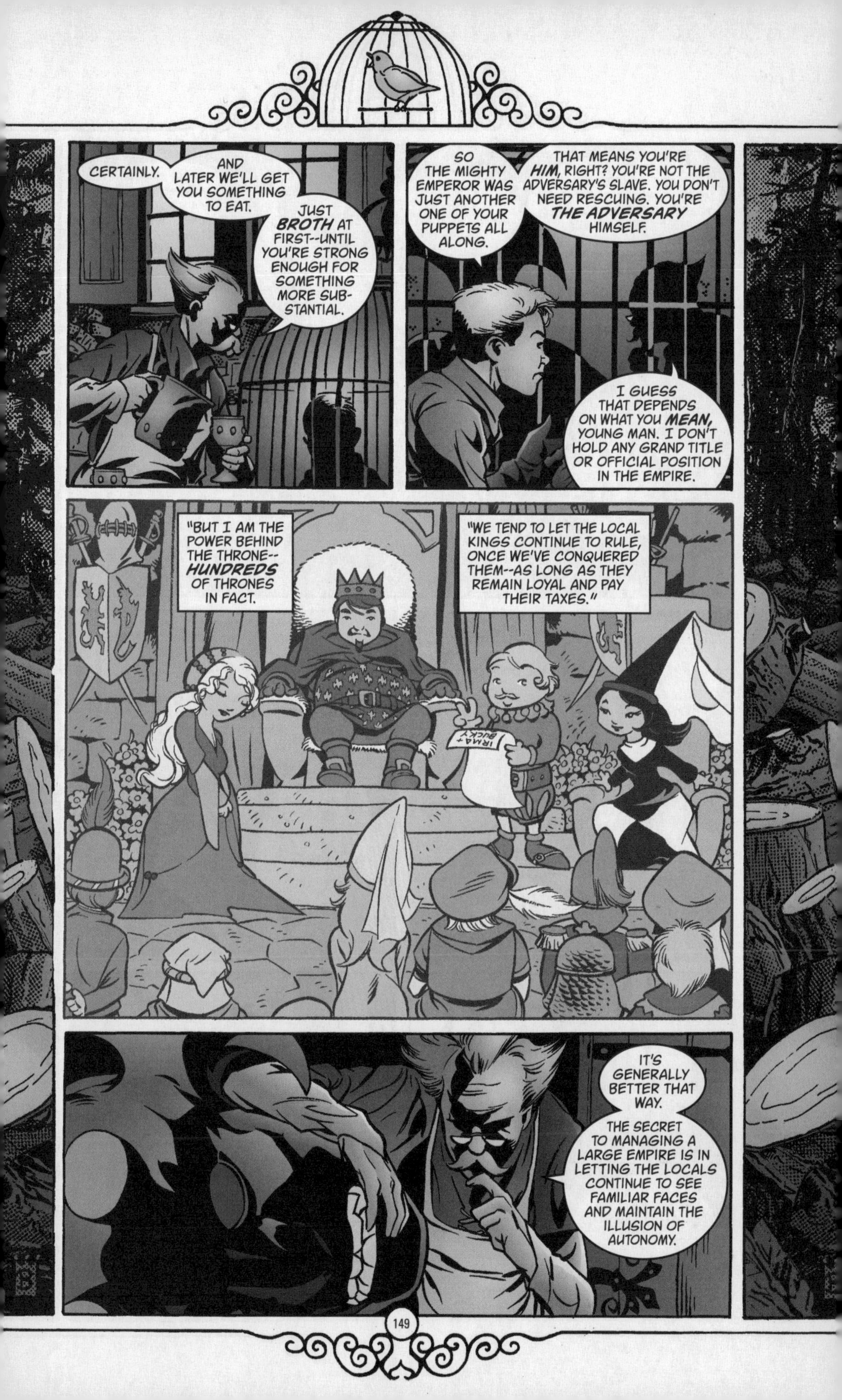
CERTAINLY.
AND LATER WE'LL GET YOU SOMETHING TO EAT.
JUST BROTH AT FIRST--UNTIL YOU'RE STRONG ENOUGH FOR SOMETHING MORE SUB-STANTIAL.
SO THE MIGHTY EMPEROR WAS JUST ANOTHER ONE OF YOUR PUPPETS ALL ALONG.
THAT MEANS YOU'RE HIM, RIGHT? YOU'RE NOT THE ADVERSARY'S SLAVE. YOU DON'T NEED RESCUING. YOU'RE THE ADVERSARY HIMSELF.
I GUESS THAT DEPENDS ON WHAT YOU MEAN, YOUNG MAN. I DON'T HOLD ANY GRAND TITLE OR OFFICIAL POSITION IN THE EMPIRE.
"BUT I AM THE POWER BEHIND THE THRONE--HUNDREDS OF THRONES IN FACT.
"WE TEND TO LET THE LOCAL KINGS CONTINUE TO RULE, ONCE WE'VE CONQUERED THEM--AS LONG AS THEY REMAIN LOYAL AND PAY THEIR TAXES."
IRMA + BUCKY
IT'S GENERALLY BETTER THAT WAY.
THE SECRET TO MANAGING A LARGE EMPIRE IS IN LETTING THE LOCALS CONTINUE TO SEE FAMILIAR FACES AND MAINTAIN THE ILLUSION OF AUTONOMY.

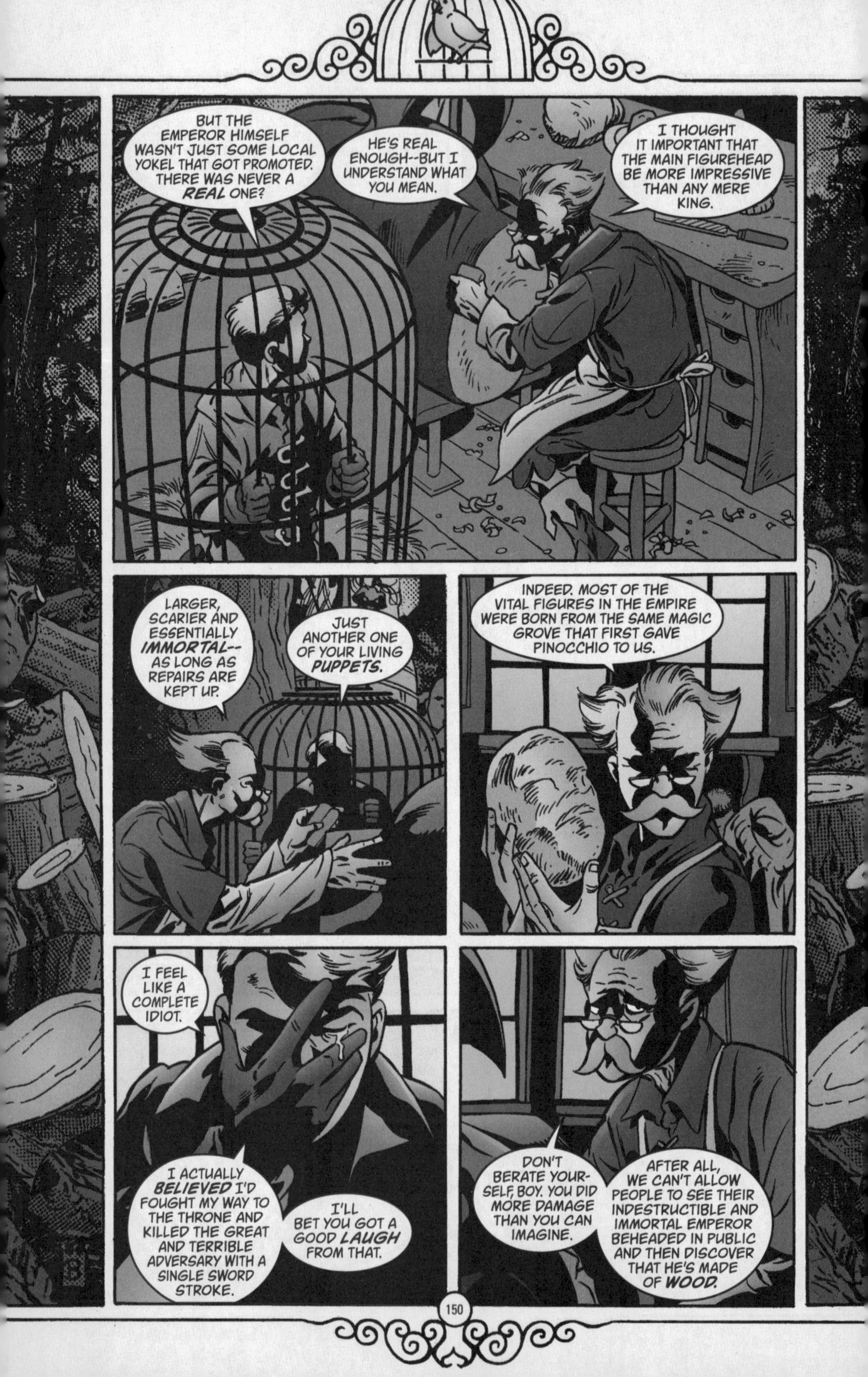

BUT THE EMPEROR HIMSELF WASN'T JUST SOME LOCAL YOKEL THAT GOT PROMOTED. THERE WAS NEVER A REAL ONE?
HE'S REAL ENOUGH--BUT I UNDERSTAND WHAT YOU MEAN.
I THOUGHT IT IMPORTANT THAT THE MAIN FIGUREHEAD BE MORE IMPRESSIVE THAN ANY MERE KING.
LARGER, SCARIER AND ESSENTIALLY IMMORTAL--AS LONG AS REPAIRS ARE KEPT UP.
JUST ANOTHER ONE OF YOUR LIVING PUPPETS.
INDEED. MOST OF THE VITAL FIGURES IN THE EMPIRE WERE BORN FROM THE SAME MAGIC GROVE THAT FIRST GAVE PINOCCHIO TO US.
I FEEL LIKE A COMPLETE IDIOT.
I ACTUALLY BELIEVED I'D FOUGHT MY WAY TO THE THRONE AND KILLED THE GREAT AND TERRIBLE ADVERSARY WITH A SINGLE SWORD STROKE.
I'LL BET YOU GOT A GOOD LAUGH FROM THAT.
DON'T BERATE YOURSELF, BOY. YOU DID MORE DAMAGE THAN YOU CAN IMAGINE.
AFTER ALL, WE CAN'T ALLOW PEOPLE TO SEE THEIR INDESTRUCTIBLE AND IMMORTAL EMPEROR BEHEADED IN PUBLIC AND THEN DISCOVER THAT HE'S MADE OF WOOD.

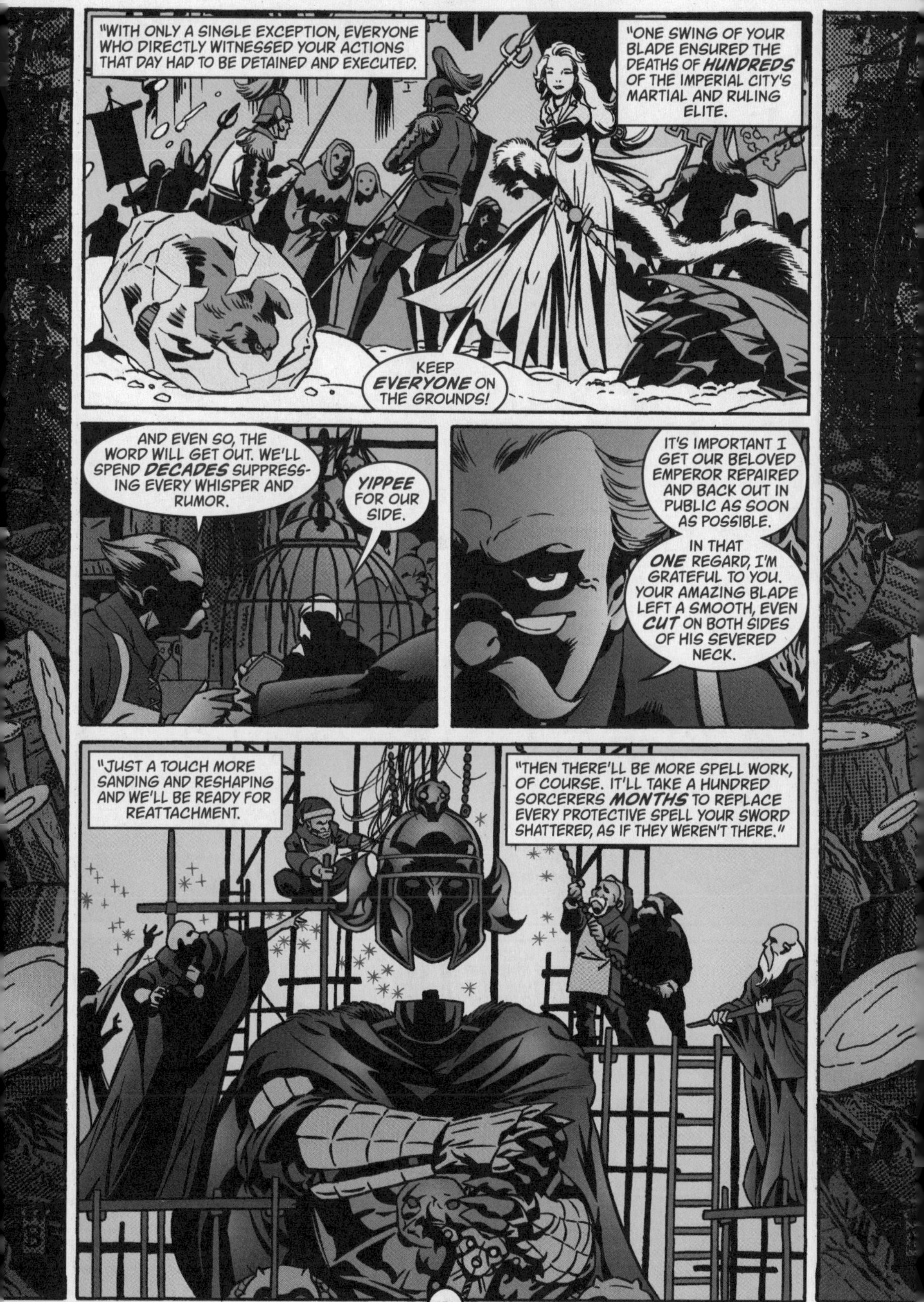
"WITH ONLY A SINGLE EXCEPTION, EVERYONE WHO DIRECTLY WITNESSED YOUR ACTIONS THAT DAY HAD TO BE DETAINED AND EXECUTED.
"ONE SWING OF YOUR BLADE ENSURED THE DEATHS OF HUNDREDS OF THE IMPERIAL CITY'S MARTIAL AND RULING ELITE.
KEEP EVERYONE ON THE GROUNDS!
AND EVEN SO, THE WORD WILL GET OUT. WE'LL SPEND DECADES SUPPRESSING EVERY WHISPER AND RUMOR.
YIPPEE FOR OUR SIDE.
IT'S IMPORTANT I GET OUR BELOVED EMPEROR REPAIRED AND BACK OUT IN PUBLIC AS SOON AS POSSIBLE.
IN THAT ONE REGARD, I'M GRATEFUL TO YOU. YOUR AMAZING BLADE LEFT A SMOOTH, EVEN CUT ON BOTH SIDES OF HIS SEVERED NECK.
"JUST A TOUCH MORE SANDING AND RESHAPING AND WE'LL BE READY FOR REATTACHMENT.
"THEN THERE'LL BE MORE SPELL WORK, OF COURSE. IT'LL TAKE A HUNDRED SORCERERS MONTHS TO REPLACE EVERY PROTECTIVE SPELL YOUR SWORD SHATTERED, AS IF THEY WEREN'T THERE."

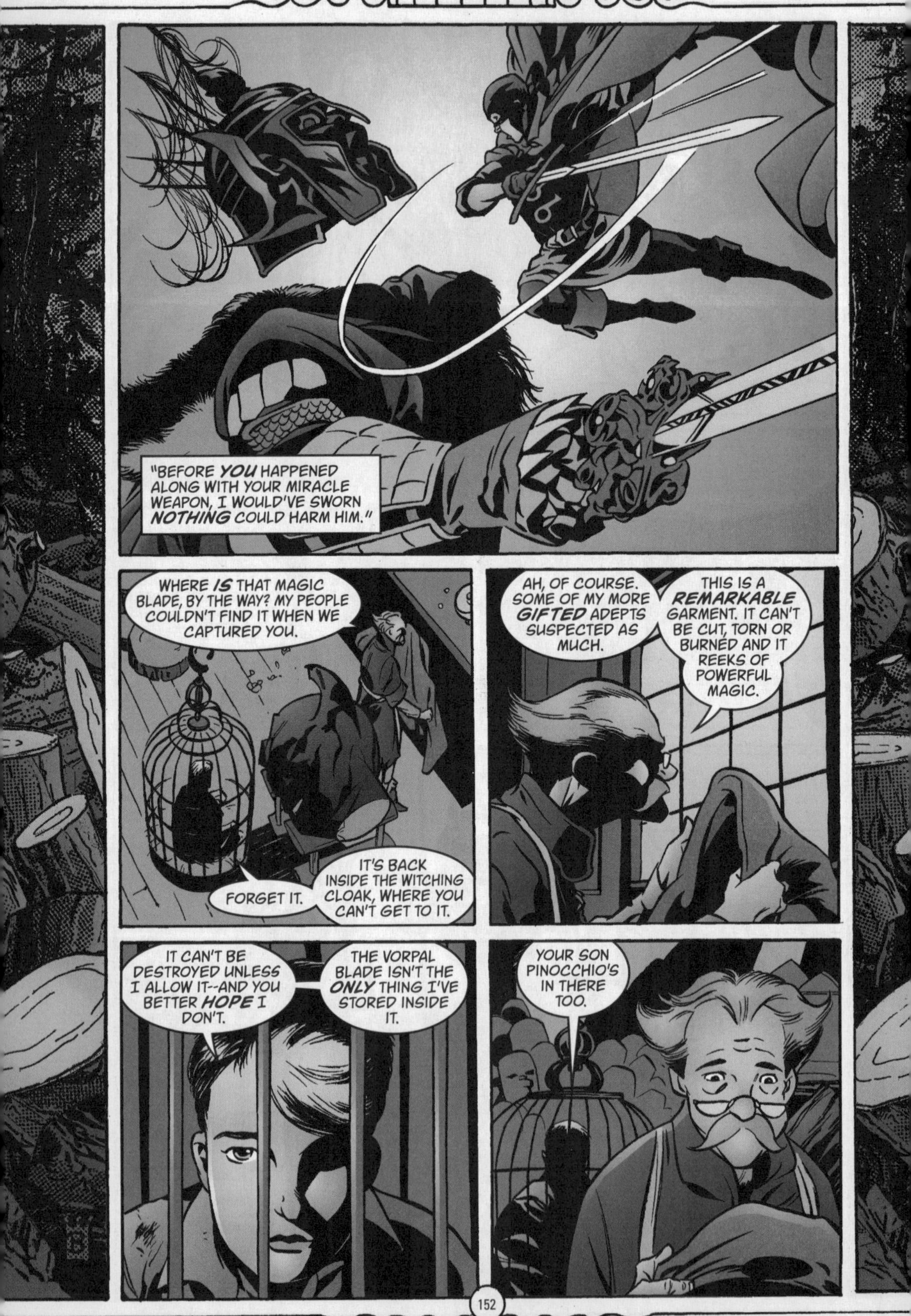
"BEFORE YOU HAPPENED ALONG WITH YOUR MIRACLE WEAPON, I WOULD'VE SWORN NOTHING COULD HARM HIM."
WHERE IS THAT MAGIC BLADE, BY THE WAY? MY PEOPLE COULDN'T FIND IT WHEN WE CAPTURED YOU.
FORGET IT.
IT'S BACK INSIDE THE WITCHING CLOAK, WHERE YOU CAN'T GET TO IT.
AH, OF COURSE. SOME OF MY MORE GIFTED ADEPTS SUSPECTED AS MUCH.
THIS IS A REMARKABLE GARMENT. IT CAN'T BE CUT, TORN OR BURNED AND IT REEKS OF POWERFUL MAGIC.
IT CAN'T BE DESTROYED UNLESS I ALLOW IT--AND YOU BETTER HOPE I DON'T.
THE VORPAL BLADE ISN'T THE ONLY THING I'VE STORED INSIDE IT.
YOUR SON PINOCCHIO'S IN THERE TOO.

HERE'S YOUR DINNER, SIR.

THANK YOU, MRS. PEASEPATTER.

HERE'S YOUR BROTH, YOUNG MAN. CAREFUL, IT'S *HOT.*

MMMMM, GIMME.

NOW, WHAT DO I HAVE TO *DO* TO GET MY FIRST SON BACK?

FIRST THINGS *FIRST*, MR. GEPPETTO. LET'S SET SOME GROUND RULES.

YOU SHOULD KNOW I SET A *NUMBER* OF MAGICAL PRE-CONDITIONS ON THE CLOAK BEFORE I EVER SET OUT ON MY QUEST.

THERE'S A CERTAIN *WORD*, IF I SPEAK IT, THAT WILL CAUSE PINOCCHIO'S BODY--BOTH HALVES--TO SPILL OUT OF THE CLOAK.

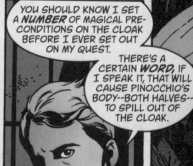

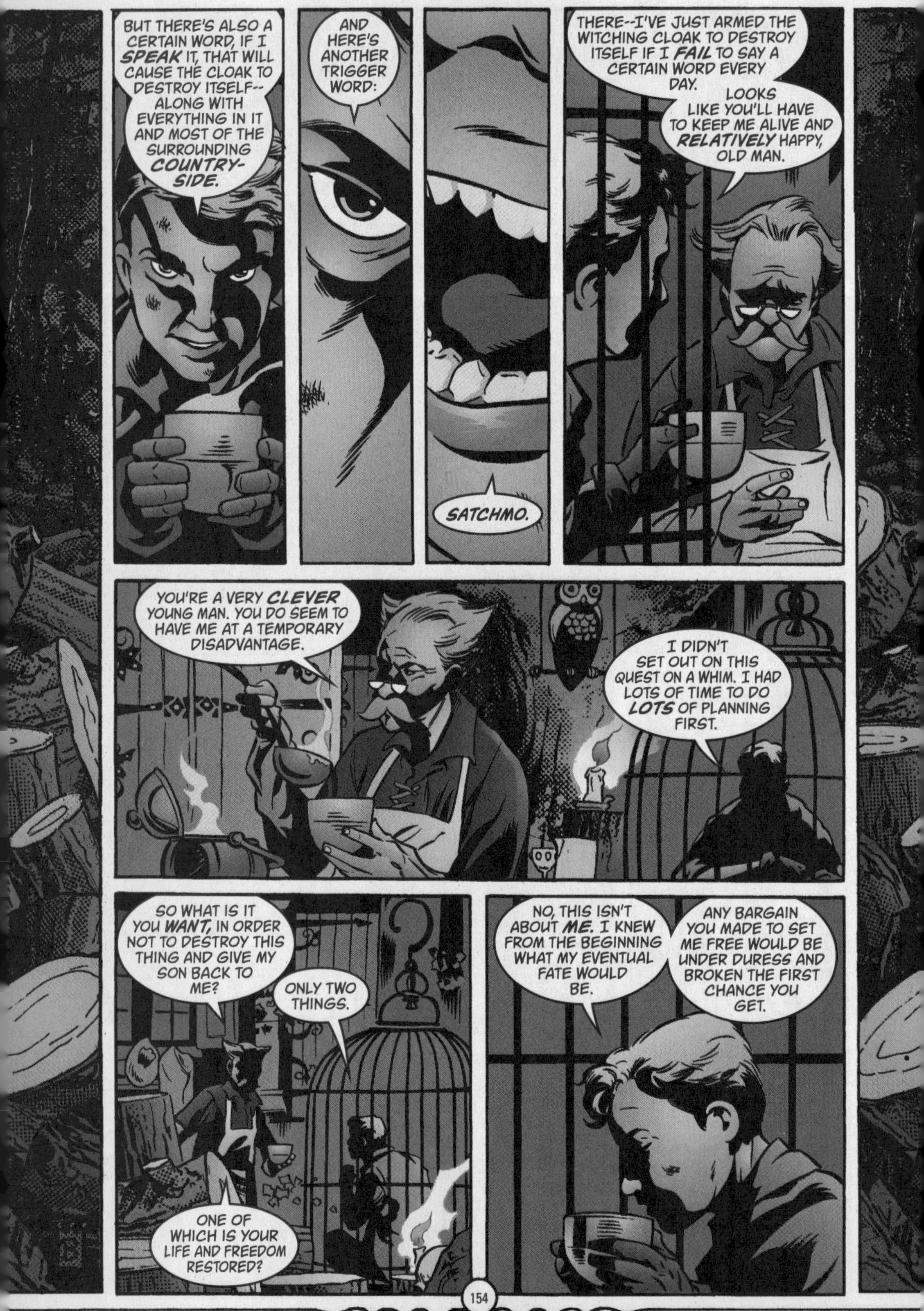
BUT THERE'S ALSO A CERTAIN WORD, IF I SPEAK IT, THAT WILL CAUSE THE CLOAK TO DESTROY ITSELF-- ALONG WITH EVERYTHING IN IT AND MOST OF THE SURROUNDING COUNTRY-SIDE.
AND HERE'S ANOTHER TRIGGER WORD:
SATCHMO.
THERE--I'VE JUST ARMED THE WITCHING CLOAK TO DESTROY ITSELF IF I FAIL TO SAY A CERTAIN WORD EVERY DAY.
LOOKS LIKE YOU'LL HAVE TO KEEP ME ALIVE AND RELATIVELY HAPPY, OLD MAN.
YOU'RE A VERY CLEVER YOUNG MAN. YOU DO SEEM TO HAVE ME AT A TEMPORARY DISADVANTAGE.
I DIDN'T SET OUT ON THIS QUEST ON A WHIM. I HAD LOTS OF TIME TO DO LOTS OF PLANNING FIRST.
SO WHAT IS IT YOU WANT, IN ORDER NOT TO DESTROY THIS THING AND GIVE MY SON BACK TO ME?
ONLY TWO THINGS.
ONE OF WHICH IS YOUR LIFE AND FREEDOM RESTORED?
NO, THIS ISN'T ABOUT ME. I KNEW FROM THE BEGINNING WHAT MY EVENTUAL FATE WOULD BE.
ANY BARGAIN YOU MADE TO SET ME FREE WOULD BE UNDER DURESS AND BROKEN THE FIRST CHANCE YOU GET.

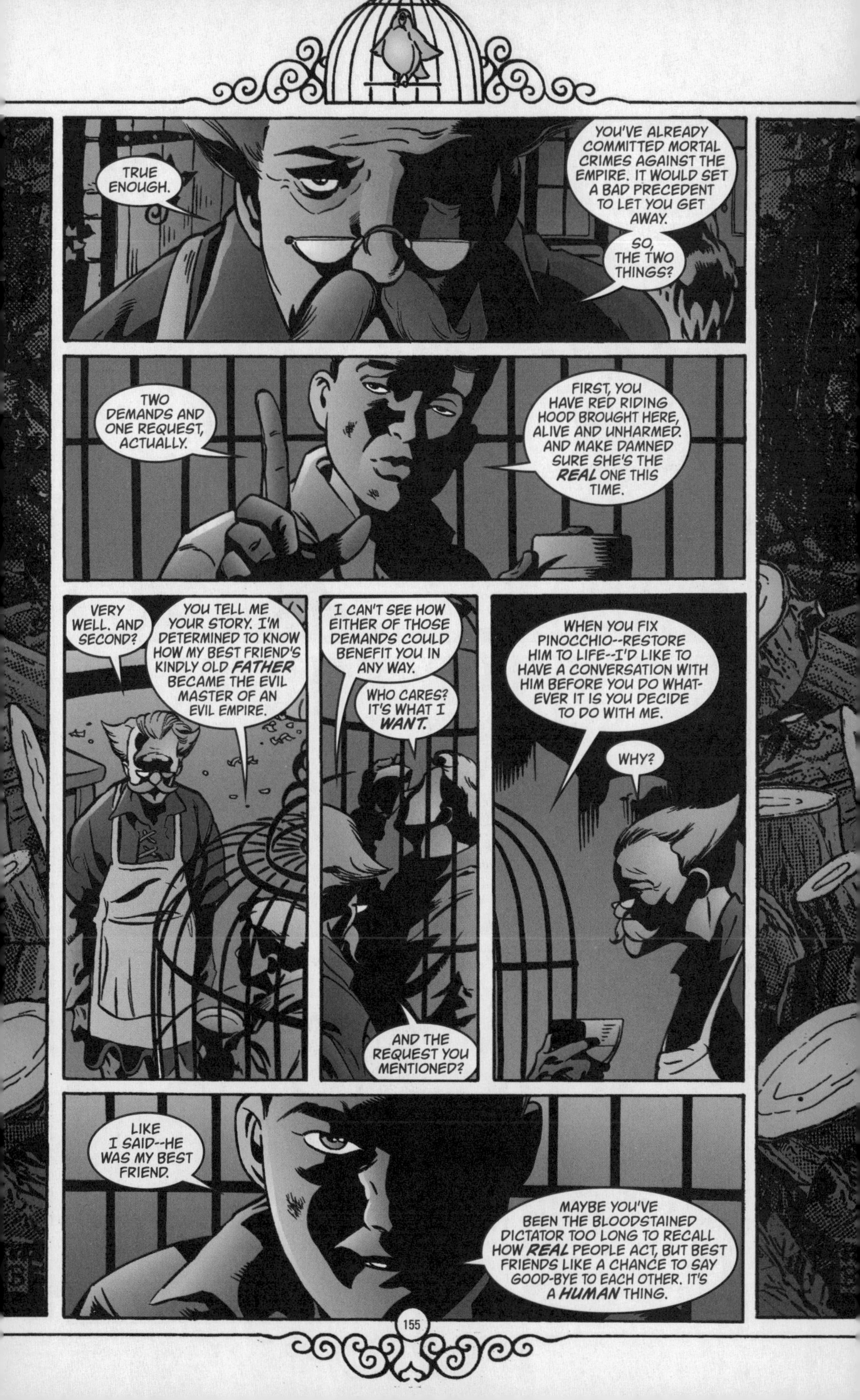
TRUE ENOUGH.
YOU'VE ALREADY COMMITTED MORTAL CRIMES AGAINST THE EMPIRE. IT WOULD SET A BAD PRECEDENT TO LET YOU GET AWAY.
SO, THE TWO THINGS?
TWO DEMANDS AND ONE REQUEST, ACTUALLY.
FIRST, YOU HAVE RED RIDING HOOD BROUGHT HERE, ALIVE AND UNHARMED. AND MAKE DAMNED SURE SHE'S THE REAL ONE THIS TIME.
VERY WELL. AND SECOND?
YOU TELL ME YOUR STORY. I'M DETERMINED TO KNOW HOW MY BEST FRIEND'S KINDLY OLD FATHER BECAME THE EVIL MASTER OF AN EVIL EMPIRE.
I CAN'T SEE HOW EITHER OF THOSE DEMANDS COULD BENEFIT YOU IN ANY WAY.
WHO CARES? IT'S WHAT I WANT.
AND THE REQUEST YOU MENTIONED?
WHEN YOU FIX PINOCCHIO--RESTORE HIM TO LIFE--I'D LIKE TO HAVE A CONVERSATION WITH HIM BEFORE YOU DO WHATEVER IT IS YOU DECIDE TO DO WITH ME.
WHY?
LIKE I SAID--HE WAS MY BEST FRIEND.
MAYBE YOU'VE BEEN THE BLOODSTAINED DICTATOR TOO LONG TO RECALL HOW REAL PEOPLE ACT, BUT BEST FRIENDS LIKE A CHANCE TO SAY GOOD-BYE TO EACH OTHER. IT'S A HUMAN THING.

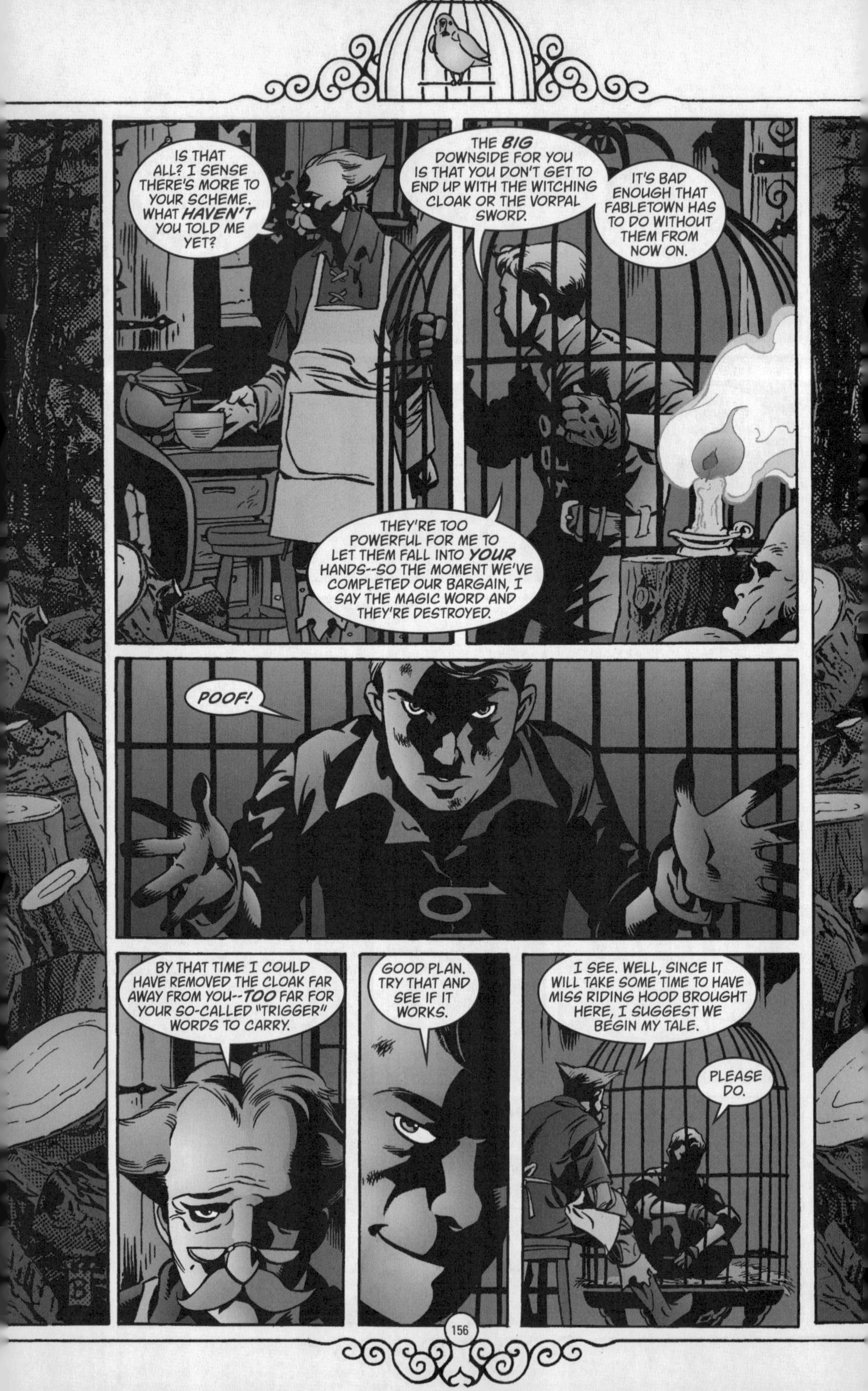
IS THAT ALL? I SENSE THERE'S MORE TO YOUR SCHEME. WHAT HAVEN'T YOU TOLD ME YET?
THE BIG DOWNSIDE FOR YOU IS THAT YOU DON'T GET TO END UP WITH THE WITCHING CLOAK OR THE VORPAL SWORD.
IT'S BAD ENOUGH THAT FABLETOWN HAS TO DO WITHOUT THEM FROM NOW ON.
THEY'RE TOO POWERFUL FOR ME TO LET THEM FALL INTO YOUR HANDS--SO THE MOMENT WE'VE COMPLETED OUR BARGAIN, I SAY THE MAGIC WORD AND THEY'RE DESTROYED.
POOF!
BY THAT TIME I COULD HAVE REMOVED THE CLOAK FAR AWAY FROM YOU--TOO FAR FOR YOUR SO-CALLED "TRIGGER" WORDS TO CARRY.
GOOD PLAN. TRY THAT AND SEE IF IT WORKS.
I SEE. WELL, SINCE IT WILL TAKE SOME TIME TO HAVE MISS RIDING HOOD BROUGHT HERE, I SUGGEST WE BEGIN MY TALE.
PLEASE DO.

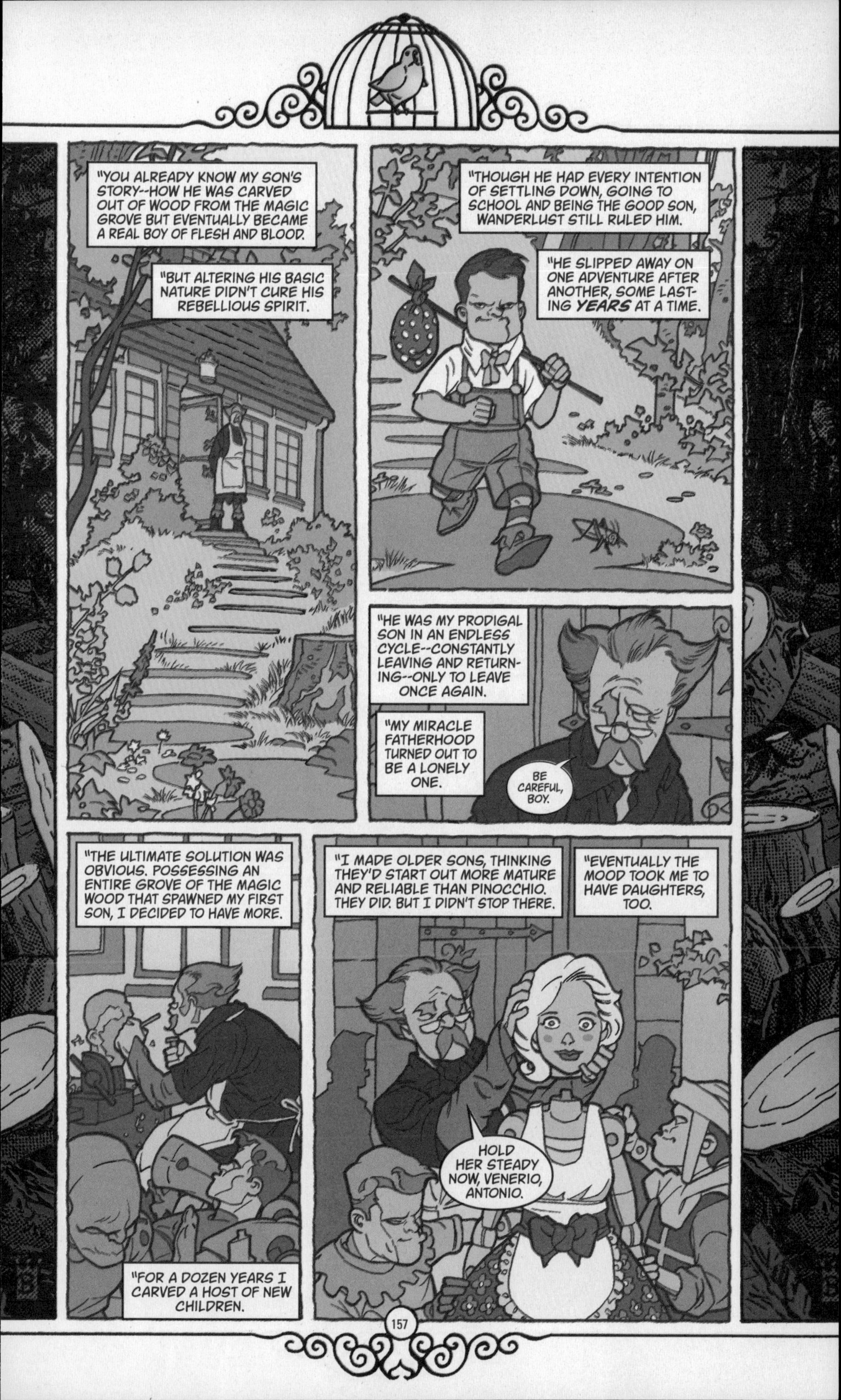
"YOU ALREADY KNOW MY SON'S STORY--HOW HE WAS CARVED OUT OF WOOD FROM THE MAGIC GROVE BUT EVENTUALLY BECAME A REAL BOY OF FLESH AND BLOOD.
"BUT ALTERING HIS BASIC NATURE DIDN'T CURE HIS REBELLIOUS SPIRIT.
"THOUGH HE HAD EVERY INTENTION OF SETTLING DOWN, GOING TO SCHOOL AND BEING THE GOOD SON, WANDERLUST STILL RULED HIM.
"HE SLIPPED AWAY ON ONE ADVENTURE AFTER ANOTHER, SOME LASTING *YEARS* AT A TIME.
"HE WAS MY PRODIGAL SON IN AN ENDLESS CYCLE--CONSTANTLY LEAVING AND RETURNING--ONLY TO LEAVE ONCE AGAIN.
"MY MIRACLE FATHERHOOD TURNED OUT TO BE A LONELY ONE.
BE CAREFUL, BOY.
"THE ULTIMATE SOLUTION WAS OBVIOUS. POSSESSING AN ENTIRE GROVE OF THE MAGIC WOOD THAT SPAWNED MY FIRST SON, I DECIDED TO HAVE MORE.
"FOR A DOZEN YEARS I CARVED A HOST OF NEW CHILDREN.
"I MADE OLDER SONS, THINKING THEY'D START OUT MORE MATURE AND RELIABLE THAN PINOCCHIO. THEY DID. BUT I DIDN'T STOP THERE.
"EVENTUALLY THE MOOD TOOK ME TO HAVE DAUGHTERS, TOO.
HOLD HER STEADY NOW, VENERIO, ANTONIO.

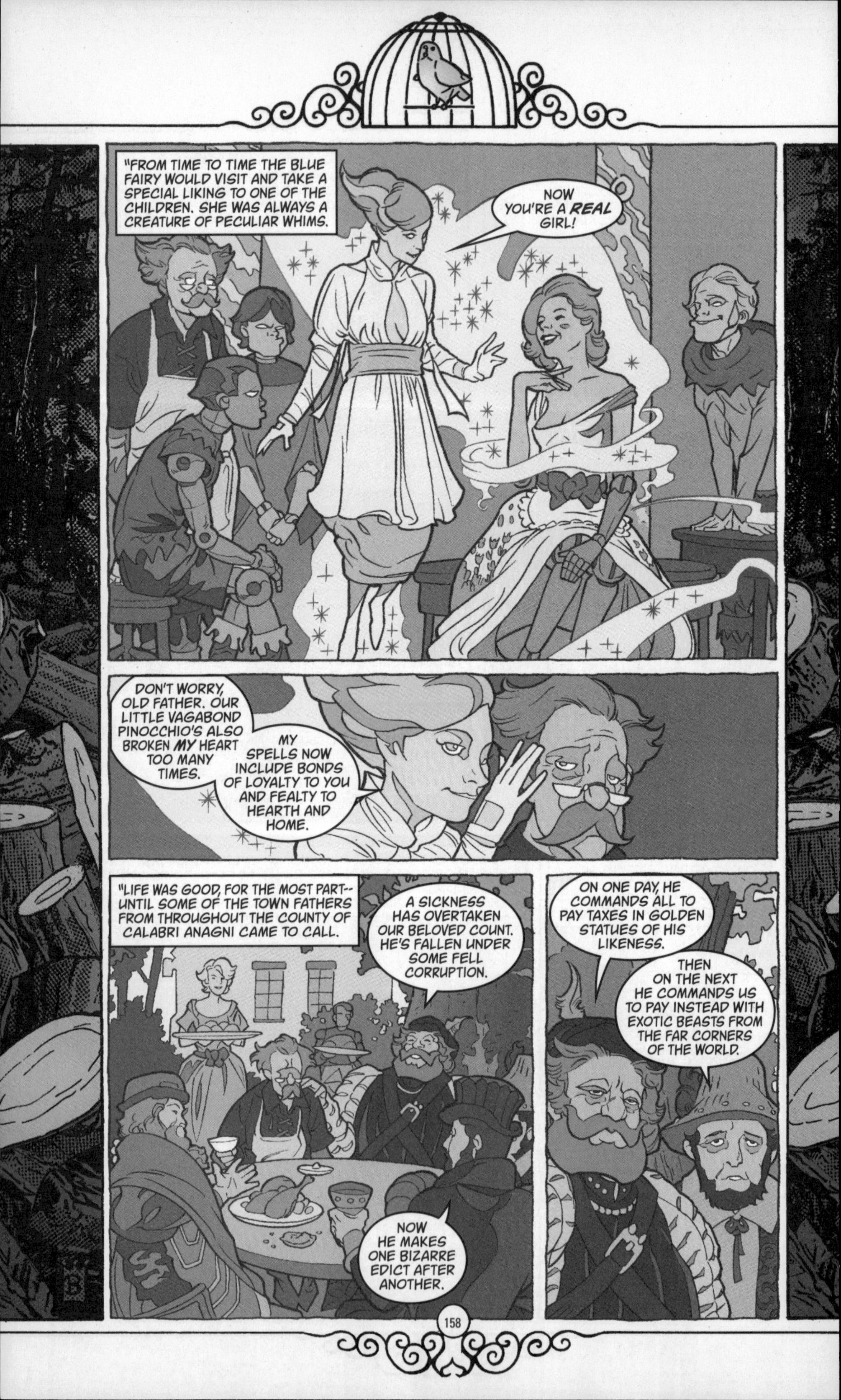
"FROM TIME TO TIME THE BLUE FAIRY WOULD VISIT AND TAKE A SPECIAL LIKING TO ONE OF THE CHILDREN. SHE WAS ALWAYS A CREATURE OF PECULIAR WHIMS.
NOW YOU'RE A REAL GIRL!
DON'T WORRY, OLD FATHER. OUR LITTLE VAGABOND PINOCCHIO'S ALSO BROKEN MY HEART TOO MANY TIMES.
MY SPELLS NOW INCLUDE BONDS OF LOYALTY TO YOU AND FEALTY TO HEARTH AND HOME.
"LIFE WAS GOOD, FOR THE MOST PART--UNTIL SOME OF THE TOWN FATHERS FROM THROUGHOUT THE COUNTY OF CALABRI ANAGNI CAME TO CALL.
A SICKNESS HAS OVERTAKEN OUR BELOVED COUNT. HE'S FALLEN UNDER SOME FELL CORRUPTION.
NOW HE MAKES ONE BIZARRE EDICT AFTER ANOTHER.
ON ONE DAY, HE COMMANDS ALL TO PAY TAXES IN GOLDEN STATUES OF HIS LIKENESS.
THEN ON THE NEXT HE COMMANDS US TO PAY INSTEAD WITH EXOTIC BEASTS FROM THE FAR CORNERS OF THE WORLD.

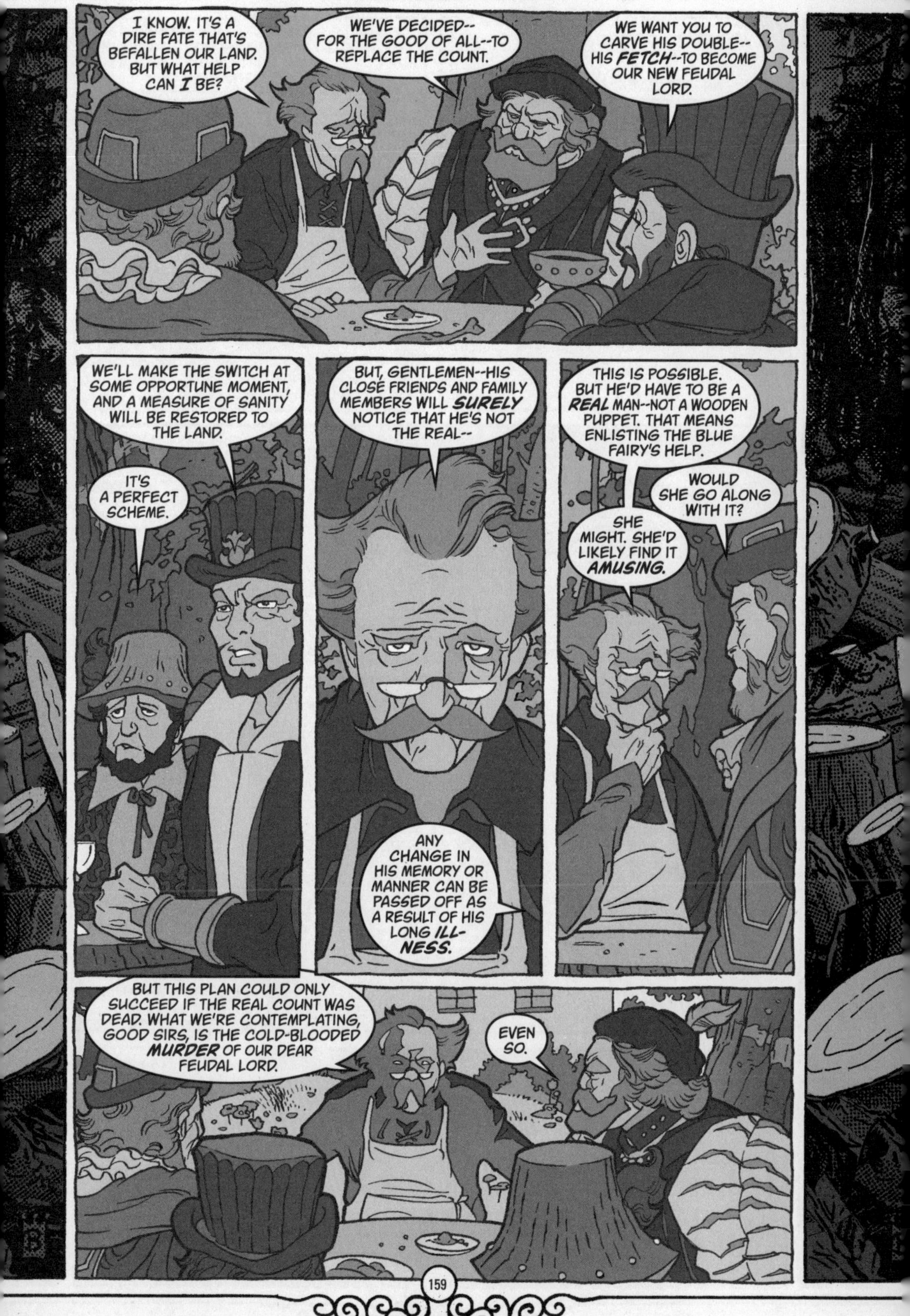
I KNOW. IT'S A DIRE FATE THAT'S BEFALLEN OUR LAND. BUT WHAT HELP CAN I BE?
WE'VE DECIDED-- FOR THE GOOD OF ALL--TO REPLACE THE COUNT.
WE WANT YOU TO CARVE HIS DOUBLE-- HIS FETCH--TO BECOME OUR NEW FEUDAL LORD.
WE'LL MAKE THE SWITCH AT SOME OPPORTUNE MOMENT, AND A MEASURE OF SANITY WILL BE RESTORED TO THE LAND.
IT'S A PERFECT SCHEME.
BUT, GENTLEMEN--HIS CLOSE FRIENDS AND FAMILY MEMBERS WILL SURELY NOTICE THAT HE'S NOT THE REAL--
ANY CHANGE IN HIS MEMORY OR MANNER CAN BE PASSED OFF AS A RESULT OF HIS LONG ILL-NESS.
THIS IS POSSIBLE. BUT HE'D HAVE TO BE A REAL MAN--NOT A WOODEN PUPPET. THAT MEANS ENLISTING THE BLUE FAIRY'S HELP.
WOULD SHE GO ALONG WITH IT?
SHE MIGHT. SHE'D LIKELY FIND IT AMUSING.
BUT THIS PLAN COULD ONLY SUCCEED IF THE REAL COUNT WAS DEAD. WHAT WE'RE CONTEMPLATING, GOOD SIRS, IS THE COLD-BLOODED MURDER OF OUR DEAR FEUDAL LORD.
EVEN SO.

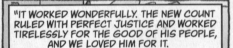

"IT WORKED WONDERFULLY. THE NEW COUNT RULED WITH PERFECT JUSTICE AND WORKED TIRELESSLY FOR THE GOOD OF HIS PEOPLE, AND WE LOVED HIM FOR IT."

"IF ANYONE EVER SUSPECTED HE WAS A FETCH, THEY KEPT IT TO THEMSELVES."

"OF COURSE HIS ELDEST SON WAS AN INTOLERABLE *ASS.* SO, WHEN WE THOUGHT IT WAS TIME FOR OUR BELOVED OLD COUNT TO PASS AWAY, I REPLACED THE SON.

"OUR PARADISIACAL YEARS OF PEACE, JUSTICE AND LOW TAXES WOULD CONTINUE, UNINTERRUPTED."

LET ME GUESS. THE PRACTICE BECAME *HABITUAL?*

IS THERE ANY DOUBT? THERE WAS ALWAYS ANOTHER NEIGHBORING COUNT, OR DUKE OR THE KING HIMSELF WHO MADE LIFE *DIFFICULT* FOR HIS SUBJECTS.

"SOON ENOUGH EVERY MAJOR RULING OFFICIAL FOR A HUNDRED MILES AROUND WAS ONE OF MY REPLACEMENTS.

"AND THANKS TO THE BLUE FAIRY'S ADJUSTED ENCHANTMENTS, EVERY ONE OF THEM WAS LOYAL ONLY TO ME."

SHE WENT *ALONG* WITH THIS?

AT FIRST.

THE FAIRY FOLK ARE OF AN ALIEN NATURE AND I'D CORRECTLY GUESSED THAT HER MORALS WOULD BE DIFFERENT FROM OURS.

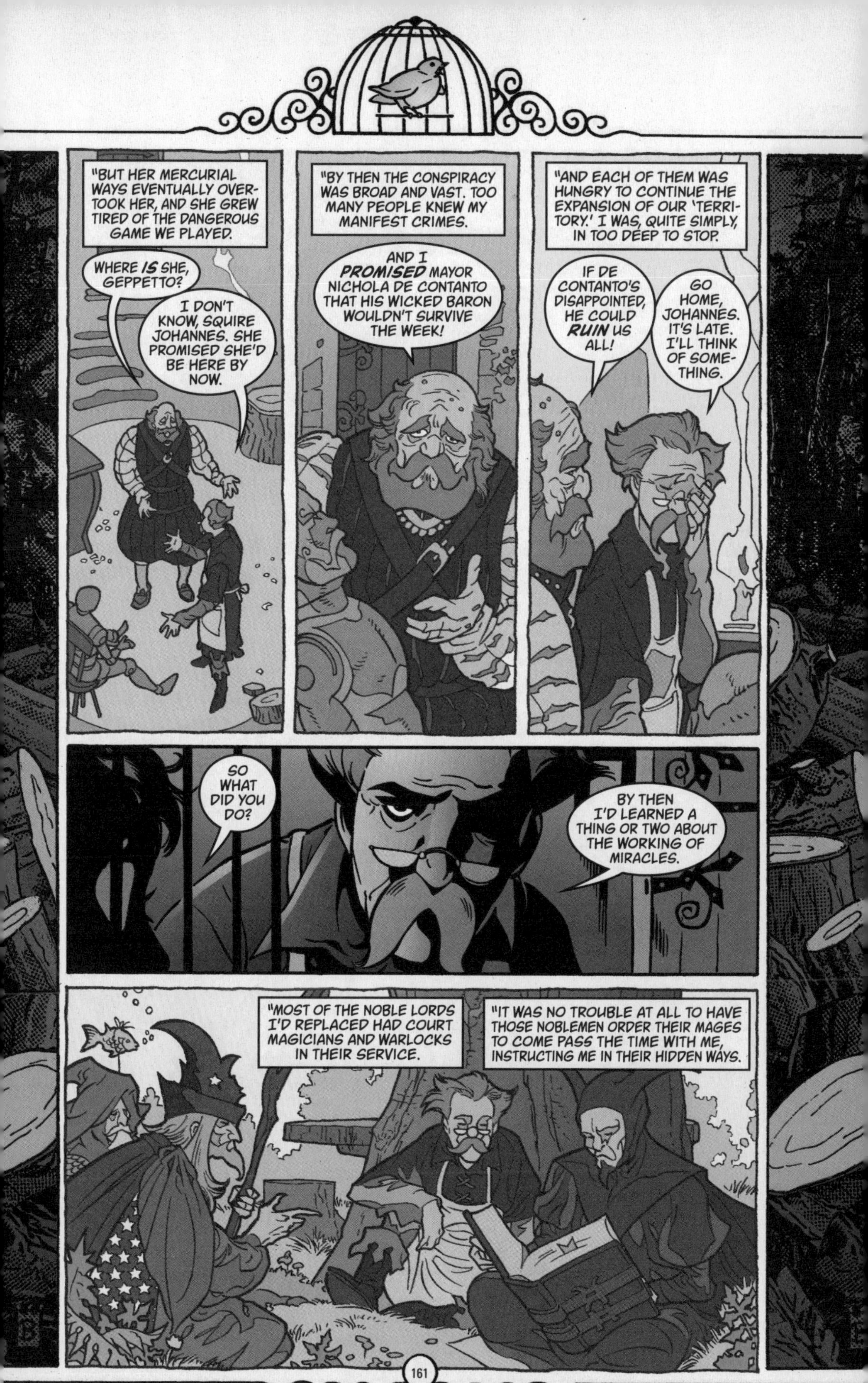
"BUT HER MERCURIAL WAYS EVENTUALLY OVERTOOK HER, AND SHE GREW TIRED OF THE DANGEROUS GAME WE PLAYED.
WHERE *IS* SHE, GEPPETTO?
I DON'T KNOW, SQUIRE JOHANNES. SHE PROMISED SHE'D BE HERE BY NOW.
"BY THEN THE CONSPIRACY WAS BROAD AND VAST. TOO MANY PEOPLE KNEW MY MANIFEST CRIMES.
AND I ***PROMISED*** MAYOR NICHOLA DE CONTANTO THAT HIS WICKED BARON WOULDN'T SURVIVE THE WEEK!
"AND EACH OF THEM WAS HUNGRY TO CONTINUE THE EXPANSION OF OUR 'TERRITORY.' I WAS, QUITE SIMPLY, IN TOO DEEP TO STOP.
IF DE CONTANTO'S DISAPPOINTED, HE COULD ***RUIN*** US ALL!
GO HOME, JOHANNES. IT'S LATE. I'LL THINK OF SOMETHING.
SO WHAT DID YOU DO?
BY THEN I'D LEARNED A THING OR TWO ABOUT THE WORKING OF MIRACLES.
"MOST OF THE NOBLE LORDS I'D REPLACED HAD COURT MAGICIANS AND WARLOCKS IN THEIR SERVICE.
"IT WAS NO TROUBLE AT ALL TO HAVE THOSE NOBLEMEN ORDER THEIR MAGES TO COME PASS THE TIME WITH ME, INSTRUCTING ME IN THEIR HIDDEN WAYS.

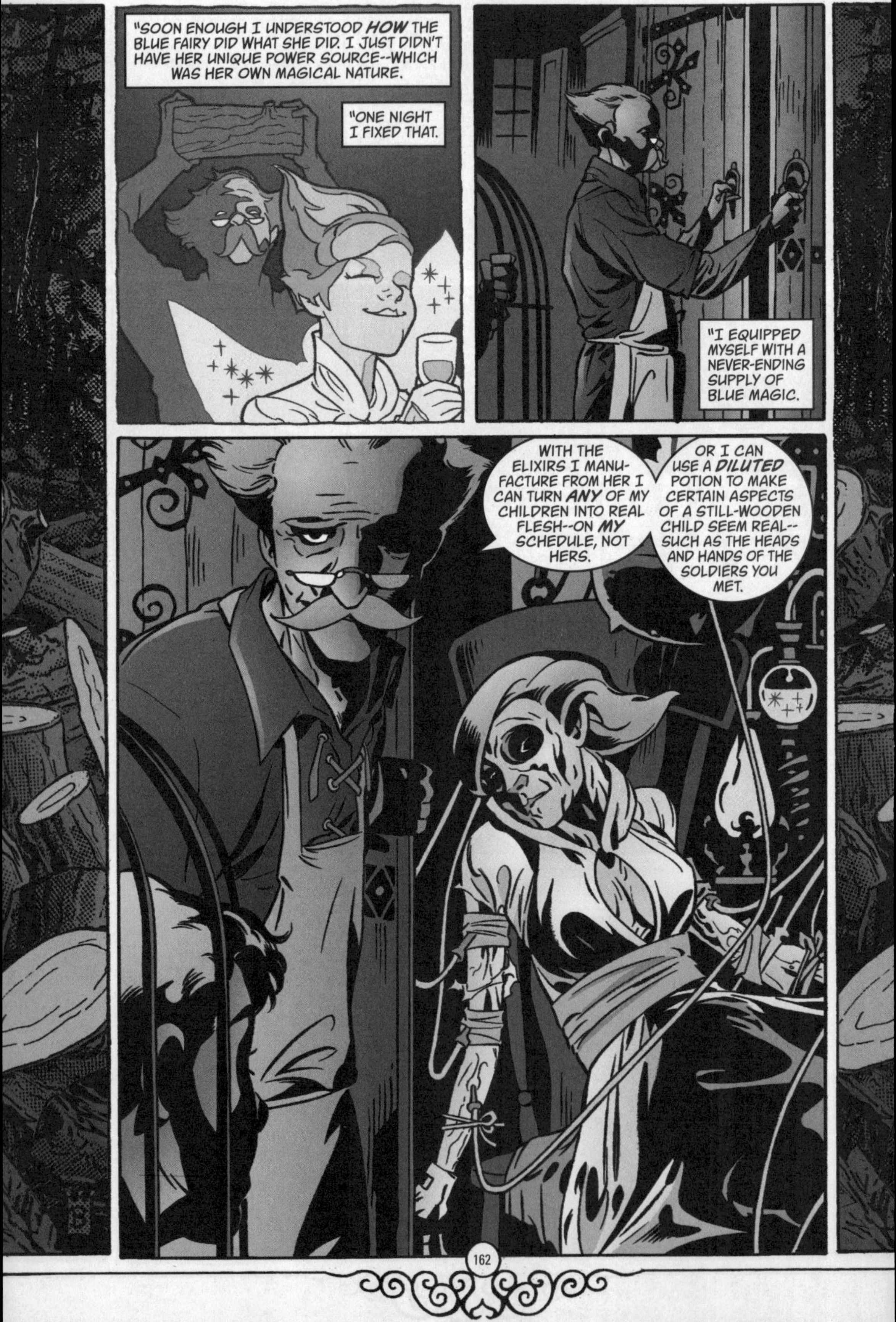
"SOON ENOUGH I UNDERSTOOD HOW THE BLUE FAIRY DID WHAT SHE DID. I JUST DIDN'T HAVE HER UNIQUE POWER SOURCE--WHICH WAS HER OWN MAGICAL NATURE.
"ONE NIGHT I FIXED THAT.
"I EQUIPPED MYSELF WITH A NEVER-ENDING SUPPLY OF BLUE MAGIC.
WITH THE ELIXIRS I MANUFACTURE FROM HER I CAN TURN ANY OF MY CHILDREN INTO REAL FLESH--ON MY SCHEDULE, NOT HERS.
OR I CAN USE A DILUTED POTION TO MAKE CERTAIN ASPECTS OF A STILL-WOODEN CHILD SEEM REAL--SUCH AS THE HEADS AND HANDS OF THE SOLDIERS YOU MET.

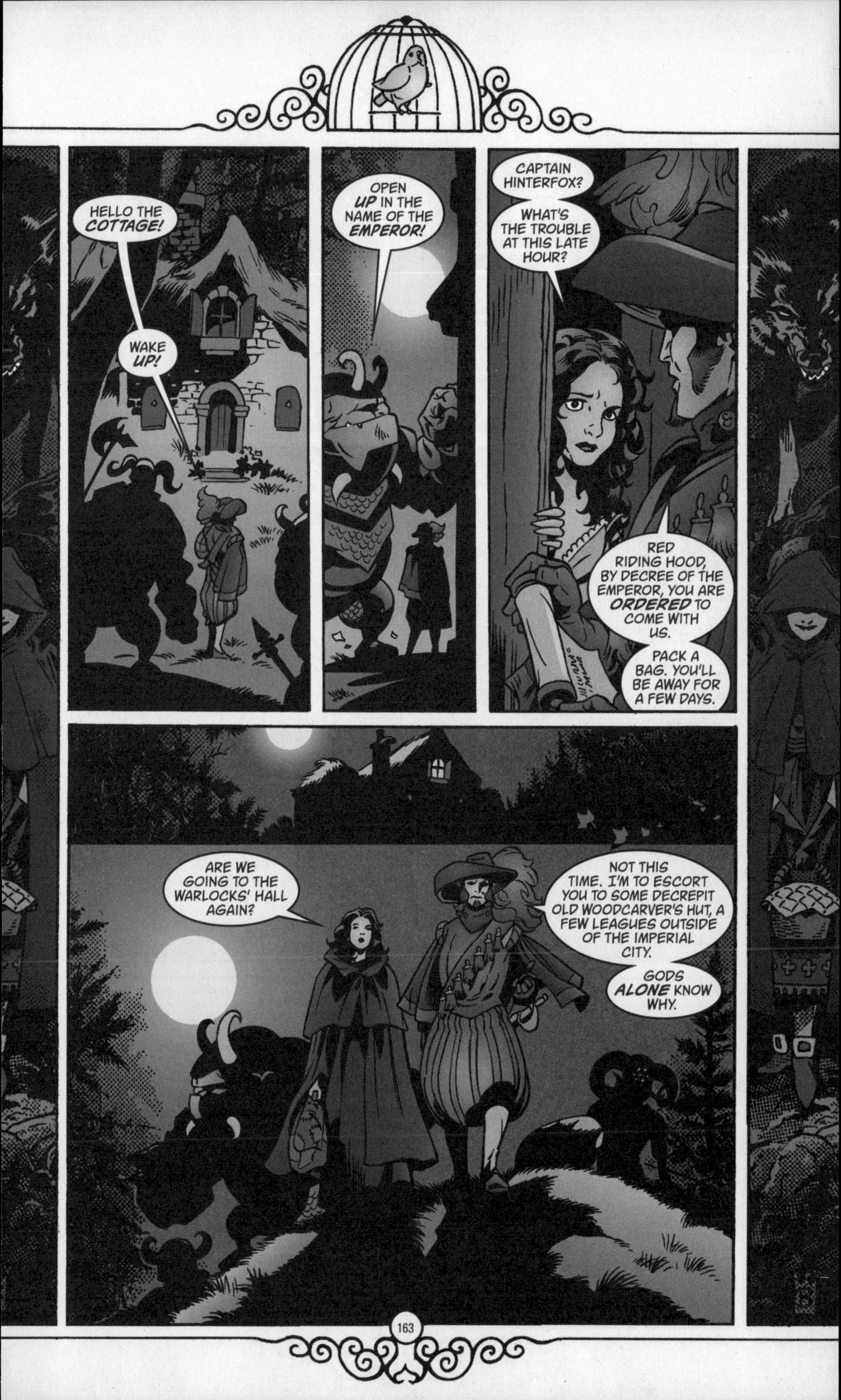
HELLO THE COTTAGE!
WAKE UP!
OPEN UP IN THE NAME OF THE EMPEROR!
CAPTAIN HINTERFOX?
WHAT'S THE TROUBLE AT THIS LATE HOUR?
RED RIDING HOOD, BY DECREE OF THE EMPEROR, YOU ARE ORDERED TO COME WITH US.
PACK A BAG. YOU'LL BE AWAY FOR A FEW DAYS.
ARE WE GOING TO THE WARLOCKS' HALL AGAIN?
NOT THIS TIME. I'M TO ESCORT YOU TO SOME DECREPIT OLD WOODCARVER'S HUT, A FEW LEAGUES OUTSIDE OF THE IMPERIAL CITY.
GODS ALONE KNOW WHY.

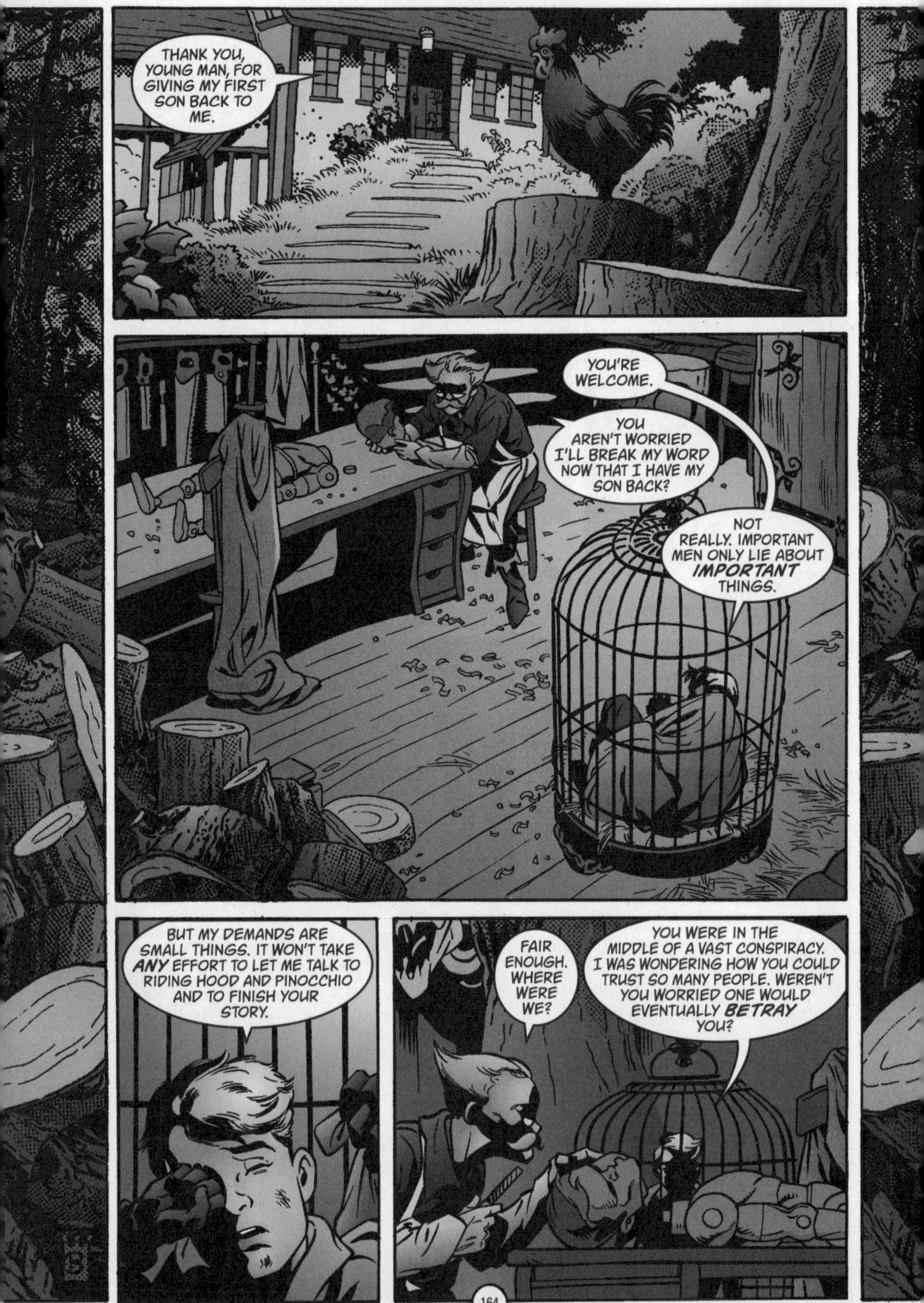
THANK YOU, YOUNG MAN, FOR GIVING MY FIRST SON BACK TO ME.
YOU'RE WELCOME.
YOU AREN'T WORRIED I'LL BREAK MY WORD NOW THAT I HAVE MY SON BACK?
NOT REALLY. IMPORTANT MEN ONLY LIE ABOUT IMPORTANT THINGS.
BUT MY DEMANDS ARE SMALL THINGS. IT WON'T TAKE ANY EFFORT TO LET ME TALK TO RIDING HOOD AND PINOCCHIO AND TO FINISH YOUR STORY.
FAIR ENOUGH. WHERE WERE WE?
YOU WERE IN THE MIDDLE OF A VAST CONSPIRACY. I WAS WONDERING HOW YOU COULD TRUST SO MANY PEOPLE. WEREN'T YOU WORRIED ONE WOULD EVENTUALLY BETRAY YOU?

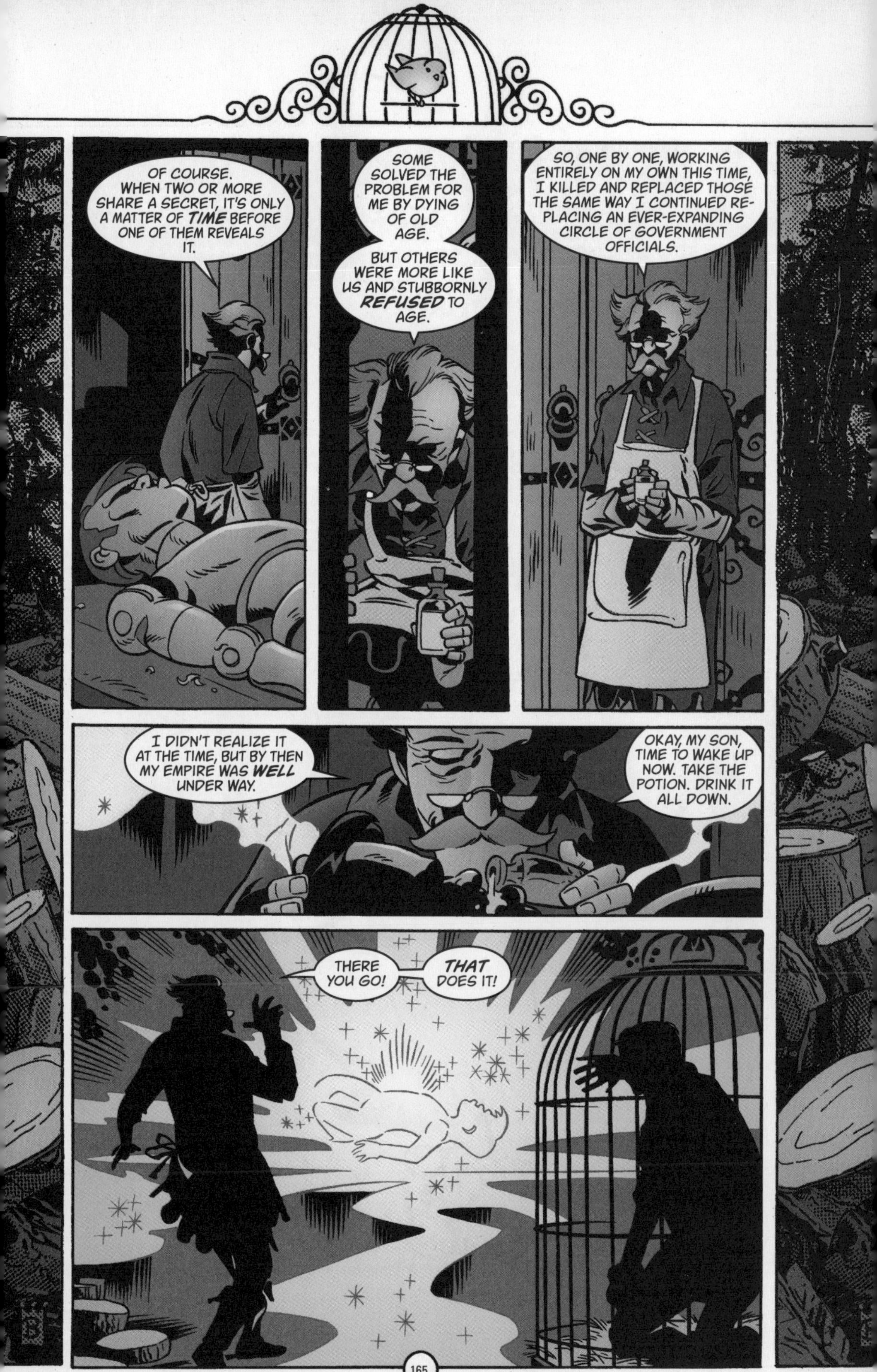

OF COURSE. WHEN TWO OR MORE SHARE A SECRET, IT'S ONLY A MATTER OF TIME BEFORE ONE OF THEM REVEALS IT.
SOME SOLVED THE PROBLEM FOR ME BY DYING OF OLD AGE.
BUT OTHERS WERE MORE LIKE US AND STUBBORNLY REFUSED TO AGE.
SO, ONE BY ONE, WORKING ENTIRELY ON MY OWN THIS TIME, I KILLED AND REPLACED THOSE THE SAME WAY I CONTINUED REPLACING AN EVER-EXPANDING CIRCLE OF GOVERNMENT OFFICIALS.
I DIDN'T REALIZE IT AT THE TIME, BUT BY THEN MY EMPIRE WAS WELL UNDER WAY.
OKAY, MY SON, TIME TO WAKE UP NOW. TAKE THE POTION. DRINK IT ALL DOWN.
THERE YOU GO!
THAT DOES IT!

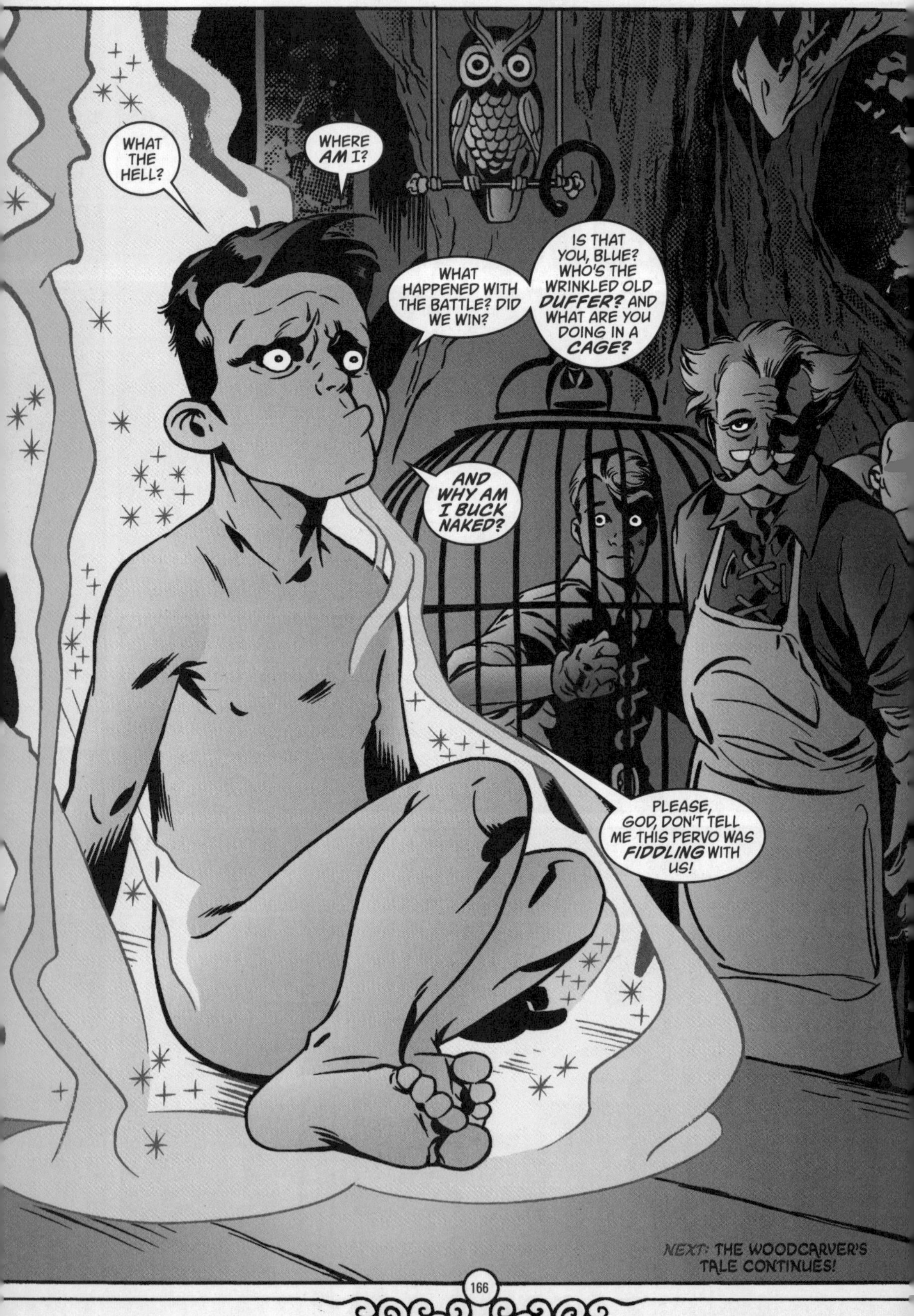
WHAT THE HELL?
WHERE AM I?
WHAT HAPPENED WITH THE BATTLE? DID WE WIN?
IS THAT YOU, BLUE? WHO'S THE WRINKLED OLD DUFFER? AND WHAT ARE YOU DOING IN A CAGE?
AND WHY AM I BUCK NAKED?
PLEASE, GOD, DON'T TELL ME THIS PERVO WAS FIDDLING WITH US!
NEXT: THE WOODCARVER'S TALE CONTINUES!

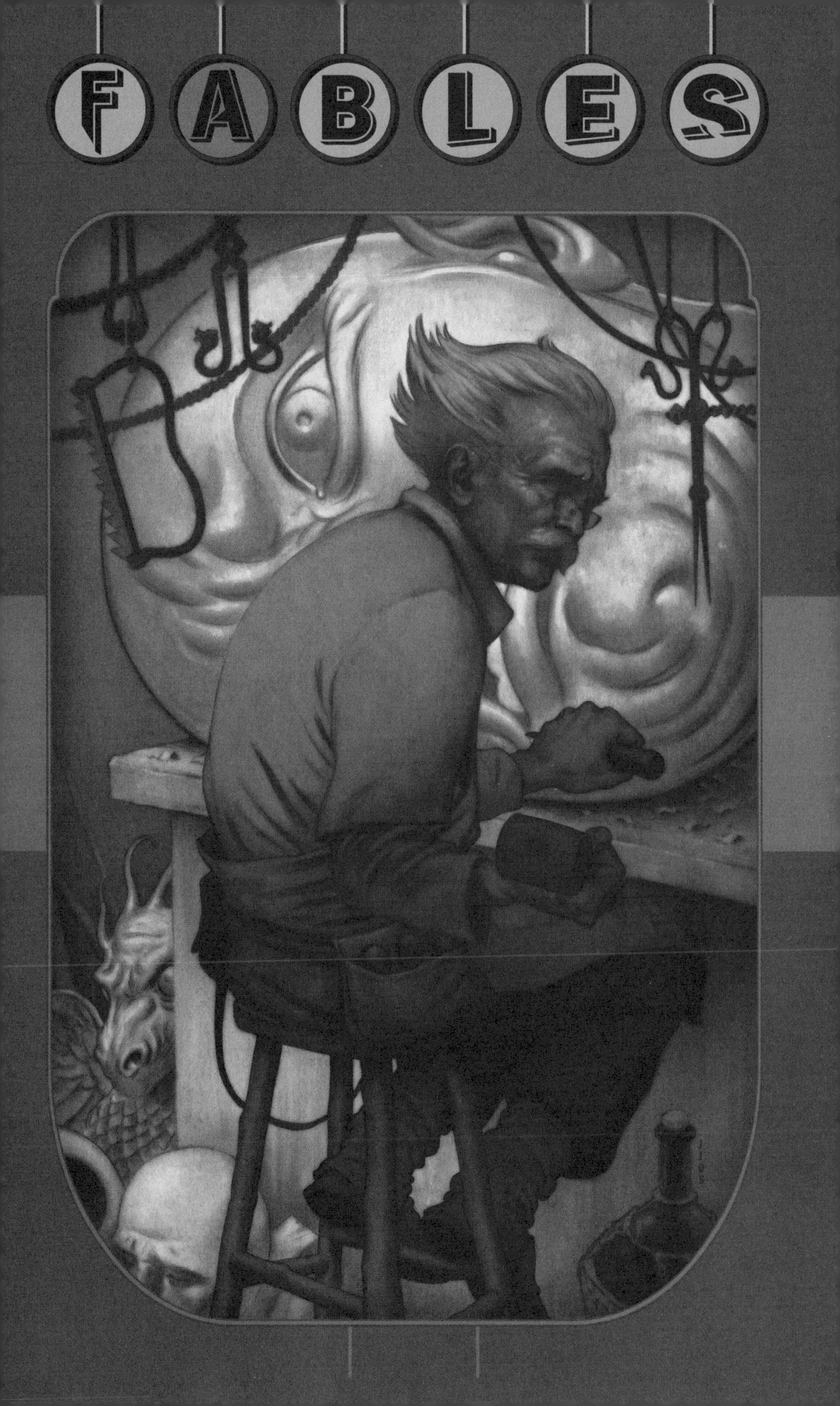
FABLES

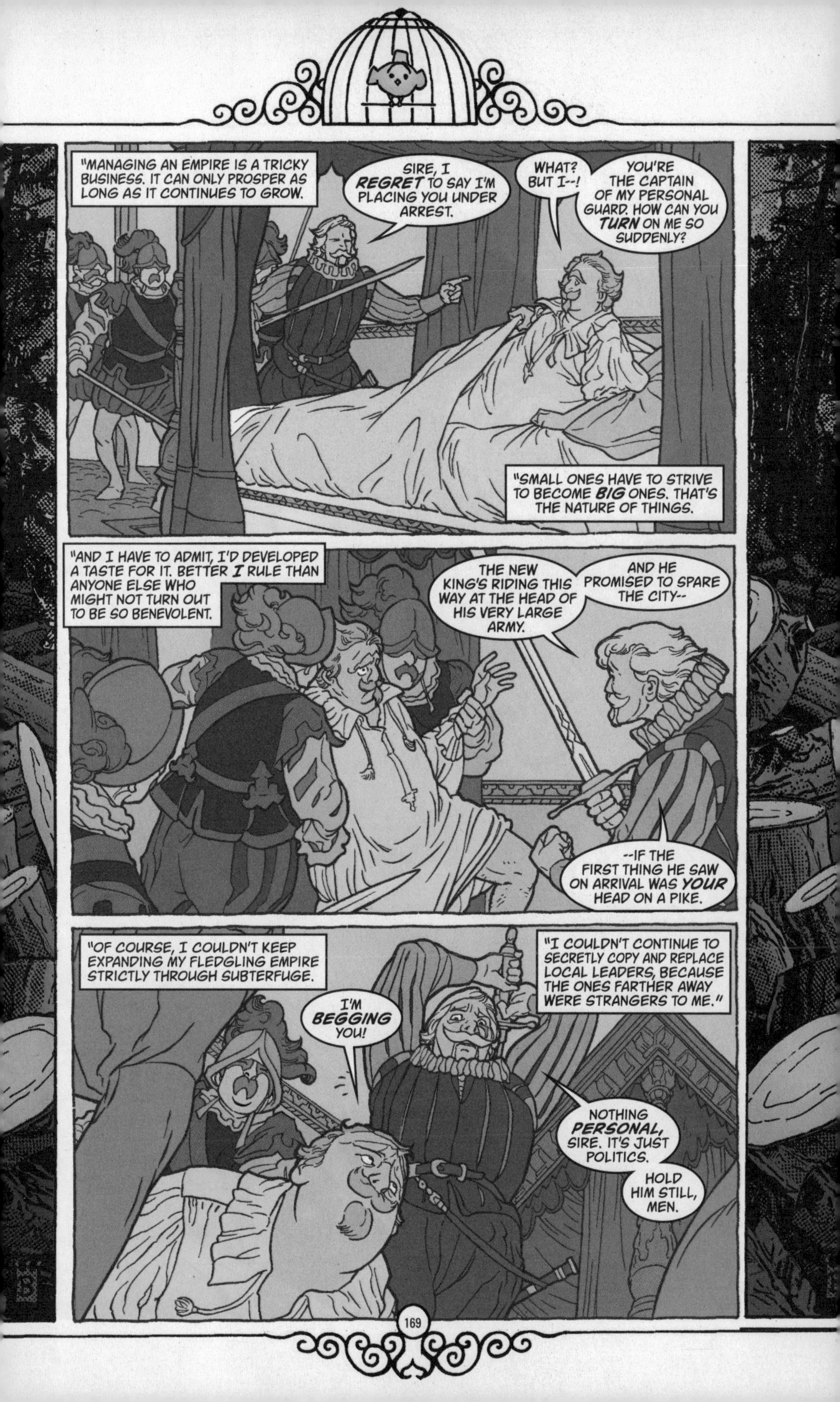
"MANAGING AN EMPIRE IS A TRICKY BUSINESS. IT CAN ONLY PROSPER AS LONG AS IT CONTINUES TO GROW.
SIRE, I REGRET TO SAY I'M PLACING YOU UNDER ARREST.
WHAT? BUT I--!
YOU'RE THE CAPTAIN OF MY PERSONAL GUARD. HOW CAN YOU TURN ON ME SO SUDDENLY?
"SMALL ONES HAVE TO STRIVE TO BECOME BIG ONES. THAT'S THE NATURE OF THINGS.
"AND I HAVE TO ADMIT, I'D DEVELOPED A TASTE FOR IT. BETTER I RULE THAN ANYONE ELSE WHO MIGHT NOT TURN OUT TO BE SO BENEVOLENT.
THE NEW KING'S RIDING THIS WAY AT THE HEAD OF HIS VERY LARGE ARMY.
AND HE PROMISED TO SPARE THE CITY--
--IF THE FIRST THING HE SAW ON ARRIVAL WAS YOUR HEAD ON A PIKE.
"OF COURSE, I COULDN'T KEEP EXPANDING MY FLEDGLING EMPIRE STRICTLY THROUGH SUBTERFUGE.
"I COULDN'T CONTINUE TO SECRETLY COPY AND REPLACE LOCAL LEADERS, BECAUSE THE ONES FARTHER AWAY WERE STRANGERS TO ME."
I'M BEGGING YOU!
NOTHING PERSONAL, SIRE. IT'S JUST POLITICS.
HOLD HIM STILL, MEN.

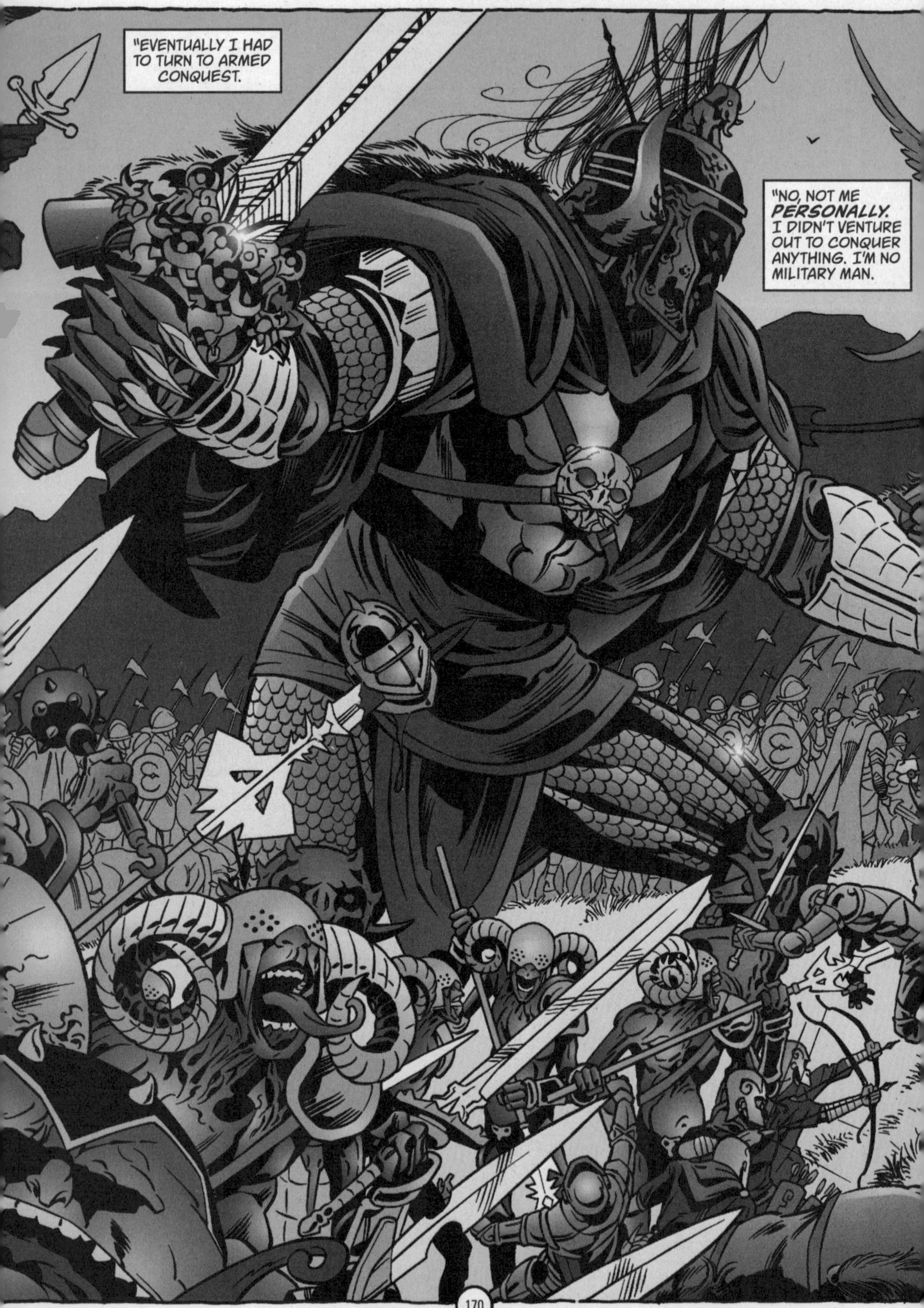
"EVENTUALLY I HAD TO TURN TO ARMED CONQUEST.
"NO, NOT ME PERSONALLY. I DIDN'T VENTURE OUT TO CONQUER ANYTHING. I'M NO MILITARY MAN.

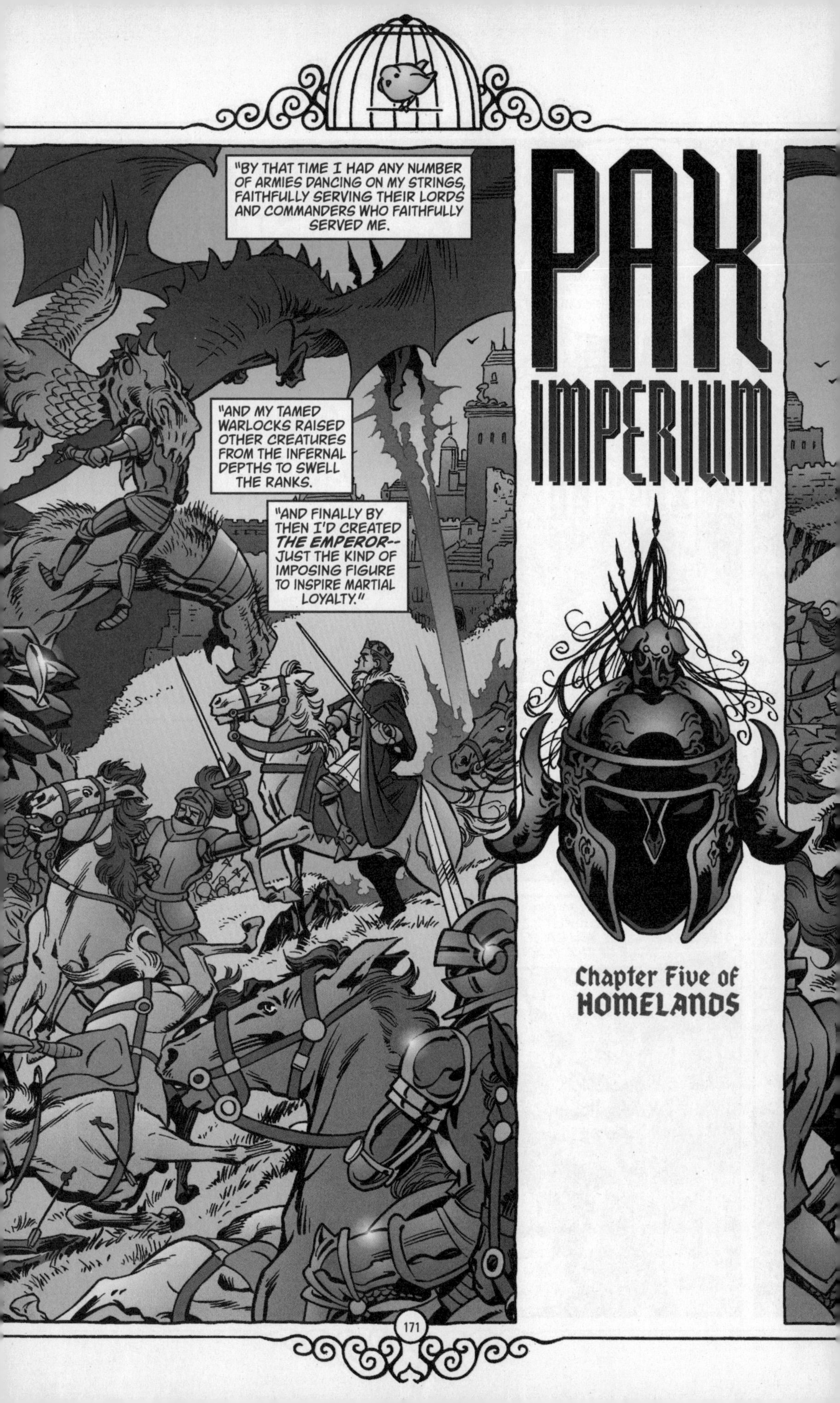
"BY THAT TIME I HAD ANY NUMBER OF ARMIES DANCING ON MY STRINGS, FAITHFULLY SERVING THEIR LORDS AND COMMANDERS WHO FAITHFULLY SERVED ME.
"AND MY TAMED WARLOCKS RAISED OTHER CREATURES FROM THE INFERNAL DEPTHS TO SWELL THE RANKS.
"AND FINALLY BY THEN I'D CREATED THE EMPEROR-- JUST THE KIND OF IMPOSING FIGURE TO INSPIRE MARTIAL LOYALTY."
PAX IMPERIUM
Chapter Five of HOMELANDS

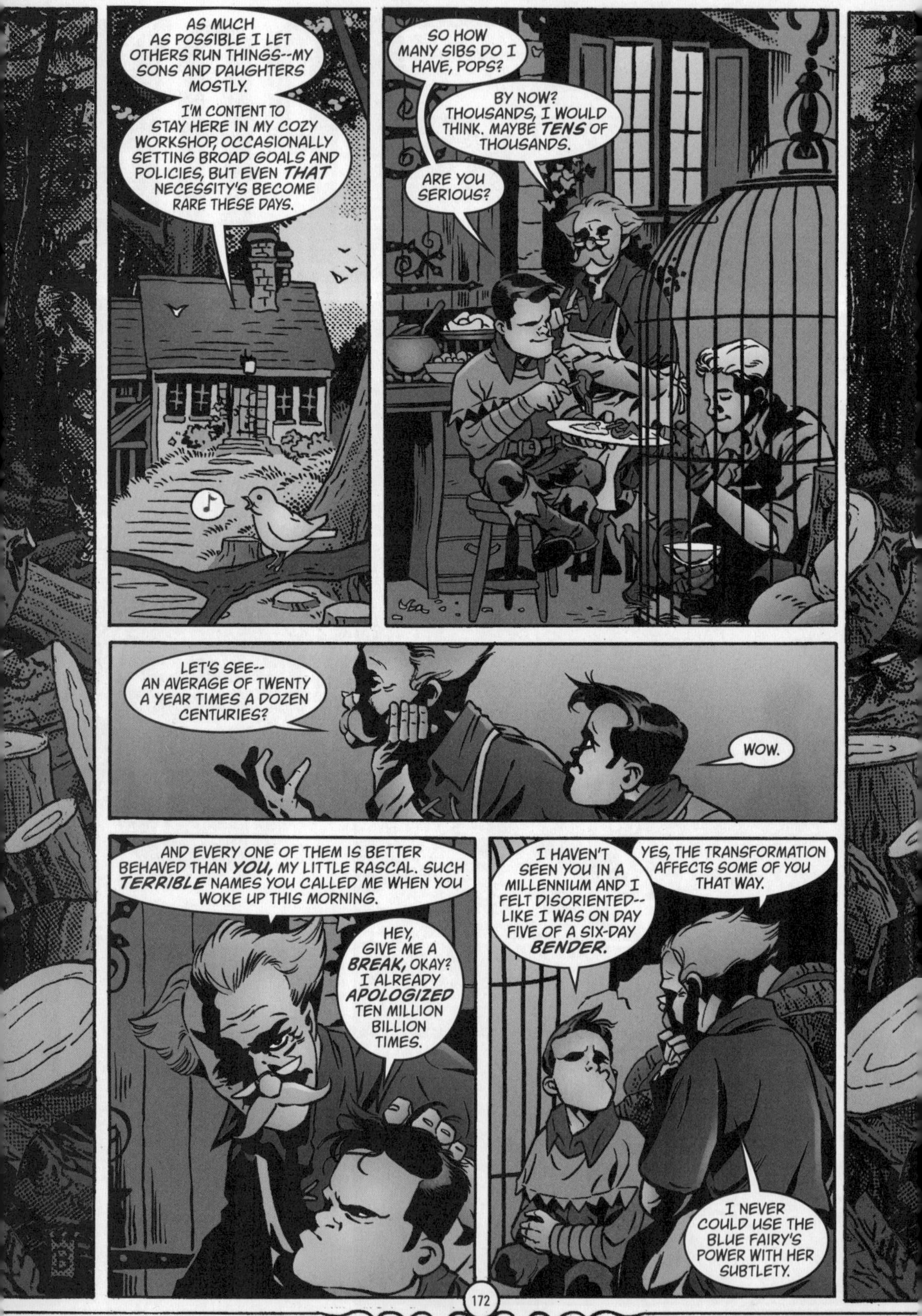

AS MUCH AS POSSIBLE I LET OTHERS RUN THINGS--MY SONS AND DAUGHTERS MOSTLY.
I'M CONTENT TO STAY HERE IN MY COZY WORKSHOP, OCCASIONALLY SETTING BROAD GOALS AND POLICIES, BUT EVEN *THAT* NECESSITY'S BECOME RARE THESE DAYS.
♪
SO HOW MANY SIBS DO I HAVE, POPS?
BY NOW? THOUSANDS, I WOULD THINK. MAYBE *TENS* OF THOUSANDS.
ARE YOU SERIOUS?
LET'S SEE-- AN AVERAGE OF TWENTY A YEAR TIMES A DOZEN CENTURIES?
WOW.
AND EVERY ONE OF THEM IS BETTER BEHAVED THAN *YOU,* MY LITTLE RASCAL. SUCH *TERRIBLE* NAMES YOU CALLED ME WHEN YOU WOKE UP THIS MORNING.
HEY, GIVE ME A *BREAK,* OKAY? I ALREADY *APOLOGIZED* TEN MILLION BILLION TIMES.
I HAVEN'T SEEN YOU IN A MILLENNIUM AND I FELT DISORIENTED-- LIKE I WAS ON DAY FIVE OF A SIX-DAY *BENDER.*
YES, THE TRANSFORMATION AFFECTS SOME OF YOU THAT WAY.
I NEVER COULD USE THE BLUE FAIRY'S POWER WITH HER SUBTLETY.

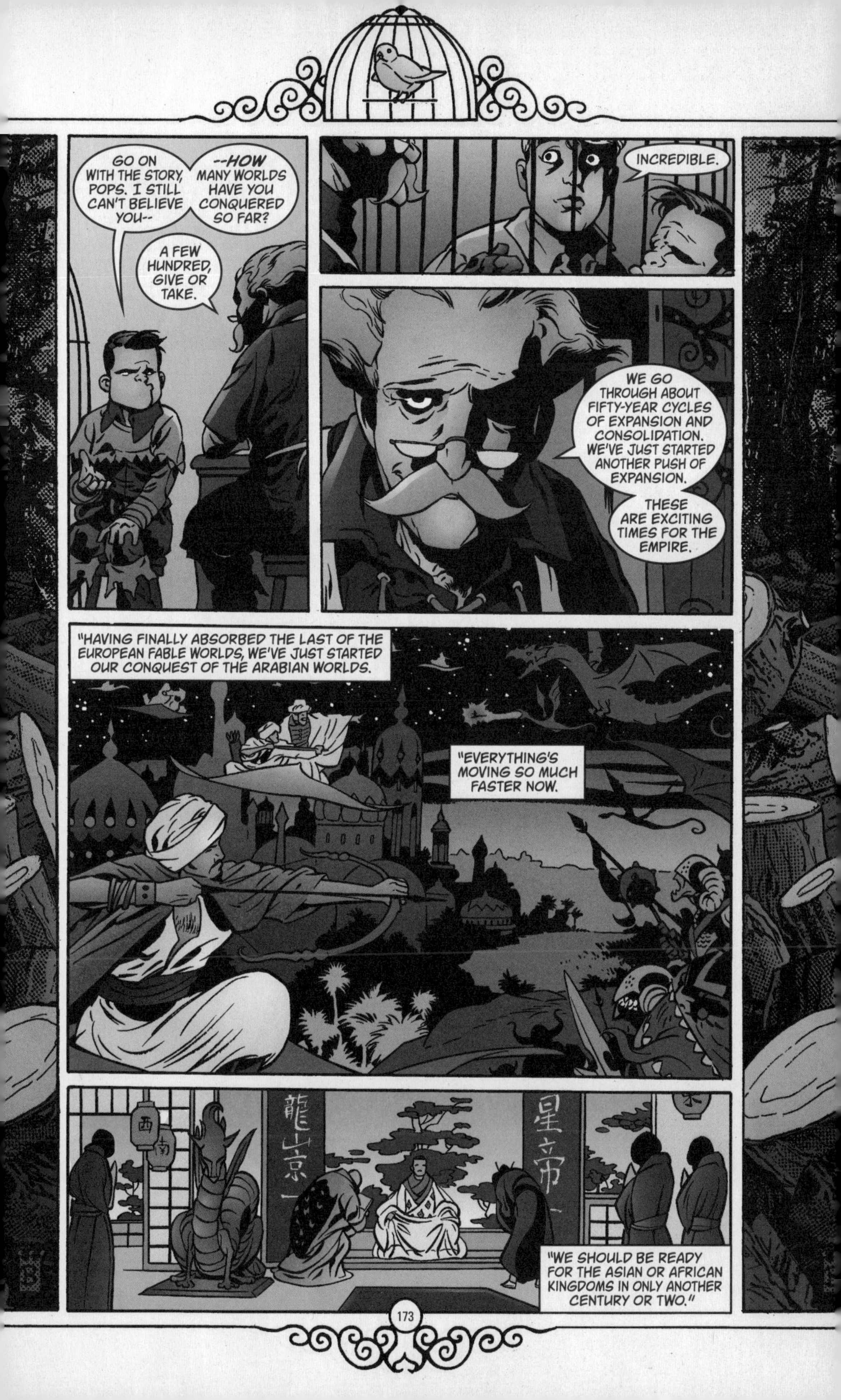

GO ON WITH THE STORY, POPS. I STILL CAN'T BELIEVE YOU--
--HOW MANY WORLDS HAVE YOU CONQUERED SO FAR?
A FEW HUNDRED, GIVE OR TAKE.
INCREDIBLE.
WE GO THROUGH ABOUT FIFTY-YEAR CYCLES OF EXPANSION AND CONSOLIDATION. WE'VE JUST STARTED ANOTHER PUSH OF EXPANSION.
THESE ARE EXCITING TIMES FOR THE EMPIRE.
"HAVING FINALLY ABSORBED THE LAST OF THE EUROPEAN FABLE WORLDS, WE'VE JUST STARTED OUR CONQUEST OF THE ARABIAN WORLDS.
"EVERYTHING'S MOVING SO MUCH FASTER NOW.
"WE SHOULD BE READY FOR THE ASIAN OR AFRICAN KINGDOMS IN ONLY ANOTHER CENTURY OR TWO."

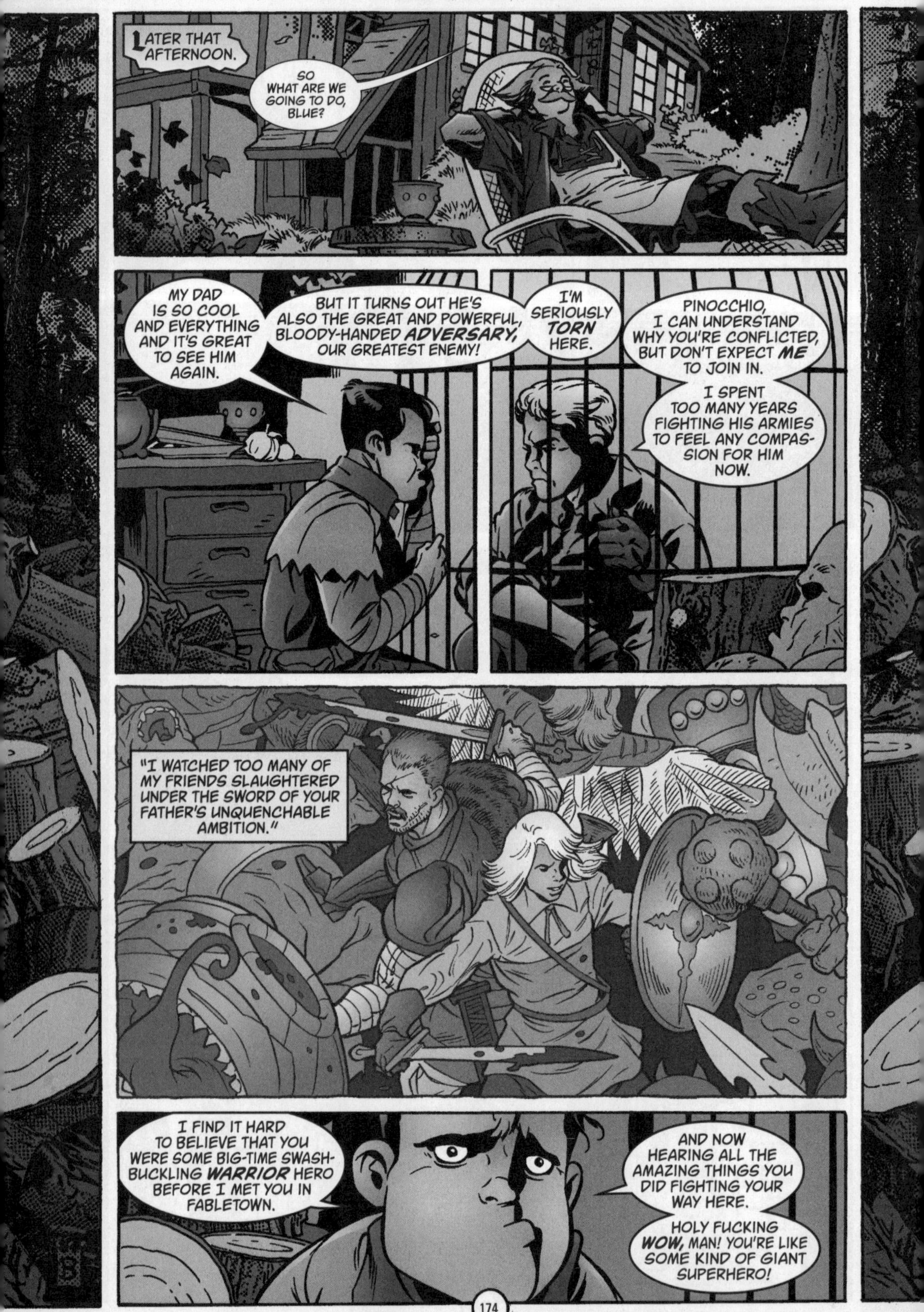
LATER THAT AFTERNOON.
SO WHAT ARE WE GOING TO DO, BLUE?
MY DAD IS SO COOL AND EVERYTHING AND IT'S GREAT TO SEE HIM AGAIN.
BUT IT TURNS OUT HE'S ALSO THE GREAT AND POWERFUL, BLOODY-HANDED ADVERSARY, OUR GREATEST ENEMY!
I'M SERIOUSLY TORN HERE.
PINOCCHIO, I CAN UNDERSTAND WHY YOU'RE CONFLICTED, BUT DON'T EXPECT ME TO JOIN IN.
I SPENT TOO MANY YEARS FIGHTING HIS ARMIES TO FEEL ANY COMPASSION FOR HIM NOW.
"I WATCHED TOO MANY OF MY FRIENDS SLAUGHTERED UNDER THE SWORD OF YOUR FATHER'S UNQUENCHABLE AMBITION."
I FIND IT HARD TO BELIEVE THAT YOU WERE SOME BIG-TIME SWASH-BUCKLING WARRIOR HERO BEFORE I MET YOU IN FABLETOWN.
AND NOW HEARING ALL THE AMAZING THINGS YOU DID FIGHTING YOUR WAY HERE.
HOLY FUCKING WOW, MAN! YOU'RE LIKE SOME KIND OF GIANT SUPERHERO!

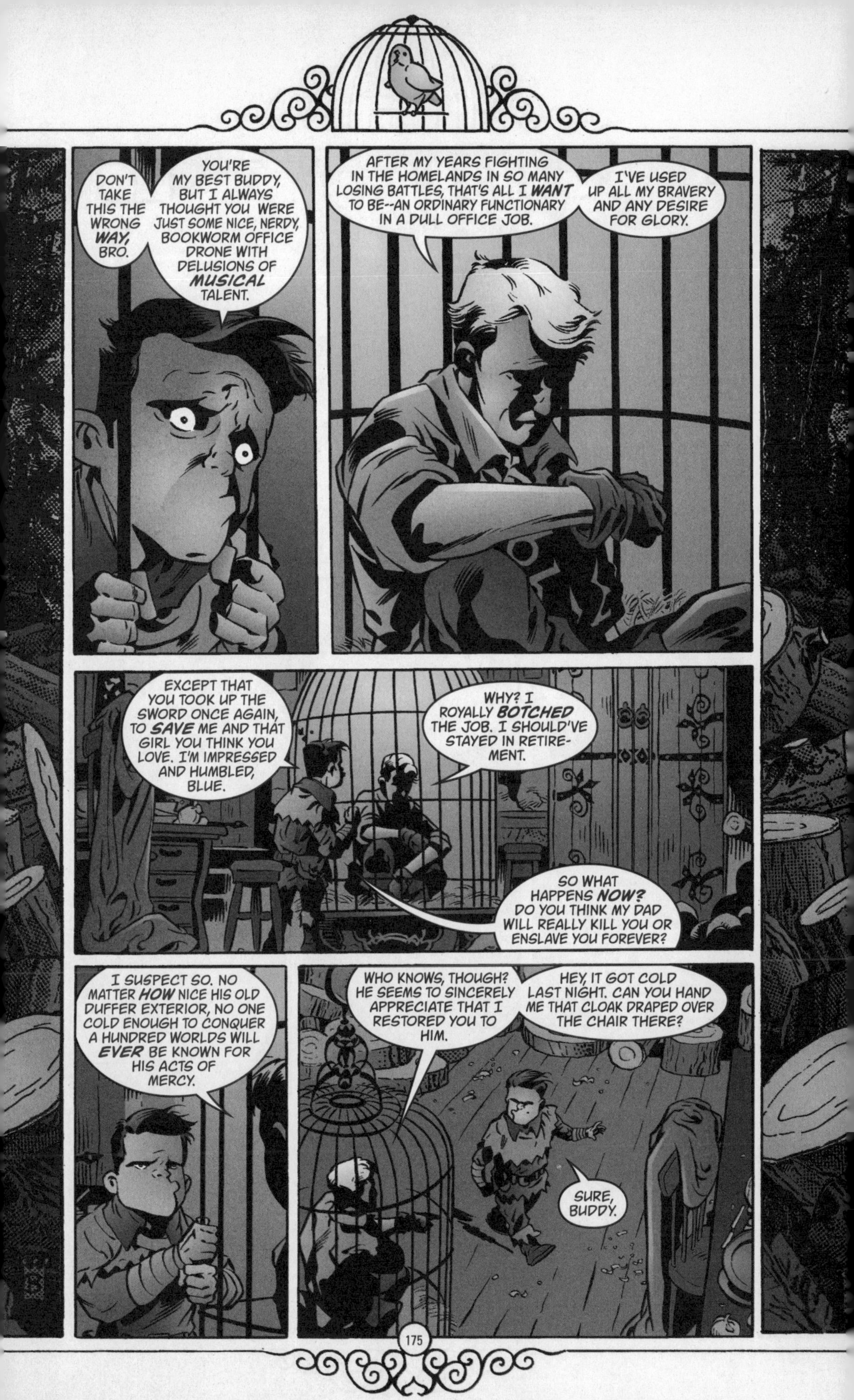
DON'T TAKE THIS THE WRONG WAY, BRO.
YOU'RE MY BEST BUDDY, BUT I ALWAYS THOUGHT YOU WERE JUST SOME NICE, NERDY, BOOKWORM OFFICE DRONE WITH DELUSIONS OF MUSICAL TALENT.
AFTER MY YEARS FIGHTING IN THE HOMELANDS IN SO MANY LOSING BATTLES, THAT'S ALL I WANT TO BE--AN ORDINARY FUNCTIONARY IN A DULL OFFICE JOB.
I'VE USED UP ALL MY BRAVERY AND ANY DESIRE FOR GLORY.
EXCEPT THAT YOU TOOK UP THE SWORD ONCE AGAIN, TO SAVE ME AND THAT GIRL YOU THINK YOU LOVE. I'M IMPRESSED AND HUMBLED, BLUE.
WHY? I ROYALLY BOTCHED THE JOB. I SHOULD'VE STAYED IN RETIRE-MENT.
SO WHAT HAPPENS NOW? DO YOU THINK MY DAD WILL REALLY KILL YOU OR ENSLAVE YOU FOREVER?
I SUSPECT SO. NO MATTER HOW NICE HIS OLD DUFFER EXTERIOR, NO ONE COLD ENOUGH TO CONQUER A HUNDRED WORLDS WILL EVER BE KNOWN FOR HIS ACTS OF MERCY.
WHO KNOWS, THOUGH? HE SEEMS TO SINCERELY APPRECIATE THAT I RESTORED YOU TO HIM.
HEY, IT GOT COLD LAST NIGHT. CAN YOU HAND ME THAT CLOAK DRAPED OVER THE CHAIR THERE?
SURE, BUDDY.

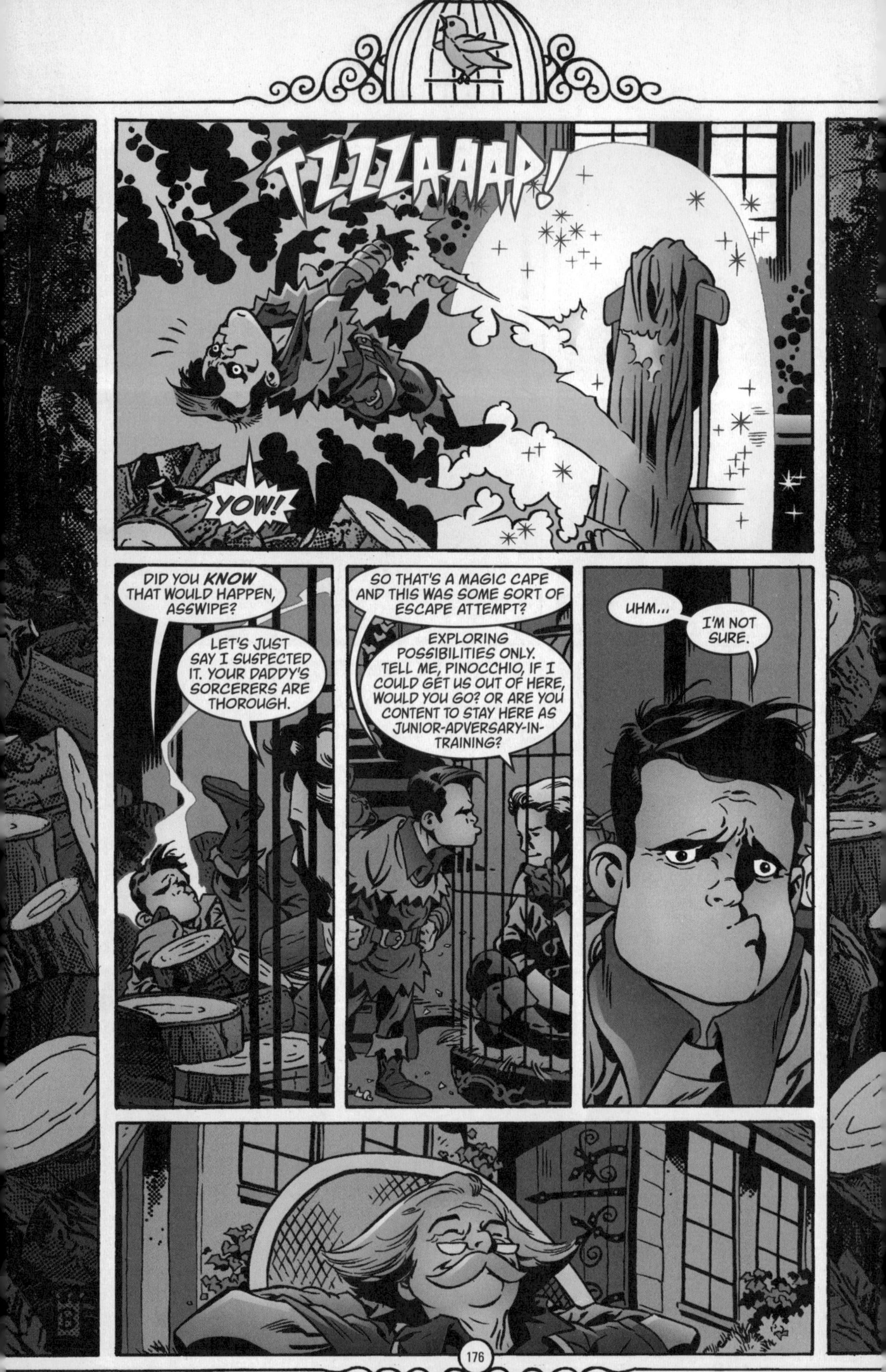
TZZZAAAP!
YOW!
DID YOU KNOW THAT WOULD HAPPEN, ASSWIPE?
LET'S JUST SAY I SUSPECTED IT. YOUR DADDY'S SORCERERS ARE THOROUGH.
SO THAT'S A MAGIC CAPE AND THIS WAS SOME SORT OF ESCAPE ATTEMPT?
EXPLORING POSSIBILITIES ONLY. TELL ME, PINOCCHIO, IF I COULD GET US OUT OF HERE, WOULD YOU GO? OR ARE YOU CONTENT TO STAY HERE AS JUNIOR-ADVERSARY-IN-TRAINING?
UHM...
I'M NOT SURE.

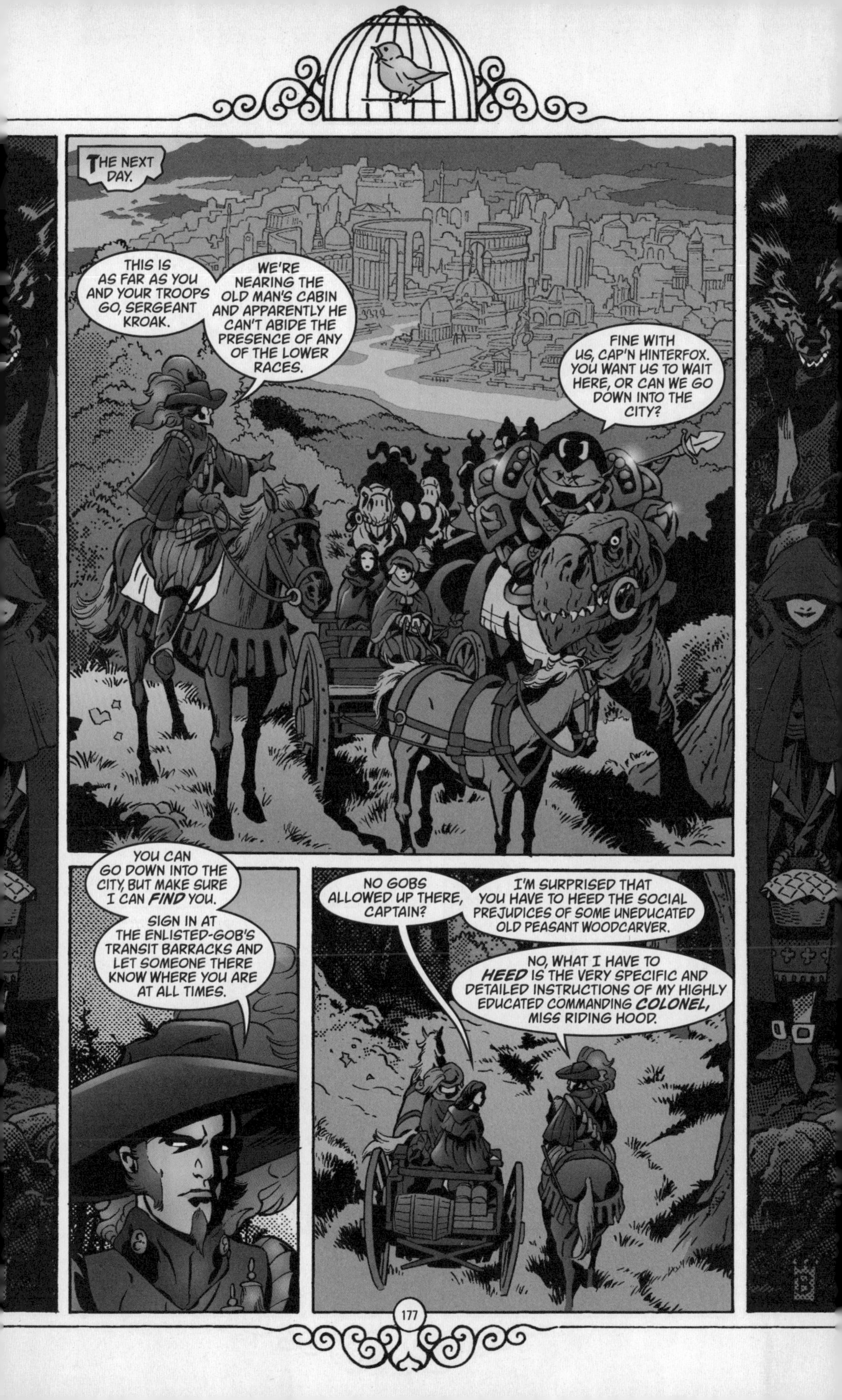
THE NEXT DAY.
THIS IS AS FAR AS YOU AND YOUR TROOPS GO, SERGEANT KROAK.
WE'RE NEARING THE OLD MAN'S CABIN AND APPARENTLY HE CAN'T ABIDE THE PRESENCE OF ANY OF THE LOWER RACES.
FINE WITH US, CAP'N HINTERFOX. YOU WANT US TO WAIT HERE, OR CAN WE GO DOWN INTO THE CITY?
YOU CAN GO DOWN INTO THE CITY, BUT MAKE SURE I CAN FIND YOU.
SIGN IN AT THE ENLISTED-GOB'S TRANSIT BARRACKS AND LET SOMEONE THERE KNOW WHERE YOU ARE AT ALL TIMES.
NO GOBS ALLOWED UP THERE, CAPTAIN?
I'M SURPRISED THAT YOU HAVE TO HEED THE SOCIAL PREJUDICES OF SOME UNEDUCATED OLD PEASANT WOODCARVER.
NO, WHAT I HAVE TO HEED IS THE VERY SPECIFIC AND DETAILED INSTRUCTIONS OF MY HIGHLY EDUCATED COMMANDING COLONEL, MISS RIDING HOOD.

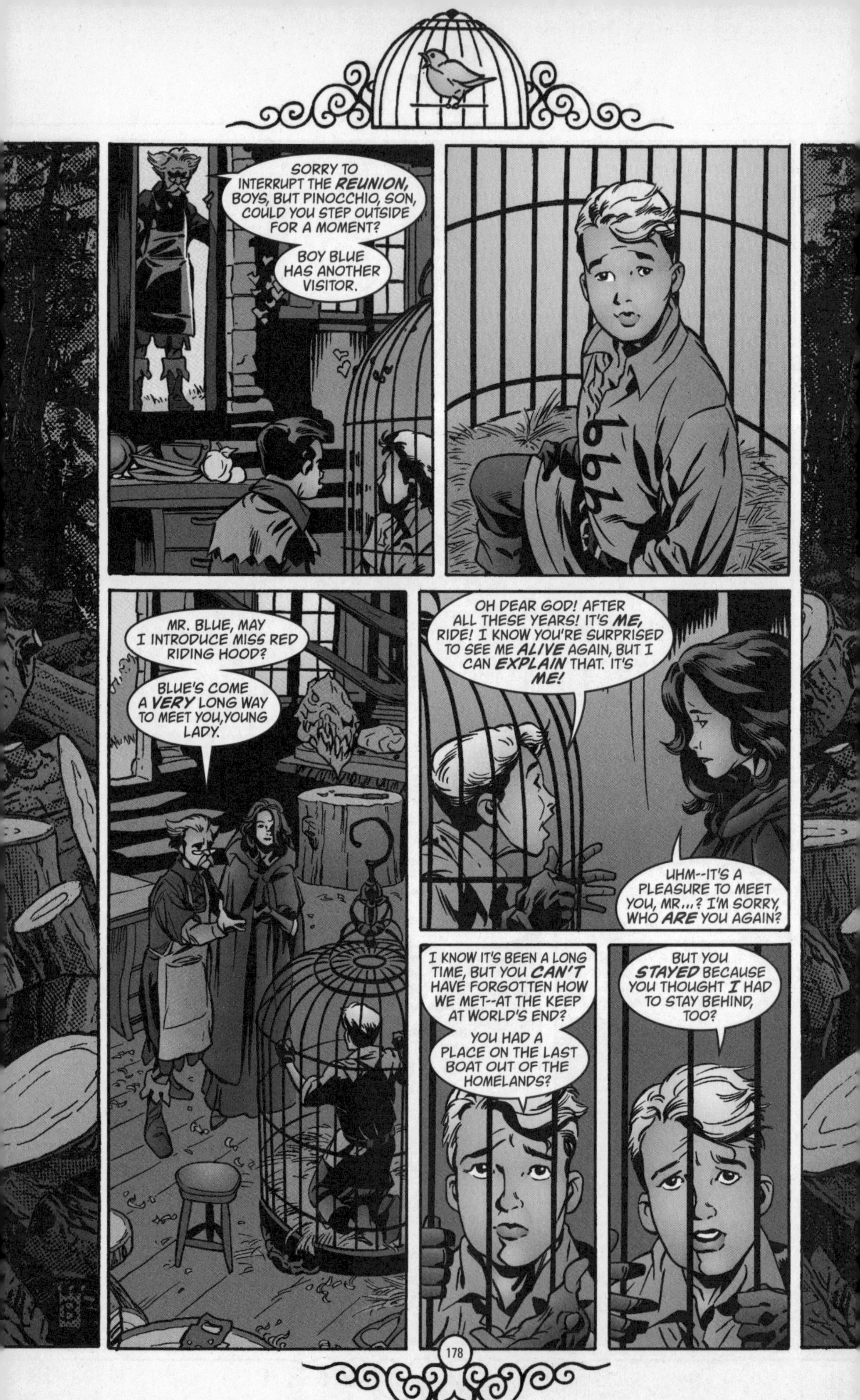
SORRY TO INTERRUPT THE REUNION, BOYS, BUT PINOCCHIO, SON, COULD YOU STEP OUTSIDE FOR A MOMENT?
BOY BLUE HAS ANOTHER VISITOR.
MR. BLUE, MAY I INTRODUCE MISS RED RIDING HOOD?
BLUE'S COME A VERY LONG WAY TO MEET YOU,YOUNG LADY.
OH DEAR GOD! AFTER ALL THESE YEARS! IT'S ME, RIDE! I KNOW YOU'RE SURPRISED TO SEE ME ALIVE AGAIN, BUT I CAN EXPLAIN THAT. IT'S ME!
UHM--IT'S A PLEASURE TO MEET YOU, MR...? I'M SORRY, WHO ARE YOU AGAIN?
I KNOW IT'S BEEN A LONG TIME, BUT YOU CAN'T HAVE FORGOTTEN HOW WE MET--AT THE KEEP AT WORLD'S END?
YOU HAD A PLACE ON THE LAST BOAT OUT OF THE HOMELANDS?
BUT YOU STAYED BECAUSE YOU THOUGHT I HAD TO STAY BEHIND, TOO?

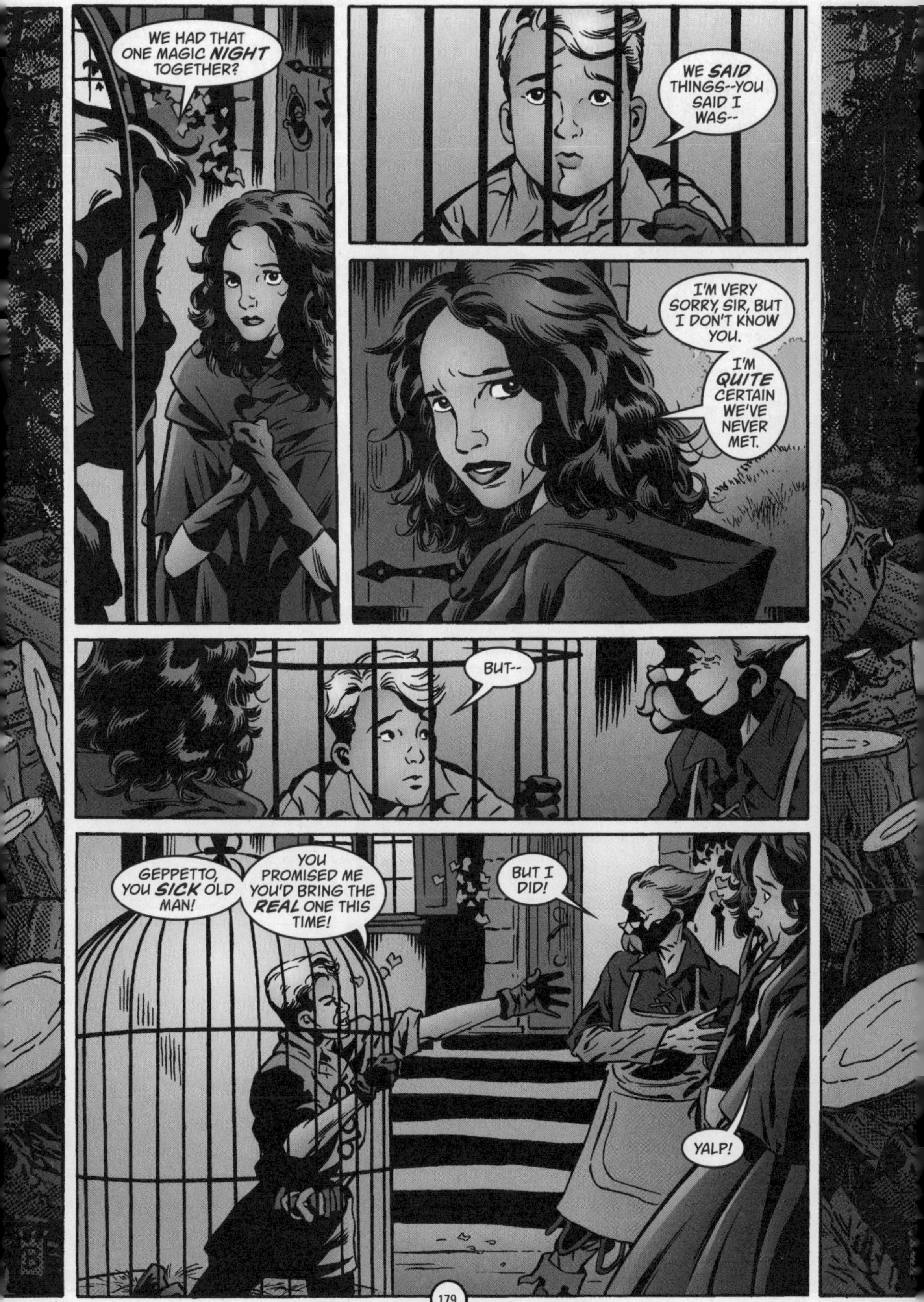
WE HAD THAT ONE MAGIC NIGHT TOGETHER?
WE SAID THINGS--YOU SAID I WAS--
I'M VERY SORRY, SIR, BUT I DON'T KNOW YOU.
I'M QUITE CERTAIN WE'VE NEVER MET.
BUT--
GEPPETTO, YOU SICK OLD MAN!
YOU PROMISED ME YOU'D BRING THE REAL ONE THIS TIME!
BUT I DID!
YALP!

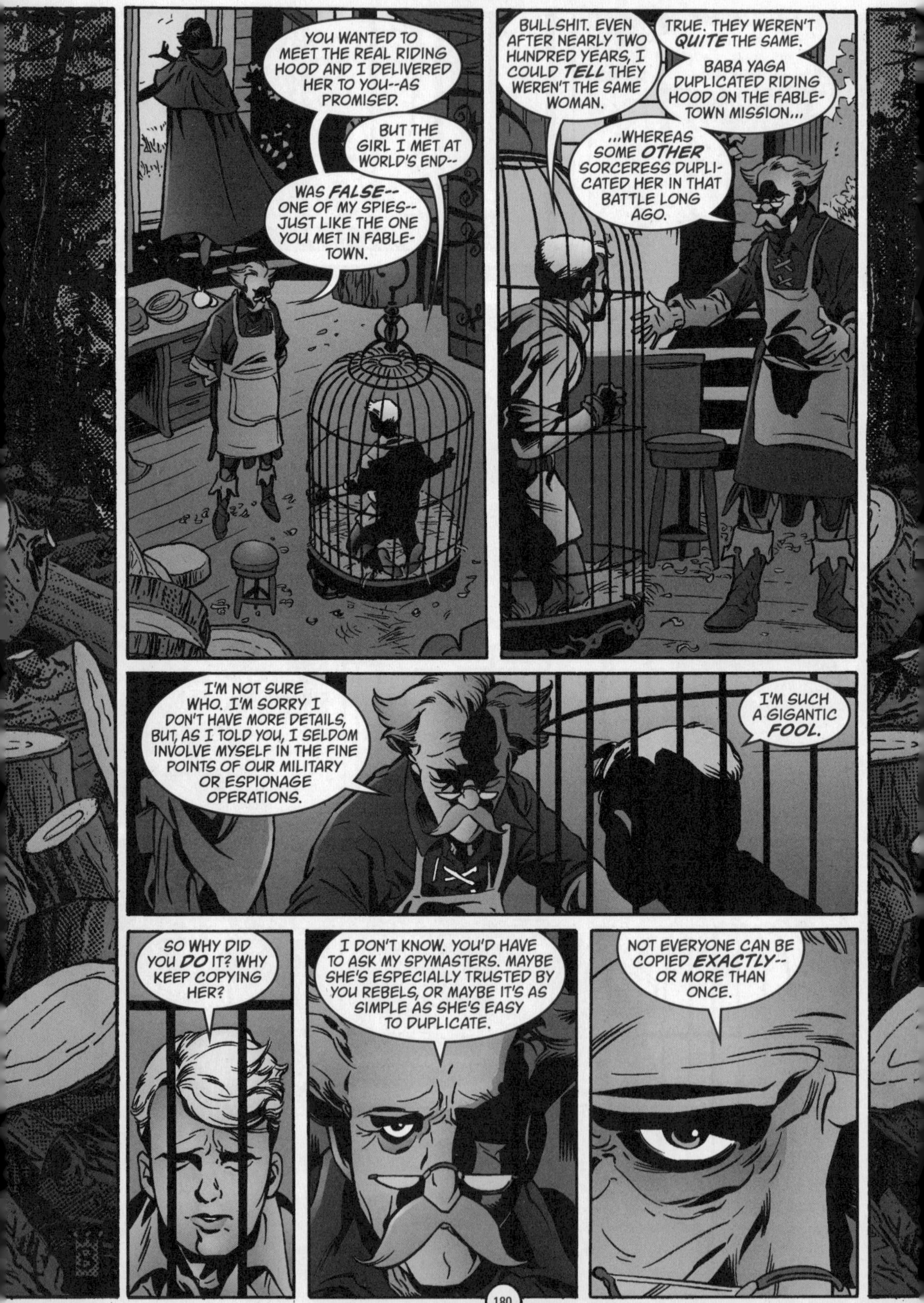
YOU WANTED TO MEET THE REAL RIDING HOOD AND I DELIVERED HER TO YOU--AS PROMISED.
BUT THE GIRL I MET AT WORLD'S END--
WAS FALSE-- ONE OF MY SPIES-- JUST LIKE THE ONE YOU MET IN FABLE-TOWN.
BULLSHIT. EVEN AFTER NEARLY TWO HUNDRED YEARS, I COULD TELL THEY WEREN'T THE SAME WOMAN.
TRUE. THEY WEREN'T QUITE THE SAME.
BABA YAGA DUPLICATED RIDING HOOD ON THE FABLE-TOWN MISSION...
...WHEREAS SOME OTHER SORCERESS DUPLICATED HER IN THAT BATTLE LONG AGO.
I'M NOT SURE WHO. I'M SORRY I DON'T HAVE MORE DETAILS, BUT, AS I TOLD YOU, I SELDOM INVOLVE MYSELF IN THE FINE POINTS OF OUR MILITARY OR ESPIONAGE OPERATIONS.
I'M SUCH A GIGANTIC FOOL.
SO WHY DID YOU DO IT? WHY KEEP COPYING HER?
I DON'T KNOW. YOU'D HAVE TO ASK MY SPYMASTERS. MAYBE SHE'S ESPECIALLY TRUSTED BY YOU REBELS, OR MAYBE IT'S AS SIMPLE AS SHE'S EASY TO DUPLICATE.
NOT EVERYONE CAN BE COPIED EXACTLY-- OR MORE THAN ONCE.

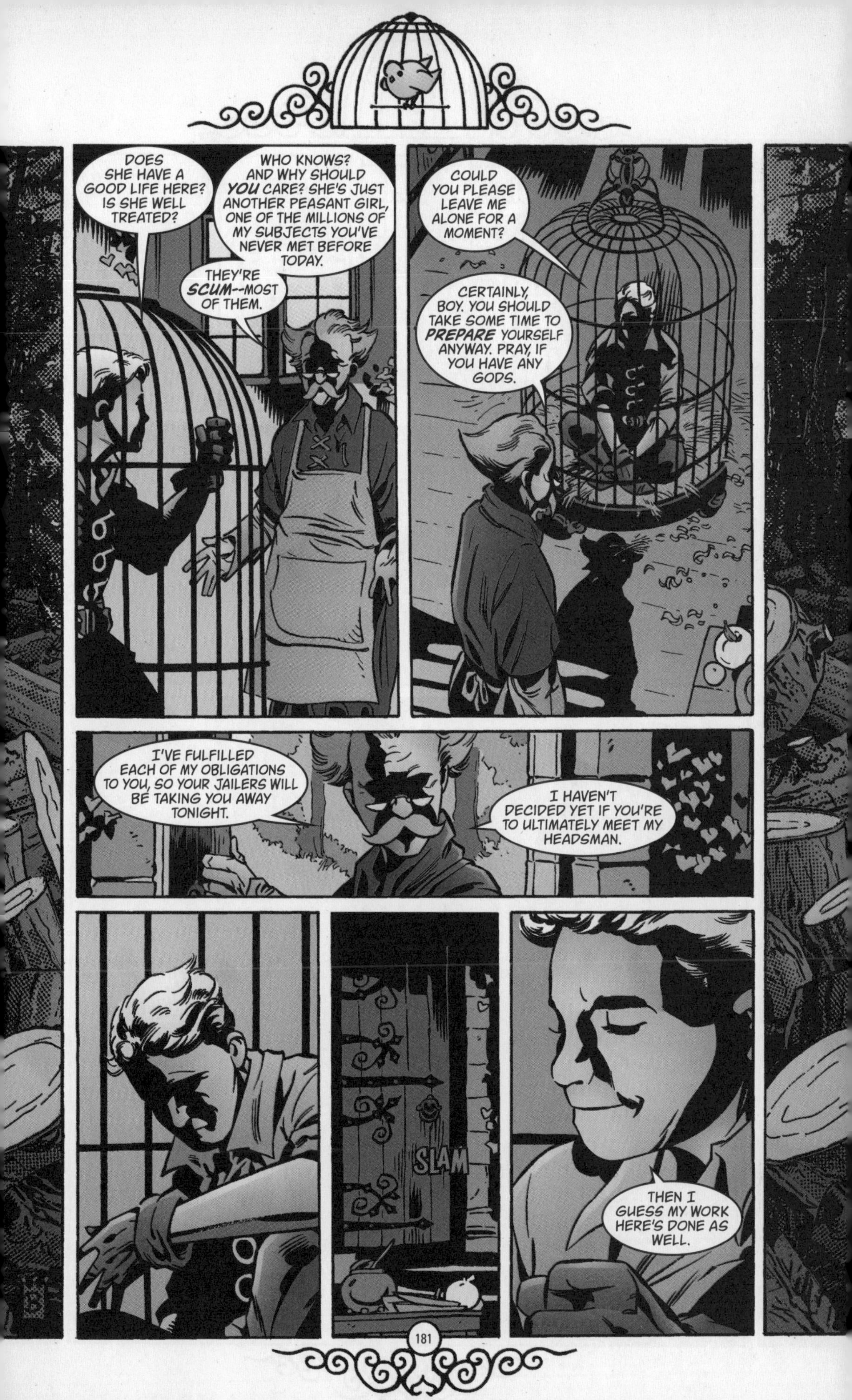
DOES SHE HAVE A GOOD LIFE HERE? IS SHE WELL TREATED?
WHO KNOWS? AND WHY SHOULD YOU CARE? SHE'S JUST ANOTHER PEASANT GIRL, ONE OF THE MILLIONS OF MY SUBJECTS YOU'VE NEVER MET BEFORE TODAY.
THEY'RE SCUM--MOST OF THEM.
COULD YOU PLEASE LEAVE ME ALONE FOR A MOMENT?
CERTAINLY, BOY. YOU SHOULD TAKE SOME TIME TO PREPARE YOURSELF ANYWAY. PRAY, IF YOU HAVE ANY GODS.
I'VE FULFILLED EACH OF MY OBLIGATIONS TO YOU, SO YOUR JAILERS WILL BE TAKING YOU AWAY TONIGHT.
I HAVEN'T DECIDED YET IF YOU'RE TO ULTIMATELY MEET MY HEADSMAN.
SLAM
THEN I GUESS MY WORK HERE'S DONE AS WELL.

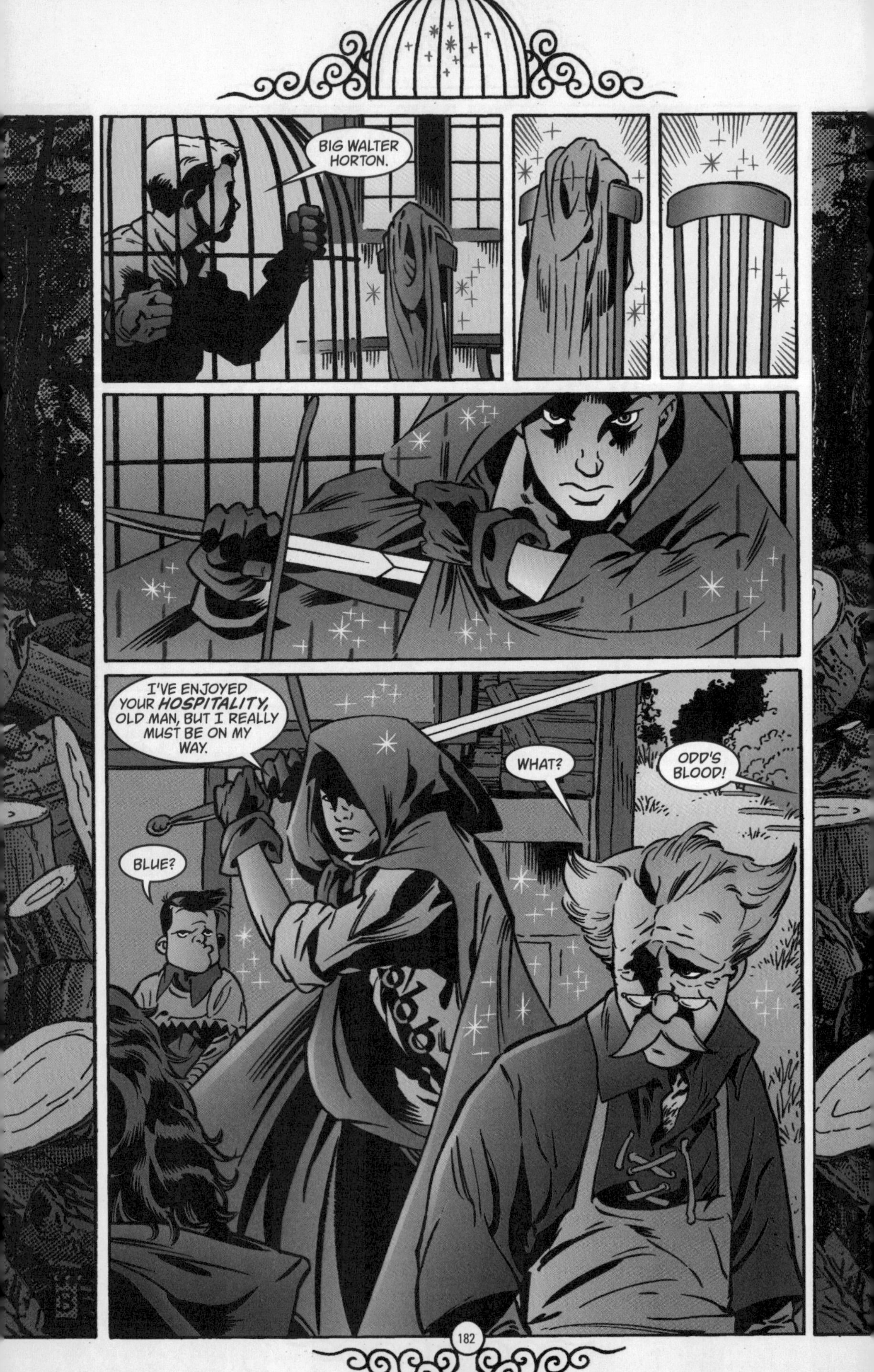
BIG WALTER HORTON.
I'VE ENJOYED YOUR HOSPITALITY, OLD MAN, BUT I REALLY MUST BE ON MY WAY.
WHAT?
ODD'S BLOOD!
BLUE?

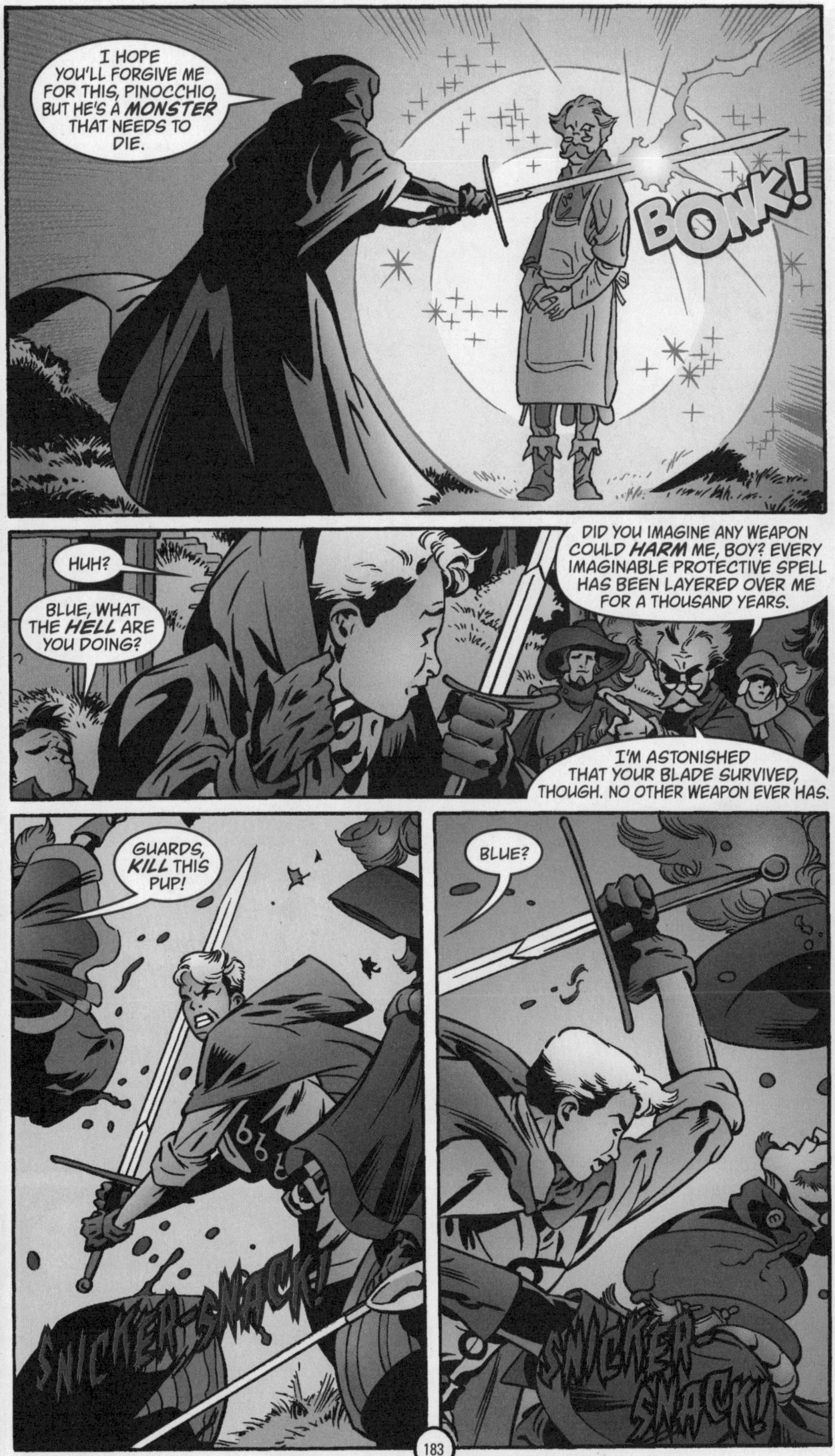
I HOPE YOU'LL FORGIVE ME FOR THIS, PINOCCHIO, BUT HE'S A MONSTER THAT NEEDS TO DIE.
BONK!
HUH?
BLUE, WHAT THE HELL ARE YOU DOING?
DID YOU IMAGINE ANY WEAPON COULD HARM ME, BOY? EVERY IMAGINABLE PROTECTIVE SPELL HAS BEEN LAYERED OVER ME FOR A THOUSAND YEARS.
I'M ASTONISHED THAT YOUR BLADE SURVIVED, THOUGH. NO OTHER WEAPON EVER HAS.
GUARDS, KILL THIS PUP!
SNICKER-SNACK!
BLUE?
SNICKER SNACK!

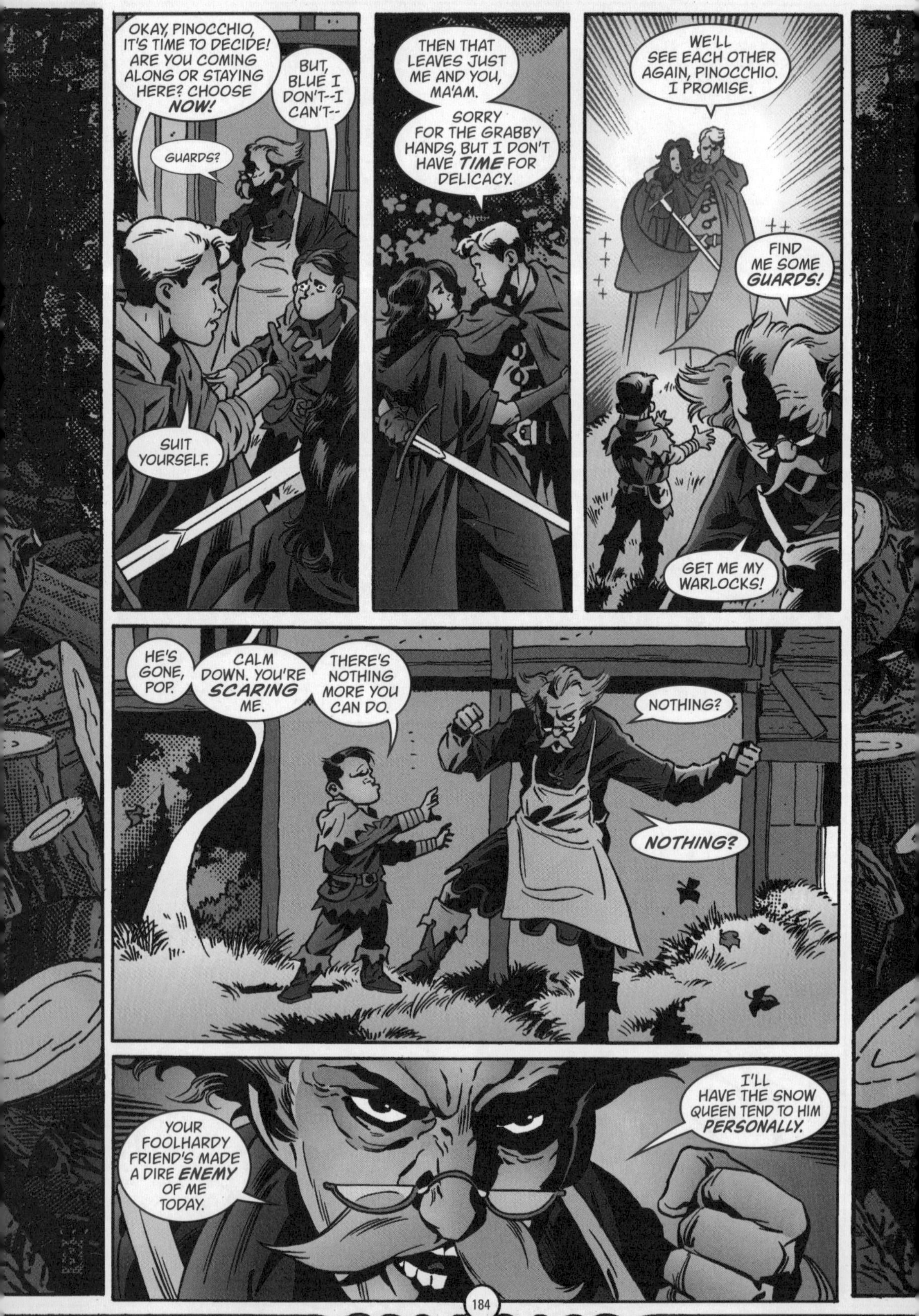
OKAY, PINOCCHIO, IT'S TIME TO DECIDE! ARE YOU COMING ALONG OR STAYING HERE? CHOOSE NOW!
BUT, BLUE I DON'T--I CAN'T--
GUARDS?
SUIT YOURSELF.
THEN THAT LEAVES JUST ME AND YOU, MA'AM.
SORRY FOR THE GRABBY HANDS, BUT I DON'T HAVE TIME FOR DELICACY.
WE'LL SEE EACH OTHER AGAIN, PINOCCHIO. I PROMISE.
FIND ME SOME GUARDS!
GET ME MY WARLOCKS!
HE'S GONE, POP.
CALM DOWN. YOU'RE SCARING ME.
THERE'S NOTHING MORE YOU CAN DO.
NOTHING?
NOTHING?
YOUR FOOLHARDY FRIEND'S MADE A DIRE ENEMY OF ME TODAY.
I'LL HAVE THE SNOW QUEEN TEND TO HIM PERSONALLY.

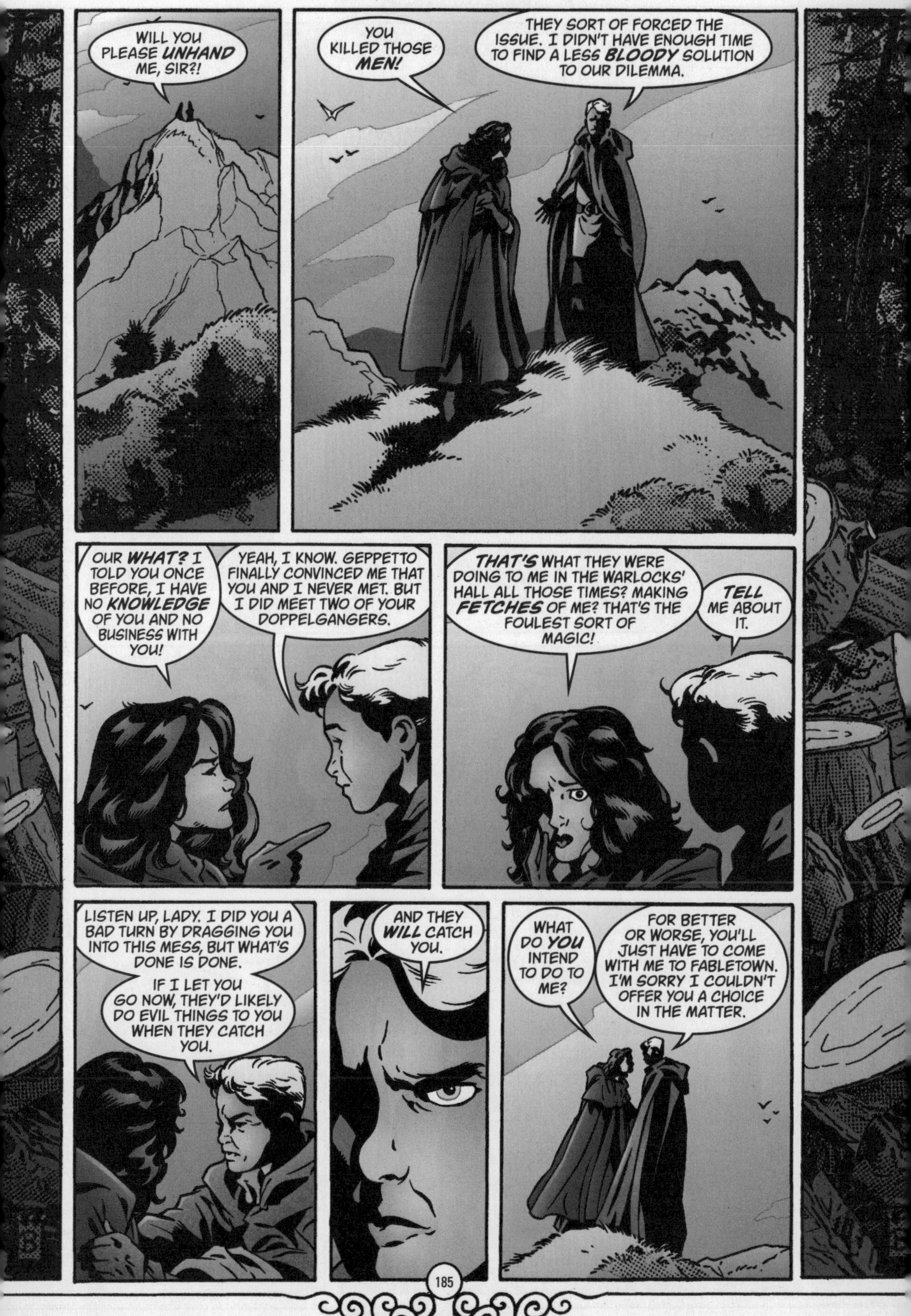
WILL YOU PLEASE UNHAND ME, SIR?!
YOU KILLED THOSE MEN!
THEY SORT OF FORCED THE ISSUE. I DIDN'T HAVE ENOUGH TIME TO FIND A LESS BLOODY SOLUTION TO OUR DILEMMA.
OUR WHAT? I TOLD YOU ONCE BEFORE, I HAVE NO KNOWLEDGE OF YOU AND NO BUSINESS WITH YOU!
YEAH, I KNOW. GEPPETTO FINALLY CONVINCED ME THAT YOU AND I NEVER MET. BUT I DID MEET TWO OF YOUR DOPPELGANGERS.
THAT'S WHAT THEY WERE DOING TO ME IN THE WARLOCKS' HALL ALL THOSE TIMES? MAKING FETCHES OF ME? THAT'S THE FOULEST SORT OF MAGIC!
TELL ME ABOUT IT.
LISTEN UP, LADY. I DID YOU A BAD TURN BY DRAGGING YOU INTO THIS MESS, BUT WHAT'S DONE IS DONE.
IF I LET YOU GO NOW, THEY'D LIKELY DO EVIL THINGS TO YOU WHEN THEY CATCH YOU.
AND THEY WILL CATCH YOU.
WHAT DO YOU INTEND TO DO TO ME?
FOR BETTER OR WORSE, YOU'LL JUST HAVE TO COME WITH ME TO FABLETOWN. I'M SORRY I COULDN'T OFFER YOU A CHOICE IN THE MATTER.

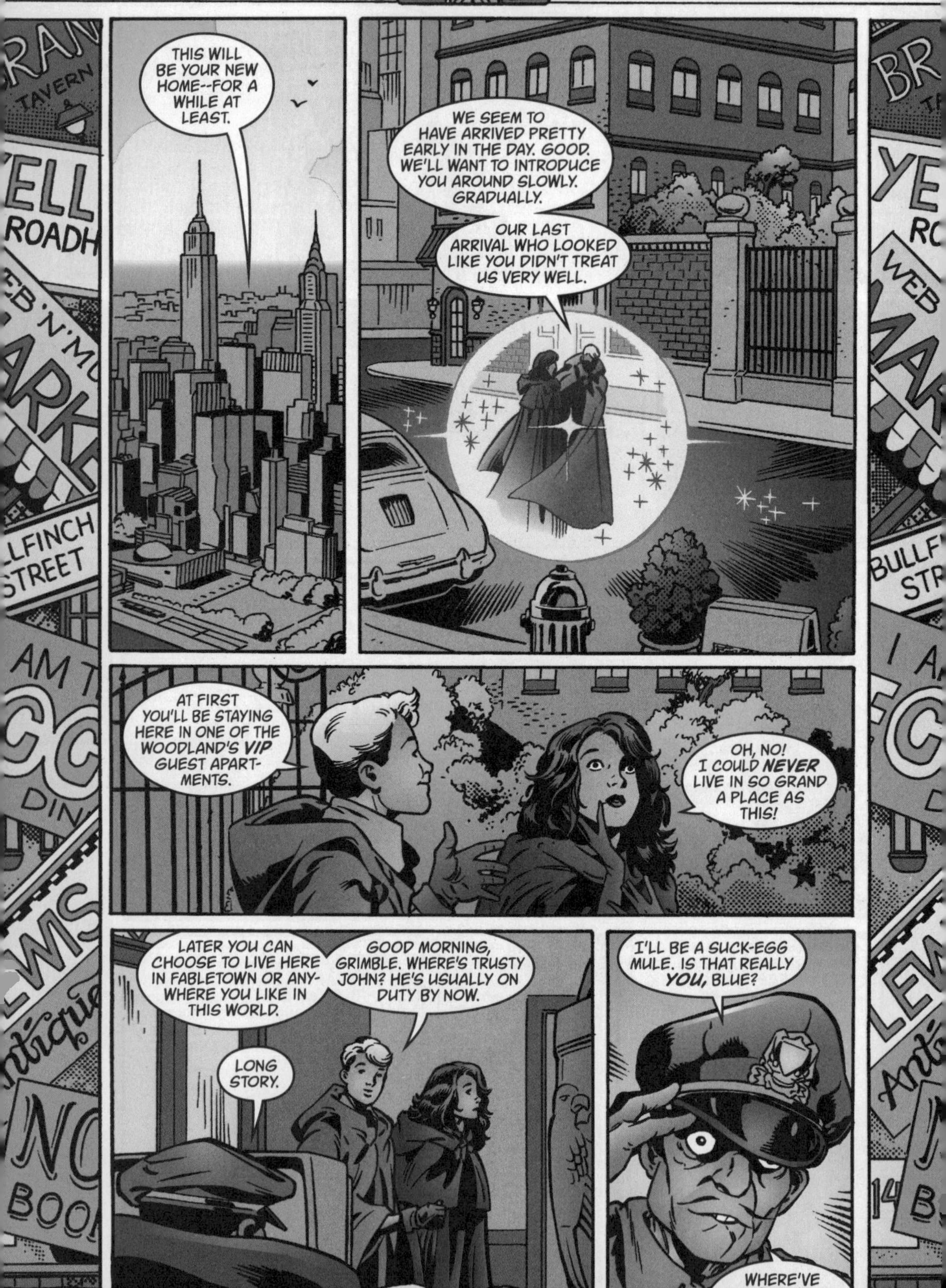
THIS WILL BE YOUR NEW HOME--FOR A WHILE AT LEAST.
WE SEEM TO HAVE ARRIVED PRETTY EARLY IN THE DAY. GOOD. WE'LL WANT TO INTRODUCE YOU AROUND SLOWLY. GRADUALLY.
OUR LAST ARRIVAL WHO LOOKED LIKE YOU DIDN'T TREAT US VERY WELL.
AT FIRST YOU'LL BE STAYING HERE IN ONE OF THE WOODLAND'S *VIP* GUEST APART-MENTS.
OH, NO! I COULD *NEVER* LIVE IN SO GRAND A PLACE AS THIS!
LATER YOU CAN CHOOSE TO LIVE HERE IN FABLETOWN OR ANY-WHERE YOU LIKE IN THIS WORLD.
GOOD MORNING, GRIMBLE. WHERE'S TRUSTY JOHN? HE'S USUALLY ON DUTY BY NOW.
LONG STORY.
I'LL BE A SUCK-EGG MULE. IS THAT REALLY *YOU,* BLUE?
WHERE'VE YOU *BEEN?* AND WHO'S THAT YOU GOT *WITH*--

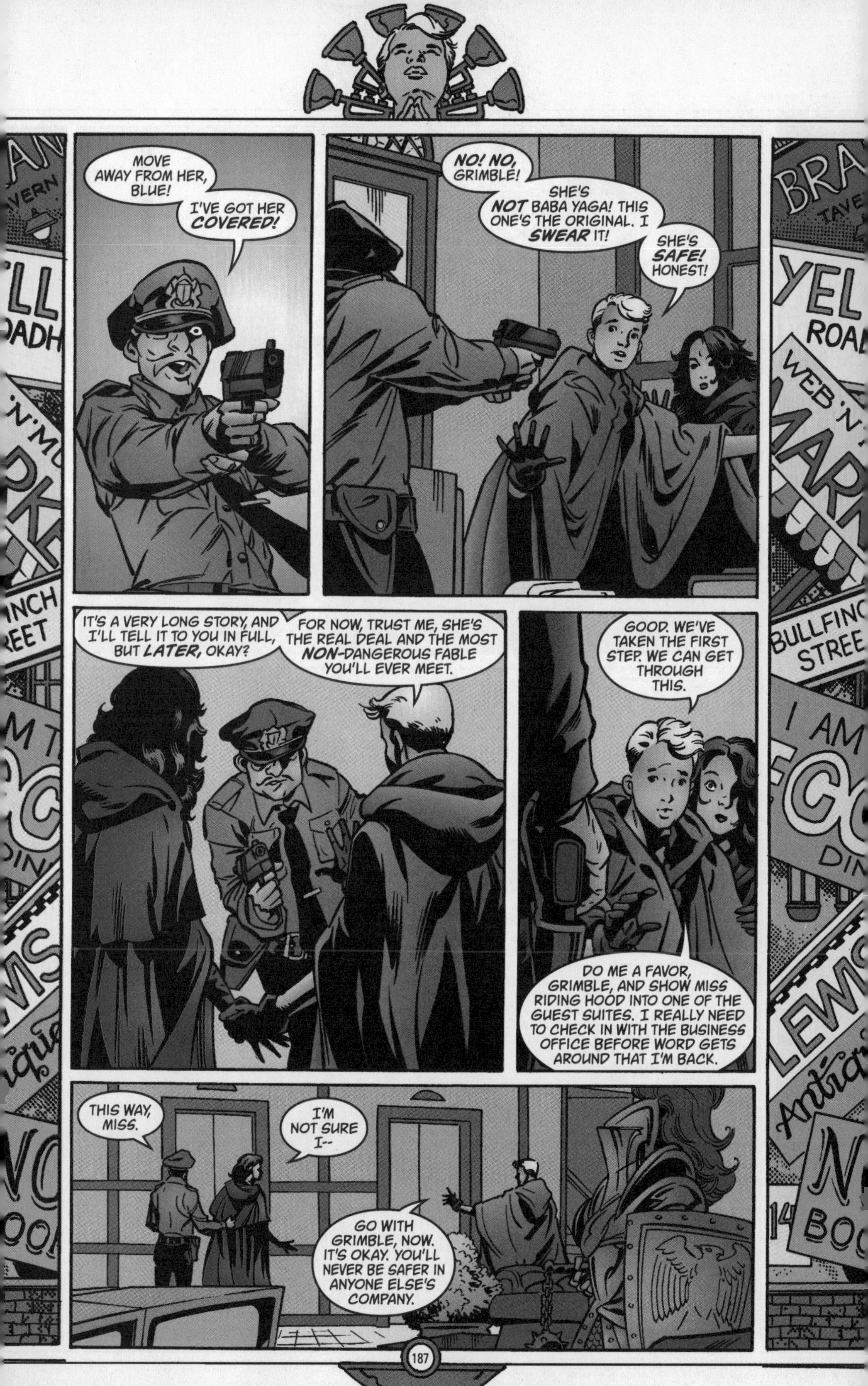
MOVE AWAY FROM HER, BLUE!
I'VE GOT HER COVERED!
NO! NO, GRIMBLE!
SHE'S NOT BABA YAGA! THIS ONE'S THE ORIGINAL. I SWEAR IT!
SHE'S SAFE! HONEST!
IT'S A VERY LONG STORY, AND I'LL TELL IT TO YOU IN FULL, BUT LATER, OKAY?
FOR NOW, TRUST ME, SHE'S THE REAL DEAL AND THE MOST NON-DANGEROUS FABLE YOU'LL EVER MEET.
GOOD. WE'VE TAKEN THE FIRST STEP. WE CAN GET THROUGH THIS.
DO ME A FAVOR, GRIMBLE, AND SHOW MISS RIDING HOOD INTO ONE OF THE GUEST SUITES. I REALLY NEED TO CHECK IN WITH THE BUSINESS OFFICE BEFORE WORD GETS AROUND THAT I'M BACK.
THIS WAY, MISS.
I'M NOT SURE I--
GO WITH GRIMBLE, NOW. IT'S OKAY. YOU'LL NEVER BE SAFER IN ANYONE ELSE'S COMPANY.

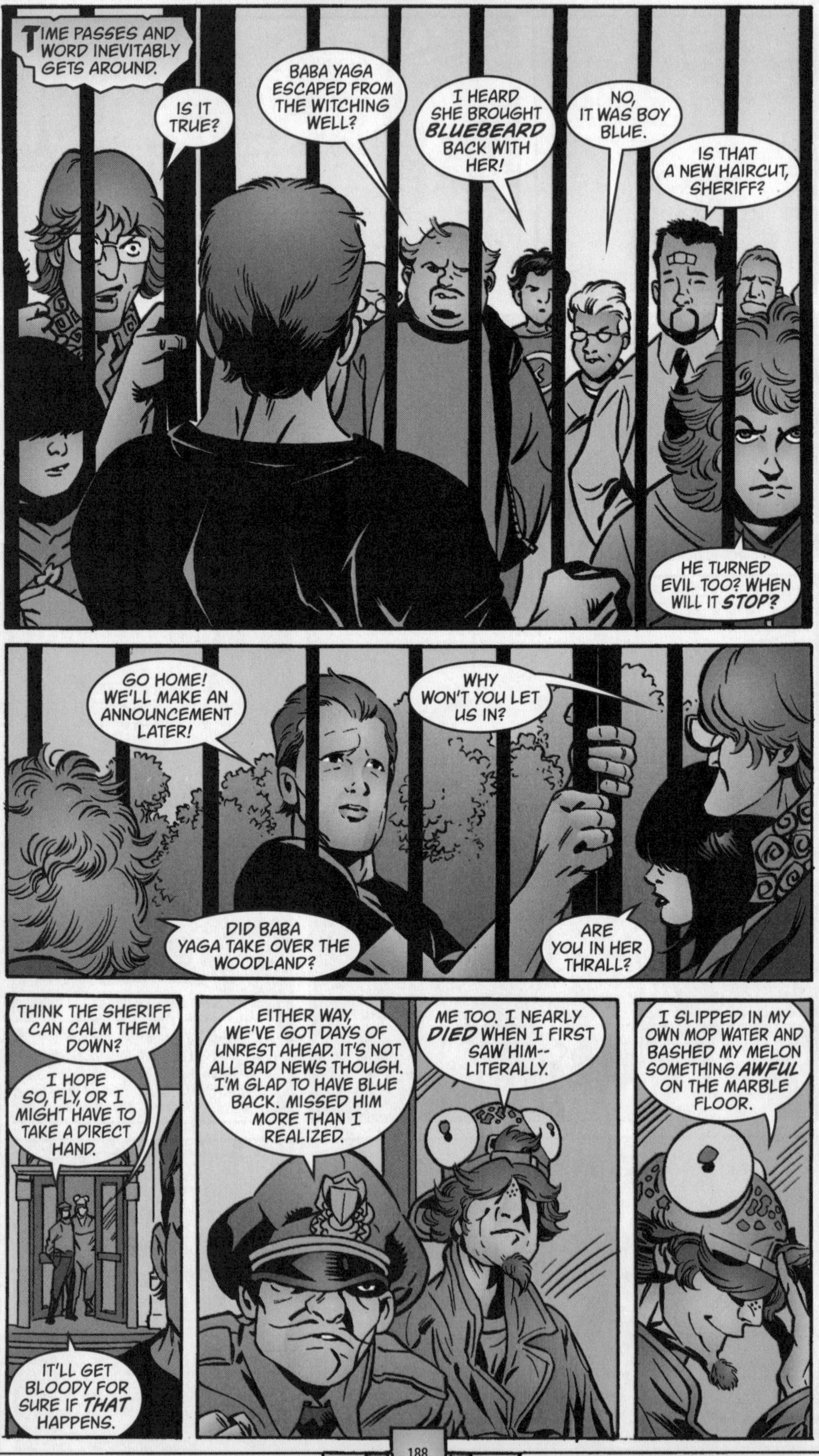
TIME PASSES AND WORD INEVITABLY GETS AROUND.
IS IT TRUE?
BABA YAGA ESCAPED FROM THE WITCHING WELL?
I HEARD SHE BROUGHT BLUEBEARD BACK WITH HER!
NO, IT WAS BOY BLUE.
IS THAT A NEW HAIRCUT, SHERIFF?
HE TURNED EVIL TOO? WHEN WILL IT STOP?
GO HOME! WE'LL MAKE AN ANNOUNCEMENT LATER!
WHY WON'T YOU LET US IN?
DID BABA YAGA TAKE OVER THE WOODLAND?
ARE YOU IN HER THRALL?
THINK THE SHERIFF CAN CALM THEM DOWN?
I HOPE SO, FLY, OR I MIGHT HAVE TO TAKE A DIRECT HAND.
IT'LL GET BLOODY FOR SURE IF THAT HAPPENS.
EITHER WAY, WE'VE GOT DAYS OF UNREST AHEAD. IT'S NOT ALL BAD NEWS THOUGH. I'M GLAD TO HAVE BLUE BACK. MISSED HIM MORE THAN I REALIZED.
ME TOO. I NEARLY DIED WHEN I FIRST SAW HIM-- LITERALLY.
I SLIPPED IN MY OWN MOP WATER AND BASHED MY MELON SOMETHING AWFUL ON THE MARBLE FLOOR.

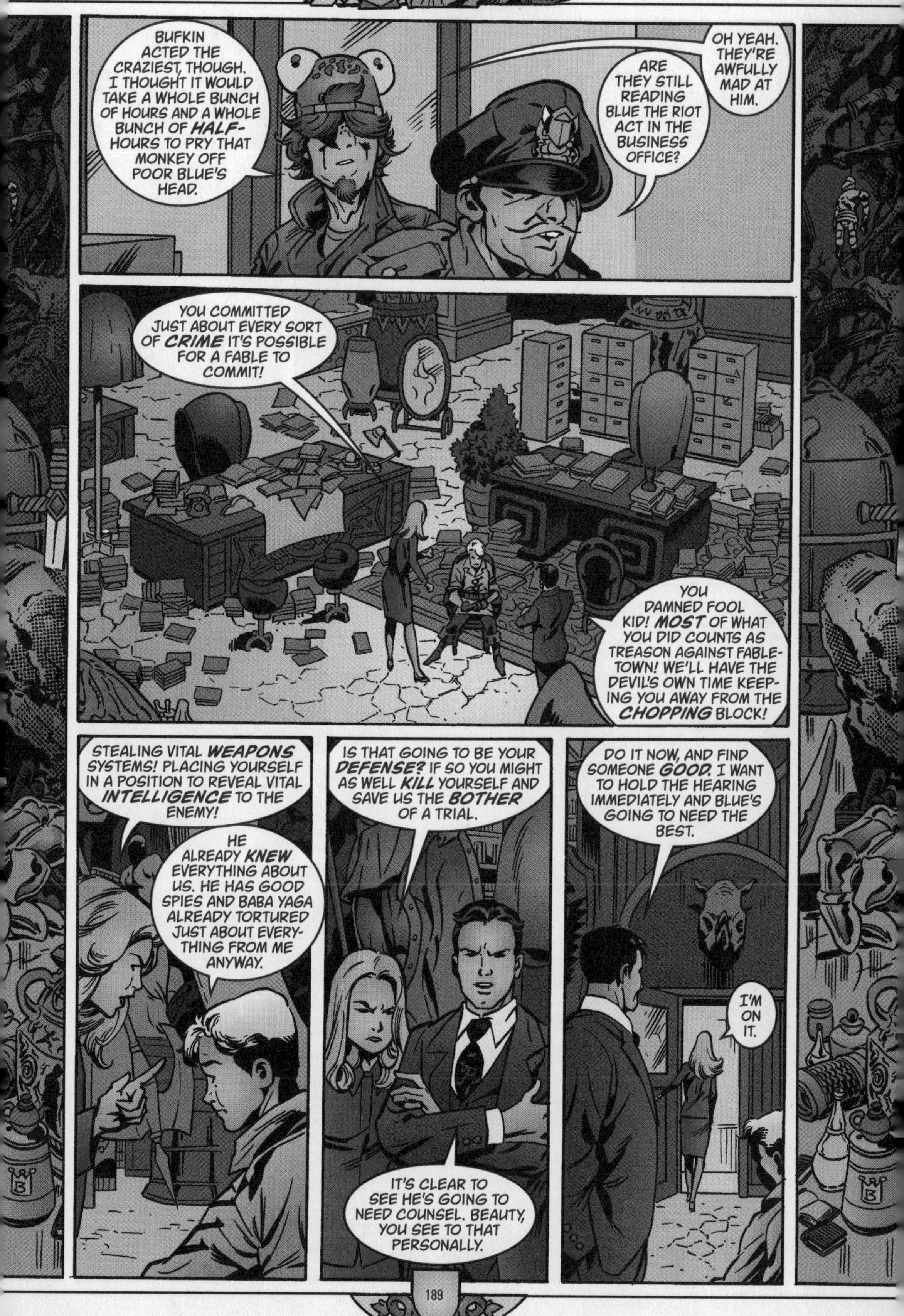
BUFKIN ACTED THE CRAZIEST, THOUGH. I THOUGHT IT WOULD TAKE A WHOLE BUNCH OF HOURS AND A WHOLE BUNCH OF HALF-HOURS TO PRY THAT MONKEY OFF POOR BLUE'S HEAD.
ARE THEY STILL READING BLUE THE RIOT ACT IN THE BUSINESS OFFICE?
OH YEAH. THEY'RE AWFULLY MAD AT HIM.
YOU COMMITTED JUST ABOUT EVERY SORT OF CRIME IT'S POSSIBLE FOR A FABLE TO COMMIT!
YOU DAMNED FOOL KID! MOST OF WHAT YOU DID COUNTS AS TREASON AGAINST FABLETOWN! WE'LL HAVE THE DEVIL'S OWN TIME KEEPING YOU AWAY FROM THE CHOPPING BLOCK!
STEALING VITAL WEAPONS SYSTEMS! PLACING YOURSELF IN A POSITION TO REVEAL VITAL INTELLIGENCE TO THE ENEMY!
HE ALREADY KNEW EVERYTHING ABOUT US. HE HAS GOOD SPIES AND BABA YAGA ALREADY TORTURED JUST ABOUT EVERYTHING FROM ME ANYWAY.
IS THAT GOING TO BE YOUR DEFENSE? IF SO YOU MIGHT AS WELL KILL YOURSELF AND SAVE US THE BOTHER OF A TRIAL.
IT'S CLEAR TO SEE HE'S GOING TO NEED COUNSEL. BEAUTY, YOU SEE TO THAT PERSONALLY.
DO IT NOW, AND FIND SOMEONE GOOD. I WANT TO HOLD THE HEARING IMMEDIATELY AND BLUE'S GOING TO NEED THE BEST.
I'M ON IT.

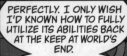

READ THE ENTIRE

FABLES

LIBRARY FROM
BILL WILLINGHAM
AND VERTIGO:

VOLUME 1: LEGENDS IN EXILE

Featuring art by **MARK BUCKINGHAM, STEVE LEIALOHA, LAN MEDINA, CRAIG HAMILTON** and others.

The immortal characters of popular fairy tales have been driven from their homelands and now live hidden among us, trying to cope with life in 21st-century Manhattan.

VERTIGO
"FABLES is a must-read for any aficionado of fantasy in a contemporary setting."
—The Magazine of Fantasy and Science Fiction
"We hope this series lasts happily ever after."
—WIZARD
FABLES
LEGENDS IN EXILE
Willingham • Medina
Leialoha • Hamilton

ALSO AVAILABLE:
VOL. 2: ANIMAL FARM
VOL. 3: STORYBOOK LOVE
VOL. 4: MARCH OF THE WOODEN SOLDIERS
VOL. 5: THE MEAN SEASONS

FABLES
ANIMAL FARM
Bill Willingham
Mark Buckingham
Steve Leialoha
VERTIGO

FABLES
STORYBOOK LOVE
Bill Willingham
Mark Buckingham
Steve Leialoha
VERTIGO

FABLES
MARCH OF THE WOODEN SOLDIERS
VERTIGO

ALL TITLES ARE SUGGESTED FOR MATURE READERS.

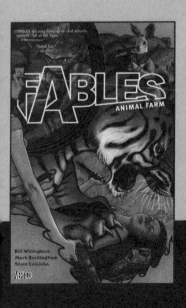

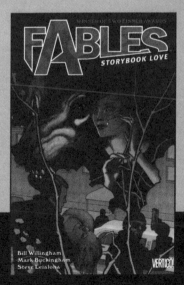

R ALL THESE
WILLINGHAM
TITLES FROM

VERTIGO

VERTIGO
FROM THE CREATOR OF FABLES
BILL WILLINGHAM
SHAWN McMANUS
the sandman presents:
THESSALY
WITCH FOR HIRE
McPherson

THE SANDMAN PRESENTS: THESSALY – WITCH FOR HIRE

With **SHAWN MCMANUS**

ALL TITLES ARE SUGGESTED FOR MATURE READERS.

THE SANDMAN PRESENTS:
TALLER TALES

from the creator of FABLES
the sandman presents
TALLer TaLES
VERTIGO

**WITH SHAWN McMANUS
MARK BUCKINGHAM
AND OTHERS**

PROPOSITION PLAYER

VERTIGO
PROPOSITION
player
FABLES
Bill Willingham ♣ Paul Guinan ♣ Ron Randall

**WITH PAUL GUINAN
AND RON RANDALL**

SEARCH THE GRAPHIC NOVELS SECTION OF

www.VERTIGOCOMICS.com

FOR ART AND INFORMATION ON ALL OF OUR BOOKS

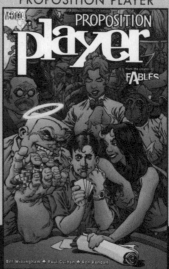